FORGOTTEN
VOICES

For my father, a child of the Blitz.

FORGOTTEN VOICES

OF THE BLITZ AND THE BATTLE FOR BRITAIN

IN ASSOCIATION WITH THE
IMPERIAL WAR MUSEUM

JOSHUA LEVINE

EBURY
PRESS

First published in Great Britain 2006

1 3 5 7 9 10 8 6 4 2

Introduction © Peter Ackroyd 2006
Text © Joshua Levine and the Imperial War Museum 2006
Photographs © Imperial War Museum 2006

Additional material taken from *What Has Become of Us?* © Channel 4/Wide Vision
Productions Ltd

Joshua Levine has asserted his right to be identified as the author of this work under the
Copyright, Designs and Patents Act 1988.

Ebury Press, an imprint of Ebury Publishing.
Random House, 20 Vauxhall Bridge Road, London SW1V 2SA

Random House Australia (Pty) Limited
20 Alfred Street, Milsons Point, Sydney, New South Wales 2061, Australia

Random House New Zealand Limited
18 Poland Road, Glenfield, Auckland 10, New Zealand

Random House (Pty) Limited
Isle of Houghton, Corner of Boundary Road and Carse O'Gowrie, Houghton, 2198,
South Africa

Random House Publishers India Private Limited
301 World Trade Tower, Hotel Intercontinental Grand Complex, Barakhamba Lane,
New Delhi 110 001, India

The Random House Group Limited Reg. No. 954009

www.randomhouse.co.uk

A CIP catalogue record for this book is available from the British Library.

Hardback:
ISBN 9780091910037 (after Jan 2007)
ISBN 009191003X

Paperback:
ISBN 970091914509 (after Jan 2007)
ISBN 0091914507

Printed and bound in Great Britain by Clays of St Ives PLC

Contents

Author's Preface

On the night of May 8, 1945, Winston Churchill stood on a balcony overlooking Whitehall and addressed the crowd below. Britain and her allies had just secured victory over the Nazis in Europe and Churchill spoke briefly of the continuing war in the Far East. Before long, however, he began speaking of an earlier period of the war; a period experienced by every member of the crowd; a period when Britain stood on the brink of defeat. As he looked down at his fellow citizens, Churchill declared:

We were left all alone against the most tremendous military power that has been seen. We were all alone for a whole year. There we stood, alone. Did anyone want to give in? Were we down-hearted? The lights went out and the bombs came down. But every man, woman and child in the country had no thought of quitting the struggle. So we came back after long months from the jaws of death, out of the mouth of hell, while all the world wondered.

Churchill was speaking of the period which began in early summer 1940 with the evacuation of the British Expeditionary Force from Dunkirk. A German invasion was expected and as the summer drew on, British civilians watched the Battle of Britain playing out in the skies above their heads. The Battle of Britain gave way to the Blitz which transformed the same civilians into front line soldiers. In the face of enormous odds, Britain survived – and she did so without assistance from the Soviet Union, and only limited assistance from Europe and the United States. She had truly fought a battle *for* Britain.

This was a period during which the British people experienced much that was new. They were not accustomed to fearing for their liberty or independence. They could never have imagined a relentless aerial bombardment on the scale of the Blitz. Nor had they experienced the social integration brought about by the shared struggle. The story of this extraordinary, intense period is told in this book by the men, women and children who were there.

When great events are viewed through the eyes of the participants, the events are no longer made up of dry fact and statistical detail. They are returned to the human level. Nor are they simplified to suit a historian's thesis. Life, after all, is rarely black and white. Memories and interpretations differ. In a criminal trial, truthful witnesses to the same event will give varying accounts. In the following pages, you will read some accounts that complement each other, some that vary and a few which are baldly contradictory. In other words, real life will be placed before you.

I have attempted to structure the accounts into a narrative which tells the story of the period. The interviewees are of all ages, both sexes and many nationalities. They are predominantly British – as one might expect – but there are many German accounts, particularly relating to the Battle of Britain and there are interviewees from India, Jamaica, New Zealand, Canada, South Africa, the United States and Poland amongst others. The stories range across the emotions. They are funny, joyful, angry and tragic. They are commonplace and bizarre. They tell of fear, courage, hatred and forgiveness. William Strachan's story of attempting to reach Britain from Jamaica in order to fight for the 'mother country', will first amuse you and then anger you. Ballard Berkeley's account of the bombing of the Café de Paris nightclub paints a picture of chilling clarity. Cyril Bamberger will teach you – patiently – how to fly a Spitfire.

Many of the individuals who feature in this book are no longer with us. As I write these words, I see that George 'Grumpy' Unwin has just passed away. In the pages that follow, you will encounter men and women, now gone, recalling their days as vital and passionate people in the prime of life. We owe a great debt to these pilots, firemen, WAAFs, bomb disposal men, air raid wardens, Home Guards, ambulance drivers, soldiers, civilians and others besides. Many of their contemporaries did not survive their youth. As Churchill drew his speech to a close on that night in May 1945, he remembered their sacrifice:

I say that in the long years to come not only will the people of this island but of the world, wherever the bird of freedom chirps in human hearts, look back to what we've done and they will say 'Do not despair, do not yield to violence and tyranny, march straightforward and die if need be – unconquered.'

Read these stories, look back to what they did and reach your own conclusions.

Joshua Levine, July 2006

Acknowledgements

Above all, I would like to thank everybody at the Imperial War Museum Sound Archive. Margaret Brooks, Peter Hart, Richard McDonough, John Stopford-Pickering, Richard Hughes and Rob White have all been more helpful than I had any right to expect. Over many months, their assistance, enthusiasm and support have made the writing of this book an utter pleasure. The Sound Archive was set up in 1972 and holds over 33,000 hours of recorded interviews. It is and ought to be recognised as a national treasure. In the photographic department, I would like to thank Rose Gerrard and Dave Parry. Terry Charman, the Museum's historian, read through the text and offered some very wise advice as did Peter Hart. My thanks go to Elizabeth Bowers and Gemma Maclagan. The good humour and efficiency of Paul Fountain, Paul Strange, Kiran Patel, Leslie Lee and Jason Strange have been greatly appreciated.

Jim Gill has provided consistent and crucial encouragement. I am very grateful to him as I am to Barbara Levy who helped to initiate the Forgotten Voices series. Ken Barlow, my editor at Ebury Press, has been a reassuring voice at the end of the telephone whenever a structural dilemma threatened my sanity. My copeditor Bernice Davison provided a helpful perspective. I would like to thank Jake Lingwood and also Caroline Newbury who has dealt efficiently and enthusiastically with publicity matters.

I must mention Max Arthur, a true friend, who set me on the path to writing this book. On September 15, 2005, Max and I attended the Salute to the Few – a dinner at RAF Northolt to celebrate the 65th anniversary of the Battle of Britain. The book began to take shape that night. As it has come together, many people have offered practical assistance. I thank Lionel Levine for his endeavours. Alyssa McDonald transcribed tapes faultlessly when time was short. I am grateful to Judy Sahm for her advice on the Rest Centres. John

Ury assisted with German translation. Suzy Klein's knowledge of the Luftwaffe proved important as did Jon Medcalf's understanding of the wartime fire services. Simon Frumkin, Harry Mount and Michael Sparkes read sections of the book and offered advice. Charles Malpass and Will Brooks gave guidance on photographs. Dorothy Sahm has never been far from my thoughts. Bridget Fallon has offered endless encouragement. Her advice has been constructive and her patience remarkable.

My thanks to Capital Radio for its superb collection of London Blitz interviews, to John and Marion Manester (and Paxy) at the Whitstable Talking Newspaper, to Channel 4 television and its programme, *Spitfire Ace*, an RDF production, to Vincent Dowd for the account of Robert Grant-Ferris. I would like to thank all of the interviewees who have given their permission for their interviews to be used.

I am grateful to Peter Ackroyd for his elegant introduction. Any errors or omissions in this book are, of course, my responsibility.

Joshua Levine, July 2006

Introduction
by Peter Ackroyd

It was a night without precedent in London's history. As darkness began to fall on September 7, 1940, the German air force commenced its attack upon London. Six hundred bombers, coming over from Europe in great waves, began an assault upon east London. A great fire storm erupted over Woolwich, Millwall, Beckton, Limehouse and Rotherhithe, signalling a first offensive that would last for a further three months. But that was only the beginning of what became known as 'The Blitz'. This book is in part a history of that fiery and bloody period. But it is not a history in the familiar sense. It is not an objective and impersonal report of the fatal bombings. It is a narrative told by the survivors themselves, the authentic and unforgettable accounts of those who lived through the slaughter and the mayhem. Listening to these voices, it is possible to hear again the sounds of these dreadful assaults – the screaming of the sirens, the drone of the planes overhead, the 'ack ack' of the anti-aircraft guns, the sound of the bombs rising in pitch as they come ever lower.

And then, in the memorable words of one of the contributors here, there came the silence. 'It was the most extraordinary thing,' he recalls. 'Everything stopped and there was complete and utter silence. It was so quiet, it was unbelievable.' After that the participants were thrown into hell. Adults and children died of shock. Limbs were torn off, and bodies torn apart. One young woman was taken on a stretcher – 'the whole of her back had been taken off – her kidneys were exposed'. Faces were blown away. Many of the wounded were given morphine and then left to die. There are many reports here of decapitations, with the heads rolling on the pavements like 'woolly footballs'. The people were drowned or burned or blasted. One father was shown the body of his dead son, its head missing. 'He looked down, bent over and stroked the body. 'So that's how you went, Jimmy?' he said. Then he shook the hand of the stretcher bearer, and thanked him for a cup of tea he had been given.

It is impossible to read these reports of the eye-witnesses without pain. These are the voices that go beyond the histories and the biographies of the period. This is raw unmediated suffering that does not abate over the years. These witnesses are more powerful than any drama, more convincing than any fiction. The chaos, the fire and the destruction killed more people than was ever known or guessed at the time. There were dropped incendiary bombs, high explosive bombs, and landmines. There was even talk of a 'great bomb' that would destroy London altogether. There was an imminent sense of apocalypse, accompanied by the experience of living day by day in an increasingly shattered and demoralised city. There were attacks upon other cities – Hull, Coventry, Manchester and Liverpool are all recalled here – but at the time it seemed to Londoners to be a war against the capital itself.

So these are sighs from hell. But of course there is another aspect recalled by these voices. It lies in the courage and vivacity of the Londoners themselves, grave in the face of peril and resilient in the face of calamity. There is an unforgettable account of a prostitute coming up from Piccadilly who, as the incendiary bombs came down, put up her umbrella and began to sing 'I'm singing in the rain'. There were occasions of great heroism, too, when at the risk of their own lives rescuers would take up the injured and the dying. Their accounts are some of the most moving in the book.

The same bravery and stamina were amply exhibited by the combatants themselves. There are many other 'forgotten' voices included here, the voices of those who participated in the exodus from Dunkirk and in that giant contest of the skies which became known as 'the Battle of Britain'. This is still living history, a straightforward narrative told directly by the participants themselves.

The war changed everything. It changed London. It changed English society. It changed the political culture of the country. For those who lived through this giant transition it was a time of terror and of turmoil. Yet the testimonies here are proof of something more enduring than war and destruction. Anyone who wishes to learn about human courage, and human endurance, should read this book.

Peter Ackroyd

Part One

DUNKIRK AND THE THREAT OF INVASION

In the early summer of 1940, Britain, her Empire and her Commonwealth stood alone against Germany. Her European allies had surrendered in quick succession and her army had barely escaped annihilation on the beaches of northern France. Her people were about to become front-line soldiers in the struggle to resist Adolf Hitler.

No nation had yet successfully resisted Hitler. In the years leading to the declaration of war, his armies had re-occupied the Rhineland and taken possession of Austria, the Sudetenland, Czechoslovakia and Poland. Britain, in common with other nations, had placed few obstacles in his path. The government of the day had lived through the horror of one war and had no desire to provoke another. Certain individuals, however, spoke out against appeasement. 'Only a few hours away by air,' said Winston Churchill in a wireless broadcast, 'there dwell a nation of nearly seventy millions of the most educated, industrious, scientific, disciplined people in the world, who are being taught from childhood to think of war as a glorious exercise and death in battle as the noblest fate for man.'

On the morning of September 3, 1939, British Prime Minister Neville Chamberlain announced that his nation was at war with Germany. His policy of appeasement had run its course but by forcing Hitler to the negotiating table, he had at least delayed the inevitable war and given Britain time to rearm. On September 9, a British Expeditionary Force of four infantry divisions sailed for France. Several months of artificial calm followed – a period which became known as the Phoney War. The calm was broken on April 9, 1940 when Hitler invaded Denmark and Norway. The British army mounted a disorganised, ill-fated campaign to liberate Norway and the consequent debate in the House of Commons led to Chamberlain's resignation.

On May 10, 1940, Winston Churchill replaced Neville Chamberlain as Prime Minister and on the same day, Germany invaded Holland, Belgium and Luxembourg. Despite fairly even troop numbers, the Germans quickly won a resounding strategic victory over the Allies. As the Wehrmacht began to move through the Low Countries, Allied forces, including the British Expeditionary Force, were sent across the Belgian border to counter the advance. The real threat, however, proved to be further south. Hitler's Panzer tank divisions thundered through the supposedly impenetrable Ardennes area, bypassing the Maginot Line – the defences constructed by the French along their border with Germany. The speed, aggression and location of this blitzkrieg astonished the Allies. Holland surrendered on May 15, the same day that Reynaud, the French premier, informed Churchill that the German army was pouring into France. Five days later, the Germans had reached the French coast.

Lord Gort, the commander-in-chief of the British Expeditionary Force, began withdrawing British troops – many of whom had yet to fire a shot – to the coast. On May 24, with the British army at his mercy, Hitler ordered his tanks to halt their advance. He had been assured by the Luftwaffe Commander, Hermann Goering, that his aircraft would be able to destroy the encircled British troops. The delay allowed the German infantry to catch up with the Panzer divisions but it also gave the British Expeditionary Force a glimmer of hope. On May 26, the order for Operation Dynamo – total evacuation – was given. By now, Dunkirk was the only possible point of departure and troops congregated on the beaches as a multitude of British vessels, answering a nationwide appeal, crossed the Channel to bring them home. Fishing boats, yachts, cabin cruisers and a substantial number of Royal Navy vessels ferried the men clear of a seemingly invincible German war machine. In all, 338,226 Allied troops were rescued. The war was not over. The battle for Britain had begun.

Dunkirk

I saw a regimental sergeant major in his knee breeches and his service dress jacket and cap – and the tears were streaming down his face.

THE RETREAT

Private Albert Dance
Rifle Brigade
I woke up very early and I could hear the general alarm being sounded on the bugle. 'The sergeant major's got the horn', as we used to say. I thought, 'What's this? A practice?' Then I heard a load of Dornier aircraft coming over at about three hundred feet and they started dropping bombs all over. We marched that morning until we got to the general area of Brussels. Then this captain came round and said, 'You may not know it but you're on the very slopes of the Battle of Waterloo.' We were told to dig trenches all along and just before dark, we got the order that we were to hold these trenches to the last man. I couldn't believe it! That night, I was propped up in the trench, listening to this tremendous noise. I was trying to make out what it was. First it sounded like men marching, then I could hear the clop of hooves and then engine noises. When dawn came up, I looked to our left and saw an entire French army had been retreating past us. Within minutes, we got the order to pull out quickly. The great retreat started at that point.

Lance Corporal Albert Adams
East Yorkshire Yeomanry
We were told to make for Dunkirk. I got to an area where the main road to Dunkirk was blocked with vehicles, troops and tanks. It was caused by a big

Lorries abandoned by the British Expeditionary Force during the retreat to the French coast.

Belgian naval gun that had toppled over. So everybody abandoned their vehicles and started walking.

Private Sidney Nuttall
Royal Army Ordnance Corps
Everybody was talking about going to Dunkirk. We didn't know where Dunkirk was.

Private Samuel Love
12th Field Ambulance, Royal Army Medical Corps
We set off for the coast. We were walking and we had to pinch hens, ducks, pigs, sheep, potatoes. We were living off the land.

Private Edward Watson
8th Battalion, King's Royal Rifle Corps
The fellers found some wine and they really started drinking it. I'd never tasted wine before. I didn't like it very much, this red stuff. It tasted very bitter. We were drinking it out of bowls – there were no glasses – and an officer said that if he found anyone drunk, he would shoot them. 'You can drink as much as you like,' he said, 'but if you're drunk, then I'm going to kill you.'

Private Sidney Nuttall
Royal Army Ordnance Corps
We started for Dunkirk and we were gradually meeting more and more people, and we started coming across vehicles in ditches and parked in fields. The majority of them had been sabotaged. People were shoving earth into the petrol tanks and trying to ruin the engines with sand. Some people were trying to set them on fire, but that caused a lot of smoke and then the dive bombers found you. It wasn't really advisable to do that.

Lance Corporal Albert Adams
East Yorkshire Yeomanry
At this tiny village, I spoke to a tall blond French soldier who spoke English quite well. I asked him which was the road to Dunkirk and he pointed to it but he said, 'Don't go down there! The German parachutists have all dropped down there!' To this day, I'm convinced he was a German infiltrator, trying to direct us wrongly, because when I went down the road, there weren't any Germans. We never saw a parachutist and we never heard a gun.

Private Edward Watson
8th Battalion, King's Royal Rifle Corps
I wanted to go to the toilet. I was really bursting but the toilet was outside in the open. There was mortar fire going on out there. After a while, I really couldn't stand it any more and I had to run out. I found the loo and opened the door and found a dead Frenchman sitting on it. I promptly slammed the door, ran back inside and did it in one of the corners of the room.

Private Albert Dance
Rifle Brigade
We'd crossed a canal and taken cover behind one of the banks. After a while, I heard a motorcycle on the other bank and I could just see the head of the driver above the reeds. I watched fascinated. Then I saw someone stand up with a map. It was obviously a German officer and I thought he was too good a target ... so I aimed at him and down he went.

Lance Corporal Lawrence Greggain
5th Battalion, Border Regiment
I was venomous against the Germans. I saw what they'd done to old people, women and children, and I thought, 'You bloody bastards! You don't deserve any mercy!' So I said to my lads, 'Now, get this, and get it clearly. If any of you ever takes a prisoner, I'll bayonet you to the bloody prisoner ... '

Flying Officer Peter Matthews
1 Squadron, RAF
I was shaken to the core when I first saw German fighter pilots machine gunning crowds of civilians on the roads. We went to pick up a chap who'd force-landed and we got mixed up with terrible strafing of the roads. It wasn't just bombers that were strafing – it was Messerschmitt 109s and 110s. That didn't seem to me to be a fighter pilot's job.

Private Sidney Nuttall
Royal Army Ordnance Corps
Somebody came out from behind a house. I'd never seen a German soldier, but after a good look at him, I thought he must be one, so I got my rifle and aimed it at him. I pulled the trigger, it went bang, and the chap kept on walking. He never even ducked. He just walked into the wood. A lance corporal came down to me and said, 'Did you just fire?' 'Yup,' I said. 'What did you fire at?' 'A bloke coming across.' 'Did you hit him?' 'No.' 'Give me a look

at your rifle.' He looked at it and said, 'Oh my God! Your sights are set to six hundred yards!' It must have gone a mile over his head.

Private Edward Watson
8th Battalion, King's Royal Rifle Corps
Someone called out, 'Gas!' and a funny smell started coming through into the basement. We thought the Germans had dropped gas and everybody whipped out their gas masks except one soldier who didn't have one. This soldier went over to an old Frenchman and took the man's gas mask off him, saying that he'd rather the Frenchman die than him. So our officer pulled his revolver out and made the soldier give the gas mask back to the Frenchman. Turned out it wasn't gas – but it was one hell of a panic.

Lance Corporal Lawrence Greggain
5th Battalion, Border Regiment
We were in this big field and in it there must have been seven or eight beautiful thoroughbred horses. The Germans mortar bombed the field and the animals were frantic, they were galloping round and round and I tried to open a gate so they could get out but they were in such a state that they galloped past the gate every time. They were terribly mutilated.

Private Albert Dance
Rifle Brigade
We went back and back until we got a town called Hazebrouck. The town was empty of French people and then suddenly the regimental sergeant major turned to us and said, 'You, you, you . . . ' and it was noticeable that he picked out six chaps from the Essex Regiment. He said, 'There's an ammunition train pulling in to the railway sidings and it's got to be destroyed. Take all the hand grenades you want!' We got down there and sure enough, there were German troops unloading the wagons. We got as near as we could and threw a hell of a lot of grenades and then scarpered. It caused a lot of pandemonium, if nothing else. As we ran, we lost each other but I remembered the route back. When I got back to Hazebrouck, there was no sign of my battalion or the headquarters. I realised that they'd gone on again. I was on my own.

Private Edward Watson
8th Battalion, King's Royal Rifle Corps
Some Germans came round the corner with an anti-tank gun. We were a hundred yards from them, at an angle, and we could see them clearly. They

were loading their gun and we were sitting in a beautiful position. I said to the officer, 'What do we do?' 'This is your job!' he said. I was an accurate shot. 'You must kill, because if you miss, they'll know where it's coming from,' he said. The position of my windowsill was such that I could rest my rifle on it and get very good aim. It was a bit frightening at first but after a while, it felt quite fun just to kill them. I vividly remember the looks on the faces of the fellows you hadn't killed, who couldn't work out where the hell it was coming from. I shot four or five before they pulled the gun away.

Private Albert Dance
Rifle Brigade
As I was walking down the road, I heard an engine. I took cover in a doorway and I saw a German motorcycle and sidecar come round. Then one or two others joined them and they stood pointing up the road. I had a rifle but I could see an anti-tank weapon in front of me. There was one round in the breech and as these Germans stood talking, I aimed at the sidecar and fired. There's a tremendous recoil and all I could see was that everything disappeared. It must have hit the bike and splattered all over the place. I ran like mad and some of them came round and started firing at me so I ran into a little house. The door was open and there was bread going mouldy on the table. I hurried through to the back room and on the table, I saw the naked body of a very old man who'd been dead for days. I rushed out the back and climbed over walls and fences until I got to the outskirts of the town. I went on like this for a day, hiding whenever I saw Germans on the road until I came across a party of eight British troops, all odds and ends who'd lost their units. There was a corporal with them but he said that we couldn't go any further and we should give up. 'I'm not giving up!' I said, 'I'm getting back! My sweetheart's back in England!' We carried on. There was a forest ahead. The light was going but I said, 'If we go now, we can make it!' In the forest, we came across a muddy trail. On a nearby tree was a daub of red paint. This paint ran right the way through the forest. It was a guide mark for the troops who had already been through. It took us a day to get through the forest but when we came out, we could see British troops heading on the road to Dunkirk. We'd gone right through the Germans.

Private Samuel Love
12th Field Ambulance, Royal Army Medical Corps
I put my hand up and stopped a convoy on the road from Lille to Poperinghe. A captain came dashing with a revolver and his obscene language was

terrible. 'Who the bloody hell are you?' 'Royal Army Medical Corps,' I said. 'You're just the bloke we want,' he said. 'We've got two blokes who made themselves a bed on top of the ammunition carrier and they've been blown up and you've never seen anything like it.' I had a look at them and told him, 'I can't do anything with these,' and I covered them over with my mac. They were in a hell of a mess. There was nothing I could do for them.

Private Edward Watson
8th Battalion, King's Royal Rifle Corps
Our officer was yelling at a sergeant to come across and join us. The sergeant ran across the road but just as he got to the doorway, he was hit by a mortar. He was completely obliterated but he wasn't dead. His whole body was peppered with shrapnel and we got him in and laid him on the floor. One of the fellers got a razor blade out and went over him, cutting and flicking these pieces of shrapnel out of him, from all over his face and body. I was very impressed.

Private Samuel Love
12th Field Ambulance, Royal Army Medical Corps
All the way up to Poperinghe, we were attacked by Dorniers and Messerschmitts. At Poperinghe, they slunk off and then you could see Jerry's tanks three or four hundred yards away coming round the bend of the hill. They started firing over open sights. After that, all these bombers came and dropped their shit on us. God, what a bloody mess. The population of Poperinghe was only five or six hundred and I don't think there were two bricks left standing, one on top of the other. We got out of there and three of us set off for Dunkirk on foot. The other nine were left behind and what happened to them nobody knows. It was about ninety miles to Dunkirk and you daren't bloody sleep. You had to keep going.

Lieutenant Arthur Curtis
7th Field Company, Royal Engineers
An ambulance came along. It was designed for two stretchers and six people sitting along a bench. Well, we managed to fit 21 people in; two stretcher cases and the rest standing or squatting round the side.

Private Albert Dance
Rifle Brigade
I passed some gunners sitting on the side of the road. One of them looked at me and said, 'I know you!' I looked at him and said, 'I don't know you.' 'You're courting a girl in Brook Hill Road, Woolwich,' he said. 'That's right,' I said, 'How do you know that?' 'That's where the married quarters of the Royal Artillery are,' he said, 'and when I was on guard duty there, I saw you kissing in the doorway. She's got lovely auburn hair.'

Private Edward Watson
8th Battalion, King's Royal Rifle Corps
The Germans started coming up the street and our officer gave us the order that it was every man for himself. I asked him what he meant. He said, 'You can do what you like. The thing is to get away. No one's in charge.' I said, 'Really?' 'Yes,' he said but then he looked at me and said, 'I want *you* to come with me!' 'No!' I said, 'I want to go on my own!' 'You come with me!' he said. So I did. We went out the back of the house and the German snipers were going at us but we got over the wall. We went into another house and there was a German sniper sitting at the window, with his back to us. My officer shot him straight away. I'd never seen it before at such close quarters. There were no questions – no 'what are you doing?' – just 'BANG'.

Wolfgang Falck
German Messerschmitt 110 pilot
I was almost a victim during a dogfight with many Spitfires. My Messerschmitt 110 was too big, not manoeuvrable or fast enough. The Spitfires hit my tail and damaged my rudder. My aircraft was shaking like it was an old tram. I held the stick with both hands and took the aircraft down to the sea. That way, I lost the Spitfire and I flew over France and the British troops below. I didn't trust the aircraft so then I tried to get up to three hundred metres in case I had to use my parachute. As I climbed up again, three or four Spitfires got behind me so I flew down again. I was flying so slowly that I lost them. The country was flat but I was flying so low that I had to jump over the dykes that were two or three metres high. As I flew over one dyke, I saw an English soldier riding a bicycle just in front of me. He fell off the bicycle and I'm sure that he's told the story: 'A pig of a German pilot tried to knock me off my bicycle!' But if he'd thrown a stone at me, I could have been his victim.

Private Edward Watson
8th Battalion, King's Royal Rifle Corps
We were cut off. We couldn't make our way any further. My officer told me to tear up all our papers. The Germans started calling out, 'Tommy, for you the war is over!' They must have been taught to say this. We were rustled up quickly and captured. I didn't know if I was going to be shot. They went through my pockets and then they sent us back behind their lines. At first, I was very impressed with the German soldiers – they looked professional compared to us. But after we had been marched to the rear, we saw their reserves, and these reserves looked like something from the Crimean War. It wasn't the same German army we'd just seen. It was all horses and carts, all higgledy-piggledy.

Private Albert Dance
Rifle Brigade
On the road to Dunkirk, we were being dive-bombed a lot. It smashed us all up and people were getting hit badly so I took to the open country. I was on my own again and I reached what must have been the last canal around Dunkirk. I walked along the bank until I found a bridge that had been blown in the middle. I slid down it, grabbed the other side and clambered up. I carried on until I could see Dunkirk.

Gunner William Davidson
5th Medium Regiment, Royal Artillery
One chap had been extremely friendly with a Belgian girl and as we retreated, he picked up this girl, dressed her up in British army uniform and brought her to Dunkirk.

Lance Corporal Lawrence Greggain
5th Battalion, Border Regiment
It took us three weeks to get to Dunkirk. In that time, I didn't have a proper meal, and I can't honestly remember having a bowel movement.

THE RESCUE

Ronald Tomlinson
Fisherman in Ramsgate
Halfway through a film, a flash came on to the screen: 'Anybody in Ramsgate trawlers, please report to the Admiralty office at once'. I took no notice,

Some of the little ships which took part in the Dunkirk evacuation, pictured on the River Thames in June 1940.

because our trawler had no water in the boilers and no coal in the bunkers. Somebody nudged me in the back and said, 'Ron, that means you!' 'It can't mean me,' I said, 'because we're blown down.' But after the film, I went down to the Admiralty office, to find out what it was all about. 'What ship are you off?' they said. I told them I was an engineer on the *Tankerton Towers*. 'Could you go round and let the crew know to be down here at half past five in the morning? Because we need a ship.' They didn't say why they needed it. I didn't know anything about Dunkirk. So I went round and by the time we got aboard at half past five, there was steam blowing from the boiler, there was coal in the bunkers and there were two lieutenants waiting for us. The Navy had done all that during the night. The lieutenants asked, 'What have you got on board?' We said, 'Nothing.' They said, 'We'll have to find something to give the boys a cup of tea when they come on board.' We didn't know what they were talking about.

Lance Corporal John Peter Wells
6th Battalion, South Staffordshire Regiment
We entered Dunkirk Harbour on the *Princessa*. We were in the middle of the main channel coming into the harbour, and there were two ships on either side and we were dive-bombed. Both of the other ships got hit at the same time and they both exploded. It transpired that they were ammunition ships. The poor little *Princessa* went down straight away. She was only a tiddly little ferry boat. The next thing I knew, I was lying on the cobblestone quayside. I was rather intrigued because I was one of half a dozen corpses that had been pulled out the sea and dumped there. The others were all in grey uniform. They were the first ruddy Germans I'd seen! And the souvenir hunters had all got their knives out and cut out the swastikas and badges from the Germans' uniforms. I felt for my Staffordshire brass knots – yes, I'd still got my buttons and emblems. I was very wet but it was a nice, sunny day and I dried out fairly quickly.

Private Albert Dance
Rifle Brigade
The beach at Dunkirk was like Margate except that the conditions were different. It was absolutely crowded with people. I could see queues of men in water up to their chins, trying to get into small boats.

British soldiers wade out to a destroyer off Dunkirk.

Private Sidney Nuttall
Royal Army Ordnance Corps
There were destroyers anchored offshore and there were little rowing boats, coming in, picking people up off the beach and taking them to these destroyers. The destroyers were being dive-bombed at regular intervals.

Ronald Tomlinson
Fisherman in Ramsgate
In the smaller boats, we were concentrating on going in close and taking the soldiers out to the bigger boats. I didn't even moor up, I just kept the engine running and let the soldiers jump aboard. I jammed them in. I had them sitting in the cockpit and on the deck. I couldn't say how many – 30, 40, could be 50. As soon as I got a boat load, I took them out to the nearest ship. It could be a cargo boat, a passenger boat, an old paddle boat, all different kinds. I dropped them, came back in and just kept filling up. I reckon we did about roughly 16 trips.

Private Sidney Nuttall
Royal Army Ordnance Corps
We had the job of carrying the wounded to the boats. We waded out into the sea, water up to our chests before the boat could reach us. And then we had to pass the bloke up into the boat. We did this for two or three nights and after each night, we were left with a white tidemark on our uniforms.

Private Samuel Love
12th Field Ambulance, Royal Army Medical Corps
Everybody was buggered. One bloke had been nine days, no grub, no water, no sleep. And then he got a direct hit. You ought to have seen his legs. He were carried on the boat and he had a really big hole in his back and he'd lost his penis. Why he didn't die, I don't know.

Lieutenant Arthur Curtis
7th Field Company, Royal Engineers
I was put in charge of a padre who'd had his jaw blown off. You could see through the gap in his bandages and he was very dicky because he couldn't see where he was going. I helped him down the steps and we went down onto the beach where we found a shed which in happier times must have had lilos and pedalos and beach stuff. The glass roof had been smashed to prevent flying glass and we settled down on the brown glass on the concrete floor. Actually,

if glass has been properly smashed up into tiny little bits, it is surprisingly comfortable to sleep on. So we lay down there for a few hours. Before dawn, we got up and joined the big crocodile. The tide was out, there was a long stretch of wet sand, and there were these big rows of people, all waiting to go forward. The wounded were given priority, so we didn't have to hang about. We went straight down to the water's edge.

Private Sidney Nuttall
Royal Army Ordnance Corps
About eighty of us got down onto the beach and we were definitely rat-tailed. We'd been sleeping in pigsties and I'd got lice in my shirt. Somebody had shown me how to run a match up the seam to pop them but it got so bad that I'd thrown the shirt away. I'd also had to get rid of the heavy parts of my kit, spare boots and stuff so I hadn't got much in the way of uniform. A regular officer came down, and said that no man of our regiment would be evacuated to the UK unless he was in possession of a full set of equipment. There was material all over the place – people had thrown stuff away, so all we did was pick up what we needed. Then the officer said that we had to shave so we shaved in sea water. Which was very painful.

Sergeant Leonard Howard
210 Field Company, Royal Engineers
I saw a regimental sergeant major in his knee breeches and his service dress jacket and cap – and the tears were streaming down his face. He said, 'I never thought that I would see the British Army like this.' And I always remember him. Poor man was absolutely shattered. He was a regular soldier and the tears were streaming down his face.

Wolfgang Falck
German Messerschmitt 110 Pilot
We received orders not to attack the British army at Dunkirk. Hitler's idea was to make Britain a friend, not an enemy. We flew only against the Royal Air Force to stop them attacking our troops. As we flew over the Channel, we watched the transportation of the British army back to home sweet home.

Able Seaman Ian Nethercott
Gunlayer aboard HMS Keith
Every time you saw a group of men in the water, the German planes came down and either bombed them or machine-gunned them.

Gerhard Schöpfel
German Messerschmitt 109 pilot
We flew against the British troops who were being rescued by little boats. We were trying to halt the boats going back to England. I tried to shoot at them. Our main thing was to go against the English.

Lieutenant Harold Dibbens
Royal Corps of Military Police
Jerry was flying down and machine-gunning us. Dozens of men were lying injured from being hit by machine gun bullets. One plane came down towards me and I jumped into a bomb hole. He missed me but the hole I chose had been used as a latrine by the soldiers.

Hans-Ekkehard Bob
German Messerschmitt 109 pilot
Goering thought that with the Luftwaffe he would be able to destroy the British Expeditionary Force.

Private Samuel Love
12th Field Ambulance, Royal Army Medical Corps
There were thousands of people on the beaches. The bombs were coming down thick and fast. One bomb would make a crater and a bloke would fall wounded in it and the next bomb would cover him over. Some of the holes were 20 foot deep – there must be hundreds of blokes lying under that beach that nobody knows nothing about.

Lance Corporal John Peter Wells
6th Battalion, South Staffordshire Regiment
In some ways, the sand was our saving grace, because the average type of bomb hitting a hard surface like a roadway, the shrapnel scatters, and you all get it. Going into the sand, there was a thud, and you'd get covered in clods of sand but that was about it. I'm not belittling it – it was bloody unpleasant.

Able Seaman Reginald Heron
Telegraphist aboard HMS Keith
There were absolutely masses of dive-bombers attacking us.

Lance Corporal John Peter Wells
6th Battalion, South Staffordshire Regiment
Firing Bren guns at dive-bombers was rather a dead loss because they were armour-plated underneath. So I said, 'What we want is an armour piercing gun.' We had an anti-tank gun with a bloody great cartridge at the back of it and a stupid little magazine with five rounds in it. We managed to scrounge a railway sleeper and we dug it into the sand. We made up a three man team, two men wedging the anti-tank gun on to the sleeper and the third one firing. We had a more or less end-on target as the aircraft dived – and it worked like a charm! It brought the buggers down! We brought two or three down like that. It's a mystery to me why it never really caught on.

Private Sidney Nuttall
Royal Army Ordnance Corps
I actually saw a dive-bomber shot down by the infantry with rifles. It was attacking a destroyer but instead of diving from the stern of the destroyer to the nose, and carrying on up the coast, the pilot arrived from the sea and finished up over the coast, very low over Bray Dunes. There was thousands of infantrymen there, lying in the dunes and they all started firing at the dive bomber. I actually saw a piece of the plane come off, and it veered off and went into the ground, well behind the town, but we saw the smoke coming up where it crashed. When you fire a thousand rifles, you can cover a lot of the sky.

Able Seaman Reginald Heron
Telegraphist aboard HMS Keith
The only British planes we saw were the Sunderland flying boats. They just steamed through very slow and majestic. We didn't see much of the RAF.

Quartermaster Raymond Trivass
1st Battalion, Coldstream Guards
I didn't see one RAF aircraft.

Sergeant Major Martin McLane
2nd Battalion, Durham Light Infantry
The RAF did a very poor job of defending us. The Germans were working in close co-operation with their aircraft. When they wanted support, they called in their dive-bombers and their fighters who strafed and bombed us to clear

the way. And what support did we have? We had no damn thing at all. Not a bloody thing. We were just left to God and good neighbours.

Pilot Officer Tony Bartley
92 Squadron, RAF

A fighter pilot I knew was shot down at Dunkirk and went in the sea. He swam out to a boat and he got on board and the navy chap said, 'Get back! We're not picking you up, you bastards, we're only picking up the soldiers.'

Wing Commander Edward Donaldson
Commanding Officer, 151 Squadron, RAF

My squadron almost lived over Dunkirk! Ten days! The army grumbled because they had a hell of a rough time but we were there. We used to patrol 10,000 feet over Dunkirk, and we went for any Germans that attacked.

Pilot Officer Ronald Brown
111 Squadron, RAF

We tried to intercept anything that was coming in. It was too late to get them if they were already attacking the beaches. So the troops on the beaches wouldn't have seen us.

Sergeant Richard Mitchell
229 Squadron, RAF

We'd set off from Biggin Hill just as it was getting light and we'd do three trips to Dunkirk by ten o'clock in the morning. There were just four of us and we weren't battle-hardened at all and I think it was the worst period of the war. We had a little field telephone and when it rang, we all thought that they must be sending us back to base but when he put the phone down, the commanding officer said, 'Come on chaps, we've got to go again.' Most of the time, we didn't reach Dunkirk. We attacked bombers or we were attacked on the way there.

Pilot Officer Tony Bartley
92 Squadron, RAF

Frankly if it hadn't have been for the RAF, the troops would never have got off. Because the German Air Force quit the beaches. We turned them back. I'm damned sure that Fighter Command had a hell of a lot to do with it.

Flight Lieutenant Gerald Edge
605 and 253 Squadrons, RAF

I fired at a Messerschmitt 109 as he came towards me over Dunkirk. I could see a lot of my tracer and bullets hitting around his cockpit but he kept on coming. I gave him another burst, thinking that must stop him but it didn't. At that moment, there was a flash and a terrific bang in my cockpit. I thought he must have blown my tail away. I tried my controls. They still worked but I flew the thing home as though it were a new-born baby. When I got back to my aerodrome, I asked the airman if there was anything left of the tail. 'Yes, sir. There's no mark on it.' I got out of the aircraft and went back to report in when the airman came running over, saying, 'Can you come sir, quick?' 'Why?' I asked. 'You wait and see, sir.' As we got to the aircraft, he said, 'You know you said there was a big bang in the aircraft? Come and look at this, sir! On the outside of the cockpit, just above your hand, there's a black line and there's a tiny splintering on the inside. And there's a little mark on the top of your throttle lever. We'd like to look at what you're wearing sir.' What had happened was that a cannon shell had gone through the side of my aircraft, nicked the top of the throttle lever, gone through my glove, nicked the rip cord part of my parachute, edged the aluminium seat and hit the armour-plating where it had blown up. The seat had caught all the shrapnel and the back of my parachute had stopped me feeling it. If anything had happened differently, I would have been killed.

Pilot Officer Peter Parrott
145 Squadron, RAF

My friend Peter Dixon was shot down over Dunkirk. We heard that he was badly wounded. I heard two stories: one that he was put on a stretcher and taken to a destroyer that was sunk, the other that the Germans took him into their hospital where he died of his wounds. You can believe which one you like.

Lieutenant Harold Dibbens
Royal Corps of Military Police

I was stopped by a very irate major who told me to get a shooting party together because two French collaborators had been picked up and they would have to die.

Private Samuel Love
12th Field Ambulance, Royal Army Medical Corps

If I'd had a rifle with me on the beach, I should have shot this one artilleryman. He took a shell that hadn't exploded and started rolling it down a hill. One of the stupidest tricks you could ever wish to do. I said, 'You stupid bastard! Let sleeping dogs lie!' If I'd had a rifle I should have shot him, honest.

Lieutenant Arthur Curtis
7th Field Company, Royal Engineers

We could see the outline of a vessel approaching. My father had been in the coastal artillery and we'd always had *Jane's Fighting Ships* on the front window so I knew how to identify ships. Somebody said, 'What's that?' I said, 'It's a French battleship.' And of course, it turned out to be a paddle steamer from Bournemouth.

Lance Corporal Albert Adams
East Yorkshire Yeomanry

I got to the beach and I joined the queue. I could see all the boats out on the water. As we got nearer the pier, I saw some drunk lads who had come up the side of the queue and were trying to muscle in. The sailors wouldn't let them on the ship. They told them to get back to the end of the queue.

Private Sidney Nuttall
Royal Army Ordnance Corps

There was a lot of drunkenness on the beaches. Soldiers had broken into *estaminets* and were stealing beers and spirits. There was a lot of bad discipline – but good discipline too. You could see orderly queues forming for going down to the boats. There was usually an officer or a sergeant or a sergeant major directing things from the beach.

Lance Corporal John Peter Wells
6th Battalion, South Staffordshire Regiment

What I remember as rather pathetic, some of these poor buggers, you'd think they were pregnant. Their battle dress blouse was full up with ciggies and bottles, all sorts of stuff that they'd picked up. Before we'd let them aboard, we'd say, 'Get rid of that lot!' And they'd have to chuck it all in the sea, all their booty.

Private Samuel Love
12th Field Ambulance, Royal Army Medical Corps

We got to the jetty and only the blokes on the boat were controlling it. As soon as they got enough on the boat, they just got hold of the gangways and pulled them away. They got hold of the rope ladders and started shaking men off. If you were on the ladders, you weren't safe because they just shook you off on to the quayside or into the water.

Lance Corporal John Peter Wells
6th Battalion, South Staffordshire Regiment

A Royal Navy destroyer was taking on some French troops. A French officer started to rush up the gangway, and the naval lieutenant on the bridge told him to stop. This bloke wasn't standing for it – he carried on running up. So the lieutenant drew his pistol and shot the Frenchman dead. It was a very sobering thing to watch.

Sergeant Leonard Howard
210 Field Company, Royal Engineers

I watched as a small boat came in and the troops piled aboard it to such a degree that it was in danger of capsizing. The chap in charge of this boat decided he must take some action. He ordered one man who was hanging on the side to get away – but he didn't, so he shot him through the head. From the people around, there was no reaction at all. There was such chaos on the beach that that didn't seem out of keeping.

Lieutenant Arthur Curtis
7th Field Company, Royal Engineers

We were rowed out to where the water was deep enough for this paddle steamer and then we were hoisted aboard. I found a nice little corner on the skylight over the passenger saloon. I didn't fancy going below. I think if a ship's going to sink I'd rather be on deck than below.

Ronald Tomlinson
Fisherman in Ramsgate

A small boat full of French soldiers came alongside our trawler. We took them and put them down in the fish hold. About fifty of them. Then a bit after that, another boatload came of English boys. Some of them were all wet and one poor lad could hardly walk. We took him down to our cabin and I thought he might as well have my bunk, because I wouldn't be using it. But when I looked round, the cabin was absolutely full – everybody had followed me down. An officer said to this lad, 'Come on, get out of that bunk! I'm an officer!' So I said, 'Look, there's no such thing as officers in these circumstances! We are all one!'

Lieutenant Arthur Curtis
7th Field Company, Royal Engineers
When we got underway I looked out, and this is a sight I've never forgotten –
a K-class destroyer, the most modern ship the navy had at that time. There we
were, dirty, unshaven, covered in blood, watching this gleaming, immaculate
ship, flying her battle ensign. She was going flat out and zigzagging because
the dive-bombers were coming down. Her Bofors guns were going, 'bump,
bump, bump'. She was a marvellous sight. I suppose she was actually diverting
the dive-bombers away from our little paddle steamer.

Private Sidney Nuttall
Royal Army Ordnance Corps
We got on to one of the little boats, and we were taken to a destroyer, *HMS
Icarus*. It was lying offshore in the dark, and they were trying to fill it up and
get off before the dive-bombers came down at first light. But they hadn't
managed, and it was still there at first light. And they had no anti-aircraft
shells left so they were just firing common shells. They had no chance of
hitting an aircraft. They'd have to hit it directly whereas an anti-aircraft shell
burst with a proximity fuse. They were just firing to keep the planes up higher.

Able Seaman Reginald Heron
Telegraphist aboard HMS Keith
I was in the wireless office of *HMS Keith* and there was a hell of a crash and
everything shook like hell. We knew we'd been hit because we were more or
less expecting it. I mean we'd been there four days – it was a wonder we hadn't
been hit before. A bomb from a Stuka went down the funnel, and blew out
the whole of the under part of the ship. We grabbed the codebooks, and put
them in a specially weighted bag and we threw it over the side. Then someone
shouted, 'Abandon ship! Throw everything floatable overboard!' So I threw a
dam-buoy overboard. A dam-buoy's a long thing, a bit like a jousting lance
with a big cork float at the end. I jumped in behind it and started swimming
with one arm. I swam over to a tug a few hundred yards away and grabbed
hold of a rubber tyre on the side. Then the tug actually started up and it got
quite speedy and I was getting dragged through the water at a rate of knots.
There was somebody above me, hanging on to the edge of the tug and a stupid
sailor was shouting at me to push him up. So with one hand I was hanging on
to the rubber tyre, and with the other I was trying to push this guy up so the
sailor could haul him aboard. After all this palaver, we got aboard eventually,
and headed back to Dover.

Lance Corporal John Peter Wells
6th Battalion, South Staffordshire Regiment
I was up in the prow of the ship when we were dive-bombed. A Stuka dropped its bomb straight down the aft funnel. Direct hit. The ship literally folded in about three seconds. I was fortunate because being up in the front end, I just fell off. The fuel tanks had been ruptured, so the sea was a mass of diesel oil. I took an involuntary swim and I managed to get ashore but I still twinge a bit with pain nowadays because I swallowed a lot of that diesel oil and most of the lining of my stomach's gone west.

Lieutenant Arthur Curtis
7th Field Company, Royal Engineers
During low tide at Dunkirk, there are banks where there's not enough water for a big ship to safely cross, but our little paddle steamer could. So we were able to go straight out northwards, and then turn left into Margate. The destroyers had to go along the coast which meant there was a danger of getting shot by artillery further down by Gravelines.

Able Seaman Reginald Heron
Telegraphist aboard HMS Keith
All the way back to Dover, we were being strafed by German fighters. We were all crowded on the deck of this thing, completely exposed. I remember an officer – who was in his pyjamas for some weird reason – standing up, waving his arms over his head and shouting, 'Survivor! Survivor!' at the fighters and then he started making engine noises. I tried to ignore him.

Private Sidney Nuttall
Royal Army Ordnance Corps
I met a sixteen-year-old ship's boy on *HMS Icarus*. I didn't realise that people of his age went into action. He was kept busy making us cocoa. We needed something, because we was very dehydrated. They also fed us bully beef sandwiches, about an inch thick, which went down very well, because I'd had nothing to eat for three or four days.

Ronald Tomlinson
Fisherman in Ramsgate
Eventually we left Dunkirk in the early hours of June 2. A sergeant major said the Jerries were on the end of the pier. He told us not to come back but we took a chance and came back for another load. He said, 'I told you not to

A deck on one of the ships returning from Dunkirk. Some soldiers are sleeping, others are eating.

come back!' I said, 'Well, jump aboard, you're not going to be left behind are you?' We got back into Ramsgate about nine o'clock the following morning.

Private Albert Dance
Rifle Brigade

On June 4, the order came along that there wouldn't be any more boats. Chaps were just sitting there, waiting to be picked up by the Germans. I headed north-east towards La Panne. When I got up there, I noticed a wooden jetty running out into the sea. It had been hit by a couple of shells but it went out quite a way. I clambered on to it and got out to the end and fell asleep. When I woke, it was dark and a boat was banging into the jetty. I heard English voices and I looked up and saw a little sailing yacht with two men aboard. One of them said, 'There's no one here! We've got to get back!' and I shouted out. As I leapt onto the yacht, I hit my head on the deck. I still had my steel helmet on and it must have banged me in the back of my head and knocked me right out. The next thing I remember was someone saying, 'Come on chum! Have a cup of tea!' I had a mouthful of tea and then he said, 'Do you want to see the white cliffs of Dover?' And there they were, right in front of me.

Lance Corporal Albert Adams
East Yorkshire Yeomanry

We arrived at Margate. By the pier where we got off, there was a soldier with a big bag. He told us to drop all our ammunition into the bag. One man dropped a couple of hand grenades in as he went by and the soldier ran off. They still had their pins in but he didn't know that.

Donald Browne
Schoolboy in Ramsgate

As the troops returned to Ramsgate, they came off the boats, on to the trains and away. The line of troops went from the harbour, up the High Street, past my school and up to the station, six to eight deep. As they were queuing, they were attacked by a Stuka but the bombs missed them and fell on the beach and the harbour. The men looked very rough indeed. They were cold and miserable until they met the ladies of Ramsgate – of all classes – who provided them with tea, biscuits and sandwiches.

Aircraftman Leslie Haines
Armourer, RAF

The Falmouth ladies were wonderful to us. They gave us sandwiches and pasties and things. Eventually, we were told that they would arrange a special train to take us all up to London to be dispersed. While we were at the station, I saw a railway inspector that I knew. 'Oh my God! Les Haines!' he said, 'Your father thinks you're dead! God! You're here!' He got on the telephone to my father in Plymouth as we got on the train. After a while, the guard came along and said, 'Is one of you Les Haines?' 'Yeah. Me.' 'Right,' he said, 'I've got news for you. This train is stopping in Plymouth Station. Look out! Your father and mother's gonna be there!' The train stopped with all these dozens of soldiers inside and there on the platform were my parents. You can imagine the scenes. They thought I was dead and gone.

Lieutenant Arthur Curtis
7th Field Company, Royal Engineers

We were all waiting on the front at Margate and I began to feel a bit hungry so I thought, 'I'll go and see if I can cash a cheque.' There was a Lloyd's Bank across the road, so I went in and formed up in a queue of people who were doing their business. They looked up and saw this chap queuing up in a red greatcoat, bloody and unshaven. I asked the cashier if I could cash a cheque, and he very apologetically said he didn't think he could do that. I only wanted a fiver.

Private Sidney Nuttall
Royal Army Ordnance Corps

After we disembarked at Dover, we were sent straight to the station. There were trains on every platform. 'Any platform, any train,' they shouted and we were pushed along. As the trains got full, they moved off. My mate and I got split up. I finished up in the train on the left, and he finished up in the train on the right. The train on the left went to Bristol and the train on the right went to Halifax. That's just the way it was. I was in Bristol for a few days in an absolute mess. I ended up sleeping in a park.

Private Albert Dance
Rifle Brigade

I got off the train at Woolwich. That's where my sweetheart, Maisey, worked. I went up to the place she was working and saw the foreman and he said, 'I know all about you! I'll tell her you're here!' and she came running out with all the other girls looking on and we embraced.

A soldier returning from Dunkirk on a train at a Kent station.

Lieutenant Arthur Curtis
7th Field Company, Royal Engineers
Our train stopped on an embankment at Lewisham. We found it rather affecting because the people in the houses by the embankment had put out signs saying, 'Welcome home' and 'Well done, lads' and all this sort of stuff. People were clambering up the embankment to the train, saying, 'Is there anyone you'd like to get a message to? We'll go and ring up for you!' But before I could give a message, the train moved off.

Francis Codd
Auxiliary fireman aboard London Fire Brigade fireboat
I think I looked a bit extraordinary when I arrived back from Dunkirk. I was wearing the reefer jacket of the auxiliary fireman and the dark trousers. I had an open-neck white tennis shirt and my cap. I'd got white plimsolls and I was extremely sunburnt. My hair was almost white and a bit long and unruly. I got to Sandwich, which is a place I've known since I was a child and has always been one of my favourite towns. I thought, 'Well, I must have a walk round in the hour I've got to wait between buses and have a look at the particularly fine church.' So I walked towards it and stood in the churchyard, looking up at the old flint tower and admiring it on this calm, beautiful summer evening. Suddenly, I was pounced on by two enormous men. I didn't know what had happened. They didn't seem to be hurting me but their obvious enmity was a bit offputting. They frisked me and looked in my pockets for something incriminating. 'We've had a lot of German spies, you know,' they said, 'and we're not satisfied.' So I said, 'Well, I'm not a German spy.' They said, 'Well, we think you might be. You look German.' I said, 'This is my standard uniform and I've been to Dunkirk.' They said, 'Well, that's your story.' I argued and remonstrated with them and said, 'I've got a bus to catch,' but they took me along to the police station. They were just enthusiastic local Sandwich Home Guard people who thought they'd trapped a German descended on them by parachute and out to take all sorts of notes about church towers and points of vantage for troops due to arrive after me. 'We'd better ring up London,' they said, 'and check that you come from there and that you're a fireman.' But they set about it in such a hopeless way, ringing the London headquarters of the Fire Brigade but unwilling to disclose my name in case it was a pseudonym. It was two hours before I was driven back to my headquarters by the police. Rumours had reached headquarters by then. It was well known that Codd of the river service had been arrested in Sandwich. For spying . . .

Private Albert Dance
Rifle Brigade
I was in a pretty poor physical condition when I got back. I'd had very little sleep and I'd not had my boots off for a week. When I eventually got them off, I was amazed. I had a ring of sock above my ankle and nothing below. Underneath the arch of my foot was all the wool packed together and congealed with blood. My feet were bloodied and blisters had burst. I could only wear slippers for a while.

Eileen Livett
Civil Nursing Reserve
We received a lot of Dunkirk casualties at my hospital. I went on duty, one morning, and sister said, 'We've a bad case on the ward, nurse, go to Staff on the end bed, and assist her with the dressings'. And when I got there, this young man was quite conscious, only about eighteen. We started to take the dressing off his thighs and he had these third degree burns, right through his flesh. He must have been in marvellous condition before he was injured because the burns were already healing. His eyes were bandaged right over, so he couldn't see us, but we could talk to him. I took the forceps to take off the bandage around his head, and his ear came away with the dressing. It was terribly charred. He'd been trapped in a burning tank. One day, his mother was sitting at the foot of his bed and after that, I was off duty for 24 hours. When I came back, he'd gone, and when I asked where he was, they said he'd died. Apparently when the nurse took the bandages off his eyes, he realised that he was blind. And although he was healing so beautifully, the shock was just enough to finish him.

Lance Corporal John Peter Wells
6th Battalion, South Staffordshire Regiment
Afterwards, one bloke was a bit bonkers. He got this thing – he couldn't keep his eyes still. They were always flickering. I was a bit bonkers myself, if the truth be known. I still suffer to this day, bursting into tears for no reason. It sounds silly at my age but it's just one of those things. I can only quote what a particular neurosurgeon said to me. He said, 'What are you complaining about? You're bloody lucky to be alive!'

Hans-Ekkehard Bob
German Messerschmitt 109 pilot
The English managed to bring back to England almost all of their men. A

The oil-covered body of a British soldier lies on the beach at Dunkirk after the evacuation.

picture presented itself that was unimaginable – how the British Expeditionary Force disappeared from Dunkirk to England using thousands of boats. I'd never seen anything like it. The entire sea was full of boats, ships, steamers and whatever. Goering's idea of attacking such an amount of boats with the Luftwaffe was absolutely not feasible and that is why I think it was possible to transport this army back to England.

Edith Kup
Women's Auxiliary Air Force, served as plotter
Dunkirk didn't seem like a disaster to the people of Britain. Once Dunkirk was lost, the feeling was, 'Oh good! Now we're on our own, we'll manage!' Which of course was probably very stupid, but that was our feeling – elation, because we were by ourselves and we could do our own thing.

The Essence of Leadership

When we heard that Churchill was to be Prime Minister,
the attitude was one of total horror.

Winston Churchill was born in 1874, the son of Tory Chancellor of the Exchequer Lord Randolph Churchill and his American wife Jennie Jerome. Until he became Prime Minister in 1940, Churchill's political career had been dogged by controversy, contradictory stances and outright failure. He first made his name during the Boer War with his accounts, published in the *Morning Post,* of his capture, imprisonment and escape from the Boers. He was elected to Parliament as a Conservative in 1900, before joining the Liberal Party. He became Home Secretary in 1910 and personally oversaw the policing of the Sidney Street siege. During the Great War, he championed the Dardanelles Expedition, with disastrous consequences, after which he served as a lieutenant colonel with the Royal Scots Fusiliers on the Western Front. In 1924, he became Chancellor of the Exchequer in Stanley Baldwin's Conservative government. He returned Britain to the gold standard and advocated ending the General Strike of 1926 by force. He was a vocal opponent of Indian independence and he remained loyal to Edward VIII during the Abdication crisis of 1936. At the outbreak of the Second World War, Neville Chamberlain appointed Churchill First Lord of the Admiralty. In this role, he proposed the mining of Norwegian territorial waters, which was quickly followed by Germany's invasion of Denmark and Norway. A failed attempt by the Allies to retake Norway led to the resignation of Chamberlain. There were two possible successors; Lord Halifax, the foreign secretary, a trusted man of integrity who had the support of most of the government, and Churchill, the adventurer, a man widely mistrusted. On May 9, Chamberlain called a meeting at which he, Halifax and Churchill were present. At that meeting, Halifax decided that his membership of the House of Lords would make it impossible for him to succeed Chamberlain. On the following day, Winston Churchill was appointed Prime Minister.

It was not a universally popular appointment – but for Britain it was a fortunate one. Churchill's political judgment may often have been questionable but his vision of Britain as the bastion of freedom and democracy, duty bound to resist evil, was not. He had been a consistent and vocal critic of the rise of Nazism when most Britons had regarded Hitler as little more than the rekindler of Germany's self respect. His speeches – on the wireless and in the House of Commons – and his air of determined calm were to fortify the nation in the face of overwhelming odds. It has been said that the essence of leadership is to dull the rational faculty and to substitute enthusiasm for it. Churchill had that power and in 1940, in Britain, it was precisely what was needed.

Flying Officer Jeffrey Quill
Vickers Chief Test Pilot and 65 Squadron, RAF
On the day that Churchill came to power, I called on an elderly couple who had been great friends of my parents. We were discussing the leadership question and I said, 'I wouldn't be surprised if old Churchill doesn't get into power.' The man, who was obviously a much older generation, said, 'Good heavens, I hope not!' It made me understand how greatly his generation of Englishmen distrusted Churchill. In their eyes, he was a rather wild man, politically.

John Colville
Assistant Private Secretary to Winston Churchill
When we heard that Churchill was to be Prime Minister, the attitude was one of total horror. There had grown up at Number 10 a feeling that he was irresponsible. We all knew about Gallipoli and his support for the White Russians and for the return to the Gold Standard which was thought to be a disaster. There was a general feeling that he was a man who would go in for wild and undigested schemes. This was also the feeling in the Cabinet Offices amongst people like Sir Edward Bridges and General Ismay. One must remember that he was held responsible in Whitehall circles for the failure of the Norwegian Expedition.

Winston Churchill and his wife Clementine.

So he arrived at Number 10 with a wall of suspicion. The senior private secretary went off with Chamberlain and Churchill brought with him two of his secretaries at the Admiralty. New people joined us in due course – John Martin and Lesley Rowan. So we were a gathering of four men and one woman – Miss Watson who'd been there since the time of Bonar Law and Lloyd George – and we were the private office. There was Commander Thompson, a sort of flag lieutenant for Churchill who arranged his journeys abroad. And there were one or two advisors and friends of Churchill such as Brendan Bracken and Desmond Morton. The remarkable thing was that we all got on extraordinarily well together. It was a very happy ship indeed.

Churchill was incredibly inconsiderate as regards hours. Without being a selfish man – because he was very generous – he was enormously egocentric. It never occurred to him that what suited him might be extremely inconvenient to other people, whether they were his colleagues in the Cabinet or his staff. But despite all that, and despite some silly things that have been said by certain biographers, he was deeply loved by everyone at Number 10 from the junior typist to the Principal Private Secretary. An example of this was Sir Horace Wilson's secretary, Miss Davis. She was a very outspoken Welsh lady, marvellously honest but sometimes rather ill tempered. She was devoted to Sir Horace and because Churchill didn't approve of him, she was violently anti Churchill at first. Yet, in due course, she became one of Churchill's greatest admirers. That he could turn her violent antipathy into devoted admiration was a tribute to Churchill's personality and ability to win people over.

Churchill always preferred the faces that he knew. It was one of his weaknesses. The call of *Auld Lang Syne* was very strong with him. He made several appalling appointments, such as Sir Roger Keyes, who was a disaster as director of combined operations. He was inclined to say, 'Oh yes, I knew so-and-so,' and he'd try and appoint him to some job.

There came an awful moment when I went away – I was always going in and out of Number 10 – and a very nice fellow was produced to take my place temporarily. I won't give his name because he had a very distinguished career afterwards but he was shown to Churchill who looked at him. After a while, Churchill rang the bell for John Martin and said, 'Take him away! I don't want to see him again!' That was very embarrassing for all concerned.

Churchill always took a great deal of trouble with young people. Whilst on *HMS King George V*, despite being very much burdened by events at the time, Churchill spent a whole hour in the gun room, talking to the midshipmen, all of whom clustered round him, asking him all sorts of questions. He treated them exactly as if they were his equals – in fact, they forgot he was the Prime Minister. He did the same on his annual visit to Harrow, his old school. He used to collect all the senior boys around him and he spoke to them for three-quarters of an hour, in an absolutely charming way. Chamberlain could never have done that. Equally, Churchill had a good relationship with the younger members of his staff – and more particularly, for some reason, with myself. I'm never quite sure why. He became, I think I can say, rather fond of me. One would have arguments with him – I remember one argument about the merits of Munich – and one really forgot that one was talking to the Prime Minister and one could let fly and he never minded a bit. He would talk man to man as if you were a contemporary. That was a remarkable attribute of Churchill that I think was very rare amongst great men.

The two main props of Churchill's way of conducting the war were Sir Edward Bridges and General Ismay. Both of them were secretaries of the Cabinet – one civil, one military. When Churchill wanted something examined, he would send a minute marked 'Action This Day' either to Bridges or to Ismay. During the Blitz, they were in the Cabinet War Rooms the whole time. In the evenings, when we dined in the mess down there, all the senior members of their staffs were there and we got to know them very well. And a lot of our work tied in very closely with theirs.

We had to take it in turns to be on duty for 24 hours at a time because of Churchill's habit of working until three or four in the morning. We couldn't all be about so one private secretary would be on late duty at Number 10. You had to know about all the papers in the Prime Minister's box on whatever subject. And of course, his box had a lot of folders in it on every kind of subject. You couldn't suddenly find yourself at Chequers on a Friday evening, there until the Monday, ignorant of the various papers.

The one exception was 'Ultra'. These were the decrypts of the German air force and, subsequently, navy and military ciphers. We weren't supposed to read these signals because they came to the Prime Minister in yellow boxes, brought personally by Brigadier Menzies who was the head of the secret service. Menzies would come in, open them with a special key, take away the ones that were out of date and he might say, 'This box has something that the Prime Minister should see urgently.' It wasn't until Churchill opened his yellow box in his car on the way from Downing Street to Ditchley, that he became aware that there was going to be this huge raid on the night of November 14. He assumed that it would be on London so he turned the car around. I happened to be on duty at Number 10 that weekend and I was looking forward to a quiet time with the Prime Minister away so I was horrified when he suddenly reappeared and sent me off to the deep shelter in Downing Street saying, 'You're too young to die. Tonight, London is going to be flattened.' Churchill then climbed on to the Air Ministry roof with John Martin to watch this huge raid and nothing happened. This huge bomber force went north of London, straight to Coventry.

The Cabinet War Rooms were built before the war and we used to get reports from the Map Room, even in Chamberlain's time. When the Blitz began in September 1940, they came into full use. A bedroom was prepared for Churchill on the first floor. There were a lot of bedrooms below that, also prepared for him, which were thought to be safer. He took a great deal of trouble over the security because he had a passion for building. I remember one evening, going down with him to the basement where workmen were strengthening the brickwork to shore up the structure against air raids. The next evening, we took our torches and went down again and by the third evening, he thought he understood these underground works pretty well and he was advising the workmen on how to build traverses. He climbed up on to one of the walls, vaulted over it and landed in a pool of liquid cement. I thought it was rather funny and I said, 'I think, sir, you've met your Waterloo.' He looked at me and said, 'My Blenheim, please . . . '.

Churchill never really liked living in the Cabinet War Rooms but he slept in his bedroom there a number of times in September and early October 1940. He also used that room for his afternoon rest. I remember vividly going into the room after the death of Neville Chamberlain to find Churchill dictating a very moving speech about Chamberlain to Mrs Hill, one of his personal secretaries. As he spoke, he was lying flat on his bed looking . . . not totally proper. He liked to lie in bed and dictate and he rather forgot who was in the room sometimes. Sometimes he used to go to the Down Street tube shelter which had been prepared by the Underground railway executive and had most comfortable accommodation. He spent the night there seven or eight times when things were very noisy.

Then, in October, an annex was built on the floor above the Cabinet War Rooms and converted into a really rather beautiful flat by Mrs Churchill, who had the most marvellous taste. So in that month, he began sleeping there. He had a bedroom and small office and Mrs Churchill had a bedroom and they shared a drawing room and a sitting room. But he still liked working at Number 10 because he liked the atmosphere. This made life very difficult for the private office because we never knew where we were going to be next; Number 10 or the annex. He used to broadcast from the Cabinet Room at 10 Downing Street where the BBC would bring their apparatus. He also carried on eating his meals at Number 10, bombs or no bombs. There was the awful occasion in October when a bomb blew in the kitchen and Churchill was very worried and he ran downstairs to see whether the cook was all right. During the evenings, he would take the a lift from the annex down to the Cabinet War Rooms for meetings of the Cabinet and the defence committee. The defence committee always met at night. As soon as the bombings stopped in May 1941, life started again at Number 10 but because Mrs Churchill said that she couldn't keep Number 10 and the annex going, they continued to live at the annex until the end of the war.

Dilwyn Evans
Worker at Armstrong-Siddeley factory in Coventry
When Churchill visited our factory, we were all told to congregate in the yard, and make two lines. Churchill came along with his homburger on, waving his hands and he was smoking a cigar which was about ten inches long. When he got near to the end of the line, he took a puff of his cigar and threw it to the ground. Nobody moved until he was out of sight – then it was one mad dash to get the cigar.

Threat of Invasion

We would really have all gone down on to the beaches with broken bottles.
We would have done anything – anything – to stop them.

Even as the troops were returning from Dunkirk, Churchill's War Cabinet was considering entering into peace discussions with Hitler. On May 25, Lord Halifax had attended a meeting with the Italian ambassador who suggested that Mussolini could broker negotiations between Britain and Germany. Over the next three days, Halifax pressed the War Cabinet to follow this course. He believed that Britain ought to consider making concessions which did not compromise her independence. So far as he was concerned, this was no longer a matter of appeasement, rather it was plain common sense. Churchill disagreed. Even to engage in mediation, he believed, would call into question Britain's willingness to fight. He felt that any terms proposed would put Britain entirely at Hitler's mercy. 'Nations that went down fighting rose again,' he said, 'but those that surrendered tamely were finished.' On the afternoon of May 28, Churchill attended a meeting of his wider Cabinet. He told the assembled politicians that he had considered negotiating with Hitler but that if he were to make peace, Britain would become a slave state. When he had finished, there was a roar of support from around the table. Churchill felt sufficiently emboldened that he was able to go back to the War Cabinet that evening and inform them emphatically that there would be no surrender.

Several weeks later, an invitation to the negotiating table was to arrive from Adolf Hitler. Hitler believed that the Germans and the British stood together as higher racial beings and he felt that the destruction of the

British Empire would benefit the United States, Japan and the Soviet Union more than it would benefit Germany. A political settlement with Britain would suit his purposes and so in a speech on July 19, broadcast worldwide, he declared that he did not wish to see the war against Britain continue but that he would pursue it to a victorious finish if that proved necessary. He waited for three days for a response. On July 22, Lord Halifax formally rejected the approach.

Yet even as Hitler was making peaceful overtures, he was preparing for the invasion of Britain. On July 13, General von Brauchitsch had presented Hitler with a plan for invasion to be carried out in August. Ninety thousand men would be sent across the Channel in an initial assault on a stretch of coast between Ramsgate and Lyme Regis. Three days later, *Operation Sealion* – the codename for invasion – came into official being with the publication of Fuhrer Directive No. 16. Only seven copies of this directive ever existed. It stated Hitler's objective – 'to eliminate the English home country as a base for the continuation of the war against Germany and, if it should become necessary, to occupy the entire island'.

At the end of July, Hitler put the date of invasion back to September 16 and two weeks later, a reduced invasion front reaching from Ramsgate to Worthing was agreed. The attack was to be carried out in two waves; the first wave of about 60,000 troops would secure the beachheads and the second wave of tanks, artillery and mobile troops would effect the breakout and establish crossings over the River Medway. Support would arrive in the form of parachute troops to be landed near Brighton and Folkestone. The ultimate goal was London which would be encircled in a pincer movement. The infantry would be brought across the Channel in barges. The German navy had already begun converting almost 2,000 cargo barges – some powered, most not – for the job.

Hitler wanted to bring Britain under his control, and he was willing to wait for his opportunity. He was keeping his options alive.

The Mood of the People

Joan Seaman
Civilian in London
I remember being very frightened indeed when France collapsed because I thought it was going to be us next. Really frightened. Until I heard the speech

that Churchill made on the radio about fighting on the beaches. I suddenly wasn't frightened any more. It was quite amazing. When people have decried Churchill, I've always said, 'Yes, but he stopped me being afraid!'

Oliver Bernard
Child in London
I can remember listening to 'We'll fight them on the beaches . . . ' That raised the hairs on the back of one's neck. It was an amazing experience. It was exciting in the way that it was exciting to listen to my heroic cricket-playing schoolmaster reading Macaulay's *Horatius* about the three men who defended Rome against the entire Tuscan army.

Joan Varley
Civilian in London
We would really have all gone down on to the beaches with broken bottles. We would have done anything – *anything* – to stop them.

Donald Browne
Schoolboy in Ramsgate
My father took his First World War pistol and tried to teach my mother to shoot it. The lessons were not successful so the pistol was returned. My mother would have done more damage to the house than to the Germans.

Ronald Oates
Civilian in London
I went into my friend's house and on her mother's wall were some beautiful carved wooden bellows. I went to examine them. 'Don't touch them!' said the mother. 'Why not?' 'They're full of pepper,' she said. 'Why on earth have you got pepper in them?' 'When the Germans come, I'm not letting them get away with it easy. I'm going to blow pepper at them.'

Marguerite Crowther
British civilian teaching English to refugees in Cluj, Romania
I was trying to get back to England from Romania. My companion and I had reached Austria and we got on a train – and it turned out to be a German troop train. When it was discovered that there were two English girls on the train, we were taken down to the officers quarters where we both passed out from tiredness. I came to, lying along the laps of a lot of German officers. One of the officers spoke good English and he said, 'Wake up! I'll show you how to pull yourselves together. You break raw eggs on your teeth and wash it down

A soldier stands watch behind English beach defences.

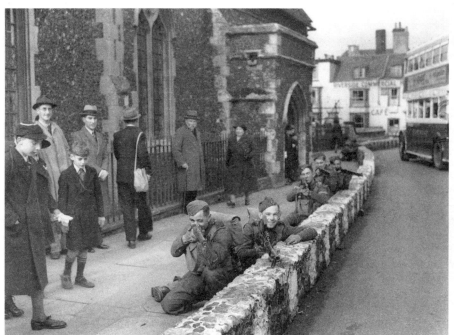

Troops defend a church during an anti-invasion exercise.

with brandy.' So we did that. Then he said, 'Where do you come from?' 'London.' 'Good!' he said, 'You must have a lot of friends in London!' 'Of course I have, I've lived there all my life.' 'Well,' he said, 'could I have the addresses of your friends? 'Why?' I asked. 'Because next month, we'll be in London!'

Hilda Cripps
Civilian in Great Wakering, Essex

I used to get up on those lovely summer mornings and look across to Foulness and wonder whether hordes of Germans would come in. It seemed so very, very possible. After a great deal of thought, I did something. I talked to my husband and we decided that our four-year-old couldn't have done anything without us. I kept a bottle of a hundred aspirins and if the Germans came, we'd have dissolved them in some milk and given them to her to drink. That's the truth. That's how real it was.

Walter Miller
Civilian in London

I remember saying to my parents, 'We've lost the war, haven't we?' And they said, 'You mustn't say that!' It was an interesting response. They didn't say, 'No, that's not right.' What they were saying was that it wasn't wise to say that sort of thing.

Private David Elliott,
Royal Army Medical Corps

The church bells were told to be silent after Dunkirk. They were going to be used as an invasion warning. There was no other method – the sirens didn't reach everywhere. So they were silent for the next few years.

Hilda Cripps
Civilian in Great Wakering, Essex

The chairman of the parish council came and asked me to be on an invasion committee. I said I would and the commander from Shoebury garrison came and told us that we must remain totally secret. He said that his garrison would have to fight over and around us, so he wanted all the people in isolated farmhouses brought into the village so that we were close together. He said, 'Your duty will be, as far as possible, to provide the essential things for living – food and drink. You won't be allowed on any roads, they will be entirely for my military. Do your best to prevent panic and keep some sort of semblance of life going.' And off he went.

We expected saturation bombing before the invasion, so we took delivery of 420 papier-mâché coffins. They were stored in the loft of a building right in the middle of the high street. The next thing we did, we placed containers of rations at strategic points around the village, that could be reached by field paths. We set aside one large house as a possible hospital, and a smaller one as an isolation hospital. We made a consensus of all the livestock – sheep, cows, pigs, chickens – and then decided the order in which they would be killed for food. Pigs and sheep first, then cows, but not those that were in milk, of course, and the chickens that were not laying. We visited every house in the village to find out whether there was anyone who might be available for cleaning, caring for people or preparing food.

We all had overall responsibility for the committee but we each had our own particular job and mine was for the water supply for the village. The first thing I did was to go to an elderly retired builder, who was able to give me information about a great many wells in the village. I went to Southend Water Company and asked if they could send someone to inspect the wells and tell me if the water in them was fit for drinking. Which they did, without any query. So I knew which wells had water suitable for drinking, and others that would do for washing. Then I found out which farmers had water carts and these carts were made available to be sterilised and used to allocate water from the wells.

We were very ordinary people but we worked hard over these weeks. We used to meet down at the Congregational church when it was vital that we knew what the next overall move was. A little yellow triangle appeared on the old village school, which told the military authorities that any information given out there would be correct, because they'd had problems with quislings giving false information. The last thing we were told by the authorities was that if the invasion did come, six of the committee would likely be shot by the Germans, so that the village wouldn't get in the way of invading German troops.

Lieutenant Arthur Curtis
7th Field Company, Royal Engineers

We wanted to put mines on the green of Brighton and Hove bowling club but the members insisted on having a last bowling match while we were laying the mines at the far end. We were terrified that somebody would roll a wood too far and it would fall on one of these naval mines, which were very sensitive. So there were these dear old ladies in their white skirts having their last bowling match, regardless of Adolf Hitler.

A village invasion committee in Suffolk.

Christabel Leighton-Porter
Model for Daily Mirror cartoon character 'Jane'

I went down to New Romney in Kent. Actually it was a closed area and I really wasn't supposed to be there. But my husband was down there in the air force and he booked me into the little Station Hotel, which was lovely. I went along the seafront and it was barbed wired and scaffolding all the way along. Hanging from the scaffolding were mines, and the beach was mined. New Romney was one of the nearest points to France and all the hotels were closed but it was beautiful weather and I used to go down and get as near to the sea as I could and sit on the esplanade and look at the sea. Then one day a crowd of soldiers marched down and they took their uniforms off and they'd got swimming gear on underneath. And they walked through a gap in the sea defences and had a swim. So I thought, well, after they've gone if I put my feet in the same marks they've made I'm OK, I'm safe to have a swim. Absolute paradise, it was absolutely lovely and I did that from then on every day. On the Saturday I went down and had my usual swim but when I came back there was a policeman stood by the side of my clothing and said that he was going to charge me and summons me for swimming off a mined beach. My court case came up on the Monday and I was fined a pound. But it was worth every penny.

Walter Miller
Civilian in London

We used to grow a lot of food on allotments and we needed a bonfire to get rid of the debris. One of our neighbours thought that the bonfire was signalling to enemy aircraft. It sounds laughable now but my family were exceedingly annoyed.

William Pilkington
Self-defence instructor

One morning, I was told to go to London. 'What for?' I asked. 'You're going to be trained to be a hangman.' I was told – and this must be the joke of the century – that if we were invaded, there would be traitors and they would have to be dealt with by judicial hanging. There couldn't be hangmen in every port, so people were to be trained to do it correctly. Four of us went to Pentonville Prison where we met the hangman, Albert Pierrepoint. He trained us in the inverse ratio of drop over weight. You divide a thousand by the number of pounds of the man to be hanged, and you get the number of feet and inches he is to be dropped. We then went on the scaffold and

Soldiers and members of the public settle down on a Norfolk beach.

prepared it, adjusted the chains, closed the doors, dropped a dummy on it, and we came out after five days as qualified hangmen. When we were leaving, Pierrepoint shook hands with us. He said, 'I wish you luck, lads but let me tell you something; this is a bloody nonsense. Because if we're invaded, the Germans would be taking the prisoners and I don't think you could go up to an SS guard and say, "May I use your gallows on one of our traitors, please?" '

There was a considerable fear of traitors in Britain at this time. Although the four accounts that follow cannot be corroborated by independent evidence, the fact that they are remembered with such clarity gives a sense of the pervasive anxiety amongst the population.

Flight Lieutenant George Lerwill
49 Squadron, RAF

I, as a flight commander, was sitting in my office one day when the telephone went. It was HQ saying that two gentlemen from the Home Office wanted to interview me about my car. I thought this was somewhat odd. They were shown in and one of them asked if I owned a Hillman Minx DT9510. 'Yes.' 'Have you ever visited Reverend Nye, the vicar at Scampton in your car?' they asked. 'Are you talking to me because the car wasn't taxed?' I said. 'because I'll get it taxed next week.' 'We're not interested in the tax,' they said. 'On a date a week previously, your car was seen at the vicar's house and a tall blonde RAF officer got out.' I looked it the date in my log book and found that I was at another RAF unit on that date. Then they told me that this conversation was strictly confidential and I was not to discuss it with anybody. And away they went. I didn't think much more about it. Until I found out that the police had gone down to Reverend Nye's house where they found him upstairs with my squadron's intelligence officer, transmitting to Germany. The intelligence officer was a reserve officer called Thompson who'd been called in when war was declared. The vicar was placed under arrest and sentenced to five years' imprisonment. Thompson disappeared. What happened to him, I don't know.

Trooper William Driscoll
12th Lancers

When we were stationed in a little village called Long Melford in Suffolk, the food we were getting was terrible so we used to go to a café called Coley's. It was run by Mr. Coley and he was a cheerful fellow, rather heavy in his jowls, always laughing and he had a lovely wife. They used to make a fuss of us. At the time, our mail was getting sanctioned – by the time we got it, it was already opened. So we asked Mr Coley if he'd accept our mail, because civilian mail wasn't getting opened. He did, and we used to go and collect our mail from him, and we'd have our lunch there. It was a lovely dinner for two shillings. Then one night, on stand-to, the alarm went. We caught it, raced down, and burst into the café with high-up officers. Mr. Coley was a spy, a German spy! And there was his transmitter up in his loft! He was such a nice chap, it amazes me. As him and his wife were marched away, he shouted out to some of the fellows, 'Best of luck!' God, he had more guns facing him – you'd have thought he was Hitler!

Lance Corporal Lawrence Greggain
5th Battalion, Border Regiment
We were located in a camp near Kingston-on-Wye, and what would happen, these light German aircraft would come over, and Welsh fifth columnists would go up on the top of these hills, and talk to the chap in the aircraft with Morse. One day I was sent out on my motorbike to try and catch a chap doing this and I could see his light flashing. You had these mountain roads that ran in a series of loops and I was in such a damned hurry to get there that I tried to cut across from one loop of the road to another. The bike went up in the air, then the bike and I went down the hill together. I ended up in the emergency hospital in Hereford. And that's the reason I got out of the army.

Eileen Livett
Civil Nursing Reserve
Barnet Hospital, where I was with the Civil Nursing Reserve, had some German nurses. After Dunkirk, when all the casualties came in, they were still with us. One day I saw one of these Germans with a beautiful bouquet, and said to her, 'Ooh! Beautiful flowers! Who gave you those? You've got an ardent suitor!' She just smiled and walked away. Anyway, the Dunkirk casualties were in the main wards, and the side wards were taken up with the officers. In one side ward we had a young Highland lieutenant who just kept talking all the time and in the other bed was a major, an older man, who didn't say anything at all. We concluded that they both had shock reactions. After a week I went off duty, and when I came back on, the major's bed was empty, and I said to one of the nurses, 'Where's the major?' and she said, 'He's gone.' So I said, 'Gone? But he wasn't ready to be discharged!' So then she told me very hurriedly that two plain-clothes detectives had arrived, spoken

to sister and gone off with him. The next day, it said in the stop press column of the paper, 'German Spy Arrested in North London Hospital', so we concluded that this must have been our major. I wondered whether the bouquet the German girl had was a signal for her that he was arriving. But by then, all the German nurses had gone. They were taken into internment.

Sergeant John Milton
Served at 'Paddock' – Cabinet War Rooms 2, Dollis Hill

When I came home from France, I was waiting for a posting and I was told to report to the Company Office, where I was told to go home and change into civilian clothes. I did and when I came back, I was told to report to Dollis Hill Post Office Research Station in North London. I arrived at this dreary building and I was shown down a long corridor to a large iron door. Sergeant Pat Kinna, a suave little man, appeared. 'Are you Sergeant Milton?' he asked. 'Yes.' 'I've been waiting for you.' I was given an office downstairs but I still couldn't work out what this was all about. Eventually Kinna told me. I had arrived at 'Paddock'. If the government was forced out of London, they would all come here. I was amazed. 'How long am I going to stay here?' I asked. 'For the rest of the war,' Pat said, 'and the first thing we've got to do is get the place furnished.'

My job was to be to keep the place fully operational. It was our duty to test all the telephones in the operations room and to test the teleprinters to all the government departments. We had scramble telephones to telephone very important people where the messages weren't to be tapped so the voice was scrambled at one end and it came out quite normal at the other end. There was a BBC broadcasting studio for transmissions by the Prime Minister. There were rooms for Anthony Eden, General Ismay, Sir Edward Bridges – there was even a room with David Niven, the film actor's name on it, but I never found out why. The best room of all was Mr Churchill's bunker. His room was hexagonal and for acoustic purposes, it was lined with straw and corrugated paper so when you went in, it was just like a morgue. The atmosphere was dead. It was enough to drive you round the bend. When we had a dress rehearsal for the evacuation – to be known as *Operation Black Move* – Churchill said to me, 'Sergeant, I want to go to the lavatory! Can you show me where it is?' 'I'm sorry sir,' I said, 'There aren't any lavatories on this floor. You'll have to climb the stairs.' He was rather annoyed about that – you know what old gentlemen are like. Churchill didn't like Dollis Hill – but if the Germans had invaded he would have had no choice.

Lieutenant Colonel Malcolm Hancock
Served with Coats Mission

The Coats Mission was an organisation which was formed for the personal protection of the Royal Family, that is King George VI, Queen Elizabeth and the two Princesses, Elizabeth and Margaret. The intention was that if a parachute landing or such eventuality should take place and the Royal Family had to be evacuated from London, they would be whisked away to one of four country houses which had been selected for them to go to. Of the houses, I can remember Madresfield Court, near Malvern, Pitchford Hall on the borders of Shropshire and Castle Howard in Yorkshire. And we – the Coats Mission – would go with them and take up the defence of that particular house. We would remain there in their defence up to the last man and the last round. Each of these houses had to be made into a local fortress. There would be a series of slit trenches placed at strategic points around the perimeter of the house and gardens so that they could not be seen from outside. There were barbed wire entanglements but these would not be put in place until we were actually called upon to defend that particular house – in order that nothing untoward should appear to be going on at these places. Everything had to be done with the greatest secrecy. It was absolutely vital that as few people as possible knew where they were. We had to be most careful of everything we said or did.

Harry Hopthrow
Assistant Director of Works at GHQ Home Forces

When the job of preparing Madresfield Court was completed, Major Coats came in furious one day and said that some of the royal entourage had come down to the house and the first thing they'd done was to produce a royal letterbox and put it in the front entrance, so everybody could see it. This was the last thing in the world they should be doing.

Lieutenant Colonel Malcolm Hancock
Served with Coats Mission

There were two saloon motor cars kept at Combermere Barracks and if the time came, Captain Morris of 12th Lancers would drive one of them with the King and Queen in and Lieutenant Humblecrost, also of 12th Lancers, would follow in the second one with the two princesses. They would make their way to whichever house had been chosen and we would make our way in a non-stop convoy from Bushey where we were stationed and we'd hope to fetch up there together. We thought it was a marvellous honour to be chosen to be part of an organisation with the object of fighting to the last round and the last man. It was a marvellous thing.

The Defence of Britain

We were told that if the church bells rang, that meant the invasion had started.

On May 27, General Sir Edmund Ironside had been placed in charge of Britain's defences. His chief strategy was to delay the invaders on the beaches, giving the badly-equipped and poorly-trained defenders the chance to counter-attack. A front line of infantry was to be deployed along the beaches which were to be defended by barbed wire, minefields, pillboxes, trenches and anti-tank obstacles. A system of over fifty defended 'stop lines', making use of topographical and man-made features, was set up further inland to halt the invaders advance. A final defence line, known as the GHQ Line, running from Somerset to Essex and then north to Yorkshire, was intended to protect London and the heart of England. Ironside was succeeded by General Alan Brooke on July 20. Brooke considered that the existing defences were too static and promoted a siege mentality. He began placing greater emphasis on the mobility of his forces.

Private David Elliott
Royal Army Medical Corps
We'd left all our weapons of any size behind in France. The country was virtually unarmed.

Major William Watson
6th Battalion, Durham Light Infantry
Our equipment was extremely short. The gunners had old French 75s with

wooden wheels, the signallers were training on a few very feeble wireless sets and some of the men were wearing the uniforms they'd been wearing when they escaped from Dunkirk.

Bombardier Douglas Goddard
Royal Artillery

It was really rather comical. We had rifles with five rounds of ammunition, we had one 1914 Lewis gun and we had three London taxis. We patrolled the coast between Camber Sands and Dimchurch – where the invasion was due to land – in taxis.

Captain Kenneth Johnstone
11th Battalion, Durham Light Infantry

I remember one officer being put on a charge by the brigadier because he didn't have a revolver, until it was explained to the brigadier that it wasn't his turn to wear the revolver, because we only had one between six of us.

Joan Varley
Civilian in London

Roosevelt was sending us munitions which had been used by the Americans for training purposes. They were pretty out of date – never mind! They were weapons.

Chief Petty Officer Ronald Apps
Engine room artificer aboard HMS Tyne

In July 1940, I joined a Royal Fleet Auxiliary tanker – the *War African* – that was anchored off Sheerness for an idea that I have always assumed was thought up by Churchill. These tankers were filled up with fuel oil and there were mines and detonators down in the holds. The idea was that we would run them over to Boulogne and about five or six miles out of the harbour, we would set the controls and lash them – with the boilers going full bore – and run them into Boulogne harbour and let them blow up, to destroy the potential German invasion fleet. It was called Operation Lucid and we spent four weeks preparing. We practised setting the controls and evacuating the ship with two speedboats alongside us which had been commandeered from Southend. These speedboats were remarkable things. They could go at 35 or 40 knots and the idea was that at the blowing of a whistle, we had to rush down, get in the boats and we were away. Those four weeks were a bit hairy because the tanker was full up with fuel oil when it came to us and it was primed and ready to explode and there were air raids at night. When you're in this tanker, sitting on all this explosive material and the Germans are coming over and dropping bombs, it's not a very . . . shall I say 'sleep inspiring' experience. It's one of those things you either get used to or you don't sleep. I got round to the idea that I had to sleep or I wouldn't be able to walk around the next day. In the end, it was decided that the operation was too risky and we would be blown up as well and the whole thing was cancelled.

Harry Hopthrow
Assistant Director of Works at GHQ Home Forces
I was dealing with the defence of Britain. When General Ironside was commander-in-chief, his strategy was to defend the beaches. He provided beach defences of many varieties, including tubes of scaffolding that were put round the beaches to prevent landings and the cutting of pleasure piers. There was also some very experimental stuff – ideas about how to set the beaches on fire – which never worked. One commander had the idea of getting hold of American bullfrogs. He said that if they all sounded at the right time, it would make the people coming ashore violently sick. I remember him telling Ironside, 'We've got to get some bullfrogs!' but whether they ever turned up, I don't know.

Eventually, Ironside was retired and made a field marshal. He was a very pleasant man to be with but he'd really passed his best by this time and he was too lighthearted to be commander-in-chief. He didn't quite fit in a big organisation and he was replaced by Brooke, who was superb. He was an excellent tactician, rather brusque but one was very confident working with him because if you wanted an answer, you got it and you were pretty certain that he was right.

After he took over, there was a very distinct tactical change from building defensive works to the idea that if there was any landing, it should be dealt with by mobile troops on offensive action rather than simply trying to stop them on the beaches. There was still defence on the beaches but Brooke's main forces could be moved about the country and concentrated wherever the enemy was concentrating.

Second Lieutenant Peter Vaux
4th Royal Tank Regiment
We were sent down to Tweseldown where each tank squadron was equipped with a train. These trains all smelt of new paint – they must have been made almost overnight. Each train consisted of 17 flats, the end one of which had a removable bogey and jacks and a lot of railway sleepers stacked on it. And

what happened was, if we were called upon, a locomotive would come to the siding where this train was waiting; the ramp would be lowered by removing the bogey and jacks and our tanks would climb up on to it. It would be jacked up again, the bogeys would be put back, the sleepers which had been put between the rails so that the tanks could swing themselves on the rails would be put back again on the flat, the crews would all get on the railway carriage at the end, and our tanks would steam off by train to meet the Germans wherever they might be landing.

We took the threat of invasion more seriously than most because we'd seen it actually happen in France. We'd seen the speed with which those Panzer divisions could hurtle across the countryside. Nobody at that time knew anything about the difficulty of seaborne landings. We always credited the Germans with being very clever in these things. We were sure that they could do it overnight. We expected that the Germans would land, the thinly spread out infantry on the beaches would withdraw and the Germans would establish a beachhead. We had to get there with our tanks before they broke out.

Private David Elliott
Royal Army Medical Corps
In Bognor Regis, I saw these rolls and rolls of barbed wire all along the front. There were stakes in the ground to stop tanks and they'd started erecting posts like giant pit props in the fields to stop the invasion gliders from landing.

Lieutenant Arthur Curtis
7th Field Company, Royal Engineers
I went around with a regimental commander, siting pillboxes. Then I would make a rendezvous with a building contractor, hand over the land, knock in a post to indicate the location required and the axis of the main loophole, and the contractor would sign the form and then he would get on with it. There were no formalities – it was very quick. But the pillboxes were very frail. They were only brick with some concrete in between the bricks, and they wouldn't have stopped anything more than a bullet. But still, they were useful because they created a firing position, and they showed up on the air photographs and we know that when the Germans were planning Operation Sealion, they grossly overestimated the strength of the defences because they assumed that these were much stronger fortifications than they actually were.

H 2988

Lord Halifax inspects an anti-invasion strongpoint on the English coast in August 1940. Two months earlier, Halifax had attempted to persuade Churchill's war cabinet to consider negotiating with Nazi Germany.

Sergeant Ronald Swann
238 Battery, 115th Field Regiment, Royal Artillery
We were sent to Beckenham in Kent, in defence of London, and we were given old four-inch naval guns. My gun position was in the car park of the Black Prince pub at Bexleyheath. It had a line of fire along the road and over the outer anti-tank defence ditch of London. Our guns were purely anti-tank and our instructions were, the moment we got to action stations, we should load the gun and be ready to fire.

One evening, at our base in Beckenham, the officer on duty came and said, 'They've come! They've arrived!' I said, 'What do you mean, sir?' He said, 'We've just had the code word for invasion! Action stations!' So I said, 'I haven't got a gun crew!' I could only find a saddler, who was responsible for the leather and webbing, and a couple of signallers. He said, 'Well, we've got to do something about it.' So he sent the signaller out into the local pubs and we got together a crew, and then we moved off to the car park of the Black Prince. I said to him I would ring as soon as I was in position and when I did, he said, 'Come back, I've got different instructions.'

This crew was made up of conscripts who'd never seen action and I said to them, 'We've got to unload the gun.' The charge came out all right, but the shell had been well rammed in to the piece and I had to go to the front of the gun, and push it out with a shell ejector. I said to two or three of the gunners, 'Be ready when I push the shell out. Be ready to catch it because it'll come out quite sharpish.' So I went up the other end and pushed it, and there was a hell of a clatter. They dropped it and jumped away, thinking it was going to go off! It couldn't of course, there are various safety measures within the shell. It amused me at the time, but to those lads it was very serious.

We travelled back to Beckenham quite slowly, with only sidelights on. I was sitting alongside the driver, open cabs of course. And when we got to Penge, some poor chap, partly deaf and partly blind, had just come out of the cinema, and he walked out in front of our vehicle. He was taken away and I gave full particulars. When we got back to Beckenham, the officer told me he'd got the wrong code word, it was only stand to, not action stations. We needn't have gone in the first place.

Second Lieutenant Peter Vaux
4th Royal Tank Regiment
There was a railway line which ran right across southern England and the question arose whether it would serve as an obstacle to German tanks or not. Nobody really knew and we were invited to drive one of our tanks over the rails

to see what happened. We sent a tank down to the station at Aldershot and the colonel drove it across the rails and absolutely nothing happened to the tank – but it stopped all the trains for a long way around. It shorted the main rail with the other rails and that blew the fuses up and down the line. If one had been standing beside the tank, and had had one's hand on the tank, you'd have been electrocuted – but as you were in the tank, you were in the same position as a bird who sits on a power line. So the Southern Railway was not an obstacle to tanks. Tanks, however, were an obstacle to the Southern Railway.

Lieutenant Arthur Curtis
7th Field Company, Royal Engineers
On the approaches to the South Downs were these quite narrow lanes and somebody had the bright idea that you could conceal a small tank of oil along the banks of these lanes and when the German tanks arrived, you could let the oil out on the road and throw a Molotov cocktail on to it and you'd frizzle the leading tank. The colonel wanted to demonstrate this, and he invited a lot of generals along to watch. He didn't want anything to go wrong, so he asked me to dress as a private soldier and lurk in the trench and light the oil. When everything was ready, he gave me the signal and I released the tank and the oil spurted out and I lit the Molotov cocktail and threw it. There was a great burst of flame but the grass was tinder dry and it immediately started a grass fire, and I was in my trench surrounded by flames, and the colonel was shouting, 'Are you alright?' Fortunately the grass wasn't very deep, and I emerged, looking rather black but otherwise unharmed. I'm not sure if the idea was ever taken up.

Private Harold Wilmshurst
5th Battalion, Royal Sussex Regiment
We had a special job. We had to go all round all these villages where there are banks and bends in the road and we had to insert these barrels of inflammable material into the banks. A charge was put behind them with a wire running behind them to the nearest cover. A detonator was put in a pipe down the back of these barrels and the idea was that if the tanks came round on the road, we'd detonate these barrels of flaming liquid over them.

Second Lieutenant Peter Vaux
4th Royal Tank Regiment
We did a lot of recce training in tanks and we covered a great deal of the country – but we didn't do it all in tanks. We used carriers and trucks as well

Flames are thrown across a river during a Fougasse demonstration.

because we wanted to conserve the tracks of our tanks. We were teaching observation – teaching the chaps to find a place on a bit of a crest of a hill, where he could see who was coming along the road on either side. I suppose you'd be able to see armoured vehicles moving at three miles or so if you were up on the South Downs. We were all very adept at using binoculars and we were all issued with these cards with the enemy tanks on them.

Lieutenant Arthur Curtis
7th Field Company, Royal Engineers
There were a lot of beach huts at Shoreham and they blocked the field of fire, so they had to be knocked down. Which was comparatively easy, except that we'd just started work when an irate gentleman came along and said that he was a personal friend of the Secretary of State for War, that his brother was an MP, and in no way was he going to allow his beach hut to be demolished, and he would make sure I was court-martialled if I disobeyed his instruction. I told him he had to go and see the general. This chap was so concerned with his wretched beach hut, so selfish, with the Germans expected any day. Britain's finest hour? Not quite everybody's finest hour.

Lance Corporal Clifford Bailey
Rifle Brigade
We were digging a weapon pit in the corner of an orchard and the fruit farmer was most irate to think that one corner of his orchard was being dug up when – let's face it – not so far away was the full might of the German army poised to come across.

Second Lieutenant Peter Vaux
4th Royal Tank Regiment
I remember being intensely irritated to see the Home Guard digging up a man's front garden, a cottage garden, and the chap was in tears, because he'd got a lot of vegetables and they were digging it all up to make trenches. There was a place on the other side of the road where they could equally well have done it and it wouldn't have upset the old man so I asked this Home Guard 'Captain Mainwaring' type, *why* he wouldn't do it on the other side of the road. He said, 'There's a war on! This man's got to understand it!' Oh dear me . . .

Second Lieutenant David Ruttledge
Duke of Cornwall's Light Infantry
We were defending a long, sandy beach near St Austell. I had what amounted

to a platoon of recruits – some of them had been in the army just a week or two and we dug positions and we stood to morning and night. There was a lot of rumours of German agents landing by boat, and we were on the lookout for them. On one very still night, the sea was like glass, and there was a beautiful moonbeam shining across the water. As we watched, an object floated across this moonbeam. And we thought, 'Ah!' I'd spotted a dinghy in a cave, so I took a section out in the dinghy with a Bren gun. We set off down the moonbeam and we rode and we rode for 20 minutes. We thought we must have missed it but then we spotted the thing, and it was slightly off to a flank. We altered course, and rode like mad towards it. As we approached it, it got bigger and bigger and bigger. And when we caught up with it, it was quite a big motor cruiser, and the gunnel was lined up with people pointing down at us with their rifles. It was an Admiralty coastal patrol. So we exchanged abuse and with our tail between our legs we set off home.

Private Harold Wilmshurst
5th Battalion, Royal Sussex Regiment
We were guarding the harbour one night and had been warned that something might happen. An exercise. Commandos came in from the sea and tried to capture some of our chaps. I was a bit bolshy at the time and when one of the commandos got hold of one of my mates, I waded in with my rifle butt and they stopped the exercise.

Second Lieutenant David Ruttledge
Duke of Cornwall's Light Infantry
As the sappers were laying mines on the beach, just below our defensive positions, one of the sappers trod on his own mine. The poor lad was blown to smithereens, and we had to shovel what was left of him into sandbags.

Private Herbert Anderson
Pioneer Corps
We had the most ridiculous duty. Every morning we set off in a lorry, all over Carmarthenshire in West Wales, and we dug holes in the soil with our spades. Into these almost man-high holes were inserted wooden kiosks, and a seat, the idea being that men would be stationed in these holes, connected to each other by telephone, in the case of an invasion. We wondered who on earth would start an invasion of Britain in west Wales? Perhaps the War Office had been influenced by Napoleon, because the French had tried to land troops at Fishguard in 1797.

Major William Watson
6th Battalion, Durham Light Infantry
I remember two old coastguards winding their way slowly along with their tin hats, their old Ross rifles and their ammunition bags. In the half-light, with their old muzzled rifles and their scruffy-looking faces, they gave me the impression that we were back in Napoleonic times.

Private Harold Wilmshurst
5th Battalion, Royal Sussex Regiment
It was a very hectic time. We were training by day and doing guards at night. We were on duty 24 hours a day.

Captain Kenneth Johnstone
11th Battalion, Durham Light Infantry
The invasion code word was 'Cromwell' and while we were in a large house deep in the countryside, this code word came through from our battalion headquarters. The admiral at Plymouth was a little jittery and whether he'd let this go by mistake, I don't know. All the men were in the stables and I was in this great four-poster bed with a rather tattered old bell rope, and the signal for a turnout was to pull the rope. So I pulled the rope, which came away in my hand and all the troops came tumbling out. We had an assortment of vehicles: we had two motorcycles and sidecars, we had a wedding car from the village, two buses, several solo motorcycles, and two trucks. So we piled into these and the whole lot went racing out of the gates. The wedding car got stuck in the gates amid the turmoil – it really was like a film. We raced down to Slapton Sands. It was absolute pandemonium. I think if Hitler had seen us, he would have had a good laugh.

James Oates
Dagenham Home Guard
We were told that if the church bells rang, that meant the invasion had started. Well, one night, when there was a raid on, my father in law and myself came up from the shelter to make tea to take down to the family. And whilst we were in the kitchen making tea, we heard bells ringing. 'Good Lord, George!' I said, 'I'd better get my rifle and report to HQ!' So I got the rifle and my 50 rounds of ammunition and set off. Suddenly I realised that these weren't church bells I was hearing – it was just the pounding of metal at Ford's factory nearby.

Ernest Clark
Wireless Operator working at RDF Stations
The Parachute and Cable Unit were rockets with parachutes and wire attached to them. They shoot about five or six hundred feet in the air and then they explode. The parachute opens and all the wire entangles the aeroplane. One night, at Poling RDF Station, the corporal in charge accidentally pressed the button and they all shot up in the air in the middle of the night. People saw the parachutes coming down and the church bells were rung because they thought that the invasion had started.

Gwendoline Saunders
Women's Auxiliary Air Force
Four of us were on the evening watch from five to midnight. When we were relieved, we were looking across to Boscombe Down and we saw all these parachutes. We watched them coming down for five or ten minutes and we said, 'They're definitely parachutes.' It was a fairly light night and they were very visible against some dark clouds. So we dashed back into the signals and hauled out the relief people who'd just taken over from us and we hauled them out to look. Then we got on to the duty officer and it became a Red Alert. We were sent back to help to man the station. I took his bayonet and stuck it in my belt. At about half past two, the alert was called off and we were allowed to go back to our billets. The next morning we were all in the NAAFI – and the jeering we got when we entered! It had got round that we said we had seen parachutes but it was all a lot of nonsense. We flew straight out of the NAAFI. Then someone came to us and said, 'I've been told under strict secrecy to tell you that you were absolutely right, but we've got to pretend you were wrong.' What we had seen was the beginning of the Parachute Regiment. They were doing their first night drops. But we had to put up with three more weeks of wigging.

Norman Smith
Caledonian Road Home Guard
We'd always been told that the Germans would come down on bicycles and we were on guard duty one night and Matthews, who was more awake than me, said, 'Hey! Bloody Germans are here!' So I thought, 'This is time to go.' He said, 'Hang on! hang on! There's Germans here! I can hear the bicycles coming!' Next minute, a bloody figure looms up right on top of us, and Matthews says, 'Halt! who goes there?' The next minute, we're on the floor and the bicycle's on top of us. It was the local police sergeant doing an inspection.

Ernest Clark
Wireless Operator working at RDF Stations

We were all issued with rifles and five rounds of .303 and we were told to carry them with us wherever we went. And then we were in the cinema in Littlehampton and a thing came across the screen, 'All service personnel to report to their units'. That emptied the cinema.

Private Sidney Nuttall
Royal Army Ordnance Corps

If an invasion occurred, our battalion had to dash from Prudhoe-on-Tyne, where we were based, to the coast north of Newcastle. To help us to get there, we were given some red civilian buses, and they came with drivers from the Midlands. We had a stand-to when we had to dash to the coast, in the middle of the night. These drivers had been living the life of Riley – they had money for food, they had accommodation in hotels and lodging houses. But when it came to the night when we were going to move off to fight, they refused to drive the buses. 'We didn't come up here to get killed.' That's exactly what they said to us in real Brummie accents. We threw them off the buses, and anybody that could drive climbed in, and I drove a Midland Red bus up to the coast. We got there and we deployed but of course it was a false alarm.

Pilot Officer Roger Hall
152 Squadron, RAF

We were woken round about three o'clock in the morning when it was pitch dark. I'll never forget this. Everyone was going up and down the corridor, and somebody came into my room and said to me, you'd better take your revolver, because the invasion is on. Off we went in the pitch dark, down to the aircraft, and we went to the dispersal and waited to take off. And it was then that I thought we were now going to be engaged in shooting people on the beach with machine guns. But it started to get lighter and lighter and nothing happened . . .

Bombardier Douglas Goddard
Royal Artillery

We were pretty sure that the Germans would invade and we had nothing to stop them. We were told that there was a strategic reserve somewhere behind us, but I reckon that it was probably just the Home Guard.

The Home Guard

We were prepared to lean out of a bedroom window, light a piece of rag in the neck of a bottle and throw it at a tank. How long would we have survived?

The defence of the country was not solely in the hands of the regular army. On May 14, the Secretary of State for War, Anthony Eden, had broadcast a radio appeal for men between the ages of 17 and 65 to offer their services as Local Defence Volunteers. Within twenty-four hours, almost a quarter of a million men had come forward to create a poorly-equipped but enthusiastic 'Dad's Army'. At the end of July, Churchill renamed the organisation the Home Guard.

John Graham
Isle of Wight Home Guard
When I joined, it had just become the Home Guard and ceased being the *Local Defence Volunteers*. Home Guard was a much better title.

Stanley Brand
Middlesbrough Home Guard
The Home Guard's uniform came as an armband first of all. This was needed because if a civilian bore arms against an occupying force, he could be shot out of hand. Would the arm band have been recognised by Jerry? I think he would still have shot us out of hand.

Stan Poole
London Home Guard
Some mates and I joined the Home Guard together. We were all about 15 or 16 but there were a lot of older blokes as well.

John Graham
Isle of Wight Home Guard
I was 17 and I was the youngest member. The oldest had been in the Boer War and he was the best shot of the lot of us. We had a chap called Smith – a gentleman of leisure – who'd only got one arm. We had a baker's boy who had TB and my particular colleague, Mick Curran, who'd been a stoker in the Battle of Jutland. Mick was a most amusing colleague but he suffered terribly from wind. Later in the summer, we used to go on night duty in a field of cows behind Nodes Fort. And what with the bombing and Mick Curran's wind, we didn't get much sleep.

Alexander Barr
Norwich Home Guard
Most of them were older men – in their forties – and you could get tales out of them. My sergeant was 'Brick' Golder, named for his red hair. He was quite a character and he told me how he'd served in Northern Ireland in the early twenties. He said he'd gone into a pub in a nationalist area of Belfast wearing his uniform and there'd been a great deal of humming and hawing. He said he'd put his hands in the pockets of his greatcoat and came out with a couple of Webley .45s and slammed them down on the bar. He'd never seen a pub empty so quick.

Benjamin Cattle
Corfe Castle Home Guard
To start with, we had to train as a platoon in the army. Drill and marching. When you start it's very difficult, it takes a lot of practice.

Stanley Brand
Middlesbrough Home Guard
We did a lot of arms drill with a broom shank. It was a waste of time. To learn how to salute an officer and all the rest of it was an absolute waste of time.

A sergeant of the Dorking Home Guard gives his Tommy gun a polish.

Major William Watson
6th Battalion, Durham Light Infantry
My opinion was, no attempt should be made to make the Home Guard into Grenadier Guardsmen. They should be what they were, Home Guard, and they should use their own individuality and ingenuity in the areas they knew. But to go further than that would upset the whole applecart, and upset the whole object of the force. They shouldn't have military parades and that sort of thing. They should be capable of dealing with tanks, and surprises at the end of the village street and searching out parachutists – which of course they did.

Stanley Brand
Middlesbrough Home Guard
We only had two Lee Enfield rifles and they probably came back with the troops from Dunkirk. Gradually weapons arrived – mostly American.

Alexander Barr
Norwich Home Guard
We had Yankee First World War rifles called P17s. They were .300. They were heavy but they were good. We had lessons on stripping and cleaning them, loading and unloading them and we were taught how to sight. We had a wooden tripod which the rifle would sit on and there was a target on the other side of the room and you'd line up your sights on the target and the instructor would come and have a look. After that we were taken to a 30-yard range – but not very often because ammunition was very tight.

Sergeant Jack Fielder
Essex Regiment
I took my Suffolk Home Guard men out on the firing range. I'd pre-marked some targets and they had to judge the distances. I went up to one chap and said, 'How far is that?' 'I don't rightly know,' he said, 'but I reckon it'd be about two acres . . . '

Stanley Brand
Middlesbrough Home Guard
I was told to strip electric wire down to get the copper wire which we used to bind First World War bayonets to broom handles. We had nothing else. After a while, we couldn't get hold of enough bayonets so we started using cleavers from the butcher – on the principle that you could get a slash at somebody when he was too close to use his gun.

The Home Guard drills with broomsticks.

Stan Poole
London Home Guard

One day, in came this major with a four-foot length of scaffold tubing with an eighteen-inch Lee Enfield bayonet welded to it. He came in and said, 'What a wonderful weapon!' I said to him, 'Excuse me sir, what use would these be against a German Schmeisser?' This major blew up. 'How dare you?' he shouted. But he's kidding these blokes about using a four foot scaffold tube with 18-inch bayonets against tough troops with MP40s!

Stanley Brand
Middlesbrough Home Guard

There was a lot of emphasis on bayonet practice. We did all the appropriate shouts, screams and gritting of teeth. You were supposed to put the bayonet in, try to twist it one way, put your foot on the victim and twist it the other way to withdraw it.

Alexander Barr
Norwich Home Guard

We had some very fantastic weapons that were dreamed up to cope with emergencies. We had a grenade launcher that was a length of drainpipe on a tripod with a handle on the back. It had a breach that opened on a spring and you took a grenade with a seven-second fuse, took the pin out and very carefully inserted it into the tube. You put in a plastic disc, which was the charge and you closed the breech. You pressed the hammer and it threw the grenade about a hundred and fifty yards. We never thought how dangerous this was – we took it in our stride.

Stanley Brand
Middlesbrough Home Guard

Because of the shortage of rifles and ammunition, I was trying other things. At the time, they were teaching us to put a rag in the neck of a bottle filled with anything inflammable, light a match and strike it – a Molotov cocktail. When I was clearing out a cupboard at ICI, where I worked, I found a litre bottle filled with yellow phosphorus immersed in paraffin. It came to me that I could make a Molotov cocktail without needing a match. So I pinched this bottle of phosphorus and we took seven-ounce bottles and tried it with paraffin but it didn't work. Eventually, somebody gave up a gallon of his petrol ration and we filled a bottle with petrol and popped in a piece of phosphorus the size of a hazelnut. Then we put a cork on it and got a fitter to machine a taper that went over the top. We threw this bottle against a brick wall and after about twenty seconds, it ignited when the phosphorus was exposed to the air. So we went to town making these things. I had twenty-four of them under the floorboards in my bedroom. Dad would have had fits if he'd known.

Alexander Barr
Norwich Home Guard
We had an old Lewis machine gun. It wasn't the normal infantry Lewis gun – it was an ex-aircraft gun. There were no end of stoppages because it had all these springs inside and they were always going wrong. I only got to fire it once because of shortage of ammunition.

Stanley Brand
Middlesbrough Home Guard
We were very keen to have our Lewis gun mounted for anti-aircraft work. I tried to get an anti-aircraft mounting but I was told that it would be unlikely to be available in the foreseeable future. But I was told to select a tall Home Guardsman, make sure that he had the strap of his steel helmet as tight as possible and I was told to rest the four legs of the Lewis gun on the brim of his helmet. I was told that with his height, I could fire up at aircraft. Well. I've never heard such a bloody stupid thing. So instead, we got about eight lengths of iron from the side of a bedbase and with a lot of welding, we made our own stands. On two occasions, I got a shot at aircraft but I think I frightened myself more than I frightened them.

Alexander Barr
Norwich Home Guard
The anti-tank grenade was a do-or-die job. You had a big ball on the end of a handle and you pulled the pin out of the handle. A metal cover fell away. It was like a big sticky ball and you were supposed to go up to the tank, put it on the side and run like hell. They were in short supply so we only practised with them once.

Stanley Brand
Middlesbrough Home Guard
We practised with hand grenades. To throw a grenade – first of all, secure your footing. Because if you're not securely poised, you're going to trip and the grenade in your hand will go rolling. Second, make sure that there is no impediment to your arm swing, nobody standing behind, nothing that could

Sappers of the Royal Engineers make Molotov cocktails from beer bottles.

Throwing a Molotov cocktail.

distract you. Distraction was the thing – if your hand met something, you were likely to drop the hand grenade so you had to make sure everything was clear behind you as well as in front. You clench the lever with your fingers – not with your palm. You pull out the pin but for God's sake don't throw the pin away – hold it in case you have to put it back.

Stan Poole
London Home Guard
We did manoeuvres where different units played the enemy. We had one big manoeuvre that went right the way through Tottenham and round by Alexandra Palace. Blokes finished up fighting each other with gun butts on the roof of the Aerated Bread Company in Camden Town. There were blokes riding past the roof on buses, throwing thunderflashes up, pretending they were hand grenades. The enemy were holed up with a machine gun at Camden Town Underground station and we finished up in a rubber boat going across the Regent's Canal, trying to get to them by the back way. It was quite good fun.

Second Lieutenant Peter Vaux
4th Royal Tank Regiment
We used to do exercises with the Home Guard and they would ambush our tanks and attack us with Molotov cocktails – which I'm thankful to say, didn't have petrol in them. And they were great! Particularly the 16-year-olds. They were great at ambushing our tanks.

Stanley Brand
Middlesbrough Home Guard
We did night exercises against an enemy made up of regulars. We learned a lot from them – we learned there comes a time when you all have to break off for a cup of tea.

Stan Poole
London Home Guard
Two of us would be sent out on patrol. We used to carry live ammunition and bayonets and we'd be looking out for people with lights on and peculiar behaviour. There was always the scare about Germans dressed as nuns and all that sort of rubbish. And we looked for looters. Looters actually were shot in London.

In training – swimming across a river.

Alexander Barr
Norwich Home Guard
We were on guard in places that were supposed to be important. You'd finish work at half five, get home and have your dinner, get changed and get up to wherever you were going to be on guard at seven o'clock. At the company headquarters, there was the main gate, and once it got dark, you shut the gate and patrolled round. At the telephone exchange, it was pretty well built up so you kept a general eye open. The golf club was a pretty big area, but as long as it was quiet, you didn't have to go too far – you knew they'd have to parachute in, so if there was no activity, it was a pretty easy guard.

Stanley Brand
Middlesbrough Home Guard
I would have liked more instruction on how to prevent anybody else getting to the thing we were guarding – on making ourselves inconspicuous. The Home Guard used to teach me to march backwards and forwards – but that was so obvious to anyone who wanted to attack. They could get in so easily if someone was doing a regular patrol up and down. And we didn't have training in house-to-house fighting yet we would have had more of that than anything else. And Jerry was good at it – he'd had lots of experience in France. We were prepared to lean out of a bedroom window, light a piece of rag in the neck of a bottle and throw it at a tank. How long would we have survived?

Benjamin Cattle
Corfe Castle Home Guard
In the evenings, we stood to in a weapons trench, ready for any eventuality – a landing of airborne forces or an invasion at the coast at Swanage or Studland. As far as we were concerned, we were the main line of defence on the coast.

Stanley Brand
Middlesbrough Home Guard
The television programme *Dad's Army* was so true. Except that we didn't have a 'Captain Mainwaring'.

James Lawrence
Trimley St Martin Home Guard
If the Germans had invaded, I think we'd have let them know we were here, but I don't think we'd have had much of a chance.

Stanley Brand
Middlesbrough Home Guard
My unit would have achieved something but nothing permanent. We couldn't ever have defeated the Germans – only delayed them. The Home Guard was really a civilian morale builder. It made us feel we could do something useful but it was really a sop.

The British Resistence

They told us our expected lifetime after the invasion started would be seven days.

Another force of civilian volunteers was formed in May 1940 with a more clandestine purpose than the Home Guard. Auxiliary Units were trained to wage guerilla war from behind enemy lines in the event of an invasion. Had the regular forces been obliged to withdraw to the GHQ Line, the Auxiliary Units, concealed by day in their underground hideouts, would have appeared at night to carry out acts of sabotage against enemy targets. The hideouts contained limited supplies and once these were exhausted, the Auxiliaries would have attempted to blend back into civilian life.

Peter Wilkinson
Chief of Staff to Colonel Gubbins during formation of Auxiliary Units
I was walking across St James's Park, slightly ruffled, when I felt a tap on my shoulder, and there behind me was Colin Gubbins, who said, 'How are things?' 'I'm pretty well out of a job,' I said and he said, 'Well, you come and join me, because I've got a new ploy, which involves setting up guerrilla units throughout southern England in case the German invasion takes place.' Which I jumped at. Gubbins had only heard of this plan that very morning, when General Ironside decided that all post-invasion preparations must be put under military control and he entrusted them to Gubbins.

We established ourselves in Whitehall Place, just opposite the staff entrance to the War Office. We were starting more or less from the beginning except that Peter Fleming had already been instructed to set up a guerrilla organisation known as the XII Corps Observation Unit, in the woods between Ashford and Canterbury. He had recruited about thirty chaps, whom he was greatly enjoying training. They were shooting deer with their bows and arrows and carrying out all sorts of other Boy Scout activities. They lived in a hideout, the entrance to which was opened by a pivot under a fallen tree. This formed the nucleus of our efforts in the south-east.

William Pilkington
Self-defence instructor

Colonel Gubbins got hold of me and said, 'I see on your record that you're pretty good in martial arts and I believe you're also quite good with a knife. Can you dream up a scheme whereby the public can be taught to defend, to attack and to kill? Something that can be learned in a matter of hours with the minimum of practice?' I said, 'Good heavens above! What are you asking me to do? I don't think anybody could do that.' He said, 'Get your grey matter on it. There's something coming your way that's quite special.' So I came up with a walking stick with ferrules made to go on the end. These ferrules had a steel tip about an inch long, fluted four ways, and you could sharpen them with a stone or a file until they were like a needle. And this could be used like a bayonet. I gave Gubbins a demonstration.

Ten days later, he introduced me to Captain Fairbairn and Captain Sykes. Fairburn said to me, 'We're police officers from Shanghai, the dirtiest, bloodiest, most corrupt city in the world. We have an average of two murders a day and we have to deal with them in our way. It's not approved by the powers that be, but it works. We want you to get the dirtiest, bloodiest ideas that you can get in your head of how to destroy a human being.' They took me to Auchinraith House in Lanarkshire. While we were there, we were given the most extraordinary training in knife fighting, garroting and pistol shooting. Fairburn was the finest pistol shot I've ever seen and Sykes was a wonderful rifle shot. They we both experts in their own field. I brought 'staff, stick and baton' to the curriculum and I also brought in the use of a pencil or pen. If you found a sleeping German, all you had to do was push it through his ear. It would immediately enter the brain, and he wouldn't wake up again. They thought this was marvellous. When they took it to the War Office, the good old boys, said, 'Oh no, that's most cowardly, we can't have that. It must not be included.' Fairbairn came back, frustrated, and he said, 'They say we can't teach it. But we will.' And we did.

Whilst at Auchinraith, Fairbairn said to us, 'We've got to have you all blooded.' So we went to a slaughterhouse with recently-killed animals, and each and every one of us had to plunge a knife into one and withdraw it, to get the feel of human flesh or animal flesh that was still quivering. To make us realise that when you put a knife into any living creature, the contraction of the sinews is such that it is very difficult to get out. It's not like you see on TV.

At the end, Fairbairn told us that he was very pleased with us, we all made the grade, and he said, 'Now you must teach members of the Home Guard to do this.' There was a branch of the Home Guard that was being specially selected, who were on Official Secrets, and who were to be specially trained by us, not only to be killers but to be saboteurs, and had we been invaded, they would have been the people who would have been coming out at night, blowing up an odd bridge, knocking off a factory, wherever they could injure the enemy. They were the Auxiliary Units.

Peter Wilkinson
Chief of Staff to Colonel Gubbins during formation of Auxiliary Units
We began to recruit people to form Auxiliary Units along the whole of the south coast, up the beginning of the east coast, and ultimately, we hoped, to cover the whole coast of the United Kingdom. First of all, we recruited a number of friends and friends' friends who could be established as local intelligence officers. Ideally speaking, it was intended that they should recruit their personnel from the Home Guard – but on a strict basis of three chaps, of whom only one knew the existence of the next-door three chaps. Of course, it couldn't possibly work like that in the country where everybody knew more or less everything that was going on, and I think the only thing that was sometimes – by no means always – concealed, was the whereabouts of the actual hideouts.

Percy Clark
Auxiliary Unit in Kent
I was at work and when I returned to the office, the office girl said that she'd had a telephone call and someone wanted to come and see me at two o'clock in the afternoon. It was a Captain Fields. He came down in the afternoon with two others and interviewed me. Before he started, he warned me that I hadn't got to say anything about the interview and that I'd have to sign the Secrets Act. The others were Peter Fleming and a man who I didn't recognise. They asked me to form a seven-man patrol. This was on a Friday afternoon and I was given until Saturday evening to find these men and ring up the Garth, which was Fleming's training centre and they would arrange transport for us to go up and start training on the Sunday.

Thomas Andrew
Auxiliary Unit in Barton on Humber, Lincolnshire
There were six in our patrol – at first. They were already up to strength but my father was the patrol leader and I started getting a bit nosey and they had to take me in.

George Pellet
Auxiliary Unit in Bekesbourne, Kent
I was having my dinner at about half past twelve one day when there was a knock on the door and there was an army captain there. He asked to have a word with me. We walked down the garden and he said that I was doing all right in the Home Guard – and would I like to do a bit more? I said I didn't know if I could take on any more and he said he didn't mean any extra. He meant something different. He couldn't tell me much about it but he said that it would be more interesting. 'Do you like a bit of adventure?' he asked. 'Yeah.' 'Then perhaps you're the chap for this.' I was told not so say anything to the wife. She used to ask a lot of questions and I used to have to make up answers. The idea was that Jerry would torture her to find out what I was doing so I wasn't allowed to tell her anything. It was a funny business. I think it broke up marriages.

Percy Clark
Auxiliary Unit in Kent
My corporal's wife was evacuated with their children and we used to go round to his house for 'card parties'. That's what we told people but in fact, we used to do training. Then occasionally, we used to invite other people and we would really have a card party so it was quite a good cover.

George Pellet
Auxiliary Unit in Bekesbourne, Kent
It was a bit awkward in the pub when I was asked what I was doing and why I wasn't with the local Home Guard unit. I used to say I was attached to headquarters. I signed the secrecy act and they checked up on us. When I arrived for training one Sunday morning, they were able to tell me how many games of darts I'd played in the pub Friday night.

Thomas Andrew
Auxiliary Unit in Barton on Humber, Lincolnshire
The role of the unit was to create as much havoc as possible beyond the German lines after they'd passed over. And for that reason, our base was underground in a hideout. It was located down a hedgerow in open country and if you didn't know it was there, you'd never find it. There was a long T-handle in the ground at a certain spot and you turned this lever. A lid then dropped down until it was horizontal and you could slide the whole thing out of the way and go down this shaft into the hideout. There were four bunks inside and a ventilation shaft – a six-inch glazed earthenware pipe in the bottom of the hedge. We had to keep as quiet as possible inside and to throw dogs off the scent we spread some kind of rat poison that came in a liquid over the hedge. So that they wouldn't smell the human beings. We didn't want them scratching at the entrance.

George Pellet
Auxiliary Unit in Bekesbourne, Kent
Our base was in the wood. You had to know the tree you stopped at and at the base of the tree, you put your finger underneath and lifted a catch and the entrance came up, weighted like a clock. It was damn well built. You never went in on your own. There were always two or more of you so that someone was looking round. If anyone had seen us going into our hideout, we were told that when the invasion started, the first thing we had to do was go and shoot them. One day we saw a bloke peeping from behind a tree as we were going in. One of us had gone in already and the rest of us packed up and walked off immediately. But we knew him and he had a gentle warning that if we caught him round there again, there'd be hell to pay. And one of the lads volunteered to shoot him when the invasion came.

Percy Clark
Auxiliary Unit in Kent
Our observation base was built by a contracting firm who were doing all the defences in the area. They built us a concrete one, dug into the ground. Inside was waterproof sealed and it had bunk beds, a water tank, tilley lamps and a little cooker.

George Pellet
Auxiliary Unit in Bekesbourne, Kent
When the invasion came, the officers would get word to us. They all knew

Group photograph of an Auxiliary Unit; the Milton Patrol, Pembrokeshire.

where we lived. We were told that we would be notified so many hours before the invasion arrived and we would then go to ground.

Peter Wilkinson
Chief of Staff to Colonel Gubbins during formation of Auxiliary Units
Once the German invasion came, the Auxiliary Units would be on their own. The observation bases were stocked with food and ammunition, and their job was to seek out their own targets and do what they could. As the Germans were establishing their bridgehead, the units could, by limited sabotage – blowing up bridges, slashing car tyres, and creating a pretty uncomfortable atmosphere behind the lines – influence operations.

Percy Clark
Auxiliary Unit in Kent
All our operations would have been under cover of darkness. We wouldn't have operated at all in the daytime.

George Pellet
Auxiliary Unit in Bekesbourne, Kent
We had to get very familiar with our area because we had all these places where they thought the German generals would make their headquarters and do their business.

Percy Clark
Auxiliary Unit in Kent
We would have travelled over the fields, not by the roads.

George Pellet
Auxiliary Unit in Bekesbourne, Kent
We had everything we needed to do sabotage work. We had plastic explosive, gun cotton, different fuses, everything we wanted. We learned how to damage transport. We learned how to blow gearboxes and back axles and how to blow the tyres off aeroplanes with gun cotton.

Thomas Andrew
Auxiliary Unit in Barton on Humber, Lincolnshire
We had blasting gelignite, detonators, various types of fuels which burned at different speeds, time pencils for delayed action and booby traps for putting under drums of petrol. A booby trap was metal and about the size of a Swan

Vestas matchbox. When you pulled a pin out, it made it live, and you walked away from it after attaching a length of fuse to an explosive charge. The fellow who moved the drum of petrol would be blown up.

Percy Clark
Auxiliary Unit in Kent
We would have booby-trapped German stores and vehicles. We'd have tried to do something about any bridges that weren't blown up. We'd have stretched wires across the road to catch necks. We were trained to be silent killers.

Thomas Andrew
Auxiliary Unit in Barton upon Humber, Lincolnshire
We trained pretty hard. Every available moment, practically. We had these commando knives with a six-inch blade and I remember one instruction was that when you tackled a German from behind, you got your fingers over his helmet at the front and his chinstrap would choke him and then you could put the knife in from behind. And we were taught how to overpower a man bigger than yourself. And then of course, we were issued with piano wire to put across a road for motorcycle troops. I remember this one thing. It was essentially a rifle bullet pointing upwards, in a container, and you pushed it into the ground. And if the German touched this pressure pad, the bullet fired like a rifle and went through his foot and his chin.

George Pellet
Auxiliary Unit in Bekesbourne, Kent
This commando bloke was giving us lessons in unarmed combat in a barn and he had one of the unit – Godfrey – on his back a couple of time. Godfrey said he hadn't been prepared. 'If I was prepared,' he said, 'you wouldn't get away with it quite so easy!' 'Yes, I would,' said the commando. So they walked around each other for a little while and all of a sudden, the commando made a grab and Godfrey grabbed him round the chest and threw him against the barn wall. 'Bugger!' said the commando. 'That's enough trouble from you!'

William Pilkington
Self-defence Instructor
I gave my first class in Glasgow. Winston Churchill was there at the time, and whilst we were in the middle of the class, he walked through the door with Major General Sir Edward Spears. Now, Spears was a very nice man, but he

was totally out of touch and he was all in favour of 'giving a chap a fair chance'. When he walked in, I was saying, 'If you have a knife which is over six inches in length, you have a weapon which is capable of killing by stabbing, or by a side slash to the throat, which will sever the carotid artery and the jugular vein, or, in the event of you being fortunate enough to be in the situation where your opponent has raised his arm, you go for the armpit, the auxiliary artery cannot be stopped bleeding, and he'll be dead in a minute.' Suddenly, a voice behind me said, 'Stop this at once Sergeant! This is monstrous!' And it was Major General Sir Edward Spears. He tore strips off me! He said, 'The Germans will think we're as brutal as they are!' Hearing this, Captain Fairburn absolutely exploded. Why he wasn't court martialled, I don't know. He called Spears all the idiots God ever made. Churchill was grinning, he looked as though he was quite drunk, he was slobbering down his cigar, and he said to Spears, 'Come and have a drink, and forget your anger, these fellows know what they're doing!' And he turned to Fairburn and said, 'You're doing a good job, I support you!'

George Pellet
Auxiliary Unit in Bekesbourne, Kent
We had training under fire and one bloke got shot. We came to a gateway and there were two hurdles up in the gateway. There were snipers on the other bank and they couldn't shoot down to us because their guns were on fixed tripods but they could shoot bits off the top of the hurdle. We were told, 'If you keep below the hurdles, you're safe.' So as we were crawling across, we'd hear 'wheeeee' over our heads. One bloke got scared and he got up and ran. Silly bugger. They killed him stone dead.

George Pellet
Auxiliary Unit in Bekesbourne, Kent
They told us our expected lifetime after the invasion started would be seven days. They reckoned that after seven days, either Jerry would be back out of it or we'd all be finished up. Because once we started blowing their equipment about, Jerry would really go mad. It didn't worry me much because I thought at least I was doing something a bit more than standing guard on a railway bridge.

Thomas Andrew
Auxiliary Unit in Barton upon Humber, Lincolnshire
We were told that when we were caught, there would be no chance. If they

found you in the dugout, they would throw a grenade in but if they wanted you for interrogation, that would be worse because they would have tortured you and then killed you anyway. If I'd been tortured, I wouldn't have known anything. There was another patrol at a nearby village but we made a point of never going to their hideout and never knowing where it was. All we knew was the name of the regular officer who was training us.

Percy Clark
Auxiliary Unit in Kent
I doubt we would have ever got away but if Britain had been overrun, I suppose we would have come out and tried to be ordinary people.

Peter Wilkinson
Chief of Staff to Colonel Gubbins during formation of Auxiliary Units
It was perfectly obvious to all of us that the moment the Germans had established themselves, the units were not going to survive very long – they would have been penetrated, and probably pretty soon. But it was a time when everybody was desperate, I mean, the country would have been defended with hayforks. One didn't really ask for anything very sophisticated, all one hoped was to be able to survive the first fortnight of the invasion and prevent the bridgehead being enlarged.

Flying Officer Roland Beamont
87 Squadron, RAF
We who'd been in the French battle came home convinced that there was only one thing that was going to stop the enemy and that would be the RAF. We could see that coming all the way through summer.

Squadron Leader Alan Deere
New Zealand pilot, 54 Squadron, RAF
If the Germans got air superiority, that would enable them to invade without much opposition. They still had to beat our navy, who would, of course, have done a marvellous job but without air cover they would have been pretty much at the receiving end of the full might of the German Air Force.

Sergeant Stanley Wright
Operations Room Deputy Controller
Consider the size of the British fleet. The size of our destroyer force alone was double that of the German destroyer force. The North Sea and the Channel

had very nasty tide rips. Both of them would cough up very rough seas in a very short time. What had the Germans got? They had beautiful big barges. Lovely things with duck-like sterns – perfect for carrying goods around but how were they going to carry troops in them? How would they get the troops across the very choppy, very unpredictable, very tide-ridden seas around England? The navy wouldn't have had to shoot them at all. They'd have belted them with destroyers and sunk them in the wash alone. I'd not like to have been a German soldier trying the job. We were hypnotised by the strength of Hitler's land forces. We'd been hypnotised by the fact that up till then, he'd done everything that he'd said he'd do. And had the Germans landed, they'd have won. But I don't think they could have landed.

Part Two

THE BATTLE OF BRITAIN

As Hitler proceeded with his plans for invasion, the Fuhrer Directive No. 16 emphasised that before Operation Sealion could take place, the Luftwaffe had to win superiority of the air over southern England. The RAF must not be allowed to threaten the invasion force as it crossed the Channel. Still hopeful of a settlement, Hitler believed that a sustained aerial attack, coupled with a blockade, might bring Britain to the negotiating table. Either way, it was clear that the RAF would have to be brought to battle and defeated. The Luftwaffe's specific aim was to lure Fighter Command into the air and wipe it out. Fighter Command – with its pilots, aircraft and carefully considered system of control – was waiting.

A Call to Arms

As the war came closer, my friends and I were wishing for it.
Let's have a war! It was a release from the boredom of going to work.

The men who flew during the summer of 1940 came from many countries and many backgrounds. Some of the British pilots had attended the Royal Air Force College, Cranwell, which provided the RAF with a steady stream of permanent officers. Others held short service commissions. Many came from the non-regular branches of the RAF. The Auxiliary Air Force had a reputation as a rich man's flying club while the Royal Air Force Volunteer Reserve was a more egalitarian organisation in which all members joined as 'airmen under training' and received commissions based on merit only. As the war approached and the need for pilots became more pressing, increasing numbers of men rose from the ranks of the regular Air Force to be trained as sergeant pilots.

The British Empire proved an abundant source of pilots. The colonies and dominions still felt a deep sense of loyalty to the 'mother country' and young men from Australia, New Zealand, Canada, India, Jamaica and many other countries overcame all manner of difficulties to reach Britain. They were joined by Poles, Czechs, Frenchmen and Belgians who wanted to avenge the defeat of their nations. A number of Americans joined the RAF even though the United States remained neutral until December 1941.

These young men shared very little except determination and a sense of adventure, qualities shared by the Lutwaffe pilots against whom they would fly.

Rupert Parkhouse
Cadet at Royal Air Force College, Cranwell, 1939
It was from my father and from his experiences, flying in the First World War, that I really conceived the ambition of becoming a pilot. My mother used to speak in awed terms of 'How daddy got his wings' and in that rather simple way, my ambition to become a pilot first appeared.

Hans-Ekkehard Bob
German Messerschmitt 109 pilot
When I was ten years old, my older sister got to know a First World War pilot, who in 1927 was performing advertising flights in a biplane. This pilot liked my sister and invited her to come flying with him and she asked him if her little brother could come too. This was a very big thing of course, because in 1927, hardly any planes at all were to be seen in the sky. My mother told me that afterwards I told her that I was going to learn to be a pilot too, that I would steer the plane with my right hand while catching eagles with my left one. This became a great and happy topic of conversation amongst my family.

Pilot Officer Archibald Winskill
72 and 603 Squadrons, RAF
I started off like quite a lot of chaps – I had a flight with Alan Cobham who used to come round to towns and cities in the United Kingdom, giving rides for five shillings. You did a trip round the airfield and back again. I sat in a little Gipsy Moth. I was in the air for about five minutes. You never saw an aeroplane in the sky unless you happened to live near an airfield or Alan Cobham came to your town. And the aeroplanes were small and hadn't improved much since the First World War. They were made of canvas and held together with bits of wire. I met Cobham, years later, in 1964. I was to be posted to be Air Attaché in Paris and I'd been sent to visit a helicopter company in Yeovil. While I was on the train, I saw an old boy in the compartment who said, 'Just look at that! There's a Mini Minor keeping up with us!' We talked and developed quite an intense aviation discussion. 'Hang on a minute!' I said, 'Aren't you Sir Alan Cobham?' 'Yes,' he said. 'Well,' I said, 'you started me off with one of your five bob flights!' 'I started thousands of you chaps off,' he said.

Sergeant Fred Gash
Boulton Paul Defiant gunner with 264 Squadron, RAF
Years before the war, I had flown in an aircraft of Alan Cobham's circus. It was an open two-seater. We had no seat belts, no seats, wind blowing all over the place and two of us sat in the rear cockpit. It was a wonderful thing and I was so thrilled that I joined an organisation called the Air League of the British Empire and I learned to fly at the Lancashire Aero Club. I got my pilot's licence there.

Ernst Eberling
German Heinkel 111 bomber pilot
As a child, I could not drive in trains, buses and cars, I had to vomit. When I started to fly, I couldn't be a flier in fighter aircraft – turning around I had to vomit. So I became a bomber pilot.

Ernest Wedding
German Heinkel 111 bomber pilot
The appeal of flying is you are free from the earth. Your horizon is unlimited. On a clear day you can see a hundred miles. Today you're tied by radar. Well we weren't. Once the wireless operator had signed off from the airfield then you were on your own. Nobody looked in your pocket. And it was a terrific feeling to be free of everything.

Rupert Parkhouse
Cadet at Royal Air Force College, Cranwell, 1939
By the time I was at prep school, I was very interested in aircraft. I knew a family with a car and they took me to the RAF display in 1930. I was immensely impressed by what I saw – squadrons of biplanes flying across the sky and a fly-past by the R100 airship. Watching the pilots climbing into their cockpits used to give me a romantic feeling. When I was at Dulwich College, I'd go into the public schools' enclosure at the Hendon Air Display where I was recognised as the 'air expert'. While I was there, two old boys showed up in their uniforms as Cranwell cadets, looking extremely smart in their white stiff collars and puttees and riding breeches. And I can remember watching two officers showing their rather glamorous girlfriends round their silver biplanes. They were helping the girls up on to the wing to look into the aircraft. I watched this and thought, 'This is one way of getting your girl . . .'.

In 1938, I took the exam into the Royal Air Force College at Cranwell. It was a long and involved process – five days of written examinations and a medical exam, after which I found myself in front of an interview board of about fourteen civil servants and RAF officers. I was very nervous and I stammered badly but my father brought *The Times* in one morning in early April 1939, and told me that I'd passed, number 17 out of 20. It wasn't a particularly good result but at least I was through. People were very surprised and one friend of my mother's sent her daughter round to see whether the rumour that Rupert Parkhouse had passed into the Royal Air Force College was true. I was awarded a Wakefield scholarship. Viscount Wakefield had established a couple of scholarships each terms for the sons of parents of limited means. My father had been thinking that he'd have to pay £300 for my two-year course but he got reduced fees because he'd been a member of the Royal Flying Corps and together with the scholarship, all he had to do was buy my uniform and books.

I joined on April 29, 1939. I was extremely proud of the hat and I used to look at myself in the mirror in my room, thinking what a handsome chap I looked. Because we'd all been in the Officer Training Corps at our public schools, we drifted quite easily into the drill and routines of our cadet squadrons. I shared a room with Warren Smith who had the bunk below me. We started flying almost immediately. While I was sitting in a ground school class, feeling a bit sleepy, there was the glorious thrill of knowing that in an hour's time, I would be up in the Avro Tutor, enjoying the flying.

I found flying a little bit difficult at first. I had rather a bad tempered Rhodesian instructor and I didn't do terribly well with him. So they gave me to a very experienced sergeant pilot and we got on extraordinarily well. He was a very tolerant and quiet chap who never lost his temper. I went solo in about three weeks.

At the end of July, the term ended and we had a passing out parade, taken by Lord Gort. My mother and father came down. The parade made a fine sight with the Cranwell band and the whole cadet wing with Lee Enfield rifles and long bayonets. But then the war broke out and the whole of our academic syllabus was consigned to the waste-paper basket. A life of adventure lay ahead. When we heard, we were in the classroom and we were so elated that a lot of the chaps tore their rather splendid slide rules to pieces and threw the ivory in the bin. I came from rather a frugal family where every penny was carefully measured and I felt that this was a great waste.

We immediately started our flying training on Avro Tutors. One day, Andrew Humphrey – who later became Chief of the Defence Staff – was slightly ahead of me on a cross-country at Little Rissington. I caught him up in the circuit and watched him land. A few minutes later, I copied him and did the same. As I landed, I bounced over a Hawker Hart that was coming towards me the other way. I can remember looking down over the side of my cockpit and seeing two agonised faces in the cockpit of the Hart. Then I found myself moving towards the hangars very quickly and I couldn't understand why and suddenly I saw the windsock out of the corner of my eye and thought, 'Oh God! I'm landing downwind!' I opened up again and went round and landed properly and was met by a very scathing sergeant pilot who told me to report immediately to the Chief Flying Instructor who tore me off a most imperial rocket. That night, I was the object of considerable derision to the short service officers at Little Rissington. About two years later, when I was in a German prison camp, Captain Pepys of the Essex Regiment told me about his training at Little Rissington and he said, 'Do you know, quite incredible, two Cranwell cadets landed downwind on the same day and the second one actually bounced over me as I was taking off! I'd certainly like to meet that bastard and tell him what I think of him!' 'You can tell me, Sam,' I said, 'because I was that chap. And I was as shaken as you were.'

One day in the crew room, a chap called Peter Howard-Williams claimed to have psychic capabilities and he went round the chaps in the crew room, saying, 'I have a knowledge of the future and I know that *you* are going to be killed and *you* are going to be killed but *you*, Rupert, are going to be saved!'

At the beginning of December, we started night flying. I found flying in the dark very, very exciting but after three solo circuits, I was tremendously relieved to land. I went back to the mess and got into bed, when I heard the most tremendous thump. I thought, 'My God! Somebody's gone in!' So I went to have a word with Alfred, the hall porter and asked him if anybody had crashed. He told me that Flight Cadet Smith had crashed. That was a bit of a shaker. Poor old Warren Smith. The boy that I'd shared my room with in the first term. The next day, we went to have a look at the wreckage of the aeroplane. There was nothing we could see inside the cockpit but there was a tremendous smell of burnt metal.

Sergeant Cyril 'Bam' Bamberger
610 and 41 Squadrons, RAF
In 1936, an ad was put in the local press that an auxiliary squadron was being formed at Hooton Park and they wanted recruits. As soon as I was seventeen, I applied. At that time, all the pilots in the Auxiliary Air Force were officers – most of them were very affluent – so I did not aspire to be a pilot and when I was offered a choice of jobs, I chose to be trained as a photographer. The amount of training you did in the Auxiliary Air Force was somewhat up to

A medical test to become a pilot. The candidate must be able to respond quickly to the movement of the examiner's finger.

yourself and how enthusiastic you were. There was Thursday evening ground training for everybody in their particular roles and then there was every Saturday and every Sunday. Work prevented a number of people coming on Thursday night or Saturday mornings – but on Saturday afternoons and Sundays, you got a fairly good turnout. I found it far more interesting than my job as an electrical engineering apprentice and it became my social life as well as a hobby. We'd go out drinking on a Saturday night.

All of the officers in the squadron were very friendly. They were in a high financial category. They all ran cars and our commanding officer had a Rolls-Royce with a chauffeur. The officers didn't socialise with us – they had their own officers' mess. The ground crew – like myself – were a very mixed bunch. Some were very good engineers who later in life ran engineering companies but others were virtually uneducated and they would do any duty like cleaning lavatories. But the majority had a loyalty and enthusiasm for the squadron and every Sunday afternoon at about five o'clock, we all paraded in the hangar and the accounts officer paid us our wages. It was a very small sum. When we went to annual camp for two weeks, we all mixed and got to know one another very well – even the officers. It brought the whole unit together. One day, at camp, we were told to parade for 'short-arm inspection'. We all paraded and we were instructed to drop our trousers, pull out our penis and the medical officer came along and held it on a ruler. To see if we had any diseases. That sticks in my mind.

In 1938, when it looked as if war was in the offing, we were told that we were to be turned from a bomber squadron into a fighter squadron. At the same time, the Air Ministry issued an order that the squadron could train four other rank pilots. I was the first one to be chosen out of 600 men. I learned to fly on the Avro Tutor. It was a very heavy wooden-framed biplane, covered in fabric, with an open cockpit. We didn't have any radio communication between the instructor and the pupil – just voice tubes – and there was no radio communication with the ground. We had no oxygen but you didn't need it because you didn't go high enough. When I went solo, it went through my head that there was I, an electrical apprentice, on my own, flying an aircraft over the Wirral peninsula. My thoughts about my life changed at that moment.

To take off in an Avro Tutor, the main thing was to line up into the wind. You didn't have runways – just a grass field – so you looked at the windsock to see which way the wind was blowing. You opened up the engine gradually, holding the stick back because you didn't want the tail to rise. As you put on full power and you were bumping along over the grass field, you eased the stick forward and the tail came off the ground. Then you'd feel the aircraft wanting to get into the air and you helped it by pulling the stick very gently back and you climbed into the air. At about a thousand feet, you would level off. Coming into land, you would throttle back the engine and approach the field in a bank curve. You straightened out with the wings level to the ground when you were about thirty feet up. You reduced your speed to something above the stalling speed and you let the aircraft settle down. The idea was to do a three point landing – so that when the aircraft stalled, you touched down on tail and wheels together, nice and gently. If you did a front wheel landing, you bounced in the air. You always landed into wind. If you came into land across wind in a biplane, you could rip the undercarriage off and wreck the aircraft.

Flying any aircraft, it was essential that you knew how to put it in a spin and get it out of a spin. To put it into a spin, you throttled back, easing the stick back and the aircraft went slower and slower. You'd start to get the effect that it was stalling and you put hard rudder in the direction you wanted to spin. And down you'd go. To recover, you equalled the rudder pedals out and put the stick forward and normally after about one and a half turns, you came out of the spin. It's a technique that you had to be taught.

To do a loop, you got up to a certain speed, perhaps 120mph, and pulled the nose up. You didn't pull it up too tightly because you didn't want to stall at the top. So you eased it around and when you were up and over and your nose was pointing down you were happy. It was a matter of easing it around rather than pulling it. There was virtually nothing to it – except keeping your wings level to the horizon.

So much of the training was about what to do if things went wrong. I remember being told by an instructor, 'When you're flying somewhere, always keep a lookout for a suitable field to land in!' Engine failure was a problem in those days so you might be flying along and the instructor would throttle back on the engine and say, 'Pick a field and land!' You'd have to pick a field that you felt that you could land in safely. As soon as you were near to landing, the instructor would say, 'I've got it!' and he'd fly off.

As far as navigation was concerned, your main thing was your compass. You had to try and fly nice and steady or else the compass would fly all over the place. You also had to know the wind direction and calculate for drift. Say you were flying on a course of 180° and you had a wind coming from port – you probably had to fly on a course of 170° to allow for the wind drift. A lot of navigation was done by railway lines and railway stations. You always carried maps but they were a problem with the open cockpits. You had to hold on to them tightly and keep the aircraft straight and level while you were doing it.

As the war came closer, my friends and I were wishing for it. Let's have a war! It was a release from the boredom of going to work. In August 1939, I was on holiday near Caen in France when I was told that a telegram was waiting for me at the local Post Office. It was dated August 26 and it was recalling me to the squadron. By the time I got back to the hotel, all the residents had heard that I was being recalled and they guessed the war was about to start so they all packed up to leave.

On returning to the squadron, things became very intense. We were now regulars and the easygoing times had gone. Sergeants and corporals were roaring orders. The first job I was given was filling sandbags. After about three weeks, the squadron was sent to its war station at Wittering. But I was sent to 8 Elementary Flying Training School at Woodley.

It was a strange change in life. About ten of us lived in a house with two batmen in white coats to feed us and look after us and make our beds. No one had ever made a bed for me before in my life. The food was wonderful and I thought, 'This is heaven!' This comfortable life carried on for about two weeks when suddenly all the instructors appeared in uniform and the whole atmosphere changed. The Chief Flying Instructor, Squadron Leader Moir, was a dreadful man. He would just shout, 'You! Get into my aircraft!' He wore black flying overalls and a black helmet and we called him the black bastard. He must have been most unhappy. The pattern of the training at Elementary Flying Training School was almost identical to what I'd done in the Auxiliary and I was only there because the Flying Training Schools were jammed up. My time at Woodley was really a total waste of time and government money.

Eventually, in April 1940, I went to 9 Flying Training School at Hullavington where I trained on the Hawker Hart. The Hart was a biplane with a fixed undercarriage but it was light on the controls. I did instrument flying where you flew the aircraft from the front cockpit and pulled a canvas hood over you so you couldn't see and were just left with your basic instruments. You had to learn to put trust in your instruments. You might be flying along at night or in bad conditions when suddenly you would feel as though you were leaning out of the side. You'd look at your instruments and they told you that you were straight and level – but still you felt as though you were leaning and you'd try and correct it. I'm sure many, many pilots killed themselves that way.

I got my wings on June 8, 1940 and I became a sergeant and I was sent to rejoin my squadron at Biggin Hill. The squadron leader asked me what I'd last flown, which was a Hawker Hart and he said, 'Well, what bloody use are you to me?' So, twenty-four hours after joining the squadron, I was sent on again to 7 Operational Training Unit, RAF Hawarden, to convert to Spitfires. The switch to a Spitfire was dramatic. When you open the throttle on a Hawker Hart, the engine gradually comes to life, you trundle over the ground and you gradually get airborne. When you push the throttle forward on a Spitfire, you roar into life, you roar across the ground and you roar into the air. I had always been conceited and I thought that I would turn out to be a wonderful fighter ace but when I rejoined 610 Squadron at Biggin Hill at the height of the Battle of Britain, I immediately realised that I knew nothing about air fighting.

Flight Lieutenant William Strachan
Jamaican with 99 Squadron, RAF

We had heard these requests on the radio in Jamaica, coming from Britain, speaking to their large family overseas that they should help to defend the Crown against the German invaders. I'm an 18-year-old, just left school and I had the ambition of getting into the RAF – but it was difficult. The British army were still in Jamaica so I went down with a friend to see them and I told them that I wanted to join the air force. We had difficulty getting past the guard but they sent us for a medical and we were both passed fit. 'Right, we want to join,' we said, 'will you send us to England?' We were laughed out. 'You find your own way there!' they said.

I knew if I'd gone to my father and said, 'I want to go to England,' he'd have completely squashed the idea. As conservative as he was, he inherently suspected Britain and I knew he wouldn't support the idea.

Wartime rules had been brought in that nobody could leave the island unless they had didn't owe the government any income tax and didn't have a criminal record. Because I was 18, just left school, I had no income and no criminal record so that was no problem. Still, how was I going to travel? I had no money so I went round all the shipping companies – they were all run by Englishmen, white men – and I said, 'Can you give me free passage to England?' I'd been listening to the propaganda on the radio saying how everybody was loyal to the crown but none of them were interested until I went to Jamaica Fruit Shipping Company, major shippers of bananas to Britain. They had a number of boats coming out from Britain with middle-class white people who were fleeing from the war to the colonies for safe haven and I was able to persuade the management to take me. Nobody was going from the Caribbean to Britain but they told me that I might have to pay for it. The full price was about £45 and I paid £15. I didn't have that so I had to sell my bicycle and my saxophone and I got about £17 for them. So I got on a ship and left Jamaica with £2 10s in my possession and a small case with one change of clothes. That's how I came to Britain.

On this ship – a vast luxury passenger ship – I was the only passenger. I was given a first-class cabin which was rather fortunate, right next to the captain, but that was for their convenience, to save opening up lot of the cabins and having cleaners and things. I ate with the captain which was regarded as quite an honour in those days. Normally those ships would have deck quoits and swimming pools, but those facilities weren't opened up so I spent my time smashing tin cans, saving metal for the war effort. The trip usually took just over two weeks in those days but it took a month because they had to do the zigzag route because of the U-boats in the Atlantic. We arrived at Bristol. I remember the train station. A porter came towards me in his uniform. 'Your case, sir,' he said and I saluted him. I thought he was a bloody admiral in his uniform. I didn't dare think that he would take my case. 'No, sir!' I said.

I got on the train to Paddington. The ticket was about thirty shillings and wartime England was dark. There was a blackout. The only place I'd heard of to stay was the YMCA on Tottenham Court Road – every West Indian that I'd ever met seemed to go there – so I took a taxi from Paddington, spending six shillings out of my fifteen. It was Saturday night, wartime, places were boarded up, wardens and Local Defence Volunteers walking round the place. I was so tired I went to bed. Come the Sunday morning, I went across to the YWCA to meet some people there. I met a lady there who was a Jewish refugee. It was the first I'd heard about these things from Germany. I went out with her for the Sunday evening and she told me what she was fleeing from and all that sort of thing.

On Monday morning, how do I get into the RAF? I've got no money, no connections, nobody. After great difficulty I found that the Air Ministry was at a place called Adastral House which was at the foot of Aldwych. So I went along to Adastral House and I spoke to the guard who I now know was a corporal. I said to him, 'I want to join the air force.' I'll never forget this. He said to me, 'Piss off.' Here am I dressed in rather lightweight colonial stuff in March – I think he thought I was drunk or a lunatic. I persisted and as he tried to get me away, a sergeant came along, and asked what was going on and I tried to tell him. He said 'You don't join the air force here, you're trying to take the mickey out of us! This is the head office of the Air Ministry!' But in my logic at that period, where else do you join the air force but at the Air Ministry? I didn't even know about recruiting stations. So I persisted in my arguments with this sergeant and he said, 'Where do you come from?' and I said, 'Kingston.' He said, 'There's a recruiting station at Kingston down in Surrey,' and I said, 'I don't come from Surrey! I come from Jamaica!' He didn't know where Jamaica was. As he stood there quite mystified, a Hooray Henry type young officer came past and heard the argument. He said, 'Oh you're from Jamaica. One of our colonial friends. Welcome! I did geography at university and I've always been impressed with you West Africans. Come in!' And thanks to his supreme ignorance I was dragged in. This bloke was a pilot officer, the lowest officer but he was above the sergeant. And thanks to his intervention, he took me in and I was taken up and saw a much higher rank, a flight lieutenant. I had to go through this story in much more detail and he really satisfied himself of its truth. And then they sent me for a medical at Euston.

I went there in the afternoon. I was told to stand in a room, 'Get all your clothes off because you're going to be medically examined.' I was shivering and freezing. I'd only been in England for 48 hours. They examined me and found me fully fit. The doctor said, 'Right now you can go home and we'll call you up when we can take you in.' I had to explain that I had no money and going home was very difficult. That took another period of argument but by about nine or ten o'clock I was on the train to Blackpool recruiting unit. I'd managed to break all regulations – to get recruited after 48 hours in this bloody country. I was joined up in 4 Elementary Flying Training School. On the Tuesday morning, I was in the RAF, in uniform, kitted out, in a group of 50 strange Englishmen. I was the only coloured person from the colonies. I was very proud of what I'd achieved.

And then these English people said, 'You're mad! You're a bloody fool! If we'd been in Jamaica, we'd still be there now! What an idiot!' It destroyed all my ideals of what I believed the whole thing was about. I was so proud of what I'd achieved and they said, 'We'd do anything to get away from the bloody war and you say you come all this way and you tell us that story.' They thought it was completely weird.

The corporal in charge of us was an ex-Bertram Mills clown. He was extremely gymnastic and fit and he looked at us in the traditional way a corporal looks at a bunch of new recruits and he said, 'Now I want you all running on the spot.' These blokes creaked into action. And then he looked at me and said, 'Right, I'm making you my deputy. Darkie, come over here!' I'd never been called 'darkie' in my life before. I was shattered because it was a term of contempt. He said, 'Darkie, you are in charge of the squad!' I had conflict in my mind. I was annoyed I was called 'darkie' but my chest swelled out because I was regarded as a man fit to be promoted, second airman in the RAF.

Pilot Officer Mahinder Singh Pujji
Indian pilot with 43 Squadron, RAF

I was born in Simla in India where my father was a government officer. I lived there until I was 14 or 15. It was a beautiful hill station. My life was bound up with the Raj. Even during my schooling I had Anglo-Indian friends. Our education was English and our dress was English but at home, we spoke Punjabi. I wasn't interested in politics but I knew what was going on and I had great admiration for my leaders, especially Gandhi and Nehru. I agreed with them but there was nothing inside me to take part in that movement. We were discouraged from meddling in those sorts of things. With my father in the government service, his position would have been compromised.

The British that I knew were the officers – my father's bosses. They were civilised and polite but we only had superficial contact. They never invited us to their houses. It was a social thing.

When my father retired from the government service, we left Simla and moved to Amritsar where I joined the local school. In 1937, I decided to join the flying club. My elder brother was learning to fly. He had decided to become a pilot. He had also started drinking. That was terrible – I thought he was ruining our family but he told my father that if you want to fly, you have to drink. I asked him why and he told me that I knew nothing about it. So I went to my father and told him that I also wanted to become a pilot. He was hesitant to begin with but then I insisted and he let me join the Delhi Flying Club. I wanted to show them that you could fly without drinking.

I was studying at college and flying in my spare time. I flew Gipsy Moths and Tiger Moths. Flying was inside me. It was a spiritual thing.

While I was in the flying club, I made friends with a British officer who was working with Shell Oil and he said that Shell had a job as a refuelling superintendent and Shell preferred people with a flying background. He asked me, 'Would I like it?' So I joined Shell in 1938 and continued flying as well. I knew that something was happening in Europe but Europe was miles and miles away from where we were. It didn't seem to affect us in any way whatsoever.

In 1940, I saw an ad in the newspaper saying that the RAF wanted qualified pilots. I immediately applied. My boss said that he would keep my job and within a month, I was in England. Twenty-four qualified pilots arrived together at Liverpool and we were all commissioned on August 1 as Pilot Officers. We arrived in London and we were billeted in temporary huts in Uxbridge. We could see the searchlights looking for the German aircraft and I was longing to fly.

When we arrived, we met a lot of people and I appreciated the spirit of Londoners. They were very friendly and courageous. It fascinated me that the people were so brave. There wasn't any prejudice in London – but on our way to London, we'd called in at Durban and Cape Town in South Africa. While we were in Cape Town, my friends and I were having dinner, dressed in our RAF uniforms, when the waiter came along and said, 'Are you from Egypt?' 'No,' we said, 'we're from India.' He looked shocked and he went away. After about half an hour, the manager came and said, 'I'm sorry, I'm not allowed to serve people from your country'. Among us there were two or three experienced pilots of international repute. They were furious. 'What do you think?' they said, 'We have come here to fight for the British and that's what you're telling us?' One pilot got very angry and hit the glass table with his shoe and broke it into pieces. A scene was created and very soon, there were police and officers and after an hour, they apologised to us and we were taken back to our hotel where it was explained that the prejudice was a local South African thing and not a British thing. But South Africa was under British rule.

We didn't see any of this prejudice in Britain at all. It was a very pleasant surprise. Everyone was nice to us. Those of us in turbans were the special VIPs for everybody because we looked very strange with the RAF wings on our turbans. We got VIP treatment in restaurants. There were no eggs and no sugar available but when we asked for them, they were produced from somewhere or other. They wanted to oblige us.

The editor of *The Times* met me at a restaurant and he said, 'What do you think of the English girls?' I said, 'I wouldn't like to know them at all,' because I had seen the 'girls' walking in Piccadilly. I was not used to these kinds of girls. I thought they were very low. The editor listened to me and then he invited me to his house. I had dinner with him and his family. He had a 17-year-old daughter and we became friends and the rest of the time I was in England, I was mostly in their house. They had the same values as my family. A few things were different, like the girls could go with us to the pictures but there was no question of behaving in an unseemly way. No embracing or kissing. I became one of the family. I gave them a couple of my turbans and I requested them that if I was ever shot down somewhere, they should drop them to me. They were very nice about it.

Throughout my air force career, I was allowed to wear my turban. I made a special request to the RAF that I didn't want to take off my turban to fly. They were curious because there were other Sikh pilots who readily took off their turbans and put on helmets. But I told them that I didn't want to because of my religion. So they allowed me to have a special headset with the oxygen mask and microphone that came over the turban. The British were very accommodating.

Pilot Officer James Goodson
American pilot with 43 Squadron, RAF

I didn't go over to England to fight. I came to Europe in the summer of 1939 to visit France. I was an American but I was studying modern languages at university in Toronto and I'd gone to summer school in Paris to perfect my French. I came back through England to see my aunt and uncle – my mother had originally been English. I happened to be in England when Joe Kennedy, our ambassador, informed us Americans that we should immediately make plans to get back to the States because there was going to be a war which England would lose. I had to get back to university anyway but I delayed a little bit and I got on the last ship to leave England before war broke out. That ship was the ill-fated *SS Athenia* which left Liverpool a day before war was declared. Just as we got off the Hebrides, we were torpedoed. There was a U-boat out there waiting for us.

I believe there were two torpedoes, one hit midships and one aft, and almost immediately the midships flooded. I was on deck when it happened and the ship immediately went dark. They put on emergency searchlights and I looked down and saw water shooshing around where the dining rooms had been. The boat had lurched to one side and there were men, women and children floundering around in the water. I said to members of the ship's crew, 'Let's go down and rescue these people!' but – amazingly to me as an American – very few of the crew of the *Athenia* could swim. So I went down into the water and started passing children and women and anybody I could help up to the crew who had let ropes down. When the ship had lurched over even further and the lights had gone out, I went to see if there were people trapped in the main section and I saw dead bodies swooshing around in the water. I think the whole thing changed my attitude. I was plunged into the whole war thing, if you like, within a few minutes.

I suppose Americans looked at the European war as something that didn't much concern them. Some Americans had bitter memories of helping in the First World War which they didn't get much thanks for. Isolationist feeling was very, very strong in the States at the time and those of us who joined the RAF lost our American citizenship. I think if I had had any of those feelings, the *Athenia* experience wiped them out.

I was rescued from the sea by a Norwegian tanker which took us to the first neutral port which was Galway in the Irish Free State. And from there I made my way to Glasgow. Arriving in Glasgow I saw some people erecting an RAF recruiting station. I asked if an American could join their RAF. Eventually, they found out that yes, I could, but since I had to swear my allegiance to the King of England, I would automatically lose my American citizenship. When I told them that I had had some experience of flying, they immediately said that I could join the RAF. Then they said, 'Of course, there's the question of pay. It's seven shillings and sixpence a day to start with.' I was very upset and said, 'I'm afraid I've lost everything on the *Athenia*. I don't think I can afford seven shillings and sixpence a day.' I was amazed when they said, 'We pay you!' I thought the English were loveable fools. To be able to fly a Spitfire and be paid for it was really something extraordinary.

The few Americans that had come over were taken down to the Air Ministry. We had a little talk saying 'Because America is not in the war and is selling us a lot of goods, you may find a little resentment. The English people are on their own and feel that they need more support from America. But please, if you run into any resentment, please try and accept it. We want you to know we very much appreciate you coming over here.' So we promised to behave. But we never, never, never ran into any anti-American feeling.

I was sent straight back across the Atlantic to Canada for training. I joined the Empire Training Scheme. We had to start off as ordinary AC2s and we did guard duty and things like that which weren't very much fun. But once the training started I thought it was absolutely excellent. It didn't give us any combat training but it certainly taught us how to fly.

We were all keen to get into combat. I can remember seeing grown men weep when they were washed out – because there was a constant process of washing people out for lack of inherent flying ability. So those that eventually ended up as pilots were very few. Most of those that did went into Bomber Command, Coastal Command or Transport Command. Those that eventually became fighter pilots were very, very few.

Pilot Officer Ludwik Martel
Polish pilot with 54 and 603 Squadrons, RAF

The beginning of the war in Poland was very sudden. I was called in and reported to my unit in Poznan on September 1, 1939. The first German bomb came down as I left the train. From then onwards we were more or less running away from the bombers. We were attacked and bombed without heart. They were just bombing every possible target with people running away from their homes. They chose the people as a target. As a reservist, I joined a unit who were going to collect aircraft from Romania. But when we reached the border on September 17, the unit was more or less disbanded. That was a very unpleasant time because we realised that everything was gone, it was finished and we had to look ahead to join the fighting in the west. I felt full of hatred. I wanted to fly and to be able to shoot the opposition. I went to France but I had a very unpleasant experience in France. As soon as the agreement between the British government and the Polish government was made, I came to England. It was a very pleasant surprise when we were allowed to go flying in England. We got access to modern equipment, which I had been dreaming of. In England, I went through preliminary training and got familiar with aviation in the west because, after all, it had been nearly six months since I left Poland and had been near aircraft. I was very pleased when after 50 minutes training on a Spitfire, I was posted to a Spitfire squadron.

Wolfgang Falck
German Messerschmitt 110 Pilot

When I left school in 1931, I joined the Reichswehr. At the time, Germany was not allowed to have an air force but the German army had a secret agreement with the Russian Red Army that every year young German officer cadets were trained as pilots at the fighter school in Lipetsk in Russia. It started in 1927 and it finished in 1933 when Hitler came to power. Our bosses were officers but everything was done in civilian clothing. Lipetsk was the air base of the Russian air force. We flew the Fokker D13, a Dutch aircraft. All the writing on the plane was in Spanish because the aircraft had been ordered by a South American state and they had been transported on a big ship from Amsterdam but the ship's captain must have been a very poor navigator because they didn't arrive in South America, they arrived in Leningrad . . .

All the flight mechanics were Russian soldiers but the supervisor was German. We were kept separate to the Russians. We had our own barracks where we lived, our own officer club and our own hangar. The Russians were very friendly to us. We had civilian friends and girlfriends too but they were not supposed to have contact with us because we were bad capitalists. So the GPU – the Soviet secret police – went to the homes of our Russian friends and asked them what we'd been talking about. The GPU told our friends to ask us questions about our organisation and life in Germany but our friends came back to us and told us what the GPU had said to them.

While we were training in Russia, there was an accident. There was no fence around the big area where we used to practise ground attacks against targets. It was always published when we intended to shoot there and signs were made so that everybody was informed. One day, the first aircraft of my crew made an air to ground attack and just after he had shot, he saw a cart with a man and two horses behind the wooden target. The man and the horses were dead. He went back and reported it to our commanding officer. The dead man was a labourer and he had a wife and three or four children and the next day there was a meeting between the Russian and German authorities. The Russians said that the dead horses were the best horses in the area and they were very expensive – 500 roubles each. Our commanding officer said, 'OK. We'll pay that.' Then the Russians said the cart was brand new – 100 roubles. 'OK.' Then the Russian officer smiled and went to leave the room. Our Commanding Officer said, 'Stop! What about the man?' because he thought that we would have to pay the widow and for the education of the children. 'Oh yes, yes,' said the Russian, '25 roubles for the funeral.' That was the Russian mentality.

This period in Russia had a great influence on our future development. Number one, we had great comradeship and number two, we all wanted to be fighter pilots – the new Baron von Richthofen. We loved Russia, the people, the language, the music, the culture and tradition – but we hated communism.

When I came back from Russia, I joined my regiment in Silesia and that was terrible because after we had been fighter pilots, we were now army recruits and the sergeants and the corporals treated us terrible. It was very hard and sometimes I was so desperate that I couldn't stand it. There were suicides because people couldn't stand it.

I remember when Hitler came to power. A little while before, we had marched through an area of Silesia that was known as being communist. People threw pots at us. But after Hitler came to power, we came back to the area and all the people welcomed us like heroes, crying, 'Heil! Heil!' There were new flags with the swastika everywhere. These people had switched in a short time. It is very difficult for young Germans and foreigners to understand why. After the First World War, Germany was in a poor condition. The Rhineland was occupied by the French, industry had gone, there were no aircraft and an army of 100,000. There were at least ten political parties, everyone fighting against the others. It was like a civil war. The communists were trying to make revolution. Millions of people were jobless with nothing to eat. It was really catastrophic. Now, all of a sudden, came a man. He promised the Germans – 'You are somebody. You are Germans. You should be proud to be Germans. I will take care that you get enough food. I will take care that you get a job. No jobless any more. No hunger any more.' And the first things he did were like that. He started building the autobahns. He marched into the Rhineland and made it German property. There were no crimes any more. Everything was safe. All these things were brand new and they impressed the people very much. Many people had a much better condition of life than before. Everyone had the feeling that now was a new time and now we are safe. Nobody knew what would happen in the future.

But we had seen the May parade when we'd been in Russia and we had been impressed. The army, the girls, the boys were marching in uniform with guns and flowers and flags. Then we came back to Germany and we saw the parades under Hitler and we saw the youth, the workers, the SA and the SS and we said, 'We saw exactly the same last year in Russia. The only difference was there they had hammer and sickles and here we have swastikas.'

On the day that I was promoted to lieutenant, I was discharged and I joined the so-called Airline Pilot School. Officially we were not soldiers – we were civilians. No soldier was obliged to salute us. But on the day that the German air force was permitted once again, I became a lieutenant and officially, I was a soldier again.

In 1936, Hitler gave the order to march on the Rhineland. Hitler said that it was German country and it was invaded. A fighter wing was built up and the most of its pilots came from the Airline Pilot School. We flew to Frankfurt. My fighter group was the only group with machine guns and ammunition. The other fighter groups flew into the Rhineland with no machine guns or ammunition. They flew into Cologne and Dusseldorf and when night came they flew back to their old base and the next morning they came back to the Rhineland to make it seem as though another fighter group had arrived. That was a tactic of Hitler to bluff other nations. He did it all the time.

Then I went to *Jagdgeschwader* Richthofen. I became an instructor for young pilots and then I became the adjutant to the commanding officer. We were visited by attachés from the UK and from France. When the British attaché came to visit, one of the hangars was closed and two guards were in front of it with guns. The attaché asked what was in the hangar. In fact it was empty but we said, 'I'm sorry, I can't say. As a soldier, you will understand.' It was another bluff – to make the attaché think we were stronger than we were. We got the order that the *Jagdgeschwader* Richthofen would be the first to be equipped with the Messerschmitt 109. My Geschwader commander and I went to the Mersserschmitt factory in Augsburg where we flew it before it was delivered. They told us to be careful with it. We were used to the Heinkel 51 which was a biplane with a fixed undercarriage, an open cockpit and now all of a sudden here is a very fast aircraft with a closed cockpit and a retractable undercarriage. It was new technology. Somebody showed me – 'This is the stick and here is the power. Be careful when you take off because it has a drive to the left.'

In summer 1937, we were equipped with the 109 and we had more accidents and losses – aircraft and pilots – than we sometimes had in wartime. But nobody was allowed to write about these losses. The 109 was a very sensitive and touchy aircraft. In my eyes, it was a wrong decision to choose the 109. When our government had wanted a new fighter, there was a competition between Heinkel and Messerschmitt. The decision was made in favour of the Messerschmitt 109. I guess Messerchmitt's connection with the government must have been much better than Heinkel's. My squadron was the only squadron in the Luftwaffe to be equipped with the Heinkel fighter;we had it for two weeks. The Heinkel was easier to fly and the undercarriage was not as high and narrow as the Messerschmitt's. Unfortunately, the decision was made in favour of the 109.

In 1937, the German air force was invited to bring a group of pilots to go to England to participate in the opening of York airfield. I was chosen to be one of the six pilots. We flew to London where we were welcomed by the Royal Air Force. On the first night, we were invited to a house on the Thames. It was a very friendly atmosphere between the Brits and the Germans. We were talking about Hitler and National Socialism. One of the British said, 'National Socialism is OK so long as you keep it at home.' We said, 'OK.' He said, 'But don't fill it up in bottles and try to export it to England or some other country.' 'No, we are not interested, you can be sure.' During this discussion, one of the British guys was playing with the radio and he picked up a German station. At the end of the programme they played the German anthem, '*Deutschland, Deutschland uber alles* . . . ' All of a sudden this British guy stood up and made the salute. Then all the other Royal Air Force officers also made the salute. We as guests couldn't do anything else but salute. In my eyes that was a typical case of English courtesy.

There were 12 or 13 nations represented at York but from the moment we landed, the Royal Air Force and the six German officers were one big group of friends. We were together at lunch and at dinner and in the bar. One night, in the hotel in York, one of the British officers came to me and said, 'We have big problems. The French have come to us and they are very offended because we are always together with you and we haven't been taking care of them. If there should be one nation we prefer, it should be the French because we have an entente. Please forgive us but tonight we have to take care of the French and we cannot be together.' I said, 'OK, I understand. But shall we join you to make the French happy?' 'Oh, that's great,' said the British officer. So a dinner was arranged for the British, the French and the Germans. After the dinner, the French were totally drunk and we left the dining room and went into a big hall. The French were sitting drunk in chairs with high backs and someone said, 'Come on! Collect the toilet rolls from every floor!' So the British and the Germans disappeared and everybody came back with toilet paper and then we wrapped the French from their chins to their legs in toilet paper. All the other nations were staying in the hotel and they laughed and laughed. The next morning, the French left York and there was big trouble for the British.

Then I became a *Staffelkapitän* in the third group of *Jagdgeschwader* Richthofen. After a visit from Goering in early 1939, we were told that we would be equipped with a new heavy fighter that would be the crème de la crème – the Messerschmitt 110. That was the first time that we had flown a two-engine aircraft and there was a second man on the back seat. We were not so happy to get a two-engine fighter but sitting here, I say thank God for the 110, because without the second engine, I would have been killed several times during the war.

When the war started on September 1, 1939, I was on a small airfield in Silesia. There was no enthusiasm. The atmosphere was very quiet. Nobody was keen on a war. The night before, we had received the order to take off the next morning at five o'clock to meet a bomber group in the air which was bomb the airfield at Krakow. It was almost dark when we took off and we didn't meet up with the bombers so we flew to Krakow, hoping to meet the bombers there to protect them against the Polish pilots. But nothing happened. We arrived at Krakow and we found no bombers, no Polish aircraft, no anti-aircraft fire – nothing. So we flew back. On the flight back, near the border, I saw a German reconnaissance aircraft taking photos. As a fighter pilot, you must protect the poor reconnaissance plane to stop the enemy shooting him down so I flew over to take care of him – but this idiot thought that I was a Polish aircraft and he shot at me. Fortunately, he didn't hit me but that was my baptism.

The same day on another mission, I saw a Polish aircraft but I didn't dare to shoot because I could only see his silhouette against the sun and there was a Polish aircraft that was very similar in silhouette to the Stuka. But then I saw red on the end of his wing so I shot. I did not hit him but then I saw that he was a Stuka. I reported to our authorities that it was easy to mix up the emblem of the Polish aircraft with the red E on the wing of the second Luftwaffe squadron. So the authorities removed the letters on the wings. That was revenge – a German had shot against me and now I shot against a German.

In Poland, I shot down three aircraft. The first one was a mixture of a fighter and dive-bomber. The second was a reconnaissance aircraft and the third was a three-engine Fokke aircraft. I remember getting the order to attack to attack ground troops some distance behind the front and we saw a Polish battery with horses. We attacked them. I hated that – the poor horses. And I saw a big city burning for the first time – Warsaw. That was terrible.

The German air force was greatly superior to the Polish air force. It didn't surprise me that victory came quickly. We had been so superior that we had compassion for the Polish people. I remember when all the population were not authorised to own a radio any more. I saw all these poor people carrying their radios. It was depressing. It must be terrible to be a civilian member of a nation that was losing a war.

Hurricanes and Spitfires

The bloke said to me, 'This is a Spitfire, get in it and fly it.'

British strategists had long been aware that aircraft would play a key role in a future war. The great fear was of a 'knockout blow' to be delivered against the British population by German bombers. A 1924 report by the Air Ministry predicted 1,700 deaths in the first 24 hours of bombing. A subsequent medical report warned of 'three to four million cases of acute panic, hysteria and other neurotic conditions during the first six months of air attack'. Moreover, there was little point in trying to defend against the menace because, as Stanley Baldwin told the House of Commons in 1932, 'The bomber will always get through. The only defence is in offence, which means that you have to kill more women and children more quickly than the enemy if you want to save yourselves.' This belief was widely held and throughout the 1930s, the Air Ministry showed little interest in air defence. Sir John Slessor, Director of Plans at the Air Ministry, had written in 1936 that Britain needed only a few single-engined fighters. Fortunately, a combination of pressure from Fighter Command's commander-in-chief, Sir Hugh Dowding, advances in science and engineering and the unlikely support of Neville Chamberlain persuaded the Air Ministry to take air defence seriously.

A substantial force of high-quality fighter aircraft was needed and Britain's leading designers were Sydney Camm of Hawkers and Reginald Joseph Mitchell of Supermarine. In 1929, Mitchell's S6 aircraft had won the Schneider Trophy, a speed and performance competition for seaplanes. The S6 was a monoplane clad in stressed steel which increased its strength and efficiency. It flew at an average of almost 329 mph. This aircraft was the forerunner of the Spitfire. Camm's Hurricane began life as the Hawker Fury Monoplane. He realised that he had neither the time nor the finance to incorporate a stressed skin into the design, so he persevered with a frame of metal tubes and wooden stingers covered in fabric.

A timely development which ensured the success of the Hurricane and the Spitfire arrived independently of Camm and Mitchell. The Rolls-Royce PV12 engine, later to be renamed the Merlin, was capable of 1030 hp and delivered a thrust that made high speeds and high ceilings possible. The Hurricane first flew at Brooklands on November 6, 1935 and impressed all those present. The Spitfire's maiden flight was at Eastleigh on March 5, 1936 – two days before Hitler marched into the Rhineland. With its striking, thin elliptical wings adding to its speed, it flew 30 mph faster than the Hurricane. The Air Ministry initially ordered 310 Spitfires and 600 Hurricanes. The first Hurricanes, with a top speed of 325 mph, came into operation with 111 Squadron at Northolt at the end of 1937 and the first Spitfires, with a top speed of 362 mph, were delivered to 19 Squadron at Duxford in August 1938.

Squadron Leader Thomas Gleave
Commanding Officer, 253 Squadron, RAF
We were badly let down by the RAF in giving priority to the production of bombers and only paying lip service to creating a viable fighter defence. I can remember the figures that people were bringing back from the continent relating to the strength of the Luftwaffe. They were very frightening and not far wrong. One chap came back with a story in mid 1939 that the Luftwaffe had 1,500 single-engine fighters. This was staggering but it was not an exaggeration. Not if you took all the front line fighter squadrons, then you allowed for three or four squadrons back up, then a maintenance depot with a lot of reserves and then the operational training units.

Of course, even in 1938, we could have produced a very gratifying figure of our own fighter defences but the snag was – only a very few of them were in the fighter squadrons.

Ronald Melville
Private Secretary to Chief of Air Staff at the Air Ministry
I had helped to prepare a memorandum to present to the Prime Minister on the size of the German air force. You might have expected the Air Marshals to

use our high figures to build a case to expand the Royal Air Force. But they didn't. They took the view that if the air force was to expand it must do so in an orderly way, slowly and gradually.

Flying Officer Jeffrey Quill
Vickers Chief Test Pilot and 65 Squadron, RAF
R J Mitchell had a lot of access to intelligence reports so he was very well aware of the threat from Germany. That's what inspired him to get on with the design of the Spitfire.

Group Captain Frederick Winterbotham
Deputy to Chief of Secret Intelligence Service with special responsibility for the security of Ultra messages
Some of my friends from the Air Ministry went down to the first test flight and they were so excited about the Spitfire. All through the Air Ministry it was terribly secret. Nobody had to know anything about it but it really looked as if we were going to have something which would match up to anything that the Germans could build.

Flying Officer Jeffrey Quill
Vickers Chief Test Pilot and 65 Squadron, RAF
I remember the first flight of the Spitfire very well. It was March 5, 1936. R J Mitchell was disappointed with the performances. It was not going as fast as it should do. The problem was mostly the propeller so a different propeller was designed and it gave us an increase of about 13 mph. Mitchell was determined that we were going to have 350 mph out of the prototype. Another problem was the riveting. It would have been much simpler to build the aeroplane with all the rivets round headed but we found that it cost us six or eight miles per hour. So we stripped them off in a methodical way to find out where it was important have flush-headed rivets. We eventually got the speed up to 362.

We had various troubles with the Spitfire – difficulties with handling and performance. If it hadn't had a large margin of speed over the Hurricane, the Air Ministry probably wouldn't have ordered it. Wilfred Freeman, who was responsible for Research and Development in the Air Ministry, rang up the flight commander, Edwards-Jones, and asked him, 'Could the aeroplane be flown by the ordinary squadron pilot?' Because a lot of people thought it was a Schneider Trophy aeroplane which only great experts could fly. Old Edwards-Jones quite rightly said, 'Yes, it can.' On the strength of that, Wilfred Freeman placed the first RAF order for it. Within a week of that conversation, we had an order for 310 Spitfires. That was very typical Wilfred Freeman. He stuck his neck out a bit. The RAF hadn't actually done any performance testing at all on it at that time.

Flying Officer Arthur Banham
611 Squadron, RAF

We took delivery of the first Spitfire at Duxford. It was the aircraft which was to be used for development flying, and our instructions were to fly it up to a thousand hours as soon as we possibly could. We had to arrange relays of us to fly it round the countryside from first light to dusk, just to get the hours in. We succeeded in doing that and I very nearly succeeded in wrecking it too. Early one morning, on the first trip of the day, I came back from the south-west, and I thought I would try and do a dead stick approach to the aerodrome. There was a warning horn in the Spitfire – when you throttled back, this horn would come on to warn you that your undercarriage was not down. But you could cancel that out if you wanted to. I made a long gliding approach to the aerodrome from a considerable height and this noise was annoying me considerably so I switched it off. And of course, at the critical moment, I came over the fence with my undercarriage firmly up. Fortunately there was a live wire in the duty pilot's office who fired a couple of red lights at me, and I realised at once what it was, and I was able to pick up my engine, go round again and come down with my undercarriage down.

Flying Officer Jeffrey Quill
Vickers Chief Test Pilot and 65 Squadron, RAF

A lot of people felt that the Spitfire had been bought at too high a price. In terms of ease of production, it was going to be a much more expensive and difficult aeroplane to mass produce than the Hurricane. In terms of ease of maintenance, it was going to be a much more complicated aeroplane to look after in service. For instance, you could lower the undercarriage off a Hurricane and take the wings off because the undercarriage was in the centre section. So you could take the wings off, put the tail up on a three-ton lorry and tow it along the road. You couldn't do that with a Spitfire. If you took the wings off a Spitfire, it took the undercarriage off as well. If we had not been able to show a really definite advantage over the Hurricane, it probably wouldn't have been ordered and we were well aware of that.

A Spitfire Mark IA of 19 Squadron.

Pilot Officer Percival Leggett
615, 245 and 46 Squadrons, RAF

I worked on the Hurricane. At the initial construction stage, it didn't look very different from the old Hawker Hart biplane. The method of construction was almost identical. It was only when we started to put the fabric over it that it started looking like another aeroplane altogether.

It was a mixture of ancient and modern. It had a steel tubular construction and then on top of that, was placed the wooden framework that attached to the steel frame with nuts and bolts. Then the fabric people came along with a great length of fabric and chucked it over the top by hand. They were dressmakers, really. The fabric was pulled down into place and stitched together. Then it went to the dope shop where it was sprayed with an acetate mixture and lo and behold, a lovely aeroplane emerged.

The big innovation in the Hurricane's cockpit was the blind flying panel. In the old biplanes, you had an altimeter, an air speed indicator and a rev counter randomly dotted around the cockpit in positions where they could be readily seen by the pilot. With the Hurricane, we had a blind flying panel with an air speed indicator, an altimeter, an artificial horizon, directional gyro, rate of climb and descent and turn and slip indicator. That panel became standard in all aircraft from that time onwards. It meant that you could hop from one type of aeroplane to another without too much difficulty.

The new Hawkers factory was opened at Langley in Buckinghamshire in mid 1939. It was built to accommodate a mass-production line. You had the nearly complete Hurricanes up near the door and at the far end, there was a pile of steel tubes being put together. It was a brand new building, built for the job. The managers had proper offices instead of poky little cubbyholes. It had a concrete floor, instead of wooden boards. It was another world.

Flying Officer Jeffrey Quill
Vickers Chief Test Pilot and 65 Squadron, RAF; worked for Chief Test Pilot of Supermarines, Mutt Summers

I can remember when Charles Lindbergh visited Supermarines as Spitfire production was getting going. He had just been on a visit to Germany where he'd obviously been impressed by what he'd seen of their aircraft industry. I met him at Eastleigh and showed him our erecting shop which was full of Spitfires in the process of final assembly. It was a fairly tatty old hangar with a big wooden truss roof. Lindbergh looked round the place, looked up at the roof and I could tell exactly what was going on in his mind. He'd been round these fine chromium-plated, modern factories in Germany and he was obviously thinking to himself, 'These bloody Brits are just playing with the idea.' What he didn't know was that we had a much superior aeroplane in the Spitfire. I bloody nearly said to him, 'You can think what you bloody well like . . . but you wait!'

Leading Aircraftman Joe Roddis
Flight mechanic with 234 Squadron, RAF
The Spitfire came out in 1936 when I was doing my flight mechanics course. A pal and I went for a walk across the airfield one day and in one corner were standing four aeroplanes. We went straight on to the wing and looked in and there on the rudder bar it said, 'Supermarine' and we knew what they were. We'd heard such a lot of talk about them. I thought, 'If I can only get on these!' It was so beautiful.

Pilot Officer Thomas Neil
249 Squadron, RAF
Most of us had never flown monoplanes before and suddenly we were faced with these fearsome aeroplanes called Spitfires. The bloke said to me, 'This is a Spitfire, get in it and fly it.' All the training you had was to sit in the cockpit with a blindfold round your eyes and you felt round, trying to identify all the tits and bits, pulling the wheels up and putting the flaps down. You spent half a day doing that. And then you were introduced to *your* Spitfire and told to get on with it.

Sergeant David Cox
19 Squadron, RAF
I was given a Spitfire and told to take off, do a circuit and land. I was used to the Harvard which cruised at 110. Well, in this Spitfire I took off and I was doing 230. My reaction was, 'Oh my God, where's the airfield gone to?'

First Officer Jackie Moggridge
Female South African pilot with Air Transport Auxiliary
I went to pick up my first Spitfire from Oxford. When I arrived, they were running it up and there were sparks and flames coming from the exhaust of the huge Rolls-Royce Merlin engine. I was absolutely petrified and I thought, 'I'm never going to manage this!' it looked so vicious. I got in and followed all my notes and I held my breath. It was fast, and it flew like a bomb when I took off. It was so powerful that I had to start with my foot full on the rudder to the side opposite to the way the propeller was rotating – otherwise it would have

done a right-angle turn before I took off. But once it was flying, it was just like a Tiger Moth. I pulled a thing from under the seat that looked like a tube with a funnel on the end. 'What's this?' I asked the engineer. 'That's only for gentlemen pilots, miss,' he said.

Flight Sergeant George Unwin
19 Squadron, RAF
The Spitfire was a super aircraft. It was so sensitive on the controls. There was no heaving or pulling and pushing and kicking. You just breathed on it. If you wanted to turn, you just moved your hands slowly and she went. She was really the perfect flying machine. She would only spin if you made her and she'd come straight out of it as soon as you applied opposite rudder and pushed the stick forward. I've never flown anything sweeter. I've flown jets right up to the Venom but nothing . . . nothing like her.

Flying Officer Jeffrey Quill
Vickers Chief Test Pilot and 65 Squadron, RAF
When you were on the ground with the tail down, you were completely blind forwards because the nose obliterated everything. You had to taxi with a zigzag motion. You swung the nose to the right and had a look over the left side to see that all was clear and then you swung the other way. Once you were airborne, the view was quite reasonable because it was in flying attitude.

Sergeant David Cox
19 Squadron, RAF
In the first Spitfires, you had a lever and you had to pump the undercarriage up. This meant transferring your right hand – which you had been using on the control column – to the lever to do the pumping and using your left hand to control the aircraft. You could always tell a new pilot because his Spitfire was going up and down as he wasn't used to flying left-handed whilst pumping.

Sergeant Cyril 'Bam' Bamberger
610 and 41 Squadrons, RAF
Taking off in the Spitfire; you taxied from side to side to see where you were going on the ground. You had to remember that you had an undercarriage to retract and you had to put your propeller into fine setting. You lined up the aircraft and eased the throttle forward – not too hard or the tail would lift up. You bounced along the grass airfield, keeping the Spitfire straight with the

rudder. Then as you got faster, you eased the tail off the ground by pushing the stick forward just a little – but not too much because you didn't want your propeller to hit the ground. Then you opened the throttle wide open, you felt the Spitfire wanting to leave the ground and you eased the stick back. There you were, airborne in a Spitfire. The first task was to pump the undercarriage up. You roared off into the blue sky and when you got about a thousand feet, you put your pitch into 'coarse' and eased back on the throttle.

When you were coming in to land at about a thousand feet, you'd let your undercarriage down. When you turned across wind, you went into fine pitch again and then you lowered your flaps. You came in on a curved approach because if you came in on a straight approach, you couldn't see anything because of the nose of the aircraft. You only straightened out, one or two hundred feet above the ground. You reduced your speed, keeping it above stalling speed. You might have to put on a little extra power if it was dropping too fast. When the ground was whistling past, you eased the throttle back and brought the control column back and aimed for a three-point landing.

Sergeant David Cox
19 Squadron, RAF
The landing was tricky because the Spitfire's got a very, very long nose and you should come in on a curve so that you're looking below and to the left of the nose but for a new pilot, coming in on a curve took a bit of getting used to.

Flying Officer Hugh Dundas
616 Squadron, RAF
During the Battle of Britain, the Spitfire still had fabric ailerons. [*Ailerons are the hinged flaps on the wings which control the roll of the aircraft.*] It wasn't until the beginning of 1941 that we got metal ailerons which made a tremendous difference to handling in the high speed of a dive.

Sergeant Cyril 'Bam' Bamberger
610 and 41 Squadrons, RAF
When you were diving at speed with fabric ailerons, the aircraft used to try to turn to the left and I hadn't the physical strength to straighten it up.

Flying Officer Jeffrey Quill
Vickers Chief Test Pilot and 65 Squadron, RAF
The aileron problem was accounted for by the fact that before the war, the Air Staff had not regarded the Spitfire as a dogfighter for fighting against other

The instrument panel and flying controls of a Spitfire Mark II.

fighters. Bombers were considered the main threat so the Spitfire was to be a bomber destroyer and a high level of manoeuvrability, particularly in the rolling plane, was not regarded as an important factor.

Pilot Officer James Goodson
American pilot, 43 Squadron, RAF

Once you got used to the Spitfire, of course you loved it. It became part of you. It was like pulling on a tight pair of jeans. It was a delight to fly. I used to smoke a cigar sometimes – against all rules and regulations – but if I dropped my cigar lighter, instead of groping around on the floor, I'd move the stick a fraction of an inch, the Spit would roll over and I'd catch the cigar lighter as it came down from the floor. That was the kind of plane it was. Everybody had a love affair with it.

Hugh Burroughes
Engineer with Hawker Company

The Spitfire was lighter, faster and better on the climb. It could get to 10,000 feet in minutes less than the Hurricane.

Pilot Officer Thomas Neil
249 Squadron, RAF

Every second German pilot who was shot down by a Hurricane will say that he was shot down by a Spitfire. That was the folklore that went on.

Pilot Officer James Goodson
American pilot, 43 Squadron, RAF

When Peter Townsend went to see one of the German pilots that he'd shot down close to the base, the German said to him, 'I'm very glad to meet the Spitfire pilot who shot me down.' And Peter said, 'No, no, I was flying a Hurricane, I'm a Hurricane pilot.' And the German said, 'Would you do me a favour? If you are talking to any other Luftwaffe pilots, please tell them that I was shot down by a Spitfire.'

Leading Aircraftman Joe Roddis
Flight mechanic with 234 Squadron, RAF

Everyone thought the Spitfire was the most marvellous thing on wings but without the Hurricane, we'd have been in real trouble. There were twice as many Hurricanes in the Battle of Britain as there were Spitfires.

Sergeant Charlton Haw
504 Squadron, RAF
When I first flew a Hurricane, I was a little disappointed. I expected it to outshine the Miles Master but it didn't really. It was only about 25 mph faster in straight and level flight and it was heavier. But as I got used to it, my attitude changed.

Pilot Officer Irving Smith
New Zealand pilot with 151 Squadron, RAF
The Hurricane wasn't easy to see out of because the canopy was divided up into little panels so I personally tended to fly with mine open so that there was no restriction to the vision. Which made you very cold because neither the Hurricane or the Spitfire had any heating.

Flying Officer Roland Beamont
87 Squadron, RAF
I particularly wanted to fly the Hurricane because I was impressed with it. The Spitfire always looked like an elegant and beautiful aeroplane but I felt that the Hurricane was somehow more rugged. You got this immense feeling of power. It had this fixed pitch propeller which gave it a rather slow and leisurely take-off performance. Once it got into its stride, it would go very quickly but its flying qualities were very simple. It was very stable and it had a wide track undercarriage which was very forgiving and it was not difficult to land. My memories of converting to Hurricanes are memories of exhilaration at all this great power and of being able to see 300 mph on the air speed indicator in a shallow dive at any point in your flight.

Flying Officer Christopher Foxley-Norris
3 Squadron, RAF
It's very often an instinct with an aircraft. You get into one and it gives you enormous confidence and then you get into another and it doesn't. The Hurricane was very stable but at the same time, manoeuvrable. If you didn't want it to do a turn, it was absolutely rock stable; if you did, it was manoeuvrable. It was a very good gun platform – better than the Spitfire. And the Hurricane could absorb enemy fire.

Flying Officer William David
87 and 213 Squadrons
To repair a bullet hole in your Hurricane, you only needed a bit of dope fabric.

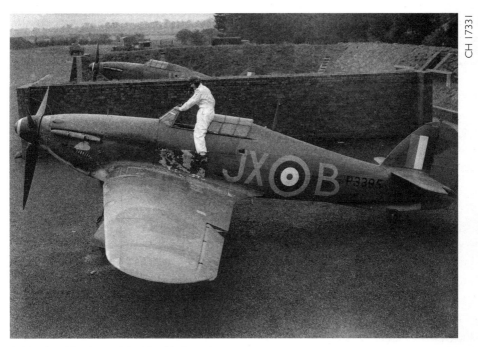

A Hawker Hurricane Mark I of I Squadron.

Whereas a Spitfire was all metal and you had to have a panel beaten in and riveted.

Fred Roberts
NCO *served as armourer with 19 Squadron*
The Hurricane was an easier plane to maintain from an armourer's point of view. On a Spitfire, you had to take eight panels off the top of the wings and eight panels from underneath the wings. When you rearmed it, you had an additional four flaps covering the underside of the ammunition tanks. In the Hurricane, you only had one panel covering each gun and one covering the ammunition tanks. And with the Hurricane, you could kneel on the top of the wing and rearm. On the Spitfire, you couldn't. You had to get on your knees on the wet grass and take all these panels off.

Flight Lieutenant Hugh Ironside
151 Squadron, RAF
The Hurricane was absolutely viceless provided you treated it right. I think from the point of view of fighting, I would have preferred it to a Spitfire, because it was so much stronger. Certainly on the early Spits, if you put an end to a very steep dive and pulled up too quick, the wings used to buckle. You could see the aluminium on the wings, little bumps. But you just couldn't fuss the Hurricane.

Squadron Leader Alan Deere
New Zealand pilot, 54 Squadron, RAF
If you were on Hurricanes they were the best. If you were on Spitfires they were the best.

Flying Officer Jeffrey Quill
Vickers Chief Test Pilot and 65 Squadron, RAF
I took the view myself that it took both planes to win the Battle of Britain. Neither would have succeeded on its own because the Hurricanes required the Spitfire squadrons to attack the Messerschmitt 109s while the Hurricanes concentrated on destroying the bombers. They were both there together and they both depended on each other. You sometimes hear people saying, 'The Spitfire won the Battle of Britain.' Well, that's absolute rubbish. The Spitfire *and* the Hurricane won the Battle of Britain.

The Air Defences

Without this system, we would have been lost.
We were almost lost with it.

The Hurricanes and Spitfires were the fighting element of Britain's air defences but to serve their purpose, they needed to be effectively deployed. That was made possible by Fighter Command's intricate defensive shield. Sir Hugh Dowding had been appointed commander-in-chief of Fighter Command in 1936 when the RAF was organised into separate commands. He was due for retirement in 1940 but was asked to remain in his post due to the circumstances. His nickname was 'Stuffy', in reference to his aloof, stubborn personality but these were precisely the attributes that served Fighter Command so well. In the face of resistance from the Air Ministry, he had created a control system capable of withstanding the Luftwaffe.

Fighter Command was divided into four operational groups. 11 Group, led by Air Vice Marshal Keith Park covered south-east England. 12 Group, led by Air Vice Marshal Trafford Leigh Mallory covered the middle part of England and Wales. 10 Group covered the south-west of England and 13 Group covered the north of England and Scotland. The groups were further divided into local sectors. Fighter Command headquarters, where Dowding kept his office, was based at Bentley Priory in Stanmore.

The key to Dowding's system was radar – known as RDF (Radio Direction Finding). A network of RDF stations, known as Chain Home Stations, had been built along the coast and were capable of tracking the approach of aircraft from over a hundred miles away. A further network of Chain Home Low stations were built which could detect low-flying aircraft. These stations would telephone the altitude, grid position and estimated strength of an incoming raid to a Filter Room at Fighter Command Headquarters which would ascertain whether the aircraft were friendly or hostile. The information would then be passed to the next-door Operations Room where the raid was plotted on a map table. The information was simultaneously passed to the Operations Rooms of the relevant groups and sectors where it was plotted on map tables. The group controller for the area under threat would choose which of his sectors would intercept the raid. The controller of the relevant sector would then scramble his squadrons and guide them to meet the raiders. Once the raid had crossed the coast, it was tracked by members of the Observer Corps – volunteers armed with binoculars, charts and altitude measuring equipment – who reported their findings to the Operations Rooms.

Pilot Officer Roger Hall
152 Squadron, RAF
Fighter Command's commander-in-chief, Air Chief Marshal Sir Hugh Dowding, was a very astute man, and when he took command in 1936, he had the foresight to build up the whole organisation almost from scratch. This comprised not only the Spitfires and the Hurricanes, but also the radar and the plotting.

Flying Officer Christopher Foxley-Norris
3 Squadron, RAF
'Stuffy' Dowding was absolutely outstanding but not in an inspirational way. He never went to an operational airfield. His leadership was superb from the point of view of the wise husbanding and apportionment of resources. He was almost entirely responsible for the command and control system which Fighter Command built up. He'd already been there for three years before the war started and the junior people like myself had enormous confidence in him. He was a sort of father figure. And you felt that as long as he had his hand on the tiller, all was going to be well.

Flight Lieutenant Hugh Ironside
Personal Assistant to Air Chief Marshal Sir Hugh Dowding
At the start of 1939, Dowding went to France. The object of the visit was to observe the French air defence system. We landed on this airfield near Lille where the grass was at least knee-high and lined up along the side were a lot of incredibly old aeroplanes with skis in between the wheels, which I didn't

Lord Dowding (taking the salute) stands alongside Sir Trafford Leigh Mallory. This picture was taken at the observance of the third anniversary of the Battle of Britain, by which time Dowding had been retired and given a peerage.

think still existed – even in France. We taxied up to the hangar, and lined up there were about a dozen beribboned French generals. 'Stuffy' got out, and he went along the line shaking hands and saying, 'The name's Dowding', 'The name's Dowding', 'The name's Dowding'. His French was extremely limited. Then we got into various motor cars and all went off to a large restaurant for a fabulous lunch, which went on for a good two hours, with an awful lot of wine, which of course 'Stuffy' didn't touch. He hardly ate anything either. I could see he was getting extremely uptight but worse was to come, because after lunch, all these jolly generals packed into cars again, and we were driven to a cellar where we sat on some hard chairs. In one corner of this cellar was a phone box with another hard chair and a French airman sitting on it. Just opposite him was a blackboard covered in squares. We sat there for some considerable time and then the phone rang. The airman answered it and there was lots of 'oui, oui, oui', and then airman put a red arrow on the blackboard. And this went on for an hour or so until the blackboard was covered in arrows of different colours. I don't think anybody knew what the hell it was all about. On the flight back, 'Stuffy' never said a word. He was absolutely silent. I think that's where he got his utter distrust of the French.

Elizabeth Quayle
Women's Auxiliary Air Force, plotter at Fighter Command HQ
We all admired our 'Stuffy' enormously. We had great loyalty to him – I think you might call it affection. He built up a tremendous esprit de corps amongst those of us in Fighter Command. One day, someone committed the heinous offence of leaving her handbag on the map table at Bentley Priory. 'Stuffy' was there and we heard him say in his rather dry voice, 'Do I see an enemy aircraft?' She removed it in a great hurry. I don't know what there was about him but it inspired loyalty. He was very remote but if you met him, he was always a gentleman. We thought of him as an extremely able and dedicated officer. And quite frankly, we felt that he saved Britain.

Flight Lieutenant Hugh Ironside
Personal Assistant to Air Chief Marshal Sir Hugh Dowding
I was PA to 'Stuffy' Dowding. I had the greatest admiration for him and I really enjoyed working for him even though he was very shy and difficult to engage in conversation. He was not a sociable chap – he hardly ever drank. His wife had died a long time ago, and that, apparently, was why he became stuffy. He lived with his sister and every few months they had a sherry party. It was my job to get people to attend it. It was really gruesome. 'Stuffy' would

have one sherry and he used to play his ancient tunes on his ancient gramophone and after a time I found it most difficult to get anybody to come.

Flying Officer Christopher Foxley-Norris
3 Squadron, RAF

Keith Park of 11 Group was a far more direct and inspirational man than Dowding. We used to see quite a lot of him.

Pilot Officer Alec Ingle
605 Squadron, RAF

Park was first rate. You'd be flying around and a lone Hurricane would come and join you with OK1 on the side of it. That was Park's personal aircraft. He'd come and see what you're up to. Join in and drop back to the squadron with you for a few words.

Flight Lieutenant Charles MacLean
602 Squadron, RAF and Sector Controller

The whole theory of fighter defence was created to avoid what they called 'standing patrols'. If you were guarding the country by having aeroplanes up all the time, you ran out of engine hours and you were on the ground when the attack occurred. So Dowding developed a system of reporting incoming raids. First, he used radar to plot the aircraft as they were approaching Britain and then he used the Observer Corps to spot them when they'd crossed the coast. All the information was fed to a filter room and then to an operations room where you got a picture of the developing raids plotted on a table. That picture would be three or four minutes old but it was sufficiently up to date to get the fighters off when they were really needed.

Hans-Ekkehard Bob
German Messerschmitt 109 pilot

I experienced a Spitfire formation all of a sudden coming up from behind, having a clear line of fire and I wondered how this was even possible. Having no visibility whatsoever, from above nor from below, how was it possible that an enemy formation was able to get into a firing position from behind? That was the first time we heard about radar. The English were able to make the best use of radar, gaining an advantage, especially in bad weather conditions.

Elizabeth Quayle
Women's Auxiliary Air Force, served as plotter at Fighter Command HQ
Radar was a word that we didn't use. It's an American word. We called it *Radio Direction Finding*.

Flying Officer Jeffrey Quill
Vickers Chief Test Pilot and 65 Squadron, RAF
In the days before radar, we used to have to fly up to Biggin Hill where they were experimenting with sound location. That was the only means they had of telling if an aircraft was approaching. We used to have to fly up and down while they tried to listen out for us. The idea was that anything that produced a non-standard sound signature must be an enemy aircraft. It never damn well worked.

Edward Fennessy
Radar expert with Air Ministry
There had been a committee set up in the 1930s under Sir Henry Tizard, to deal with the air defence of Great Britain. They were wondering how on earth they could defend this country against an air attack. Intelligence information suggested that the Germans had developed an 'engine stopping ray' – a radio beam that could stop aircraft engines. Goodness knows where that intelligence came from. So a paper was put round to various establishments in this country, asking whether this was possible.

At that time, Robert Watson-Watt was in charge of the radio research establishment at Slough and he was engaged in ionospheric research. That meant that he was sending radio signals up into space and measuring the time it took for them to be reflected back from various ionospheric layers. By that you could determine the height and size of these layers. So this question came to Watson-Watt and together with his assistant, Arnold Wilkins, he showed beyond any doubt that you couldn't produce anything like enough radio energy to stop an aircraft engine. That was ridiculous. They had noted, however, that on their ionospheric tests, they were getting reflections from something below the ionosphere. They knew that these reflections must have been aeroplanes but they'd put that to one side – they weren't engaged in that work.

Now, it occurred to them that they could use their system to detect aircraft. Watson-Watt wrote a paper, setting out the whole concept of RDF – sending out pulses of high intensity radio energy on suitable frequencies, getting a reflection back from the metallic structure of the aircraft and measuring the distance, bearing and height of the aircraft. His report went to the committee in late 1934. The committee told him to demonstrate it so he and Wilkins gathered together some equipment in a van and took it up to Daventry where they used the transmitter as their source of energy. An aircraft was flown from Boscombe Down and – true enough – it was well observed at a range of some thirty to forty miles. With that demonstration, the Air Ministry agreed that Watson-Watt would set up a research unit at Orford Ness on the east coast.

Flight Sergeant Jack Nissen
Engineer working on radar systems
We had two basic types of RDF station. We had the big Chain Home stations. By the time war came, about twenty of these stations were going, down the east coast of England and stretching round to the south, because the attacks were going to come from that area. These Chain Home stations could see aircraft out to 180 miles at 18,000 feet. But they could not see any aircraft below 3,000 feet, so that was an awful blind spot. As a result, stations of a new kind were created, called Chain Home Low. These stations could see down to 500 feet out to about fifteen or twenty miles. So the gap from 3,000 feet downwards was nicely covered. Without this system, we would have been lost. We were almost lost with it.

Edward Fennessy
Radar expert with Air Ministry
On August 2, 1939, the Graf Zeppelin airship was observed on our RDF screens, tracking up the east coast from the Thames Estuary to the Firth of Forth. It gave a very different response to an aircraft; it was a massive echo on the RDF screens. There was a visual identification of it by a lighthouse keeper and Fighter Command intercepted messages being passed from the Graf Zeppelin back to base. We assumed it was on a reconnaissance and that it was aware that we had a RDF system in operation. We thought that its function was to measure our frequencies so that the German could locate our RDF stations as potential bombing targets and generally get a good view of what we were up to. But it puzzled us why they didn't bomb the RDF stations at the beginning of the war. It was only many years after the war, that I had my answer when I met General Martini. He had been the Chief Signals Officer of the Luftwaffe and I asked why the Germans hadn't attacked the stations at the beginning of the war. 'Because the stations were not operational!' he said. 'Then how did we track the Graf Zeppelin?' I asked and he nearly shot out of his chair in surprise. 'You tracked us?' 'Yes.' It was a very significant

The Chain Home RDF installation at Poling, Sussex.

intelligence failure by the Germans because had they succeeded in measuring the transmissions from the stations and confirming that they were operational, it might have altered the whole course of the war.

Flight Sergeant Jack Nissen
Engineer working on radar systems
The Germans only really confirmed that we had RDF when they got to the coast of France in May 1940. From Calais they took photographs of our RDF stations – massive masts that bore no resemblance to their own German radar.

Edward Fennessy
Radar expert with Air Ministry
By the outbreak of the war, we had 18 large Chain Home stations covering the whole of the south and east coast of England from the Isle of Wight up to Scotland. We could track aircraft coming in from a distance of 100 miles. We could measure their bearing, their height and a good estimation of the number of aircraft in a formation.

Aircraftman Wilfred Slack
Engineer working at Poling RDF Station
Quite early in the war, British aircraft were equipped with equipment known as 'IFF', 'Identification – Friend or Foe'. This meant that when our RDF pulses struck British aircraft, there was an immediate response from the aircraft transmitter which was picked up by the RDF station on its cathode ray tube. This operated every few seconds, indicating that the response was coming from a friendly aircraft. Any other aircraft being plotted were assumed to be enemy.

Edward Fennessy
Radar expert with Air Ministry
If Watson-Watt had never had his concept, war would have come and we would have been utterly incapable of fighting the Battle of Britain.

Jackie Moggridge
RDF Operator with Women's Auxiliary Air Force
I was trained as an RDF operator. They told us that on no account were we to say who we were, what we were and what we were doing, and if anyone asked us, we were cooks.

We each had an RDF screen which was like a television set with a whole lot of wiggly lines going across the middle. Somewhere in those wiggly lines, we had to find what was called an 'echo', which was a little V-shaped thing which kept popping up every now and again. That was the aircraft that we were trying to find. We had this little wheel at the side and you turned it so that the echo would disappear. As soon as it disappeared, you looked at your wheel and noted the direction from which it was coming and the height it was at. Then you had to call up your headphones and say, 'We've got an echo at such and such a height, such and such a direction, such and such a heading,' and they would plot it on a plotting machine.

Ernest Clark
Wireless Operator working at RDF Stations
One day, like a bloody fool, I put my hand inside the modulator at Poling RDF station. We're talking about 30,000 volts and a pulse of about 350 per second. Some WAAFs came along from the receiving hut and found me standing frozen with my hands in the air. One of them touched me and I fell flat on the floor. This is what they told me later because I can't remember a thing. I was out for about two hours. The WAAFs were told on the telephone by a doctor that they had to get me warm so they wrapped me in blankets and one of them lay next to me on either side. Although they might have been pulling my leg about that.

Edward Fennessy
Radar expert with Air Ministry
A problem with RDF was that it could track aircraft very efficiently approaching from over the sea but it was not very good at tracking them over land because of irregularities in the terrain. So the aircraft were tracked over the land by the Observer Corps. In the spring of 1939, we demonstrated RDF to Winston Churchill when he was still out in the political wilderness. He said, 'Gentlemen, what I've seen today is the most exciting thing I've seen for many years. I've seen the weapon with which we're going to beat the Germans. But gentlemen, you have a problem to solve! I'll put it this way: I'm a German airman. I'm briefed to bomb London and I'm flying across the North Sea. I'm scared stiff. I know that I'm being watched by RDF, this marvel of the twentieth century. But when I cross the coastline and I haven't been intercepted, I'm a happy German airman! I throw my flying helmet over the side! Why, gentlemen? The reason is that I've flown from the twentieth century – RDF, into the early stone age – the Observer Corps. And that, gentlemen, is the problem that you've got to solve.'

Sergeant Stanley Wright
Operations Room Deputy Controller
An Observer Corps post was simply a sandbagged hole in the ground. There'd be two or three observers sitting in a little hole with hats, microphones and earphones on. Someone would have a theodolyte affair at the ready to look for aircraft. They were the fastest people I'd ever seen at recognising aeroplanes. Just give them a glimpse and they could say, 'Junkers 88.' Each Observer Post was connected to a main centre by telephone.

Squadron Leader Roger Frankland
Sector Controller at RAF Biggin Hill
The Observer Corps were a great help. And they could sometimes give you better weather reports than the Met Office.

Rosemary Horstmann
Women's Auxiliary Air Force, served with Y Service at RAF Hawkinge
One day, a notice was put on our Orderly Room notice board, asking anybody who could speak German to report to the adjutant. Although my German wasn't good, I went along and said I could speak German. The adjutant turned out to be a very good German speaker and he shamed me by putting me through a very searching interview at the end of which he said, 'But you told me you could speak fluent German!' I blushed somewhat, and he said, 'Never mind. It's nothing to do with me, I have a railway warrant for you to go to Air Ministry for an interview. Here you are. Have a 33 hour pass, go to London and enjoy yourself.' So I got on a train, went up to London, and was interviewed by a board of brass hats who decided my German was acceptable for the Y Service.

In the Y Service, there were a dozen of us WAAFs who took it in turns to sit in a little suburban house off the perimeter of Hawkinge aerodrome and listen to the radio conversations of the German fighter and bomber pilots. We had to be taught how to operate our receivers, how to search the band until we picked up a conversation and how to tune in carefully. Then we had to write down what the pilots were saying to each other and to the ground station. When there was a pause, we would write a translation underneath. I was an official eavesdropper.

Fanny Jones
Women's Auxiliary Air Force, served with Y Service
The pilots spoke with every known German accent so you had to be fluent

enough to be able to understand an East Prussian or a Bavarian. If they said anything that could be of any use, we had to report it immediately to the controller at 11 Group.

Rosemary Horstmann
Women's Auxiliary Air Force, served with Y Service at RAF Hawkinge
There were occasions when you just couldn't make out what they were saying. Then you just had to write down an impression of what you thought you'd heard, and indicate that you'd not heard it fully.

Fanny Jones
Women's Auxiliary Air Force, served with Y Service
The Germans used similar sorts of code words to the RAF. Where the RAF used *Angels* as code for height, the Germans used *Kirchturm* – 'church tower'. So it wasn't really conversation. It was mostly the leader giving instructions to his section or talking to the ground station. And they gave their position quite often. They had their map of England divided up into grid squares and we had to interpret that on our own map to find their correct position.

Rosemary Horstmann
Women's Auxiliary Air Force, served with Y Service at RAF Hawkinge
It was very dramatic because several of the girls working with us had boyfriends who were pilots and so they would find themselves in the situation of monitoring a battle in which their fiancés were fighting. We were writing down what the German pilots were saying and they were saying things like, 'I've got him!', 'He's gone down!' and you would hear people screaming.

Fanny Jones
Women's Auxiliary Air Force, served with Y Service
The pilots' voices came through a great deal of loud static. Which is why I now wear two hearing aids.

Petrea Winterbotham
Women's Auxiliary Air Force, plotter at Fighter Command HQ
I'd gone along one day to join the Wrens because I've always loved the sea but a snooty female told me that the only job open at the time was as a stewardess. I didn't think I'd like that – and I hated her – so I left and I went to have lunch with my father. During the meal, he said that he'd been reading *The Times* and he'd seen an advertisement for 'Intelligent, educated women of

British origin' who were wanted for a special job. So, after lunch, we looked at the advertisement and we went along. I wasn't told what the job was but I was asked if I could keep a secret. 'Yes,' I said, 'I've kept secrets before.' Then, I was given a lecture on how serious this job was. I was told that I would never be allowed to tell anyone what I was doing. At this point, I got rather scared. I had visions of being dropped into the French countryside. After that, I went for several more interviews. I was accepted and I was sent off to Leighton Buzzard where I was to be trained as a plotter. The warrant officer who was looking after us told us that there was a belief amongst the authorities that women always chattered and couldn't keep a secret. He was determined to prove that we could keep secrets. Of course we could.

Flight Sergeant Jack Nissen
Engineer working on radar systems
Once the RDF stations around the coast had plotted the aircraft, they would then pass all their plots by open landline to the Filter Room at Fighter Command Headquarters at Bentley Priory, Stanmore.

Anne Duncan
Women's Auxiliary Air Force, plotter at Fighter Command HQ
In the Filter Room, there was a great big table with the map of England on it and the whole of the map was marked out in a grid. The man speaking to you on the other end of the telephone, he was reporting things coming in and he'd give you two letters and four numbers and from that I'd put down a little round disc on the map, like a tiddly-wink. Then a few minutes later there would be another one, that would be a bit further on and you could see the course gradually building up of something coming in.

Felicity Ashbee
Women's Auxiliary Air Force, plotter at Fighter Command HQ
Each of us would receive information from a different RDF station and then the Filter Officer filtered all the scattered tiddlywink plots from the different RDF stations and worked out what was called 'the true track' of the incoming aircraft and put arrows down.

Then the teller sent the front point of each arrow through to the Operations Room next door who put it on to their map. The Operations Room was connected in turn with all the sectors and air stations which would send up the fighters to intercept the incoming German raiders.

Joan Seaman
Women's Auxiliary Air Force, plotter at Fighter Command HQ
Plotting was different at Fighter Command Headquarters to the groups and the sectors. In the sectors, you only had a small piece of the country on the map in front of you and the grid was enormous. You pushed a little plaque around on which a sergeant put the number of the raid and the height and strength. In the group, you had a bigger area on the map and a smaller grid, whereas at Stanmore you had the whole country and a much much smaller grid which made the work much more precise.

Petrea Winterbotham
Women's Auxiliary Air Force, plotter at Fighter Command HQ
We had to follow a clock that changed colour every five minutes. As the clock clicked to the next colour, the colour of the plotting arrows we were using changed. This was so that when they looked down from the balconies on to the table, they instantly knew that the plots were not more than five minutes old. Everyone watching had an up-to-date picture of what was going on.

Jean Mills
Women's Auxiliary Air Force, plotter at Duxford and Fighter Command HQ
We enabled the senior officers to direct the aircraft when they saw something coming in. They would know exactly in which direction to send them and the height and speed at which they should fly. Some people think that the fighter boys just used to leap into their aircraft and fly off into the wild blue yonder. Of course it wasn't like that at all.

Petrea Winterbotham
Women's Auxiliary Air Force, plotter at Fighter Command HQ
The air raid warnings went out from us; the Home Office were there, watching.

Rosemary Horstmann
Women's Auxiliary Air Force, plotter at RAF Filton
All sorts of strange things used to happen. One evening, we had a totally puzzling map reference. The Observer Corps couldn't make out what it was and we found eventually that what we were plotting was the moon.

The Operations Room at 10 Group, Box.

Jean Mills
Women's Auxiliary Air Force, plotter at Duxford and Fighter Command HQ
Plotting took quite a lot of getting into because you hear unfamiliar voices coming in over the headset, coming at quite a good speed. You had to concentrate fairly hard until you were familiar with it.

Petrea Winterbotham
Women's Auxiliary Air Force, plotter at Fighter Command HQ
When we were plotting, we used to plot the German raids and see the raiders going over our own homes. I heard many girls saying, 'God! There's poor old Ma up again.' That was what made us realise that we had to be utterly accurate. The table was divided into squares and if you took the wrong square, you'd send all the people into a shelter who needn't be and the people who should have been, would have been bombed. There was a story that was always told about a WAAF who took the wrong square and went off her head when a school was bombed. That story might just have been a frightener but it certainly worked. We were all terrified of making a ghastly mistake.

Jean Mills
Women's Auxiliary Air Force, plotter at Duxford and Fighter Command HQ
From the little wireless and radio rooms behind the controller, we could hear the crackly voices of the pilots. Although our work was quite intense, we managed to ease one earphone off so that we could hear what was going on. We listened out for 'Tally Ho!' which meant they'd sighted the enemy and we could hear them talking to each other – 'Look out, Blue Two! Bandits to your right!' which seemed to bring it right into the room.

Edith Kup
Women's Auxiliary Air Force, plotter
You didn't always know who was flying what unless you recognised their voices. It was a very anxious period, especially if they were shouting to each other, 'Look out, so-and-so on your tail, or so-and-so's gone down.' It could be very traumatic.

Petrea Winterbotham
Women's Auxiliary Air Force, plotter at Fighter Command HQ
'Stuffy' Dowding was such a darling to us. When there was a tiny lull, he used to look at his 'girlies' as he called us – nauseating but sweetly meant – and he'd say, 'That poor girl looks absolutely exhausted!' The 'poor girl' was probably

exhausted because she'd spent the night dancing in London and she hadn't been to bed. But he didn't know that.

Edith Kup
Women's Auxiliary Air Force, plotter
We worked in four-hour watches. It was four hours on and two hours off. There was one watch of eight hours, one night in three, so that you could have a full night in bed. Everybody worked very hard. Everybody wanted to do their best. I mean, we didn't think about it, we just did it.

Marian Orley
Women's Auxiliary Air Force
A lot of the plotters' health went to pieces because of the funny hours. I had a lot of WAAFs with stress – which was called 'Anxiety Neurosis'. They were in tears and couldn't do anything. You'd hand them a broom to sweep up the hut and they'd lean on the broom and cry. The medical profession could do nothing for them so in the end they'd probably have a compassionate discharge on medical grounds.

Petrea Winterbotham
Women's Auxiliary Air Force, plotter at Fighter Command HQ
We plotters were a bit of a sideshow. King George VI came along to watch us. So did Winston Churchill. We were the first girls doing this amazing thing.

Squadron Leader Peter Devitt
Sector Controller at RAF Tangmere
The controller – as I was – controlled the aircraft once they got off the ground. I might be told by group to get them up to a height of 18,000 feet over a certain place and to wait for further instructions. We used to get the further instructions and then we would tell the pilots where to go, what to expect and the number of German aircraft coming through. We were controlling them to get into the right position to attack the enemy. When I heard, 'Tally Ho!' from the pilots, I was finished with them and ready for anybody else going up.

Flying Officer Harold Bird-Wilson
17 Squadron, RAF
We had jolly good controllers and when we scrambled we were in their hands. You knew that what they were telling you over the radio was accurate.

Flight Sergeant Jack Nissen
Engineer working on radar systems
I was working on an RDF station in Scotland and I knew that nothing could happen unless Bentley Priory gave orders to scramble. A Dornier had flown up and down Union Street, Aberdeen, machine gunning people and tramcars. People who had seen me in my RAF uniform asked, 'Why don't you do something about it?' I didn't like what was happening so I set up an arrangement with the fighter pilots.

I couldn't officially tell them that we had an RDF station and we could see a plane – RDF didn't officially exist and they would think you were a nutter if told them you could see an aeroplane hundreds of miles away. So what I said was, 'We're radio-telephone operators, we've got the forward relay of your VHF on our station, and we see these aeroplanes, so when we see them, we'll tell you, and you make a plan to do a cross-country and then we'll give you a simple code.' So *apple angel screaming* meant enemy aircraft at 3,000 feet over Fraserburgh.

We gave them instantaneous reports which were fed into the radio telephone but this caused a lot of misunderstanding because the people keeping the logs couldn't understand where the extra radio telephone messages came from. But the pilots who had taken off knew what they meant, and very quickly they started to make contact with Germans and they scored a series of successes.

Then the Germans got annoyed with us, and they started to carry out bad attacks on Fraserburgh. And during one of these raids I was arrested as a spy and taken down to London under close escort. They thought I was a spy because the administration staff on an RDF station were never allowed into the operations room and in those days, everybody was hyper about spies. When I got to London, people knew exactly who I was from my pre-war days working on RDF and it was all a big giggle but I was told to stop trying to run the world by myself. 'You're not allowed to do things without official permission!'

Harry Hopthrow
Assistant Director of Works at GHQ Home Forces
As I went into my office, I was told, 'We've got a visitor next door, and you're the chap he wants to speak to.' So I went in and met this chap who was from the west country and he said, 'I know these Germans very well, and the worst thing that can ever happen to them is that they're disappointed. If you disappoint them, you can beat them.' We didn't seem to be getting very far.

Then he said, 'If we could produce a material to spray on to the Germans' airfields so that when their aircraft go back, they get bogged down and could never take off again, they'd give up this war altogether.' He was very serious about this. So I said to this chap, 'What sort of material is it you're proposing?' 'Oh, *I'm* not proposing anything,' he said, '*you've* got to find the material.' I closed the interview as quickly as I could and went home.

The Start of the Battle
'The Channel War'

We found Stukas very easy to get out of the sky. We tackled them from the back end and the poor bastards just fell out of the sky.

Throughout June, Luftwaffe crews had flown over Britain, reconnoitring airfields, practising navigation and creating nuisance on the ground as air raid sirens were sounded. In July, the Luftwaffe began a sustained attack on British coastal convoys. Known to the Germans as the *Kanalkampf*, its aim was both military and economic. The attacks would draw the British fighters up to battle, damage to shipping would impair Britain's war effort and clearing the Channel of British shipping would prepare the way for minelaying prior to invasion. The ports which received British shipping and which would harbour the British fleet in the event of an invasion were also attacked. When deciding how to respond to these attacks, Britain had the advantage of Ultra. This was secret German intelligence that was received by decrypting German radio messages sent by the Enigma machine. Frederick Winterbotham organised the distribution of this material from Bletchley Park and the information he passed on undoubtedly offered an insight into German strategical thinking.

Group Captain Frederick Winterbotham
Deputy to Chief of Secret Intelligence Service with special responsibility for the security of Ultra messages
We realised from Ultra that we were going to have the Battle of Britain because the Luftwaffe started getting on the air. We knew, more or less, what the strength of the Luftwaffe was and we got the positions of all the Luftwaffe.

So we had the whole line-up of the German air force easily planned before they started. Some of them were still up in Holland, and others stretched right down to Brittany. The functions of each of their squadrons became quite obvious because the whole of the rearrangement came through on the air.

Once the battle had started we got the orders from Goering through to his squadrons that now they were going to conquer Britain and that the Fuhrer had given permission for Operation Sealion to be undertaken. We started getting all the movements of the German troops up to the coast and we got the installation in Holland of a number of what they called 'air loading points' where an aeroplane would come in, and rather like railway platforms, there would be platforms either side of it, so that it could be loaded with troops or equipment in a matter of minutes and then turned around and sent off again. The invasion was obviously to be on these lines, an immense amount of equipment dropped by air, and all the time the German air force would be bombing behind – the whole plan of the invasion was there.

Then we got Goering's statements – he was at odds with the army about this because he told Hitler that the army wouldn't be needed, that he could bring Britain to her knees merely by the Luftwaffe. It was a tremendous boast. We had a signal from Goering establishing his strategy with his commanders. He told them that they were to fly over Britain and bring the whole of the Royal Air Force to battle because only that way could it be destroyed in the time that they had. That was the key for Dowding to fight the battle with very small units every time they came over and gradually wear them down. But always to have aeroplanes to send up. It became evident that Hitler and his generals wouldn't contemplate an invasion unless they had absolute control of the air over the Channel. We also got that intimated to us as well as Goering's assurance to Hitler that this would be done and that he would bring Britain to its knees with his Luftwaffe alone. These appeared in Ultra and Churchill adored them because here was the whole strategy.

Pilot Officer Roger Hall
152 Squadron, RAF

The first German strategy of the Battle of Britain was to starve the British out and demoralise us. They started to attack convoys of ships so that we wouldn't get any food. They had quite a lot of success in the Channel, but it wasn't effective enough – they didn't starve us and the convoys went through regardless.

Sergeant Leslie Batt
238 Squadron, RAF
The reason that I survived the Battle of Britain is because I was in at the beginning. We started off protecting the British ships that were stupid enough to come down the Channel. These ships were attacked by Ju 87s – Stuka dive-bombers.

Werner Roell
German Junkers 87 pilot
The Stuka was the sharpshooter amongst the bombers. Whereas the horizontal bombers dropped an enormous amount of bombs on an area, the Stuka had a small target and with a small number of bombs, it could erase a target of importance. A bridge was a typical target. Of course Stukas were slow. They had to be sturdy because they came out of the dive sharply. And the pilot had to be accustomed to that. It was easy to black out when you redressed the plane because the blood went out of your head. You could hear in the earphones when you were down to 1,000 metres and then you started redressing the plane and you levelled off about 700 metres above the ground. The Stukas had sirens in front of the wings, one on each side. When the speed was increasing during the dive, the sirens started making a terrific noise. And we had air brakes which would not let us go over 650 kph. There were also cardboard whistles on the tail rudders of the bombs so that when the bombs were released, the bomb itself started whistling. That gave quite a psychological effect but all these things worked only at the beginning of the war. After that, people developed resistance to it. The Stuka was slow so you needed fighter protection. The fighters would be circling the dive-bomber group all the time. When you approached the target at a special altitude before you went into dive, some of the fighters would be up there with you, some would accompany you down and some would be down below for when you redressed the plane. You needed the fighters so you could concentrate on the target and have not to look around for the enemy. It was frightening until you were in the dive but the minute you were in the dive, you forgot about the fear.

Heinz Lange
German Messerschmitt 109 pilot
Stukas were flying only at the beginning of the Battle of Britain – their speed was too low and they couldn't help themselves.

Bombs fall away from a Junkers 87 Stuka dive-bomber.

Wing Commander Edward Donaldson
Commanding Officer 151 Squadron, RAF
We found Stukas very easy to get out of the sky. We tackled them from the back end and the poor bastards just fell out of the sky. I think I got eight of them. I tried to get them before they started to dive-bomb. They had very brave crews. They'd go on towards their target with a squadron of Hurricanes chasing them.

Flying Officer Alan Geoffrey Page
56 Squadron, RAF
In one action I remember attacking a large force of Stukas. It was quite fun because as the Stukas peeled off to attack the ships, we peeled off to attack the Stukas. It was rather like shuffling a pack of cards. One German, one Hurricane, one German, one Hurricane and I think we got about six Stukas. Don't forget, after the Stukas pulled out of their dive at sea level, they had to fly back to France, at about ten feet above the waves. In our Hurricanes, by throttling back the engines, we could sit behind the Stuka and there was the poor rear gunner with just one pop gun to defend his aeroplane while we were sitting there with eight machine guns. They were a pretty easy target and I'm not proud of the fact that one just knocked them off like skittles.

Flight Lieutenant Charles MacLean
602 Squadron, RAF and Sector Controller
People used to say that the Stukas were easy planes to shoot down but in fact, quite a lot of us got hit by the blighters. Their rear gunners were quite good. Ian Ferguson was shot down by one and I was given an account of his bad language when he was pulled out of his aeroplane.

Pilot Officer Richard Leoline Jones
64 and 19 Squadrons, RAF
If the Stukas were diving over the sea, it was quite on the cards that you could overshoot and dive into the sea after them. When you're in a dive and you pull the stick to come up, you don't come up straight away. If you're over the sea, unless there's a ship to give you a sense of height, you could be at 5,000 feet or you could be at 100 feet. I saw people dive into the sea, pulling up too late.

Ronald Walsh
Seaman served aboard HMS Foylebank

I was on board *HMS Foylebank*, an anti-aircraft ship. She was moored in Portland Harbour and served as the harbour's anti-aircraft defence. She was very big and looked like a merchant ship. On July 4, my mate and I were scrubbing out the mess, when we heard a lot of running around and shouting on the upper deck. All of a sudden, they sounded action stations, so my mate and I ran. He went out first and as I was stepping over the combing, there was an almighty bang and I found myself flying across the canteen. I got up, went back to the mess and saw the hammock nettings burning, the double ladders twisted with blokes inside and the tables I'd been scrubbing with their legs twisted. It was a terrible sight.

My mate was still with me so we went down the port side and got about half way down when a bomb was dropped down the funnel, which blew the side of the ship out. I could see the docks through the side of the ship. We went round the other side – still below decks – and after a while we could see bright sunshine coming down through a hatch. We'd reached the master-at-arms office. As we passed it, they all ran out of the office to climb the stairs on to the deck. Just at that moment, the Germans opened up with machine guns and everyone on the stairs got it. We climbed over them and reached the aft end of the ship where all the non-combatants were mustered in the sickbay flat. All the sickbay attendants and wardroom stewards were there. There was a ladder going up so my mate and I climbed it. I was ahead of him and I heard an almighty bang. The Germans had hammered one through the upper deck into the sickbay flat and that cleared all that lot. It also killed my mate.

I got up on to the upper deck and I looked up and saw the Stuka bombers coming down and dropping their bombs. None of my gun crew was there and the guns were all bent to hell. I heard someone shouting and I looked over and saw 'Badger' Otley, a leading seaman, going to town on his gun. The coconut matting around his gun was on fire but he had two crew with him and he was shouting, 'Give us some ammo! Give us some ammo!' and the crew was shouting, 'We've only got the practice shell!' 'Well, give us that then!' and he poked the practice shell in and hammered that up as a Stuka came down. Whether it did any good or not, I don't know – I never stopped to see. The deck was riddled with bomb holes and bodies and twisted metal. At that point, a first lieutenant said, 'We're going to abandon ship.' I went over to a ladder but it had been blown away and it only went a few steps. So I dropped about ten feet and landed on an anchor. At the time it didn't bother me but I smacked a couple of vertebrae at the bottom of my spine. It was only in later years that it bothered me. I was nearly along to the starboard pom-poms when I came across a mass of dead men piled up. I climbed over them and came across Jack Mantle firing his gun. A plane had dropped a bomb and killed his gun crew and shattered his left leg but he had pulled himself back on to the gun. He was having difficulty moving the changeover lever on the gun because it was slightly bent but he had kept an eye on the plane that had bombed him and he was cursing and swearing at it as it went out over the bay and approached him again. He managed to move the lever and he fired four barrels of pom-pom into the Stuka just as it machine-gunned him. He flaked out over his gun, hit in the chest by bullets. The Stuka blew apart and Mantle was posthumously awarded the Victoria Cross for what he did.

I noticed our surgeon sitting on a bollard with his guts in his hands. I went down below with a first lieutenant to see if there was anything we could do. He went over to a couple of men who were sat against the bulkhead and shook them by the shoulders but they just fell apart so we went back up on deck. By now, Mantle had been brought down from his gun and he was lowered into a boat and we dropped into another boat. All the boats in the harbour had hung around. We were taken ashore and within half an hour of the attack starting, the *Foylebank* was on the bottom. Six or seven coaches arrived in the early afternoon, loaded the survivors up and took us all to Portsmouth barracks.

Squadron Leader Alan Deere
New Zealand pilot, 54 Squadron, RAF

Early in July, my flight was sent out to intercept a German seaplane. It had a red cross on it but the government had told Germany that we couldn't observe Red Cross movements unless we were given warning about them. How were we to know it wasn't mapping the coastline? Anyhow we shot it down and the crew were picked off in a rubber dinghy and taken off to a prisoner of war camp.

Charles 'Pat' Kingsmill
825 Squadron, Fleet Air Arm

One day in July, a friend of mine in the RAF had a day's leave and he suggested we should play golf. So we were hacking round the golf course at Norwood when an aircraft came over flying very low. We looked at this aircraft with a certain amount of interest to see what it could be. Once it reached 300 feet we saw it was German and then he opened up his machine gun on us which was singularly unfriendly. Fortunately he got nowhere near either of us particularly as I was playing truant on that afternoon and I should have had difficulty explaining what I was doing on the golf course when I was supposed to be at work.

Flying Officer Alan Geoffrey Page
56 Squadron, RAF

My first time in combat; six of us – half a squadron – were sent up. As we climbed, the controller advised us that there were 20 bombers coming in to attack a convoy and 60 fighters above them, acting as their escort. Our leader ordered Taffy Higginson to take three aircraft down to attack the bombers and he ordered the other three of us to climb to attack the 60 fighters. As we climbed, I caught sight of this enormous swarm of aircraft. They were above us and this was dangerous. When you're climbing, your speed is low whereas the enemy is way up in the sky and flying quite fast. He has a tremendous advantage over you. Anyway, we got up and we saw two types of aeroplanes, both fighters. One was a twin-engine fighter, the Messerschmitt 110 and the other was the single-engine Messerschmitt 109. The Messerschmitt 110s started flying in a defensive circle when they saw the three of us. That made me chuckle to myself, despite my mouth feeling rather dry with fear. I dived into this circle, firing rather wildly through absolute inexperience and then the 109s came down on us. Suddenly came the phenomenon that I saw again and again throughout the war. You're in a dogfight with so many aeroplanes about and then suddenly it's as if the hand of God has wiped the slate clean and there's nothing else in the sky. I found myself alone except for one speck of an aeroplane in the distance. I approached the speck and he approached me until I saw that he was a Messerschmitt 109. It became the equivalent of tilting at the lists in medieval times. We attacked each other head on and I could see the little white flashes on the leading edge of his wing as he fired at me. I was feeling a bit stubborn that morning so I didn't budge. He flashed over the top of me and I returned to base and landed.

Flight Lieutenant Hugh Ironside
151 Squadron, RAF

On July 9, we were scrambled to patrol a convoy in the Thames estuary. The convoy had been through the Channel and was on its way up north. We'd been on patrol for about an hour when I called up North Weald, and said, 'There doesn't seem to be much about. How much longer are we going to stay here?' At that moment, someone said, 'Tally Ho!' and we saw a great mass of German aircraft coming over. The bombers were below and the fighters –

Messerschmitt 109s and 110s – were up above them. There were about 70 or 80 aircraft. As we went flat out into them, the 110s formed a circle. The 110s always formed a circle where they covered each other's tails. Our idea was to burst through the circle and get to the bombers underneath. From my point of view, that didn't work out, because I got shot. I don't know where it came from, but it blew the windscreen away. I couldn't see anything – my eyes were full of bits of glass. The only thing to do was bail out, because I couldn't land the bloody thing if I couldn't see. I was tugging away at the hood to try and get it open but it wouldn't. There was no hope then for bailing out but luckily, one of my eyes cleared and I flew towards North Weald. I had no undercarriage, no lights, no radio and very little in the way of instruments so I flew over the control tower, waggling my wings to ask if the undercarriage was down, which fortunately it was, and I landed. I taxied the thing up to a hangar, and there was the commanding officer, Tony Donaldson, waiting for me with a fireman's axe. He started hacking away at the hood and I thought he was going to kill me. I looked far worse than I was. I'd got tiny little pinpricks of glass all over my face and I was a mass of blood, but when that was cleared up, all I had was a bad right eye. The station doc pulled a piece of glass out of it but it didn't do any good. It's still duff today.

Sergeant Leslie Batt
238 Squadron, RAF
If the Royal Navy were in the Channel and your aircraft went anywhere near them, they shot at you. Even if we fired the colour of the day, they didn't take a blind bit of notice. I take a dim view of the fact that they couldn't recognise the difference between a Hurricane and a Messerschmitt.

Flight Lieutenant Hugh Ironside
151 Squadron, RAF
I was patrolling a disabled British cruiser in the Channel and every time I got near the thing it fired everything it had at me. That was very unfriendly.

Flight Lieutenant Duncan Stuart MacDonald
213 Squadron, RAF
Jackie Sing, flight commander in 213 squadron, was shot down attacking Germans in the middle of the Channel. 'That's the end of him,' I thought. Not a bit of it. That evening, I was sitting in the mess, thinking about poor old Jackie, when he came on the telephone from Portsmouth. He'd been picked up by a tanker bringing 100 octane fuel over from America for the

fighters. He said he'd been sitting in that tanker, full of flammable fuel, thinking how much happier he'd be up in the air fighting.

Flight Lieutenant Hugh Ironside
151 Squadron, RAF

As we were above the Channel, we saw a big tanker below us. Some Junkers 88s approached it and we went after them but we were too late and they dropped a bomb on the tanker. She just exploded. It was a terrible sight. The 88s turned up to 10,000 feet and we chased but I got a bullet in my prop from the back end of one as it disappeared into cloud.

Flight Lieutenant Thomas Dalton Morgan
Commanding Officer 43 Squadron, RAF

Myself and my number two were attacking a Junkers 88, when my engine failed and I had to ditch my Hurricane 20 or 30 miles out in the North Sea. I very foolishly undid my safety straps and then I put the Hurricane down on a wave. There was no forward movement – I went straight into the wave and my face hit the gun sight, breaking my jaw and pushing all my front teeth in. The Hurricane floated for long enough for me to get my dinghy, which I only had because I'd been a test pilot at Farnborough and they'd given me the first prototype. I undid the carbon dioxide bottle to inflate it and nothing happened. So then I went to get the hand pump and when I looked at it, it was in small plastic pieces. I managed to hold it together enough to get a little air into the dinghy – not much – and I clambered into it so that my feet were sticking out one end and my head the other.

The Junkers 88 had also ditched and every time I came to the top of a wave, I could see the crew in their round dinghy a few hundred yards away. My number two had got a fix on me and he flew very low over me, pointing to the west, where I could see some smoke on the horizon. It was a four funnel destroyer. He brought the ship towards me and they picked me and put me onboard, in the sick quarters. The Commander told me that an air sea rescue boat would come alongside and take me ashore. But each time it came out, it was late on the interception. We missed it at Lowestoft and when we got to the Firth of Forth we missed it again. The commander said that if we didn't get a boat next time, then I'd have to go across to America with them. 'Oh God!' I thought.

When we got to Aberdeen, the Commander saw the herring fishing fleet coming in and he took me up on deck, tied me up in a hammock and lowered me on to one of the herring boats. Then a Junkers 88 appeared on the scene and started strafing and dropping his bombs. I was lying in the hammock and couldn't see anything except the sky. Only the fishing boat skipper and me were exposed and he was hit in the arm. We went ashore and an ambulance was there to take me down to the naval hospital in Aberdeen where the dentist wired all of my teeth back into position.

Flying Officer Roland Beamont
87 Squadron, RAF

On July 24, a brilliant, sunny afternoon, we were scrambled on a major German raid and vectored after a plot that was coming in over the Isle of Purbeck. We saw them coming in over Swanage, a great line of twin-engine bombers, Dorniers in the front, Junkers 88s behind, probably 70 or 80 of them, with a fighter escort that we couldn't see. We had plenty of time to position ourselves and our squadron commander took us in for a beam attack, diving from about 5,000 feet above them.

By this time, we were beginning to get some tactical experience and I'd realised that the wrong thing to do in these major battles was to stick in there, milling around in the middle of all the confused fighting. The thing to do was to make a firing pass on your selected target and then to dive out of it, take stock of the situation and then get stuck in at something else. And I did just that; I did a long straight firing pass at a Dornier, right into point-blank range and I hit him well. He streamed smoke and rolled out of the formation and I rolled away into a spiral dive. I pulled out about 5,000 feet lower down, looked out, cleared my tail and there was nobody there.

I could see the rest of the formation up above and I thought, 'Right, well, I'll climb back up and see if I can pick up a straggler.' But before I did that, a target presented itself. Right down across my front came a single Messerschmitt 109. I rolled in after it, half thinking for a moment that it might be a Spitfire because it was so unusual to see a Messerschmitt by itself. Whether he'd been hit or not I don't know. He wasn't showing any smoke and he was travelling fairly fast, diving towards the sea as if he was getting the hell out of it and going home. I got on to his tail and fired a long burst. He slowed up and then rolled very violently up to the right. I could see that his undercarriage was coming down and he was streaming grey smoke which might have been coolant. We were down to about 1,200 feet and he started to side slip fairly violently and then did a diving turn towards the ground. We were over land by now and I held off and he went round a field, lost speed and landed rather hard. He buckled the undercarriage, slipped on his belly across the field and ended up at the far end in a hedge.

I dived after him and watched him lift his canopy, jump on to the wing and then jump off and lie flat on the ground. I wondered whether he thought his aeroplane was going to blow up but then I realised that he must have thought I was going to strafe him on the ground. I flew round him again and by this time he was standing on his wing root delving into the cockpit. I could see the aeroplane smoking and soon after that it caught fire properly. I was later told by the army unit who took him prisoner that he was very appreciative that the pilot who shot him down didn't strafe him on the ground and he asked these army chaps to give me his Luger pistol, which they duly did.

Pilot Officer Peter Parrott
145 Squadron, RAF
We began patrolling a convoy early in the morning just west of Beachy Head. The convoy had been attacked by E-Boats and one of the ships was on fire. We were sent out at dawn to check on them. They were smallish ships. One little ship, leading the landside column, was flying a barrage balloon and a small destroyer was laying a smokescreen. We flew over them for a little while and gave them a bit of moral support. Then we came back and landed. We were scrambled again at breakfast time. By now the convoy had reached Selsey Bill where it was being attacked by Stuka dive-bombers, protected by Messerschmitt 109s. We flew towards them and we could see 80 to 100 Stukas and 109s, in two waves. The squadron commander put us into line astern and we picked our own targets. I picked a Stuka that was finishing its bombing run. I followed it and started firing. He'd begun to turn to the south to go home but as I fired, he straightened up. I kept with him and gave him a short burst every now and again to make sure he knew I was there. He landed on the Isle of Wight near Ventnor. I'd killed the rear gunner and the pilot became a prisoner of war. We did another sortie that afternoon over the convoy and by the end of the day, most of us had got something.

Flight Lieutenant Arthur Banham
264 Squadron, RAF
I was posted to 264 Squadron at Duxford, flying Boulton Paul Defiants. The Defiant was like a very big Hurricane except that it had a gun turret with rearward firing guns. There's little doubt that when it first appeared in action, it gave the Germans a very nasty surprise to find something shooting out of its side at them.

Pilot Officer Roger Hall
152 Squadron, RAF

I thought the Defiant was the worst aircraft ever built. It had the same engine as the Spitfire and the Hurricane, but the gun turret weighed half a ton – even without the gunner. It had no forward firing guns and so from a pilot's point of view, it was of minimum currency. It had a comparatively high stalling speed and if you did stall, it went upside down because of the turret, and I saw a friend of mine killed like that – coming into land too slowly.

Sergeant Fred Gash
Boulton Paul Defiant gunner with 264 Squadron, RAF

I was a Defiant gunner but I was only given half an hour's training before I went on operations in it. I had four Browning .303 guns – 600 rounds a minute each gun. I was allotted to Pilot Officer Hughes at 264 Squadron and we flew several convoy patrols together out in the North Sea but the first aircraft I opened fire on were three of our own. Mr Hughes had been in some other part of the airfield when we were scrambled and I had to jump in an aircraft piloted by some other pilot. We were flying round the convoy when the pilot suddenly yelled to me, 'Look out! Here they come!' I looked up and saw three aircraft diving out of the clouds towards the convoy, so I opened fire. The pilot said, 'Stop, you silly man! They're ours!' I didn't hit them but they fired off a Very light pistol and dived away so I must have frightened them.

Pilot Officer Roger Hall
152 Squadron, RAF

The intention of the Defiant was quite sound from the point of view of a chairborne tactician. Prior to the war the chairborne tactician thought that all we'd got to do in order to shoot German bombers down was to sit in front of them and shoot backwards from the cockpit. But they ignored the fact that the Germans were going were going to have fighters to stop us from doing that. At first, the Defiant had great success – the Messerschmitt 109s thought they were Hurricanes and they got the surprise of their lives when they were fired on by four machine guns as they were coming down behind. They got about ten 109s initially virtually without loss. But the next time that squadron went up, the Germans got wise and tackled them head-on and the reverse thing happened.

Boulton Paul Defiants in flight.

A Boulton Paul Defiant gunner in his gun turret.

Flight Lieutenant Arthur Banham
264 Squadron, RAF

I was shot into the sea off Margate. I was up with two other Defiants when a complete squadron of Stukas came in. We attacked them and shot one down but I was hit and set on fire. Eventually, I managed to turn the machine upside down and I fell out. I thought my gunner, Sergeant Baker, had got out as well but unhappily he was never seen again. I came down in the sea, about eight miles off land and by a stroke of luck an inshore fisherman had seen some parachutes come down into the sea, and he put his last two gallons of petrol in his little motorboat, and drove out to pick anyone up. And by grace of God it was me he picked up. He thought he'd seen another person in the sea and I hoped that it was my gunner but we found him and unhappily it was a German pilot. We were the only two rescued.

Sergeant Fred Gash
Boulton Paul Defiant gunner with 264 Squadron, RAF

My squadron of Defiants became very sadly depleted as was another squadron of Defiants with us in the south – 141 Squadron. The Germans got to know of the Defiant aircraft and how easily they could knock it down. After a while we were so badly depleted we only had three aircraft that were serviceable. And then one day, we were ordered out on patrol to meet a flight of a hundred plus German aircraft which were corning over the east coast. But the only Defiant available at that time was ours. Just the one! And we actually took off and went out to meet them. After we'd been in the air for about half an hour, we got a call from control saying, 'Return to base. The enemy seem to have gone back.' We were a bit grateful. Goodness knows what would have happened if we had met them. In August the Defiants were withdrawn from the Battle of Britain and we were sent to retrain as night fighters. The Defiant was a wonderful aircraft but it was really close to the bottom of the barrel as far as being a fighter aircraft was concerned. But we filled the role. We did what we had to do.

In the Air

You were so darned frightened but you couldn't let anyone else
see that you were frightened so you put a bold front on it.

The popular perception of the Battle of Britain is of an encounter between the British 'few' and the German 'many'. In fact, British aircraft production was booming under Minister for Aircraft Production, Lord Beaverbrook and by August 10, Fighter Command had slightly more single-engined fighters than were available to the Luftwaffe. The Royal Air Force appeared outnumbered because Dowding chose to send small numbers of fighters up at any one time and because the German raids consisted not merely of single-engined fighters but also twin-engined fighters and bombers and dive-bombers.

The German single-engined fighter was the Messerschmitt Bf-109. The 109E-1 had contained a Daimler Benz DB 601-A engine which produced a maximum of 1,150 hp – more powerful than the Rolls-Royce Merlin. Despite its metal fuselage and wings, it was considerably lighter than the Spitfire and the Hurricane. The 109s were deployed to escort the German bombers which were no match for the British fighters. The Heinkel 111 had a top speed of only 227 mph. The Dornier 17 was more manoeuvrable than the Heinkel but only slightly faster. The Junkers 88, the newest bomber, had a top speed of 292 mph and a greater range than the Heinkel and the Dornier. At the beginning of the Battle, the Luftwaffe had pinned great hopes on the performance of a twin-engined fighter, the Messerschmitt Bf-110, but in practice its manoeuvrability was poor and it caused Fighter Command few problems.

The Luftwaffe was able to fly from airfields along the coast from

Norway to Brittany but it was compromised by the fact that the 109s had an extremely limited range. They could only remain in the air for about ninety minutes which allowed them very little time over southern England. Drop fuel tanks had been developed which could have increased their range but these were highly inflammable, highly unpopular and rarely used.

Flight Sergeant George Unwin
19 Squadron, RAF
We had been lectured by Taffy Jones who was a First World War ace of some renown. He stuttered terribly and I'll never forget his words: 'When you g-g-get into your f-f-first f-f-fight, you'll be f-f-fucking f-f-frightened. Never f-f-forget that the chap in the other c-c-cockpit is twice as f-f-fucking f-f-frightened as you are.' It was a good morale booster.

Flying Officer Christopher Foxley-Norris
3 Squadron, RAF
A very well-known fighter ace named 'Cobber' Kain came over to lecture us on fighter evasion. At the end, somebody got up at the back and said, 'You've told us how to evade one fighter, sir. What if you meet two?' To which the answer was, 'Most unlikely. They haven't got many aircraft and they're very short of fuel.' I last saw the man who asked that question being chased round a church steeple by six Messerschmitt 109s.

Hans-Ekkehard Bob
German Messerschmitt 109 pilot
On our side of course, there were people who had already experience of war in Spain and people like myself who had seen action in Poland. The English were good pilots, they simply had not had any previous experience of war.

Pilot Officer Antony Thompson
85 and 249 Squadrons, RAF
The last thing I did before my first combat – I went up with Peter Townsend to do a dogfighting session. A dogfighting session is rather like jousting. You approach each other head on and try to get on the other's tail. He got on my tail three times but on the fourth time, I got on to his tail. I was highly delighted because he was an extremely experienced fighter pilot. In retrospect, I'm bloody sure that he allowed me to do that because he's that sort of man. So I went into the Battle of Britain with my tail well in the air.

Flight Lieutenant Denys Gillam
616 and 312 Squadrons, RAF
Our day would begin when we were called about four in the morning and we went down to dispersal in the half-light. Breakfast was brought down to us.

Flying Officer Harold Bird-Wilson
17 Squadron, RAF
We sometimes used to sleep at our dispersal points. Some pilots actually scrambled and flew in their pyjamas.

Flying Officer Charles Brian Kingcome
92 Squadron, RAF
Our squadron commander came down to dispersal one morning and used a bit of petrol from the bowser to clean some oil off the sleeve of his tunic. Then he lit his one cigarette of the day. And he went up in flames.

Flying Officer John Reginald Young
249 and 603 Squadrons, RAF
Readiness meant that you were sitting in the dispersal hut, togged up in your 'Mae West' life vest, your aeroplane all ready for instant departure. *Standby* meant that you were sitting in the cockpit with your helmet on, your hood slid back, listening on the radio for start-up.

Aircraftman Douglas Rattle
Flight Rigger with 19 Squadron, RAF
I remember one chap who got bored while he was sitting in the cockpit at standby and his fingers wandered and he took the firing button off safety and he fired all eight Browning guns. Bullets went whizzing all over the airfield. The poor chap was as white as a sheet and he was put on a charge.

Sergeant Cyril 'Bam' Bamberger
610 and 41 Squadrons, RAF
The most stressful thing in the Battle of Britain was sitting at readiness waiting for the scramble telephone bell to ring. I couldn't relax. You tried to read a book or you tried to play draughts or you pretended to doze. The phone would ring and immediately you jumped up but it was probably to say that the NAAFI van was coming with tea. Then you flopped back and tried to relax again.

Pilots at readiness pass the time with a game of draughts.

Sergeant Fred Gash
Boulton Paul Defiant gunner with 264 Squadron, RAF
While we waited to scramble, we did the usual things. We played cards, we played darts, we talked to each other. We argued a bit if we weren't the best of friends.

Sergeant Charlton Haw
504 Squadron, RAF
I believe in some squadrons, they used to have a drink at dispersal – but I wouldn't like to say for certain . . .

Wing Commander Edward Donaldson
Commanding Officer 151 Squadron, RAF
There was one pilot who used to take a bottle up with him. I was told it was whisky but it didn't alter his flying.

Sergeant Cyril 'Bam' Bamberger
610 and 41 Squadrons, RAF
Every day seemed to be a nice sunny day during the Battle and people would lug these chairs out and sit outside. The sun didn't agree with me so I used to stay inside.

Ulrich Steinhilper
German Messerschmitt 109 pilot
Before you sat in your aircraft and started the engine, you asked yourself the question, 'Is this going to be the day when I don't return? Am I going to be back again from this mission?' Each time.

Pilot Officer Alec Ingle
605 Squadron, RAF
I was apprehensive rather than frightened of going up. The first flight you made in the morning, you would get a sinking feeling in the pit of your stomach until you saw the enemy. The minute you made your first interception, for the rest of the day it didn't matter what happened. The adrenaline had flowed and it kept me going for the rest of the day. But the first flight of the day was always the worst.

Hans-Ekkehard Bob
German Messerschmitt 109 pilot

The ones who were very apprehensive – in other words the ones who remained afraid during the actual battles and flew cautiously – they were the first ones to get it.

Flight Lieutenant Peter Brothers
32 and 257 Squadrons, RAF

You were so darned frightened but you couldn't let anyone else see that you were frightened so you put a bold front on it. I think that went for a lot of us.

Pilot Officer Archibald Winskill
72 and 603 Squadrons, RAF

'Sailor' Malan was older than most of us, thirty odd, he'd been in the merchant service and he was a tough chap. He was the highest scoring chap in the Battle of Britain. I once asked him, as an old friend, 'Were you ever frightened?' 'Of course I was frightened,' he said. 'Right in the heat of the battle, I went to my room and there were tears in my eyes.' Even the toughest chaps felt the strain. It wasn't surprising.

Flight Lieutenant Denys Gillam
616 and 312 Squadrons, RAF

We had one pilot that went to pieces on the ground just as he was getting into his aeroplane. The doctor went up to this chap and hit him hard on the chin, knocking him out. He had to do that. The chap was making a drama out of taking off and one couldn't have that in front of all the other pilots.

Sergeant Charlton Haw
504 Squadron, RAF

We had one case who just refused to fly and he was stripped down to the lowest rank, his wings were taken away from him and he was put on to cleaning latrines. He was taken out of the sergeant's mess so we didn't have any more contact with him and then he was posted away and I never heard of him again. I think he was one of these people who wanted the glamour of the job without actually having to do it.

Marian Orley
Women's Auxiliary Air Force

In the officers' mess at Northolt, we were all eating together – the WAAF officers with the pilots. There'd be a scramble in the middle of a meal and the chaps would say, 'Goodbye. I may not see you again . . . '. And a lot of them didn't come back.

Sergeant Cyril 'Bam' Bamberger
610 and 41 Squadrons, RAF

When you were scrambled, you ran to the aircraft. The commanding officer's aircraft was the closest and mine was about a hundred yards away so I had to run as fast as I could to make certain I was ready in time. The ground crew handed you your straps and your helmet and shut the cockpit door for you. From the moment you scrambled, you weren't scared because you had so much to think about; getting into the aircraft, strapping yourself in, turning the oxygen on, hoping that the engine would fire properly, taking off in formation, listening to the controller . . .

Pilot Officer Archibald Winskill
72 and 603 Squadrons, RAF

When you jump into the aeroplane and start up the Merlin engine, there's a bang and a roar and you're hyped up and you know no one's going to shoot *you* down. That's for sure.

Flying Officer Harold Bird-Wilson
17 Squadron, RAF

We flew in ordinary uniforms. We had no overalls in those days. We had jolly good sheep-lined flying boots, leather gloves and helmets. We had sheepskin leather jackets and Mae Wests.

Sergeant Cyril 'Bam' Bamberger
610 and 41 Squadrons, RAF

I always flew with a silk scarf round my neck so that I had the freedom to turn my neck through 360°.

Pilot Officer Thomas Neil
249 Squadron, RAF

I always wore goggles and gloves. The Hurricane got to within two to three thousand degrees centigrade in a matter of seconds after being set on fire and that's why so many people were terribly burned. When I'd first gone into action, I wore short sleeves and no goggles, but I soon changed that, believe you me.

A Spitfire pilot in mask and goggles.

Sergeant Cyril 'Bam' Bamberger
610 and 41 Squadrons, RAF
When you got airborne, the first communication was the squadron leader using the squadron call sign, communicating with control, asking, 'Have you any information for me?' The controller might say, 'We have 20 bandits coming in at such and such a height and such and such a course. Vector 180°.' Everyone was listening to this and you all knew what was going on.

Sergeant Charlton Haw
504 Squadron, RAF
The wireless sets in the early Hurricanes were chronic. You could hardly hear what was being said.

Sergeant Cyril 'Bam' Bamberger
610 and 41 Squadrons, RAF
The average pilot wouldn't say a word on the radio from take-off to touchdown unless he had engine problems or he saw enemy aircraft. You couldn't allow chatter. Sometimes the Poles would chatter between one another on the radio and they'd block all communications. As it was in Polish, it didn't mean anything to anybody. The CO of the squadron would scream, 'Shut up!' but he couldn't be heard because they were all talking. That was an inconvenience because it was important for the first person who saw the enemy to shout out and alert the others.

Pilot Officer Antony Thompson
85 and 249 Squadrons, RAF
The Poles were remarkable people. They always seemed to see the enemy ten seconds before anybody else.

Sergeant Cyril 'Bam' Bamberger
610 and 41 Squadrons, RAF
Normally there were two or three people in a squadron who were better than the others at spotting enemy aircraft. One improved with experience. It was believed that Australians who had lived in the outback were much better at picking up things in the distance than the average English townie. Once somebody spotted an enemy formation, the order from the CO was, 'Break!' It was no use staying in close formation so you broke up.

Flying Officer Charles Brian Kingcome
92 *Squadron, RAF*

The enemy looked like a bloody great swarm of bees. You were probably doing 400 in your Spitfire and they were doing around 180 so you were approaching each other at not far short of 600 mph and the gap closed very quickly. Very soon the swarm of bees became a lot of bloody great aeroplanes.

Flying Officer Harold Bird-Wilson
17 *Squadron, RAF*

You cannot help but get worried when you look around you and see eleven of your aircraft and look ahead of you and see hundreds of enemy aircraft coming towards you.

Flying Officer Roland Beamont
87 *Squadron, RAF*

As we headed straight towards the mass of black dots, I just had time to think, 'I wonder what sort of tactic the CO's going to employ? Is he going to try and dive out of the sun at them or go round to the right and come in behind?' While I thought that, it became quite apparent that he wasn't going to do anything. He bored straight on into the middle of this lot until we seemed to be going into the biggest formation of aeroplanes you ever saw. Then his voice came on the radio and said, 'Target ahead! Come on chaps, let's surround them!' There were nine of us. We went right into the middle of them. Out of this great mass you would have two things to do. First thing would be to watch your immediate leader and make sure you didn't run into him and make sure you hadn't chosen the same target as he had. I picked my own target and went in on a firing pass. The second high priority was to avoid a collision in this great mass of aeroplanes. The Germans in turn would start breaking formation under fire. The whole place was a mass of aeroplanes going in all directions. I fired at a Stuka at point-blank range and I hit it. I don't know what happened to it. I could see my tracers going into it and I rolled away as I went by because I was going much faster than he was. While I did that, I came under attack from below. It turned out to be a Messerschmitt 110 doing a zoom climb straight up at me, firing as he came. He missed me. I rolled away from him straight behind another of his mates, a Messerschmitt 110. I fired a long burst at him and his port engine stopped and started to stream smoke and fire.

A still from a camera-gun on board a Spitfire, taken as the pilot closes in on a formation of Dornier bombers. Tracer bullets from the Spitfire can be seen heading towards the Dorniers.

Another still from a camera gun, showing a Spitfire's tracer hitting the starboard quarter of a Heinkel bomber. This combat took place during the Luftwaffe raid on the Bristol Aeroplane Company's factory at Filton, Bristol on September 25, 1940.

Squadron Leader Alan Deere
New Zealand pilot, 54 Squadron, RAF
There were little black specks weaving all around the bombers. Those were the Messerschmitt 109 fighters.

Hans-Ekkehard Bob
German Messerschmitt 109 pilot
The Messerschmitt 109s used the *Schwärme* four aircraft formation. Two aircraft would fly together at the same altitude with a distance of 50 metres between them. Another two aircraft were flying alongside, further away, again with a distance of 50 metres between them, so that we were flying in a broad row about 200 metres long. Each of the pilots was able to monitor to the rear and to the front and so see what was where.

Heinz Lange
German Messerschmitt 109 pilot
The main job of the Messerschmitt 109 was to escort the bombers – it was important to stop the British fighters shooting at the bombers. For me, it was more important to fulfil the task of escorting the bombers than it was to have personal success against the Spitfires.

Ernst Eberling
German Heinkel 111 bomber pilot
There were five people in the crew of a Heinkel 111 bomber. The pilot, the bomber and navigator, the radio operator, the technician and the gunner. And the technician had to become another gunner at the site.

Ernest Wedding
German Heinkel 111 bomber pilot
I flew my Heinkel 111 bomber in formation and I had to keep to my station. Even when the British fighters started attacking me, I couldn't do any intricate manoeuvres within the formation or else I would crash into the other bombers. It was a tedious job. All I was doing was watching the aircraft in front and on the left and right and hoping the chap behind was doing the same so that he wouldn't take my tail off. A bomber pilot had to be as steady as a bus driver.

Flying Officer Charles Brian Kingcome
92 Squadron, RAF

A head-on attack did far more to destroy the morale of the German bombers than anything else. It upset the poor old pilot so much that he turned tail. When he was sitting and couldn't see the attack and he was protected by a nice sheet of metal behind him and he could hear his gunners firing away, he was in a much more relaxed state of mind than when we were coming straight at him and he had nothing between himself and the guns.

Flying Officer Harold Bird-Wilson
17 Squadron, RAF

We had a squadron commander who believed in the head-on attack. 'The next raid we go up to intercept, we will do a head-on attack,' he said. So he attacked an ME 110 head-on and I'm afraid Jerry got the better of him and all we found of him was his shirt.

Pilot Officer Tony Bartley
92 Squadron, RAF

In my view, the best way to attack a bomber was to come down from above, out of the sun. If I couldn't do that, I used to come in from the quarter. Dead astern was tricky because they had all their guns firing backwards. Coming in from the quarter, I used to aim a little bit in front and as it went through, I'd catch him.

Ernest Wedding
German Heinkel 111 bomber pilot

If my bomber was attacked by a Spitfire, the rear gunner might say, 'Ten o'clock high.' That means that the Spitfire is high on the right-hand side of the aircraft, curving in for an attack. So to spoil his aim, I turn into his attack. As I fly into his path, he has to make sure that he doesn't collide with me. You see, you're playing chess in the air. You try to out think him and he tries to out-think you. You don't want to turn too early. Normally a fighter will open fire at 400 yards maximum, but you can let him come in closer and then turn into him. Or get to the nearest cloud because the fighter boys didn't like clouds. They were not trained for blind flying. But as a bomber pilot, I knew how to rely completely on my instruments and I hopped from one cloud to the next. The fighters were probably waiting for you at either end of the cloud in case you came out. It's not a very comfortable feeling, I can assure you.

Pilot Officer Irving Smith
New Zealand pilot with 151 Squadron, RAF

I once shot a Heinkel 111 down in cloud. As I descended, I saw what I can only describe as a 'mole run' along the top of the cloud and the 'head' was moving. The Heinkel was in this cloud, close enough to the top surface for his propellers, the heat and the engine exhaust to produce a discernible pattern on top of the cloud. I stabilised my speed to match the head of the moving 'mole run' and lowered myself into the cloud straight behind it. When I felt the slipstream, I gave it a quick squirt. I went below the cloud and waited for it to pop out which it duly did. One engine was feathered. I did another quick attack from the quarter and shot the other engine out. It ditched in the sea.

Ernest Wedding
German Heinkel 111 bomber pilot

A British fighter always had the upper hand over our bombers because of speed, manoeuvrability and fire power. The fighters will always try to have the sun at the back so that you have to look into the sun. And your gunner faces the problem of estimating the speed of the fighter and how much he has to fire in front of the nose to get a hit. He can't fire constantly like he's using a fire hose. He only fires bursts and follows the tracer. But it's very difficult for a gunner to actually pick a fighter up and shoot him down unless you're in a bomber formation when you have four, five or six aircrafts' combined fire on a fighter.

Flying Officer Roland Beamont
87 Squadron, RAF

The way the Germans used their Dornier and Junkers 88 bombers was excellent. Their accuracy was good. Their formation flying was very good. And they produced quite powerful crossfire.

Pilot Officer Thomas Neil
249 Squadron, RAF

The German bombers were coming from different airfields, and they all had to take off loaded down with bombs, and they'd climb until they got to their fighting height, which was about 17,000 feet. The Messerschmitt 109s, the fighters, had to escort them. The bombers could go for five or six hours but the Messerschmitt 109s – which were escorting them – had a range problem and could only go for an hour and 20 minutes.

The Junkers 88 A-1.

Heinkel 111s in formation.

Three Spitfire Mark I aircraft of 19 Squadron.

Hans-Ekkehard Bob
German Messerschmitt 109 pilot
The Messerschmitt 109 was an extremely beautiful aircraft. A handsome, racy machine. It handled very impressively in the air.

Gerhard Schöpfel
German Messerschmitt 109 pilot
Although the 109 was not as manoeuverable as the Spitfire, it was faster and it was better in the dive because it had fuel injection. When a Hurricane or Spitfire was behind us, we could dive away from them.

Hans-Ekkehard Bob
German Messerschmitt 109 pilot
The British still had carburettor engines whereas we already had fuel-injected engines. The difference was that when the Spitfire's carburettor engine went into a dive, the flow of fuel stopped and the engine ceased to produce power. Whereas the 109's fuel-injected engines could run at full power in any situation. So if there was a Spitfire attacking me from behind and I wanted to avoid the attack, I would simply push the nose of the plane down and go into a nose-dive at full speed. The English plane was not able to do that.

Flying Officer Jeffrey Quill
Vickers Chief Test Pilot and 65 Squadron, RAF
The Spitfire had a great advantage over the 109 insofar as it could turn well inside it. In a dogfight, you were always turning all the time, trying to get on the other's tail. The aircraft that had the better turning circle had the advantage.

Walter Krupinski
German Messerschmitt 109 pilot
In my view, the Spitfire was a much better aircraft than the Messerschmitt 109. The turning rate was fantastic compared with the 109. The climbing rate was also very good. The visibility out of a 109 was better than out of a Spitfire but what does that give? It's not so important because you can handle your aircraft to see everything that's going on in the air.

Gerhard Schöpfel
German Messerschmitt 109 pilot
The English fighters had four machine guns in each wing. The 109s had several cannons in the middle so we could aim better.

Hans-Ekkehard Bob
German Messerschmitt 109 pilot
Our three-centimetre cannons used special ammunition so we only needed to score a few hits to bring an English plane down. In a fraction of a second, I could bring down a Spitfire. If I could hit it twice, I could destroy it. The English had to score a great many hits with their machine guns to bring a plane down but they didn't need to shoot as accurately.

Squadron Leader Alan Deere
New Zealand pilot, 54 Squadron, RAF
The 109 was a tough customer and they were well flown. They were good – they were damned good. No question about that.

Ulrich Steinhilper
German Messerschmitt 109 pilot
'Spitfire on my tail.' I heard this cry from 109 pilots on the radio quite a few times. From then it sometimes didn't last that long until that voice didn't exist any more. 'Spitfire on my tail' was usually a very bad surprise. And sometimes you panicked.

Hans-Ekkehard Bob
German Messerschmitt 109 pilot
I know my fellow 109 pilots were very fearful of the Spitfire. When the message *'Watch out! Spitfire!'* came, everyone shuddered – but not me. By dragging the plane up, swinging it round and then slipping into the curve, I was able to fly in tight curves. And the 109 was always just that little bit faster than the Spitfire so I repeatedly managed to gain an advantage. I managed again and again to score air victories. I shot down eight Spitfires.

Pilot Officer Dennis Armitage
266 Squadron, RAF
To attack you had to get close to the 109. Your optimum range was 250 yards and you would hold it as long as you could.

Hans-Ekkehard Bob
German Messerschmitt 109 pilot
I generally flew as close as 20, 30 or 40 metres behind a British fighter, and then from behind I would dip slightly, aim at the plane from underneath and then fire a quick round. In order to hit the back of the plane, I would naturally aim more in the direction of the front part, because some time would elapse before the shots hit the target, and during that time the other plane would have covered some distance.

Sergeant Cyril 'Bam' Bamberger
610 and 41 Squadrons, RAF
If the 109 that you were firing at was in a turn, then there was no use shooting directly *at* him. You had to get a lead on him – you had to pull through his line of flight and fire ahead of him. That was called *deflection shooting*. Tracer helped a little because you could fire the gun and wave the tracer through him and get a lead using the tracer to guide you.

Hans-Ekkehard Bob
German Messerschmitt 109 pilot
The most successful fighter pilots specialised in shooting down British planes that were banking. If the enemy craft was banking, he was able to shoot it down from a long way away. You had to keep the plane in your sights and you had to make a calculation of the distance that the plane would cover before the shots that you've fired hit it. So you said to yourself, 'I need to keep the other plane 100 metres in front of my sights.' By the time you fire the rounds, the enemy will have covered those 100 metres and your shots will coincide with the plane. Lots of pilots failed because they kept the banking plane too short a distance in front of their sights.

Sergeant Cyril 'Bam' Bamberger
610 and 41 Squadrons, RAF
I'll make a bold statement. Eighty per cent of pilots during the Battle of Britain were firing out of range – over 250 yards. But even when I was firing out of range, I was hoping that it would make the enemy weave and slow down.

Sergeant Leslie Batt
238 Squadron, RAF
We were usually outnumbered by four or five to one. So a squirt here, a squirt there and then get the hell out of it.

Squadron Leader Alan Deere
New Zealand pilot, 54 Squadron, RAF
Once you became engaged with a German formation it was every man for himself. One minute there were Spitfires and 109s going round in circles, the next minute you were all by yourself. If you were still alive.

Sergeant Cyril 'Bam' Bamberger
610 and 41 Squadrons, RAF
The most important thing that you learnt was that you never flew straight and level. If there were a lot of aircraft around and you wanted to see if there was someone on your tail, you pulled the aircraft into a tight turn but that meant you lost your speed so the next thing you would do would be to dive down to try and get some speed up.

Flying Officer Basil Stapleton
South African Pilot, 603 Squadron, RAF
You had to learn when to run away. When somebody's shooting at you – you take off. Germans had green tracer and if you saw green tracer coming past you, you were off as quick as you could make it. Being a live coward is better than being a dead hero.

Squadron Leader Alan Deere
New Zealand pilot, 54 Squadron, RAF
I used to say to new pilots, 'Don't do anything by yourself. Stick with your leader and just watch and unless you're attacked yourself just stay out of trouble a bit until you get the feel of things.' It's pretty hard for a young chap to follow that dictum. In fact generally what happened was they'd follow their leader and the next thing they knew they were in a parachute because a 109 got up behind them.

Pilot Officer James Goodson
American pilot, 43 Squadron, RAF
I remember the first time the squadron was in combat. I was glued to the tail of my number one, figuring that the safest thing to do was to stay with him. Over

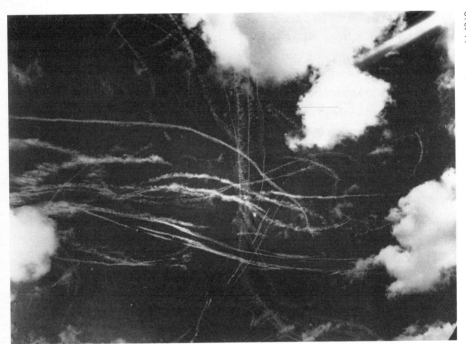

H 4219

Condensation trails left in the sky after a dogfight.

the radio, I heard, 'Bandits coming in at eleven. Break right . . . ' When I landed, I realised that I had not seen any of these Germans. I hadn't known what in the world was going on. All I'd seen was the tail wheel of my number one, which I'd glued myself to. Most of the people that got shot down in the battle were the inexperienced ones. They usually never saw the plane that shot them down.

Pilot Officer Roger Hall
152 Squadron, RAF

New pilots flew at the back. We used to call them 'Arse-end Charlies'. They were supposed to cover the tails of the experienced pilots. They had to weave about, looking behind. It was really rather silly when you come to think of it because the new boys had never seen a German aircraft before and yet they were expected to identify one. When I had just joined the squadron, six aircraft were scrambled on the report that there was a hostile formation in the Plymouth area. We never contacted them so we were told to return to base. I was at the back of one line, in parallel with the other when all of a sudden, all of our aircraft disappeared. I just couldn't see them. I looked up and down but they'd gone. When I got back to the airfield, I said, 'Why did you suddenly disappear?' What had happened was that a Messerschmitt 109 had come out of the sun and shot the chap opposite me into the sea. My flight commander had then shot the 109 into the sea. We had been 'bounced'. I was supposed to have been the lookout but nobody had ever told me that was my job. The turnover of pilots was so high that the 'old hands' simply hadn't time to tell the new pilots what to do. After that, I learnt.

Flight Sergeant George Unwin
19 Squadron, RAF

The first time I was shot at, I froze. I saw a Messerschmitt coming up inside me and I saw little sparks coming from the front end of him. I knew he was shooting at me – and I did nothing. Absolutely nothing. I just sat there. I was frozen for ten or fifteen seconds. I just sat there and watched him shoot at me. He hit me but just knocked a few little holes in the back of my aircraft. From then on, I realised what a mug I'd been and I never did it again. I suppose one isn't used to being shot at in any walk of life and if most people found somebody shooting at them, they would freeze.

Sergeant Iain Hutchinson
222 Squadron, RAF

On my first engagement, I was separated from the rest of my squadron and I

Flight Sergeant George 'Grumpy' Unwin and squadron mascot, 'Flash'.

saw these yellow-nosed aircraft going past me and I started admiring them – they looked so pretty. I suddenly realised that they were the enemy but by that time some of them had got on to my tail and I heard a series of loud bangs and my engine started pouring smoke.

Sergeant Charlton Haw
504 Squadron, RAF

On my first trip, I got a bullet right through the windscreen. How it missed me, I'll never know; three of us came through layers of grey cloud and there was this Heinkel 111. My leader dived after it, his number two dived after him and I followed them. As we got close, what looked like red hot chain links started coming from the rear gunner and the Heinkel dived into cloud. As he broke away, one bullet came right through my cockpit. When I got back, they were all slapping me on the back, telling me how lucky I was.

Flight Lieutenant Eustace Holden
501 Squadron, RAF

I remember one young chap, a very nice young man. It was easy for me to see that he should not have been there. He wasn't a strong enough character. He thought it would be marvellous to be in this front line squadron but I could see him being shot up in no time at all. I told him that I wasn't sure that he was up to it. It would be better if he left the squadron. The poor chap was very nearly in tears. That day, he came up with the whole squadron, over the Channel at 31,000 feet. He was lagging behind – I don't know why. There were three 109s up above. We could see them. I kept telling him to come on, come on, catch up. And sure enough, one of the 109s came whizzing down and shot him into the Channel. He was never seen again.

Flying Officer Charles Brian Kingcome
92 Squadron, RAF

It wasn't necessarily the number of hours you'd spent in the air – it was the number of hours you'd actually spent in combat and if you lived the first three, four, five or six sorties, you cottoned on very quickly and you learnt the business of rubbernecking. Because far more pilots were shot down by aircraft they never saw than by ones they actually did see – people creeping up on you because you weren't looking round. That was how I finally bought it – sheer overconfidence and being blasé. I was practising a forced landing from 15,000 feet and I never saw what shot me.

Pilot Officer Roger Hall
152 Squadron, RAF
I remember two new pilots coming into the squadron. As soon as they arrived, they were scrambled in formation with the flight commander to a pretty high altitude – about 30,000 feet – but both of them had forgotten to turn their oxygen on, and of course they both passed out and went straight into the ground. They'd only been there a day.

Flying Officer William David
87 and 213 Squadrons
Two kids were given to me to train. Sergeant Thorogood and Sergeant Wakeling. We gave these youngsters as much flying as we could. I managed to get them about twenty hours with me on dogfighting and weaving and getting ready for the German onslaught. Then they both came with me on a very nasty fight. Four or five of us went in against 300 Germans. Wakeling got separated from us. He called up about ten minutes later to say that he'd had his left hand shot off but that he thought he'd be able to make base. But of course, he lost blood and spun in.

Squadron Leader Alan Deere
New Zealand pilot, 54 Squadron, RAF
Generally speaking, when you were in combat you weren't thinking of the chap. You were thinking of the aircraft. 'I've got to get that aircraft.'

Hans-Ekkehard Bob
German Messerschmitt 109 pilot
I wasn't thinking that I had injured or harmed a human being, I was only thinking about the plane I had destroyed. I was thinking about gaining an advantage for the Fatherland by destroying equipment which might have harmed my country.

Wing Commander Edward Donaldson
Commanding Officer 151 Squadron, RAF
When I shot down an enemy aircraft, I felt elated. Wonderful. Him and not you.

Hans-Ekkehard Bob
German Messerschmitt 109 pilot
It's like when a hunter in the forest has felled some game, he feels a flush of success.

Pilot Officer Dennis Armitage
266 Squadron, RAF

The controller said, 'They're bombing Portsmouth, go to it,' so we went along and found Heinkel 111 bombers and no fighter escort. We had a field day. When we arrived they were below us, just where we wanted them and we attacked from behind the stern, a little above, a little below or a little to one side. I'd aim at the nose of the enemy aircraft which allowed for a little deflection. They didn't usually blow up in a great ball of flame and go straight down. More often, you got them trailing smoke and flying away. We recorded three or four of these Heinkels and we all thought it was easy. We were fairly pleased with ourselves.

Pilot Officer Thomas Neil
249 Squadron, RAF

The second aeroplane I was credited with was a Heinkel 111, which crash-landed in a field and some of the crew got out. I fondly expected them to wave to me but they didn't. They weren't in a state of mind to wave.

Flight Lieutenant Peter Brothers
32 and 257 Squadrons, RAF

I've always been a quiet chap. I don't often lose my temper but I did when I pressed the button in combat and nothing happened. The armourers had forgotten to rearm the aircraft and I had no ammunition. I always had my pistol in my flying boot and when I got back on the ground, I sent for the armourer. I banged my pistol on the table, pointed it at him and said, 'I've a bloody good mind to shoot you!' I shouted and waved my pistol and said, 'If this happens again, I *will* shoot you!' I think he got the message.

Pilot Officer Irving Smith
New Zealand pilot with 151 Squadron, RAF

I once frightened a 109 into the ground without firing a shot. Two of us chased this chap. He hadn't seen us and he was just haring home and he was diving towards the ground when he suddenly saw these two Hurricanes following him. He'd forgotten that he was close to the ground and he half-rolled and went straight in.

Flight Lieutenant Duncan Stuart MacDonald
213 Squadron, RAF

I was sent off to attack at between 30,000 and 35,000 feet. The poor old

A Messerschmitt Bf-109, shot down on the south coast of England, about to be moved from its crash position.

Hurricane was getting near its ceiling there – and a 109 attacked me from above. As he came over my head, I fired at him. He went down and I followed him, firing like mad. I saw him crash into the sea. As I was circling around to see if the pilot had escaped, a second 109 came down and started firing. He shot all the canvas off my fuselage, from the back of my seat right to the tail. It was only when I landed back at Tangmere that I realised that my aeroplane was naked from the seat to the tail end. There was no canvas at all – just a series of ribs.

Flight Lieutenant Charles MacLean
602 Squadron, RAF and Sector Controller
I caught up with a Junkers 88 and fired every round I could into it and it kept on flying. I flew up alongside it and I could see that everyone was killed in it except for the pilot and he was obviously wounded. There were bullet holes everywhere but somehow this old thing plodded on. I let it fly on because if it ever got back to Germany, it would have been a bloodbath when they opened it up, and it would have frightened the aircrews who saw it.

Pilot Officer Frank Carey
43 Squadron, RAF
On one particular sortie, the human angle predominated for a while. The formation in which I was flying came upon a rather lonely Heinkel 111 way out in the North Sea which we naturally proceeded to deal with. After a few shots, a fire was seen to start in the fuselage and the flight commander immediately ordered us to stop attacking it. The enemy aircraft turned back towards Wick and we escorted it on its way with me in close formation on its port side where the fire was. Being only a few feet away from the Heinkel it was all too easy to become sympathetically associated with the crew's frantic efforts to control the fire and I even began to wish that I could jump across and help them. I suddenly converted from an anxious desire to destroy them to an even greater anxiety that they survive. We had got to within a few miles of the coast and had really begun to hope that they would make it, when we were all outraged to see a Hurricane from another squadron sweep in from behind and without a single thought about us all around, poured a long burst of fire into the Heinkel which more or less blew up in our faces and crashed into the sea without any survivors.

Pilot Officer George Bennions
41 Squadron, RAF
My room mate was a devout Roman Catholic – Tony Lovell. He used to get very upset when he shot something down. He used to go and see the RC

padre. He was a first-class pilot and realised that he had a job to do. It was just that he was a very, very nice young man.

Pilot Officer Alec Ingle
605 Squadron, RAF
There may have been some odd birds who had a personal animosity against the German pilots. I hadn't.

Gerhard Schöpfel
German Messerschmitt 109 pilot
There was no hatred. We had respect for the British pilots. The war in the air was different to the ground war. There was a difference between pilots shooting at each other when they couldn't see each other and infantrymen shooting at each other on the ground. I once shot down a British pilot and we later buried him. There was a definite respect between pilots.

Flight Lieutenant Denys Gillam
616 and 312 Squadrons, RAF
I hated the Boche for what he was doing. I blamed the lot of them. In other words I had no time for the Germans and still haven't.

Flying Officer Benjamin Bowring
600 and 111 Squadrons, RAF
I lost my best friend. Somebody that I was so fond of that I could never make such a good friend again. He and I did everything together. To lose him was a great shock. I was extremely angry with the enemy.

Flying Officer Peter Matthews
1 Squadron RAF
The Poles were a great bunch of chaps but they felt they really had to kill Germans. And they did. They'd seen their own country get practically obliterated by Germany and they came here pretty keen to end the war.

Leading Aircraftman Joe Roddis
Flight mechanic with 234 Squadron, RAF
Two pilots a lot of us had more respect for than anybody else were two Polish sergeant pilots – Klein and Szlagowski. When nobody else would fly, they wanted to. At Middle Wallop, one day, it was a pea-souper. The birds were walking. A Jerry came over, buzzing the field and these two Poles were out and

into the cockpit, screaming at the CO to let them go. 'No!' he said and went back inside but they signalled to the ground crew and off they went into the fog. They hadn't gone ten yards when they disappeared. They knew there was nothing in front of them for half a mile so they got airborne. The CO was biting lumps out of everything and then we heard the Jerry come over and immediately behind him, we heard two Spitfires and they were both firing and there were bullets everywhere and they shot it down. When they landed – were they in trouble! But that's why we liked them. They were there to do a job and nothing was going to stop them.

Flight Lieutenant Gerald Edge
605 and 253 Squadrons, RAF
There was a Pole in my squadron called Samolinski. He told me how he had been pegged on to a door with a bayonet through his shoulder while his mother and three sisters were raped to death by the Russians. Even after they were dead, the Russians kept raping them. After he got out of Poland, he had joined the Royal Air Force. One day, just the two of us were flying along the south coast. Samolinski was flying about fifty yards on my starboard beam. After flying about half an hour, he gave the sign to change sides. He came in and as I saw his wing come underneath me, about fifteen feet below me, I was filled up with incendiary shot. Immediately I went on fire. The flames came from under the tank and rushed up between me and the sight. According to the Observer Corps, there was no other fire from around there. Just the one burst of shell from Samolinski. We had been friends and I'm sure that he just cracked – but before we went up he'd shown no sign of cracking at all. I fell into the Channel and he was never seen again. I don't blame him. But I wish he hadn't done it.

Flying Officer Christopher Foxley-Norris
3 Squadron, RAF
I think I can claim that my record in the Battle of Britain is one of the few that was never, ever disputed. Because I claimed nothing. I certainly never had sufficient justification to say, 'I shot that down.' So I claimed nothing at all. And that was by no means as rare as some people would imagine.

Pilot Officer Thomas Neil
249 Squadron, RAF
There were three areas in which you could claim. Firstly – if you destroyed an aircraft. The second category was a probable – when you thought you destroyed it but you didn't see it crash. And the third was a damaged.

Sergeant Cyril 'Bam' Bamberger
610 and 41 Squadrons, RAF

In air combat, things happen very quickly. With so many people shooting at so many aircraft, genuine duplication went on. But an element of pilots – for whatever reason – felt that they couldn't come back to base without having claimed something and false claims were put in.

Flight Lieutenant Gerald Edge
605 and 253 Squadrons, RAF

I remember one case where a man made a claim – even though he hadn't spent any ammunition.

Sergeant Cyril 'Bam' Bamberger
610 and 41 Squadrons, RAF

You'd land and you were shattered. Sleepy, tense – you didn't know what you were. You just wanted to flop into a chair or a bed. The intelligence officer would come around and ask, 'What happened to you?' If you thought that you may have shot at something and got it, you'd tell him your little story and then he'd complete his records by finding out from the armourers how much ammunition you'd shot. But there was an element who would always go searching for the intelligence officer. Everybody's different.

Hans-Ekkehard Bob
German Messerschmitt 109 pilot

In the Luftwaffe, it was the practice to award different classes of award depending on the degree of victory. So you got the Second Class Iron Cross if you had shot down just one plane, the First Class Iron Cross for five air victories and the Knight's Cross for 20 air victories. My name was submitted for the Knight's Cross in 1940, during the Battle of Britain, and the award ceremony was held in March 1941. It was presented by Goering himself. I was invited to his supreme command headquarters, in a train in France that consisted of ten carriages of saloon and sleeping cars. I went there with a bomber pilot and neither of us knew what exactly was supposed to happen.

We reported in at Goering's office but he wasn't there. He was on his way back from Paris but then he showed up wearing a raw silk shirt with puffed sleeves, a silk cravat with a great big emerald on the throat, light grey riding breeches and red boots. Even by today's standards, it was a pretty daring get-up. He received us with the words, 'What is your business here?' We both thought, 'What's going on?' but suddenly he dived into his pocket, pulled out the Knight's Cross and said, 'This is for you!'

Group Captain Frederick Winterbotham
Deputy to Chief of Secret Intelligence Service with special responsibility for the security of Ultra messages
Goering was rather fussy about decorating his pilots and we received one excellent Ultra that asked that it be ensured that all the pilots that Goering was going to decorate should be properly deloused before he came near them, so that he wouldn't catch anything.

Squadron Leader Alan Deere
New Zealand pilot, 54 Squadron, RAF
We never had much respite from the battle really. We were taken out of the line once for a short period. In mid-July we went out for a week up to Catterick to get new aircraft and new pilots. But while at Hornchurch, it was just dawn till dusk, non-stop. You were either at readiness or you were in the air. It was pretty tiring. I was up as many as five times in a day for 45 minutes each time.

Flight Lieutenant Duncan Stuart MacDonald
213 Squadron, RAF
We were tired, but ready to go on if it was necessary. We had our ups and downs of course, but nothing serious. There was never any question of being defeated.

Flight Lieutenant Gerald Edge
605 and 253 Squadrons, RAF
I don't know if you've ever driven a car and gone to sleep while driving but it happened to me when I was leading a wing. I shook my head and turned on my oxygen full. I just could not keep awake.

Ulrich Steinhilper
German Messerschmitt 109 pilot
I believe we were exhausted too much which is why we had the so-called *Kanalkrankheit* – Channel sickness. In the beginning, Channel sickness was just a funny expression, more or less a nickname, nobody would ever thought it would occur. But after a while, some pilots really were vomiting before flight or in flight, some of them got ulcers and had real problems with the stomach. I too had a high temperature.

Flying Officer John Reginald Young
249 and 603 Squadrons, RAF
You never hear a word about what happens as a result of the constant high G forces; haemorrhoids were quite common amongst fighter pilots.

Squadron Leader Peter Devitt
Sector Controller at RAF Tangmere
There was a pub near Swanage and the landlord made an offer that any pilot who needed a rest could come and stay at the pub for 48 hours. I utilised that to a very great extent.

Wing Commander Edward Donaldson
Commanding Officer 151 Squadron, RAF
I really was tired during the Battle of Britain and I became really quite sick of it all. There didn't seem to be any end to it. I couldn't see how we could win . . . but I didn't show these feelings.

Fred Roberts
NCO served as armourer with 19 Squadron
About seven or eight of us young airmen watched a plane coming in. The pilot's flaps didn't work and when he landed, he tipped up on his nose and overturned. We just stood there watching him burn to death. He was 19. 19! If you've seen seven or eight airmen crying – that's how we felt.

Pilot Officer Thomas Neil
249 Squadron, RAF
We had a chap named Constable-Maxwell. A delightful boy. He was one of the world's fall guys, he was always being shot down. He was talking to me one day and there was a bloke sitting next to me, listening to our conversation and after Constable-Maxwell had gone away, this bloke stood up and said, 'Can't you persuade him to fight for the other side?'

Flying Officer William David
87 and 213 Squadrons
I remember the smell of cordite. When an enemy was shooting at you, you could smell hot lead. To smell that in a cockpit meant a very near miss.

Pilot Officer Thomas Neil
249 Squadron, RAF

Sometimes you had this sixth sense that something was happening behind you. Some people didn't have that, and they were the people who got shot down regularly. They just didn't have that awareness.

Pilot Officer Alec Ingle
605 Squadron, RAF

I was coming back on my own, minding my own business. Not a thing in the sky as far as I could see. The next thing I knew, I had a cannon shell through the wing. Black oil covered my entire windscreen so I couldn't see out of it and then the propeller stopped. I'd have to make a forced landing but when I tried to turn, the aircraft wouldn't respond. The aileron controls weren't working. I looked up and saw a hole in my starboard wing and the two aileron controls sticking up out of it. I slid the hood back and unfastened my straps which enabled me to lean forward and peer out to see where I was going. That was not very encouraging actually, because when I looked out all I could see ahead was a row of trees and a railway line. I thought, 'This is an impossible situation,' and I watched my knees knock together. My knees literally knocked together until they hurt. I pulled myself together and I jumped the aircraft over the railway line and landed with a bang in a wooded bit on the edge of a field. I bashed my head and suddenly there was absolute silence. Except for the hiss of the coolant escaping.

Flying Officer Alan Geoffrey Page
56 Squadron, RAF

There was a big bang and my aircraft exploded. I instinctively reached for the harness and slid the hood back. I rolled the aircraft on to its back, kicked back the control column so the nose pointed upwards, but as I was upside down, I popped out like the cork from a toy gun.

I stupidly wasn't wearing any gloves so my hands got a terrible burning. My face did as well. My mouth and nose were saved by my oxygen mask. I found myself tumbling head over heels through space. I remember looking at my right arm and extending it, forcing myself to pull the metal ring of the ripcord on my parachute. That was agony. It was like an electric shock through my burnt hand.

Then, I noticed a funny thing. My left shoe and my trousers had been blown off completely by the explosion. I was almost naked from the waist downwards. I could hear the fight all around me and it took me about ten minutes to float down into the water.

I had various problems to deal with. First of all I had to get rid of my parachute. It was difficult because I was badly burnt. Next I had to blow up my life jacket. I got hold of the rubber tube over my left shoulder but when I blew into it, all I got was a lot of bubbles. It had burnt right through. By now my face was swelling up and my eyesight was bad because my swollen eyelids were closing up. The distant view of England, which I could see a few miles away, was blurred but I started to swim vaguely in the right direction.

Then a happy thought came to my mind. I remembered that in my jacket pocket I had a brandy flask that my dear mother had given me – which I had filled with brandy as an emergency measure. I thought that this probably qualified as an emergency, so I rolled on my back. This was a painful process but I got it out and held it between my wrists and undid the screw cap with my teeth. I thought, 'Well, life is going to feel a whole lot better.' But as I lifted it up to take a swig, a dirty big wave came along and the whole lot went to the bottom of the Channel. I was a bit annoyed but there was nothing I could do so I continued swimming.

I heard a boat. There were two men in it and they kept asking me questions. By this time I had been swimming for half an hour and I was fed up with the whole affair, so when they asked me if I was a Jerry, I'm afraid I let loose with every four-letter word that I could think of. They picked me out of the water and took me to the big ship where the captain dressed my burns and gave me a cup of tea. Then the Margate lifeboat came out and took me in to transfer me to Margate Hospital. For the first time in an hour or more, I was able to laugh, because waiting on the quayside was the Mayor, dressed in his top hat and tails, saying, 'Welcome to Margate!'

Sergeant Leslie Batt
238 Squadron, RAF
Before you bailed out, you had to unbuckle, remove your radio plug and remove your oxygen feed. That took about ten seconds. Then, so that you didn't hit the tailplane as you went, you had to roll the aircraft over on to its back, push the control column forward with your feet and eject yourself upside down.

Pilot Officer Thomas Neil
249 Squadron, RAF
If the Hurricane was set on fire, you were out double quick because you'd be incinerated within three seconds. You had three petrol tanks, one in front of the cockpit, one to the left and one to the right. Invariably, it was the wing

tanks that were hit. And in the early Hurricanes these were non-self-sealing tanks and they immediately caught fire and the flames were drawn in through the wing roots right up into the pilot's face.

Flying Officer Alan Geoffrey Page
56 Squadron, RAF
The scientists reckon the temperature inside a burning aircraft goes from a cool room temperature to 3,000°C in about ten seconds. When you consider that water boils at 100°C, you've got quite a temperature change there on your hands. So if you don't get out in just a few seconds – you're not going to get out.

Sergeant Iain Hutchinson
222 Squadron, RAF
I'm quite sure it was another Spitfire that shot me down. I was watching behind me, and I saw this aircraft with a familiar shape and I turned to show him my wings. But it was too late and he'd shot off his bolt and hit me in the petrol tank. The thing was on fire and the flames were coming up my right side and obviously the thing to do was get out of the aircraft as quickly as possible. I opened the hood, undid my safety belt and tried to struggle to my feet. The moment I got my head clear of the aeroplane, the wind flattened me along the fuselage, and my parachute jammed in the hood. I was stuck and the flames were burning my uniform and bits of me in the process. And the next thing I knew, I was falling through the air. I pulled the ripcord and hit the ground with a thump. A group of lovely ladies came along and asked me how I was. One of them put some brandy on my lips but she refused to put it any further.

Pilot Officer Alec Ingle
605 Squadron, RAF
On one sortie, the man who was supposed to be guarding my tail was – for some unknown reason – ahead of me. I was watching him and thinking, 'He should be by my tail, what's he doing there?' and the next thing I knew, there were five large splats on the armour plate behind me. They were cannon shells hitting me. The noise they make is just like boiling water dropped onto a metal surface. You don't feel anything, you just hear this splat. I pulled the thing up into the air, lost some speed, turned it on its back, kicked the stick forward and projected myself out of the aircraft. I came down in a parachute. It was a little difficult because I'd come out in such a hurry that my parachute harness was dragged over my shoulders and was pushing my head into my

chest. So I couldn't move my head nor get my arms up to control the parachute. I could see a big electric power line below and I was drifting down onto the thing. I missed it but I hit the ground flat on my back. I was winded and I'd just missed a large tree stump.

Leslie Stark
Civilian in Sussex
On a Saturday afternoon, we saw a Spitfire coming down. Just as we lost sight of it behind the trees, we saw the pilot coming out. We went over to it and we found him hanging up in the trees by his parachute. His feet were just touching the ground and the plane was about fifty feet away up against another tree, pointing straight down. It was smoking but it didn't catch fire. He had a scar across his head that was bleeding, the top of his ear was missing and his shoulder and leg were wounded. My dad got him out of the tree, picked him up and carried him home.

Flight Lieutenant Billy Drake
421 Flight, RAF
'Pussy' Palmer was the most extraordinary bugger. The first time he bailed out, he was seen at about 1,000 feet, smoking a cigarette as he came down. I don't know how he lit it.

Flying Officer William David
87 and 213 Squadrons
When John Cock bailed out of his Hurricane, he looked down and saw half of his radio embedded in his arm. He was amazed that he'd been hit. The pain only happens later on.

Pilot Officer Roger Hall
152 Squadron, RAF
A friend of mine got shot down and bailed out – but his parachute didn't work and he was killed. They went and picked up the parachute. The way the parachute works is that two pins go through the eyelets, and when you pull the ripcord, these pins are withdrawn, and the whole thing expands. Now, these two pins had been bent right round so you couldn't pull the ripcord. And in addition to that, they found that the silk inside the parachute had been ripped with a knife. And that was done by the IRA. Rather ridiculously, Irish labourers were employed on Warmwell airfield. It couldn't have been anyone else. Who would want to do that sort of thing?

Flying Officer John Kaye
Polish pilot, 302 Squadron, RAF
As I came out of the cloud, I saw a Hurricane pilot jumping from his burning plane. And as he came down in his parachute, a German started firing at him. I was above and I saw the parachute coming down and the man was not moving. I thought, 'You're not getting away!' so I went for the German. I fired a few rounds and his left wing exploded. The German tried to jump but I thought, 'You're not going to do that!' and I fired at him. He never got out. I did it only because I saw him firing at the parachute. When they found the body of the Hurricane pilot, he had a couple of holes in his head and his shoulders.

Gerhard Schöpfel
German Messerschmitt 109 pilot
I was disappointed after the war that the British pilots believed that when the British parachuted out of their planes, the Germans continued shooting at them. We never did this.

Flying Officer William David
87 and 213 Squadrons
In a fight over the oil tanks at Weymouth, I looked up and saw a Hurricane pilot bailing out at 20,000 feet. I immediately got the wind up when I saw a 109 going to shoot at the pilot in the parachute. The pilot – John Cock – heard his shroud lines pinging as the 109's bullets went through them. Extraordinarily worrying. I saw him safely down to the ground.

Flying Officer Peter Matthews
1 Squadron RAF
I went home on leave and I was teaching my fiancée to drive, and when we got up on to Epsom Downs, I saw fights going on above and I saw Hurricanes shooting down Germans in parachutes. I knew jolly well who they were. They were 303 squadron boys – Poles. And they owned up to it; 'the only good German's a dead German'. Our view was, they were in this country, they were going to be kept as prisoners anyway. But the Polish idea was to shoot them down. And that made the holiday quite interesting.

Sergeant Leslie Batt
238 Squadron, RAF
One of our Polish pilots shot down a bomber. The crew escaped into a dinghy

but he shot them up. The CO said to me, 'If he must do that, then I don't want to see it in writing in any report.'

Pilot Officer Dennis Armitage
266 Squadron, RAF

Would I have shot somebody coming down in a parachute? Not over England. I never did it. I don't know if I would have done it over Germany. I don't know the answer to that. I don't think so, and yet why not? I mean what's the difference between shooting them like that and shooting them in the aircraft or shooting them in a tank on the ground. I don't know what the difference is. Perhaps we would. Perhaps it would have been stupid if we hadn't.

Pilot Officer Peter Parrott
145 Squadron, RAF

Over the coast at Deal, my engine stopped and I picked out three fields to put down in. I went sailing over the first one so I shoved the stick forward and went down. Unfortunately, I hit two sheep. Spectators arrived but they didn't approach. Then the local bobby arrived. He came across and I asked him to keep people away from the Hurricane – the guns were still loaded – while I went to find a telephone. As we were talking, a farmer arrived in a horse and trap. He got out and the first thing he said was, 'Who's gonna pay for them sheep?' In a lordly tone, I said, 'Try the Air Ministry.' He got back in his cart and off he went. I still needed to use a telephone so I had to walk over to his farmhouse, the nearest building, to face him again. By the time I got down there, he and his wife were having tea and there was a large ham on the table. It looked super. I made my telephone call to Manston for them to come and pick me up and then the farmer pointed down the corridor and said, 'You can sit in there!' I wasn't offered any ham. Eventually, his wife did ask if I'd like a cup of tea but by then I'd rather have had a whisky.

Sergeant Iain Hutchinson
222 Squadron, RAF

One of my comrades came back to our airfield one day, looking rather shamefaced. He said he'd got shot down and crash-landed in a field with his wheels up. A lady came running up to him and she stopped, took a look at the aircraft and said to him, 'Is that a Spitfire?' 'Yes,' he said. She looked at him and said, 'Is that what we raised £5,000 for?'

Squadron Leader Peter Devitt
Sector Controller at RAF Tangmere
I crash-landed in a field near Dartford. I couldn't get out of my Hurricane until an ARP man came along with an axe and chopped me out. A crowd of people had come along and once he got me out, the people pounced on me to try and get souvenirs. They tore my clothes off. There was nothing I could do because I was wounded and I'd been blinded by petrol. It's amazing what a crowd will do.

Anonymous
The saddest thing as far as my squadron was concerned; the whole squadron was scrambled to orbit at about 10,000 feet and then bounced by a hell of a lot of 109s. One man got shot down and bailed out. The fields were full of harvesting people and they killed him with pitchforks and farm implements. He didn't have a Royal Air Force suit on and he was chucking money down and papers to try and convince them who he was but they wouldn't have it. We took that very bad.

Pilot Officer Richard Leoline Jones
64 and 19 Squadrons, RAF
I was attacked by three or four farm labourers with pitchforks. They were absolutely determined that I was a German because I wasn't wearing uniform. Rumours had been going around that British aircraft left behind in France had been repaired and were being used by the Germans to infiltrate our airspace.

Flying Officer Christopher Foxley-Norris
3 Squadron, RAF
I landed in a nice grassy field where I was pitchforked by the local yokels. I was concussed and grabbed rather roughly by some splendid chaps in smocks. Eventually a police car turned up and a yokel said, 'Ah, there you are, sergeant. We've got the bastard!'

Flight Lieutenant Thomas Dalton Morgan
Commanding Officer 43 Squadron, RAF
I bailed out and landed on the side of a hill near Medhurst. I was gathering up my parachute when a voice behind me said, 'Have you got any identification?' I turned round and there was a uniformed policeman. 'No I haven't,' I said, 'but I'm from Tangmere.' 'I think you'd better come to the police station with me,' he said. The police had those lovely little MG sports cars in British

racing green and we got in it and went down to Medhurst Police Station. We saw the sergeant who asked me again if I had any identification. 'No,' I said, 'but my station is Tangmere. Ring my adjutant and ask him to come and collect me!' 'You're under suspicion,' they said and they put me in a cell with four Germans. One of these Germans could speak English fluently and we chatted, exchanging things about our aircraft. I suspected that they were the crew of a bomber I'd shot down that morning – they were already there when I arrived and the policeman who picked me up had been wandering around the area. After I'd been there a couple of hours, my adjutant showed up. He looked across at me and I'm sure I saw a smile on his face. The sergeant said to him, 'Can you identify this man?' and he said 'Never seen him before in my life.' And they put me back in the cell. Two hours later, I was allowed out. My adjutant was there again and as we went to leave, the sergeant turned to him and said, 'Be very careful where you try your little jokes in future!' Then he looked at me and said, 'And *you* carry some identification!'

Sergeant Iain Hutchinson
222 Squadron, RAF

I had lost a shoe in baling out, I hadn't got a cap and my parachute was tied up with string. I had a bandage on my foot and a bandage round my head – all in all I was rather conspicuous as I left the hospital. And I was just dumped on the platform and left to catch the train back to my airfield. I got on the train and I was promptly adopted by two sailors, who insisted on giving me a drink of the rum they'd saved up. When we got to Gravesend, we tried to get on the ferry but the skipper said, 'I'm not going across tonight – there's an air raid on.' The two sailors pointed at me and said, 'You must take this man across, he's a secret service agent and he's got to get back to his station. You can see, he's just baled out.' So, I was taken across to Tilbury on this great big car ferry. At the other end, I was picked up and taken to an an ack-ack unit where I was given dinner and something to drink, which I really could have done without, and a big cigar, which nearly made me sick. Eventually, I was brought back to my own airfield and my own bed. And then, the next morning, when I went to wash my face, I was greeted by someone who looked at me shocked and said, 'I thought you were dead, you bastard!'

Flying Officer William David
87 and 213 Squadrons
You were losing your friends at such a rate that after a while, I didn't make any real friends. I knew jolly well that I'd lose them. I made a lot of 'hail fellow, well met' friends but I didn't bother with close relationships.

Sergeant Fred Gash
Boulton Paul Defiant gunner with 264 Squadron, RAF
I'm not being callous or anything but I didn't have any feeling when a comrade was lost. Except obviously sorrow that a friend had gone. He'd gone but where he'd gone or why I couldn't imagine. There was no depression amongst us. We just said, 'Poor so-and-so's had it.' And that was it.

Flying Officer Basil Stapleton
South African Pilot, 603 Squadron, RAF
Everything was so exciting and exhilarating that we didn't have time to think deeply. Everything was happening on the surface. That's why we didn't think about it when friends were killed.

Heinz Lange
German Messerschmitt 109 pilot
What we heard of our comrades downed over England – they were treated correctly. This was our smallest worry, to come into prisonership. It was more frightening to be shot, to be wounded or killed.

Walter Harris
Non-commissioned Officer, Royal Army Ordnance Corps
We saw a German pilot coming down with his parachute, and we went off in different directions to try to locate him. I got to him first, holding my rifle, shaking in my boots. I challenged him and he unhooked himself from his parachute, and because I was pointing a weapon, he handed over his pistol. The others had joined me then, so we put him in the utility wagon and he was taken to headquarters for interrogation. He didn't resist at all but what could he do? He was in a strange land and he was probably pleased he was still alive.

Christabel Leighton-Porter
Model for Daily Mirror cartoon character 'Jane'
When I was in Lyme Regis, there was a raid over the sea. They shot down a German plane and I remember all the people on the beach getting in a circle

Captured German airmen.

and then a boat brought in the Germans that had bailed out. Everybody was shouting. Even the little kiddies were encouraged to join in and boo. But when the Germans got out of the boat, people saw that these were very frightened young blond boys and everybody went very quiet.

Unknown German Heinkel 111 pilot

I landed my plane in the sea off Margate. It was difficult to land my plane in the sea because I hadn't trained to do it. I couldn't remember how to do it. The aeroplane was floating on its wings. One of my crew had tried to escape by parachute and had jumped out of the plane before we landed. His parachute caught the tail of the machine and he was dead. I remember going to the coast in a dinghy with my two comrades. On the coast stood three people, crying, 'Hands up! Hands up!' I was arrested and I asked for a comb to comb my hair. I wanted to look like a proper man.

Leslie Stark
Civilian in Sussex

A Dornier crash-landed near Wadhurst. The crew got out with their little bags, all prepared to be taken prisoner. The Black Watch 'saw them off'. I wouldn't like to say any more.

Pilot Officer Thomas Neil
249 Squadron, RAF

One German who was shot down was a real dyed-in-the-wool Nazi, so proud and so much a Hitler person, that he wouldn't be attended to by our doctors and he died, horribly injured.

Margaret Rumbold
Women's Land Army

I remember watching two Spitfires come back from a sortie and they'd obviously had a good day. They were doing victory rolls. I remember so well saying, 'I wish for God's sake they'd straighten up and go. The sky's not big enough for them. They'll have an accident!' I'd hardly said it when one of them tipped the wings of the other and the plane dropped like a stone. As it dropped, we ran forward to the plane but it didn't burst into flames and we tried to get the pilot out but the cockpit was jammed. People ran from everywhere and the village copper was there and he was shouting at us to get away from the plane. The blacksmith said to this policeman, 'No! There's some mother's son in there and I'm going to get him out before this thing goes up in flames!' 'But he's dead!' said the copper. 'I know he is,' said the blacksmith, 'but I'm still going to get him out. He doesn't have to stop in there and cook!'

Sergeant David Cox
19 Squadron, RAF

I saw a Hurricane on his own near Folkestone being attacked by four 109s. Before I could do any good the Hurricane crashed and the four 109s immediately devoted their attention to myself. They were no doubt experts because two got above me and two below me. I realised I was in a tight corner and I did a lot of firing which was more to boost my own morale and frighten them than to have any chance of hitting them. Then there was a loud bang in my cockpit and I was momentarily sort of dazed. When I came to, the aircraft was going straight down and I thought, 'Oh this is it.' Then I suddenly decided it wasn't, and I grabbed the control column and shot straight up again, and as I slowed down, I opened the hood, turned the aircraft over and baled out. It was very cold and obviously I was suffering from shock and then I looked at my right leg and saw that there was blood seeping through my flying boot. Subsequently it appeared that I had nine pieces of cannon shell in my right leg and I was taken to an emergency hospital near there, and that was the end of the Battle of Britain for me.

Sergeant Maurice Equity Leng
73 Squadron, RAF

You never think it's going to be you next. But you could sometimes see a deterioration in one of your pals. They're not quite the same person that you knew. Morose, quiet, non-talkative – they're losing the motivation to carry on. Although they probably wouldn't know that themselves. And you'd think, 'Poor old George. I don't think he's going to last long.' And very often, he didn't.

Sergeant Fred Gash
Boulton Paul Defiant gunner with 264 Squadron, RAF

I can remember one of our gunners, Maxy Maxwell, quite a character. One day, I was standing by the window at Duxford, looking out over the airfield when Max came up to me and said, 'Fred. I'm not going to come back from this.' 'For goodness sake, Max, don't be silly! What are you talking about?' 'I won't come back!' he said. And he was right. He didn't.

Flight Lieutenant Duncan Stuart MacDonald
213 Squadron, RAF

Sergeant Bootle was an interesting character. He had been a tea taster with some big firm in London and they said to him that he would get his job back at the end of the war and that he would get a financial retainer when he was on leave but they told him that he wasn't allowed to drink or smoke. And he never did as far as we can remember. He was a wonderful little pilot and it was just so sad when he spun in as he was coming in to land. We don't know what happened, whether he had a blackout or what. He never went back to do any tea tasting, except *up there* perhaps . . .

Squadron Leader Thomas Gleave
Commanding Officer 253 Squadron, RAF

I was taken to Orpington Hospital on August 31. I remember it because I was in agonising pain. All the skin on my right leg and practically all on my left was burned – the legs were just like balloons. And my hands and my face. I was taken to the hospital by a very kind-hearted chap in an old Austin 12. They put me in the back of this car, practically no clothes, all burnt off. I kept saying, 'How much longer? For Christ's sake do something!' We got to the hospital and somebody rushed out and saw me and said, 'Don't bother! Put him in the barrow!' So I was wheeled into the hospital in a tin wheelbarrow, dumped on the floor and they gave me morphia. They saved my life. I was there two months. I don't remember the first two weeks of it – I was barmy, but after two months I was fit to move. In those days the only cure they had for burns was to put stuff like lard on you, cut all the old skin off, and put bandages on top. And the bandages used to stick – oh God, it was hell!

Igraine Hamilton
Women's Auxiliary Air Force

When Tom Gleave's wife came to see him for the first time after his crash, she said, 'I don't know! Playing with matches again?' Anyone who had a wife like that was very lucky.

Flying Officer Douglas Grice
32 Squadron, RAF

I was taken to the Naval Hospital at Shotley. A little nurse came along and cut me out of my uniform. I was shaking like a leaf. I was very embarrassed and I said, 'I'm terribly sorry I can't keep still!' and she smiled and said, 'Well, don't worry you're only suffering from shock.' I was seen by a naval doctor, and wheeled into the operating theatre. I eventually came to, hearing a voice saying, 'It's all right Mr Grice, it's all right Mr Grice, it's all right Mr Grice,' and this voice went on and on. What had happened was that the naval surgeon had cut away the bits of loose skin around my face and put a mask over it from just under my hairline to below my chin. He had pierced a couple of holes for me to breath through and there was a little hole where my mouth was. They were frightened that I would come to from this operation, realise I couldn't see and start scratching at my face. So they had put an orderly by my bed to keep saying 'It's all right, Mr Grice, it's all right.'

A couple of days went by and the surgeon came and said 'I'm going to cut away a bit of the mask, so you can see,' and very, very gently he scraped away at the mask until I could see quite a bit. And he scraped away a bit more around my mouth. And came the day when I got out of bed and had a look at myself in the mirror. Never had a bigger shock. My mouth had been covered in gentian violet and there I was, absolutely purple, with this terrible-looking mask, with these holes in it. Talk about Frankenstein, it really was a terrible sight.

Flight Lieutenant Gerald Edge
605 and 253 Squadrons, RAF

At Cosford Hospital, the first thing they did with my burnt leg was to send a chap round with a heat treatment lamp. He blistered it from top to bottom. It had been healing so beautifully and now it was another fortnight until it healed again. When the same chap came back the next morning, I wasn't very pleased to see him. My father came along and spoke to the doctor in charge and I was moved away from Cosford Hospital.

Squadron Leader Thomas Gleave
Commanding Officer 253 Squadron, RAF

A very nice chap came to see me in hospital and he said, 'I'm McIndoe from East Grinstead.' East Grinstead was the burns centre where they had marvellous new treatments so I thought I might as well go there with him. I'd lost all my eyelids. I had a little bit of nose left. Archie McIndoe said, 'We'll give you four new eyelids, a new nose, and we'll put skin grafts on both legs. It'll all take time, but we'll start off with your bottom eyelids, then the top eyelids and then your nose.' That afternoon, the sister, a marvellous Irish girl who stood no nonsense, looked at my burns and said, 'Oh, we've had worse than that!' It was a famous opening remark.

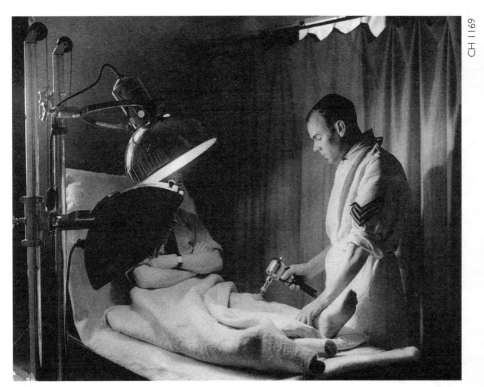

A patient receives physiotherapy at an RAF hospital.

Flying Officer Douglas Grice
32 Squadron, RAF
I was taken to a Masonic Hospital in London where Archibald McIndoe came to see me. I still had my mask on and I had been burnt round my wrist and ankle, too. He looked at me and said, 'Well, quite shortly I'm going to take a piece of your bottom. That's where I take skin when I have to do grafting.' He came again a week later and after a very good look, he said, 'You're one of the very lucky chaps. You're not going to need me. You're going to grow a new skin. The main reason is you came down in the sea. And we've learnt from you chaps that a brine bath is the best initial treatment for a bad burns case.'

Squadron Leader Thomas Gleave
Commanding Officer 253 Squadron, RAF
In the corner of this ward at East Grinstead, behind some curtains, there was the sort of bath you see lying outside a demolished house. A thing on four legs with bits of pipe on it. McIndoe had had one of these brought into the ward and the hot water pipe went through a little instrument which rang a bell if the temperature went half a degree higher or lower than blood temperature. And a light came on which told you if the specific gravity of the salt in the water went up or down. A rough gauge was four pounds of white salt to nine inches of water. This was the famous burns salt bath. I was taken there in the afternoon – outwardly a picture of fantastic courage but inwardly, scared stiff. Being a squadron leader, I had to look very brave and I was put in the bath and the effect was so fantastic. I had raw flesh everywhere – no skin on my hands, great raw patches on my face – but in the bath I just felt fine. But the greatest thing about it was, it healed skin.

Marie Agazarian
Voluntary Aid Detachment
McIndoe was wonderful because with burns a great deal of it is morale. People get very depressed when they're burnt. He'd have things done his way. He'd come in and look round the ward and say, 'I'll have that nurse, that one and that one,' and he'd choose the prettiest and the most cheerful. And we did as he did because you had to cheer these patients up.

Igraine Hamilton
Women's Auxiliary Air Force
The woman who brought round the library books at East Grinstead took one look at a Czech pilot and said, 'Ooh, you look like a monkey!' He disappeared

under his bedclothes and it took a very, very long time to get him out. He wouldn't see anybody. I talked to him and told him that the woman was ridiculous and that he was all right and that I would stay there until he came out. Eventually, he did.

Pilot Officer George Bennions
41 Squadron, RAF

I felt terribly isolated. I couldn't see, I couldn't hear very well. I couldn't recognise people unless it was somebody very close to me. My wife and mother came down. But I was feeling extremely sorry for myself which I think is a very bad thing for anybody. I felt so deflated just as though half my life had been taken and the other half wasn't worth bothering with. It was I think the worst period of my life. But you get over it. I think the people in the hospital, one person in particular, put me on a much more even footing. He'd been shot down flying a Hurricane. He was in Ward 3. He'd heard that I'd been admitted to the hospital and he'd sent a message along, 'Could I go and see him?' He couldn't get out of bed because his legs were badly burnt. I was on crutches at the time but I managed to get over there with a hell of a lot of struggle and self pity. As I opened the door in Ward Three I saw what I can only describe now as the most horrifying thing that I've ever seen in my life. That was this chap who been badly burnt, really badly burnt. His hair was burnt off, his eyebrows were burnt off, his eyelids were burnt off, you could just see his staring eyes. His nose was burnt, there were just two holes in his face. His lips were badly burnt. Then when I looked down his hands were burnt. I looked down at his feet also and his feet were burnt. I got through the door on the crutches with a bit of a struggle. This chap started propelling a wheelchair down the ward. Half way down he picked up a chair with his teeth. That's when I noticed how badly his lips were burnt. Then he brought this chair down the ward, threw it alongside me and said, 'Have a seat old boy.' And I cried. And I thought, 'What have I to complain about?' From then on everything fell into place.

Igraine Hamilton
Women's Auxiliary Air Force

One patient had lost his leg and his wife came in and said, 'You won't be able to dance again.' He said, 'No, I won't.' She said, 'Well, I'm not going to be married to somebody who can't dance!' and she left. And that was the last he saw of her.

Squadron Leader Thomas Gleave
Commanding Officer 253 Squadron, RAF

Wherever you looked at East Grinstead, there was a chap worse than you. So you had this marvellous camaraderie. McIndoe broke every well-known hospital rule – this silly business of lying to attention, all that nonsense. If someone didn't want to wake up in the morning, you didn't wake him up. Just leave him alone. And provided you didn't have an operation the next day, you could go on a pub crawl in East Grinstead. You took wheelchairs to wheel the non-mobile people. And the people in East Grinstead were marvellous. McIndoe spread the word, 'These chaps are ordinary blokes. Don't stare at them. Look after them!' And they did. You had a hell of a job trying to pay for a pint yourself.

Flying Officer Harold Bird-Wilson
17 Squadron, RAF

The best way I can describe McIndoe is that when he came to see you before an operation, he gave you such confidence in his capabilities and his dynamic personality that regardless of what he did with you under operations, you'd be quite happy.

Igraine Hamilton
Women's Auxiliary Air Force

If McIndoe wasn't God himself, he was certainly his right-hand man.

Flying Officer Douglas Grice
32 Squadron, RAF

There was a time, for a year or two afterwards, when I had a red line round the bit of my face that hadn't been covered by the mask. If I had a drink too many and got the old bloodstream working, this line would appear. But its all grown away now, and when people learn that I was burnt during the war they can't believe it.

Pilot Officer George Bennions
41 Squadron, RAF

My left eye was lacerated but I was a bit anxious that they should try and save it – that they should try and do something with it and not take it away altogether. I was being unreasonable. The specialist tried explaining to me that if it wasn't taken out, I would go blind in both eyes. He said, 'It'll get worse and eventually a cataract will form on the good eye if I don't take it out immediately.' So I had this momentous decision to make. I knew then that that would stop me from flying which was the only thing I wanted to do. In that respect it was a very traumatic period. I resisted his advice for 48 hours. That was an eternity to me. But after I'd had the operation and had the bad eye removed my sight improved very rapidly. After about three months, I could see well enough to do almost anything.

Sergeant Stanley Wright
NCO *served on aircraft interception radar work*
There was a particularly nasty cry in the Royal Air Force that people who 'chickened out' became known as having 'lack of moral fibre'. There'd been an air gunner in Bleinheims at Manston who'd had 'Lack of Moral Fibre' stamped across his papers. He went off one morning in one of twelve aircraft. He went off later that morning in one of the six that remained. In the afternoon, he was told to go up in one of the three that was left – and he said, 'No!' That made him 'Lack of Moral Fibre'. I reckoned he'd earned his pay already.

Flying Officer Harold Bird-Wilson
17 Squadron, RAF
I had cases of chaps coming up to me and saying, 'I can't take it'. These were chaps who hadn't been with us very long. I'd say, 'Right! You're going to do one more sortie and then I will post you.' And you'd put him as your number two and you'd watch him the whole time but I made sure that he did one mission. For his own mind and his own human being part of himself. If I had said, 'All right you can go off on rest,' he would never be a man again.

Flight Lieutenant Peter Brothers
32 and 257 Squadrons, RAF
One chap was imagining all the worst things that could happen and burst out in perspiration. I thought he had flu so I sent him to the sick quarters. The doctor came and said, 'He's had it.' He couldn't face the enemy but he had a different courage. He was put on to testing rebuilt Hurricanes and Spitfires and he had the most ghastly crash in one. He smashed himself up and was nearly a year in hospital. When he came out, he went back to test flying. That was great courage, I reckon. A different sort of courage.

Flying Officer Harold Bird-Wilson
17 Squadron, RAF
After I was shot down, I went on rest to a unit at Sutton Bridge. You saw chaps who had really taken shock extremely badly. They'd come into the bar and they'd have a terrible facial twitch or a body twitch and there was

nothing you could do to help them except to act back again the same twitch. While you're drinking your drink, you did the same thing back to them. And so they realised that they were doing it. It was a very cruel way to be kind and it cured these chaps in the end.

Edith Kup
Women's Auxiliary Air Force, served as plotter
I remember seeing this very tall young man out of the corner of my eye, and he sort of sagged down the wall. I said, 'Would you like to lie down? We have some beds in the Ops Room.' He said, 'Yes,' so I asked someone to keep an eye on him. The boy had cracked but nobody said anything. Later, I went back into the Ops Room, and he was asleep. We tried to wake him and we couldn't, so we rang the medical officer and asked him to come. And when they picked him up, he was stiff, from head to toe, you know, he didn't sag in the middle. And the medical officer said to me, 'You're looking at someone who's literally scared stiff.' Nobody saw him again – he was whisked off.

Flying Officer Harold Bird-Wilson
17 Squadron, RAF
Fatigue broke into a chap's mentality in the most peculiar ways. Some really got the jitters and facial twitches and stuff like that. Others, as I did, had nightmares. I used to wake up in the dispersal hut, sleeping within 25 yards of my Hurricane. I was night flying! And this went on quite a long time.

Hans-Ekkehard Bob
German Messerschmitt 109 pilot
I don't really understand how anyone could have nightmares. I suppose that very sensitive people might suffer in that way.

Sergeant Iain Hutchinson
222 Squadron, RAF
The last time I got shot down, I was stuck in my aircraft and it was going down rather rapidly. I didn't think I could get out and I was just waiting for the big bang. I actually remember wondering whether the bit of me that was sticking out of the aircraft would be more pulverised than the bit that was inside, which is rather an odd thought, but you think odd thoughts at these times. And then I found myself floating through the air. After I came out of hospital and got back to the airfield, the nightmares started. And they've persisted over the rest of my life.

On the Ground

During the Battle of Britain we got stuck into the beer.
Each night we managed to get away eight pints.

Flying Officer Christopher Foxley-Norris
3 Squadron, RAF
The public attitude to fighter pilots was almost exaggeratedly adulatory. It's rather like the attitude towards a really big footballer nowadays.

Sergeant Fred Gash
Boulton Paul Defiant gunner with 264 Squadron, RAF
When we celebrated our hundredth victory, the Boulton Paul people invited us to their factory for a dinner and then they took us to the theatre in the evening. It was very embarrassing because whoever was on the stage mentioned the fact that the air crew of 264 Squadron were in the audience and everyone started to applaud. Then they asked us to stand up, which we did and everybody started to cheer.

Pilot Officer Roger Hall
152 Squadron, RAF
The public couldn't get enough of us. They were all over us, we could do no wrong. It was just like a pop star now. You were a star. Except for the army who still couldn't stand us after Dunkirk.

Leading Aircraftman Joe Roddis
Flight mechanic with 234 Squadron, RAF
To be on a Spitfire squadron was the ultimate. Especially when the King let the fighter pilots undo their top button. We knew then that we'd made it.

Pilot Officer Alec Ingle
605 Squadron, RAF
We were a pretty extrovert lot, you know. A very arrogant lot. I was old for my squadron. I was 24 in 1940.

Flying Officer Basil Stapleton
South African Pilot, 603 Squadron, RAF
We had people to look after us. Batmen and batwomen. The batwomen were all mother figures who used to scold us, 'Why haven't you put your dirty clothes outside for me to wash?'

Flight Lieutenant Frederick Rosier
Commanding officer 229 Squadron, RAF
When I went to Northolt, I found that the wives of some of the chaps were living in the vicinity. It wasn't long before I stopped chaps living out and I said it would be far better if their wives moved away. It was affecting morale in that these wives would count the number of aeroplanes leaving and the number of aeroplanes coming back. And they were on the telephone to find out whether Willie was all right. It was far better when we were all living together in the mess and developing a first-class squadron spirit.

Pilot Officer Tony Bartley
92 Squadron, RAF
When the bombing of Biggin Hill got bad – the officers' mess was bombed – we were moved into temporary accommodation which was a sort of prefab. Then Fighter Command became nervous that there were three squadrons on the airfield so they said that we couldn't live on the airfield at night and we were billeted in country mansions three miles from the airfield.

Sergeant Richard Mitchell
229 Squadron, RAF
We were based at Northolt but just before dusk, we had to fly to a little airfield nearby. It was just a grass field. We used to get there before dark, tie down our aeroplanes and cover them up. There was nothing there in those days – no telephones, no fuel, no ammunition, nothing – but after the war it became Heathrow Airport. After we'd tied up our aeroplanes, we got into a lorry and we were taken to a pub where we had a meal and then we were taken to a selected house somewhere in the countryside, where we spent the night. My colleague and I stayed in a fair-sized house, run by a market gardener and his

wife. The wife was very kind to us. She used to order us to bed when we got in because we were so tired. Sometimes, during the night, she would creep in and leave us a Thermos flask and a couple of biscuits that we could have in the morning while we were getting dressed and the driver was throwing stones up at our window.

Rosemary Horstmann
Women's Auxiliary Air Force, served with Y Service at RAF Hawkinge
The house where I was billeted was a bungalow up an unmade track, The woman had put up an air raid shelter in the hall of the bungalow and this shelter was inhabited by a butcher who had been bombed out from Gravesend. And he never washed. The smell was something absolutely frightful. We used to take a deep breath, hold our noses and dash through the hall to our bedroom.

Flight Sergeant George Unwin
19 Squadron, RAF
When we were patrolling the convoys, Douglas Bader and I slept in a little bungalow. I was trying to sleep one night and he was trying to adjust his tin legs with a file and a tin of oil. The file was going, 'scrape, scrape, scrape'. Then he would strap the legs on and he would go, 'squeak, squeak, squeak', as he walked around. After hearing the scrape, I was waiting for the squeak and eventually I said, 'For God's sake! If you must do that, go outside and do it!' *Snow White and the Seven Dwarves* was on locally and he said, 'Oh shut up, Grumpy!' From then on everybody knew me as 'Grumpy'.

Pilot Officer Richard Leoline Jones
64 and 19 Squadrons, RAF
We lived in tents and Nissen huts. We lived as though we were on a big camp, living in one another's arms. The sergeants and officers were living in close quarters and we became one family. We all lived together and we were all a team.

Flying Officer Christopher Foxley-Norris
3 Squadron, RAF
In the average fighter squadron, one third of all the Battle of Britain pilots were sergeant pilots. They were good old sweats with bald heads and moustaches and they'd been in before the war. They were very steady and professional and completely contrary to the dashing young silk-scarved

A pilot's living quarters.

cigarette holders. That picture was built up to boost morale. It's rather along the lines of the dashing knight-at-arms going in and swatting down the professional Germans. But it wasn't true.

Sergeant Cyril 'Bam' Bamberger
610 and 41 Squadrons, RAF

I was a sergeant while I was at Flying Training School at Hullavington and on the course with me, were a lot of officer pilots and I got to know them. I can always remember meeting a man called Winnie. He mentioned Charterhouse to me and I didn't know what the hell he was talking about. It was his public school and he was staggered that I'd never heard of it. It gradually sank in to me that there was another world out there that I knew nothing about. One day, six of us were chosen to be interviewed to become officers. Though I say it myself, I was probably one of the best pilots at Hullavington but as the others were interviewed, I was left waiting and eventually I had to knock on the adjutant's door. They'd decided not to interview me because I'd left school at 14. I started to realise the importance of background. It occurred to me that at Hullavington, I had been given a sergeant instructor while all the officers had been given officer instructors – and until then I hadn't been aware of it at all. After we got our wings, the officers moved away from the sergeants. We were living in the married quarters and eating in the airmen's mess and they moved to the officers' mess. These were people who were flying with me but they were living a different life.

Ernest Wedding
German Heinkel 111 bomber pilot

We were getting replacements – young officers coming from the academy. One morning at briefing, all the flight commanders were senior sergeants. One of the second lieutenants, equivalent to a pilot officer, said, 'Sir, why is it that we officers have to fly wing men and the sergeants are flight commanders?' He was told, 'We want to get the aircrafts there and we want to get them back. Once you prove that you can do that then you can be a flight commander. Until then you fly wing man.' And that was the end of the story. Once you were on an apron on an airfield there were no ranks. You didn't salute any more, you didn't call anybody sir. Ranks completely disappeared. It was Tom, Dick, or Harry. In our case Hans, Fritz and Oscar.

Sergeant Cyril 'Bam' Bamberger
610 and 41 Squadrons, RAF
If you were an officer, you got the same aircraft every time – but when I was a sergeant, I very rarely flew the same aircraft two days running.

Sergeant Fred Gash
Boulton Paul Defiant gunner with 264 Squadron, RAF
The difference between commissioned and non-commissioned didn't make a difference as far as my squadron was concerned. I remember I went into Maidstone one morning to buy some toothpaste and shaving equipment and I got hauled in by the provost marshal for being improperly dressed. He told me to report back to the guardroom to be reprimanded by my CO. But when I got to the CO's office, he was sitting at his desk and behind him was my pilot and two or three other pilots. As I stood to attention and started reporting what had happened, the pilots started sticking out their tongues and sticking their fingers up their noses. I tried to keep a straight face as I told the CO what had happened and then he rang through to the provost marshal, telling him in no uncertain terms to keep his hands off his crew. Then he said, 'It's all over and done with. We'll buy you a beer next time.' That was the attitude. They were a great bunch of people and that's why we got on so well.

Sergeant Cyril 'Bam' Bamberger
610 and 41 Squadrons, RAF
When I became an officer, the controller and the wing commander would drop into our mess and we were up to date with what was going on. We were very well briefed. But the sergeants didn't know what was going on. This separation was a big weakness. When I was a sergeant, I had no grudge or animosity because it was what I was used to. But looked at with hindsight, the sergeants should have been told more about what was going on. For instance, if someone had said to me that a 109 could only have stayed over the country for twenty minutes, I'd have jumped for joy. But no one mentioned it to me so I didn't know. These were basics that the sergeants should have been briefed on.

Pilot Officer Roger Hall
152 Squadron, RAF
We always used to go out as a squadron. Whenever we went out at night, the whole squadron went. There was no distinction in rank at all. We were a very close-knit unit. And this was common to all fighter commands, there was no distinction in rank really. Well, there may have been in some units . . .

19 Squadron relaxes in its squadron crew room at Manor Farm, Fowlmere.

Flight Sergeant George Unwin
19 Squadron, RAF
The famous Red Lion pub in Whittlesford was regarded as the officers' pub – without any orders being given. I was a flight sergeant and although there was no question of forbidding us, we just politely kept away. We went to another pub in the village.

Pilot Officer Archibald Winskill
72 and 603 Squadrons, RAF
How did we control the fear? We couldn't suddenly say we didn't like it. So we became rather jolly chaps. 'Let's have another beer!' 'Let's go after girls!' 'Has anybody got a fast motorbike? Let's race round the perimeter track!' Anything – it didn't really matter. We had the reputation of being a little flighty, not very serious – and that's how we behaved.

Sergeant Maurice Equity Leng
73 Squadron, RAF
You had this adrenaline rushing through you. It was a state of euphoria. It wasn't real but it was very enjoyable. You went along to the pub in the evening and you were feted by all the local people.

Pilot Officer Dennis Armitage
266 Squadron, RAF
We occasionally had a bit of a rough party but I wouldn't call it hooliganism. Of course, there was a tendency to go out and get a belly full of beer and find out the local female talent. You needed a relaxation – a mental change.

Pilot Officer James Goodson
American pilot, 43 Squadron, RAF
My memories of those days are the jokes, the fun in the mess, the camaraderie. If people were frightened, tired, neurotic, disillusioned and despondent there was an unwritten law in Fighter Command that you did anything rather than show it. Probably those that were cracking the jokes the most, who were making silly schoolboy pranks in the mess, they were probably the most frightened but they never, never showed it.

THE BATTLE OF BRITAIN

Pilot Officer Antony Thompson
85 and 249 Squadrons, RAF

This sounds bloody stupid now but three of us had an imaginary dog called 'Bismarck'. We had a lead and a collar but no dog on the end. One night, we were having a party with the Spitfire boys from Hornchurch at a pub in Chigwell and a dear old lady saw the lead and collar and said, 'Where's the dog?' We said, 'That's 'Bismarck.' We thought no more about it but she went home and came back with a newspaper full of bones. We had to tell her our dog was imaginary. She wasn't best pleased.

Wing Commander Edward Donaldson
Commanding Officer 151 Squadron, RAF

During the Battle of Britain we got stuck into the beer, Each night we managed to get away eight pints. We used to call that a quota. But there didn't seem any point in staying sober.

Pilot Officer Roger Hall
152 Squadron, RAF

The thing was, the anxiety of what could happen tomorrow would prevent you from sleeping. But if you had a good wad of beer, you'd go out like a light.

Sergeant Iain Hutchinson
222 Squadron, RAF

The tension was such that when I got back, I couldn't relax in bed. I found one way out of it was to run a hot bath, get in the bath, and just fall asleep. I had an alarm by my side, and when I woke up three hours later, the bath was cold and I had time to get dressed for the next day. I'd be in the bath between twelve and half past two, a relaxed time, and I was fit and fresh for what went on in the morning. I suppose sleeping in the bath could have been dangerous but it didn't seem to be.

Sergeant Charlton Haw
504 Squadron, RAF

I found, throughout the war, that the people who went to bed early to read a book and who didn't chase the ladies or drink a few pints were much more likely to be killed than people who were a little bit on the wild side.

Fighter pilots relax. The crooner on the far right is Flight Lieutenant James Nicolson, the only man to win the Victoria Cross during the Battle of Britain. He died later in the war.

Flying Officer Basil Stapleton
South African Pilot, 603 Squadron, RAF
When we were at Hornchurch, we went into London and got up to all sorts of high jinks. I'd joined a wine club and I'd been given a card. When you went to a nightclub, you presented this card to one of the waiters who went round to the liquor store and got what you ordered. That was you set for the night. We usually finished up at about one o'clock and we'd go to the Turkish baths on Jermyn Street. It was the perfect hangover cure. You had a massage on your cot, you'd sleep there for six shillings and sixpence and next morning, you were as fit as a fiddle. On one occasion, Maxwell, Olver and myself went down to the baths and we all had massages. The masseur had left the spirit rub on Olver's cot-side table. Olver looked over the top of the partition and saw Maxwell lying naked on the next cot so he poured the spirit rub over Maxwell's more sensitive parts. Maxwell leapt up with one thought in his mind – to get into the cold plunge pool but he slipped and finished up with his back against some hot lag pipes. He fell on his backside and we picked him up and threw him into the pool. Then we followed him in. Six hours later, we were all flying.

Flight Lieutenant Peter Brothers
32 and 257 Squadrons, RAF
Most of the pilots were enthusiastic hard drinkers and hard players and they pulled together well. I had the occasional problem with chaps who went off to the Kit Kat Club in London after we finished flying. They'd go to the club in uniform and they'd be there at readiness the next morning, asleep in deck chairs after drinking and partying all night. Jolly good fun for them but I didn't reckon they'd be all that reliable in the air so I used to get a bit cross.

Sergeant Charlton Haw
504 Squadron, RAF
If you had a bit of a hangover, you sat in the aircraft and put the oxygen full on and it worked like magic. It cleared your head straight away.

Pilot Officer Irving Smith
New Zealand pilot with 151 Squadron, RAF
One night, I'd promised to meet a whole lot of my New Zealand friends for a grog at the Tivoli Bar, across the road from the New Zealand High Commission in London but there'd been a bomb on my quarters at North

Weald so I had to land at Stapleford Tawney. I was divorced from my clothes. I didn't have a collar or tie and I didn't have any shoes – only flying boots. I borrowed a tie from one of the airmen who happened to have one tied round his trousers and made a collar out of newspaper and I got a train at Epping to get to the Strand before the Tivoli shut. By the time I arrived, I'd lost the collar and I was so late that they all thought that I'd been shot down. They saw me, shut the bar up, shut the public out, opened it again and we had a great thrash. At the end of the night, the two barmaids went off down the road, holding each other up, giggling, 'Our hubbies are going to murder us!'

Heinz Lange
German Messerschmitt 109 pilot
If it was bad weather and no fighters could fly, we sometimes got free. The pilots drove to Lille where there was a small bar. I remember it very well – the Rio Bar. There were very nice French girls and this was a relaxing event for us but it was only sometimes. Later on in the autumn when weather was worse we had a little more relaxing than before. After the war, I asked an English friend who had fought in the Battle of France, 'Do you know the Rio Bar?' and he said 'Of course, we were always there!' Those girls were the first international Europeans who had friends on both sides.

Sergeant Leslie Batt
238 Squadron, RAF
One night, I was drinking with the Poles and Czechs. We were drinking whisky and cherry brandy with a beer chaser. We were called up the next morning and brought to readiness within half an hour. Normally, I could fly up to 15,000 feet without any oxygen but on this day at 10,000 feet, I started feeling groggy and before I got to 15,000, I realised something was wrong. I couldn't move. Fortunately, I always trimmed my aircraft slightly nose heavy and I just released my grip and came down. I circled the aerodrome and landed OK. I said to the flight sergeant, 'I think there's something wrong with my oxygen,' but he couldn't find anything wrong and by now I felt perfectly all right. About a fortnight later, I read in a booklet circulated to pilots, the perfect explanation for what I had suffered . . . excess alcohol.

Marian Orley
Women's Auxiliary Air Force
The pilots taught the WAAFs to drink and smoke a lot. Everybody was on the edge. We never knew what was going to happen next.

Pat Pleasants
Women's Auxiliary Air Force

A whole crowd of WAAFs and pilots went down to the Cock Hotel in Epping every evening. The pilots were French, Americans, Czechs, Polish – I can't remember many English. We used to relax and drink and after a while you'd be talking for them because they got stuck on their words. They couldn't speak English very well. I had plenty of boyfriends. It was brilliant.

Pilot Officer Richard Leoline Jones
64 and 19 Squadrons, RAF

Some of our jokes could be on the naughty side. When we were at Turnhill, those of us who were promoted to Acting Pilot Officers had to wear a three-inch armband over our sergeant's stripes. We used to go into the town for dances but I found – and so did the other Acting Pilot officers – that it was almost impossible to get a girl to dance. It was as if we had BO. In the end, I met a girl who was prepared to talk. 'What is it?' I said, 'Here we are at these dances and we find it virtually impossible to get a partner!' 'Oh,' she said, 'I suppose I'd better tell you. We've been told by members of the sergeants' mess to keep away from the sergeants with white armbands. They told us you've all got VD.'

Pilot Officer Antony Thompson
85 and 249 Squadrons, RAF

One day, I had to land in a field and the first person on the scene was an exceedingly pretty girl. I said to this girl, 'Do you live nearby?' and she said, 'Yes, I live in the house over there,' so then I asked, 'Have you got a telephone I can borrow?' 'Yes, I have.' So I went off with her and I rang North Weald where I was based and they told me that it would be at least two hours till they came to pick me up. So I said to the girl, 'Is there a pub near here?' 'Yes,' she said, 'the Green Dragon, just across the road.' So I said, 'How about coming over for a beer?' 'I'd love to!' She turned out to be one of the nude models for *Men Only* magazine and in a manner of speaking I saw quite a lot of her over the next few months.

Marian Orley
Women's Auxiliary Air Force

The Poles were charming but very naughty. They were the dancing cheek-to-cheek types. I remember walking home to my billet with one who fell on his knees, put his arms round my legs and said, 'I love you!' I said, 'You've got a fiancée back in Poland, you'd better think about her!'

Pilot Officer Richard Leoline Jones in the cockpit of his Spitfire at Fowlmere.

Flight Lieutenant Gerald Edge
605 and 253 Squadrons, RAF
When we moved to Turnhill, we weren't welcomed at all because the Polish squadron that had been there before had been a proper pest. The Commanding Officer and another officer had been found breaking in to the WAAFs' officer quarters. When we arrived there, they were both in cells.

Marian Orley
Women's Auxiliary Air Force
When we had new postings of Poles on the station, I used to tell the WAAFs that there was only one Polish word that they needed to know: 'Nie'. And not once did I have a pregnancy on that station.

Alison Hancock
Women's Auxiliary Air Force
Most of the WAAFs were interested in the opposite sex – which was only natural. You had to try and keep your end up a bit.

Victor Hester
25 and 532 Squadrons, RAF
The Squadron Commander asked me if I had a car. I said yes. He gave me a local purchase order and asked me to go the chemist in the High Street and buy 400 French letters. It was ridiculous. I think I'd kissed a girl by then but that was about the limit and the idea of walking into a chemist shop and buying French letters was beyond me. I'd much rather have gone up and faced some Germans. I went into the shop and lots of pretty young ladies came up – the air force was quite popular at the time. I asked for the manager and I whispered to him, 'French letters.' 'Yes, I understand,' he said, 'how many?' '400,' I said. That knocked him sideways. 'I'll have to go and see if I've got 400,' he said. He obviously told the girls what it was all about because they all came back full of smiles to see this man who could use 400 French letters. To the unenlightened – we used to put them over the ends of guns to keep the rain out.

Alison Hancock
Women's Auxiliary Air Force
At one station, a couple of WAAFs got pregnant and they both came in to me to say goodbye and one was quite a tough girl and the other one was a sweet girl. Blow me if the tough one didn't point at the sweet one and say, 'It wouldn't have happened if it hadn't been for her . . . '

Marian Orley
Women's Auxiliary Air Force
I had a WAAF corporal who volunteered all the time to go on the ration lorry that bumped up and down everywhere. I couldn't understand why until one day, in the middle of PT, she gave birth. She was a very fat girl – we'd never have known.

Flying Officer Basil Stapleton
South African Pilot, 603 Squadron, RAF
We weren't thinking about wives and kids. We had no responsibility other than being in the air force. We had no distraction apart from the ones we made ourselves.

Flying Officer Harold Bird-Wilson
17 Squadron, RAF
After one patrol, the wives of the missing men came daily to the officers' mess and hung around waiting for information as to the return of their husbands. I think some of us vowed at that point that we wouldn't marry until things got more settled.

Elizabeth Jones
Wife of RAF fighter pilot
It was not really allowed for pilots to get married but Richard managed it. We got married two weeks after the end of the Battle of Britain. It was rather quick because Richard only had a fortnight's leave and I got married in a suit and a hat. We only had four people at the wedding and then a lunch afterwards and then we went straight to Hornchurch where we rented a bungalow and it became a mecca for all the pilots. It was nothing to come home from shopping to find three of them asleep on the sitting room floor. I fed them and got on very well with them.

Alison Hancock
Women's Auxiliary Air Force
I met my husband at the first station where I was commissioned. In wartime, it was all very different and he said to me, 'If you don't marry me, I don't know what I'll do!' He'd lost his parents and he touched a soft spot in me. But after we married we had very little in common.

Edith Kup
Women's Auxiliary Air Force, served as plotter

A young pilot threw a handful of sand on to the fan belt of my tractor one day
when I was laying flare paths. So I made him start it again. That's how I first
met Dennis. He was 20, I was 21. He used to take me to dinner in Cambridge.
He took me to the Rose and Crown where I wasn't allowed to go because
other ranks were banned but he said, 'If I want to take you, I'm taking you!'
And he did. We became engaged. One morning, there was a big attack. I was
actually on duty and it was about eight miles off the south east of Orford Ness.
I can't remember how many Germans but it was quite a lot. Our lot attacked
and I heard somebody say, 'Blue Four going down.' And suddenly I thought,
'My God! I know who it is!' And I knew, I really knew it was Dennis. I was
just devastated. Oh God. We were just about to come off duty and go for
lunch but I just went off by myself. When I got back, the flight sergeant was
waiting for me. She told me. And of course I knew already. But they were
wonderful. Everybody was wonderful.

Supporting Roles

Believe you me, there was nothing worse than
trying to change a tyre on a Spitfire.

GROUND CREW

The No. 1 School of Technical Training had been founded in 1920 at Halton Park in Hertfordshire to train ground crews for the Royal Air Force. Aircraftmen trained at Halton were amongst the mechanics, riggers, fitters and armourers who served during the Battle of Britain. These men were responsible for the aircraft that flew against the Luftwaffe.

Sergeant Cyril 'Bam' Bamberger
610 and 41 Squadrons, RAF
The ground crews worked very long hours and frequently through the night. They'd been up, working on the aircraft before dawn and when we stood down, they had to put the aircraft to bed. They worked longer hours than the pilots. On the other hand, they didn't have to go up and be shot at.

Aircraftman Douglas Rattle
Flight Rigger with 19 Squadron, RAF
At the crack of dawn, ground crews would be out wearing balaclavas. The flight mechanic would get in the cockpit and the flight rigger would lie on the tail. It was really hard going. There was nothing better for waking you up in the morning.

Leading Aircraftman Joe Roddis
Flight mechanic with 234 Squadron, RAF
I'd do a 'pre-flight exam' on the engine to see that we'd missed nothing; to see the oil tank was full, that there was 85 gallons of petrol in the tank, that everything was all right in the cockpit. Then they'd bring the aircraft to readiness.

Aircraftman Douglas Rattle
Flight Rigger with 19 Squadron, RAF
At readiness, I'd sit by the starter trolley and the mechanic would sit in the cockpit ready to start up the motor when the claxon went.

Fred Roberts
NCO served as armourer with 19 Squadron, RAF
After the planes took off, you'd either have a game of football, a game of cards, or put your head down and sleep on the grass.

Leading Aircraftman Joe Roddis
Flight mechanic with 234 Squadron, RAF
When the aircraft returned, I'd refuel the engine and put oil in it. If there was a snag and it was within my capability to fix it, I would and then I'd run it up to see that I'd resolved the problem. I would always do an 'afterflight'. That meant giving the engine a real good going over. You might look at it and think that nothing's happened but a bullet could have gone through the cowling or the propellor. It would take about half an hour and they'd bring us back on readiness when all the other trades had finished their jobs.

Fred Roberts
NCO served as armourer with 19 Squadron, RAF
There were red patches over the gun ports to stop the guns freezing up in high altitudes. When the aircraft came back and the red patches were gone, we'd say, 'Something's happened!' but we didn't know what until the intelligence officer had finished talking to the pilot. Unless the pilot held one or two fingers up to us. If he'd fired the guns, I'd take the empty ammunition tanks out and put new ammunition tanks in. While I was doing that, the assistant cleaned the barrel out. When we were all done, we put the panels back on the plane, and that was it. It would take two armourers and two assistants about three and a half minutes to rearm a Spitfire. We loaded 300 rounds into each gun. So a full rearm was 2,400 rounds. Every squadron prided themselves on being able to rearm a Spitfire quick.

A Hurricane being armed.

Leading Aircraftman Joe Roddis
Flight mechanic with 234 Squadron, RAF
Some people's jobs took longer than others. The instrument man had to replace the oxygen bottles. The radio man had to check such a lot. The rigger had responsibility for the wheels, tyres, airframe and the hood. He had to polish the hood so much; if there was a speck on the hood, it could be mistaken for a German aircraft. They were very keen on polishing that hood. So the rigger was running around with a cloth and polish.

Aircraftman Douglas Rattle
Flight rigger with 19 Squadron, RAF
Believe you me, there was nothing worse than trying to change a tyre on a Spitfire. Without any modern tyre-changing equipment, it was just RAF boots and brute force. It was a terrible job.

Flight Lieutenant Duncan Stuart MacDonald
213 Squadron, RAF
The ground crews were marvellous, the way they worked, the speed with which they managed to refuel and rearm. When you landed, the panels were off before you'd stopped the aeroplane. You see it now in the Formula One motor races – you see the driver coming in, and the car's jacked up and the wheels are taken off – that's how they worked. The ammunition was poured into the guns, the guns were cleaned, patches were put over the front of the guns, all the panels put back on, the aeroplane was refuelled – it was all done so quickly.

Leading Aircraftman Joe Roddis
Flight mechanic with 234 Squadron, RAF
You couldn't get close to the pilots. At the start of the war, nearly all the pilots were university graduates, clever lads from well-to-do families, and they'd not been brought up to mix with mechanics.

Fred Roberts
NCO served as armourer with 19 Squadron, RAF
The only contact we had with the pilot was when he came out and had a look at the plane in the morning. He went over the plane and took the covers off and saw that everything was secure. We used to have a few words, you know, 'Everything alright, Flight Sergeant?' And when he'd landed, after he'd finished with the intelligence officer, we used to go and have a chat about

what they'd done and if he thought anything wasn't right, we would put it right for him. Other than that we didn't have any contact with him.

Sergeant Cyril 'Bam' Bamberger
610 and 41 Squadrons, RAF
A close bond built up between myself and the ground crew. I generally knew them by their nicknames or Christian names.

Leading Aircraftman Joe Roddis
Flight mechanic with 234 Squadron, RAF
I would never ever call an officer by his first name. But we got on with them because they realised our worth as much as we realised theirs. In our opinion, they were the most important thing on the squadron but without our help, they wouldn't have had an aeroplane to fly. We didn't go out drinking with them. It was pilots and ground crew and that's the way we liked it.

Fred Roberts
NCO *served as armourer with 19 Squadron, RAF*
Some of the officer pilots were a bit stand-offish. 'I'm an officer, you're not.' I remember one pilot officer who pulled rank on you. He wasn't very well liked among the ground crew. But, on the whole, we looked up to the pilots – and we looked up more to the NCO pilots because they understood us better, they had been through the ranks with us.

Leading Aircraftman Joe Roddis
Flight mechanic with 234 Squadron, RAF
The pilots used to say that the Spitfire was the kindest aeroplane that they'd ever flown. It would never do them any harm. But they were purely flying it. We sometimes got into situations where it could hurt you. But that was purely out of carelessness. We had an aircraft tip up on its nose and the prop flew off and cut a bloke in half. I've got a mark on my chin where I walked into a prop tip – when it was stopped. But it was an excellent aeroplane and provided you treated it with the respect it deserved, it wouldn't hurt you.

Fred Roberts
NCO *served as armourer with 19 Squadron, RAF*
I got attached to individual planes. Out of the five Spitfires that I had, the first one was the best of the lot. It had the best set of guns. They were lovely. Pre-war, made by BSA in Birmingham. The Spitfire was an old Mark 1 but it

was replaced. I think one of the pilot officers taxied into the back of it and tore the tail off.

Leading Aircraftman Joe Roddis
Flight mechanic with 234 Squadron, RAF
I wasn't bothered about the Spitfire – I wanted the pilot back. You could replace the Spitfire but pilots were very hard to come by. If he could bail out and get away with it, I couldn't care less about the Spitfire.

Pilot Officer Tony Bartley
92 Squadron, RAF
The ground crew were part of the team. The armourer, the fitter, the rigger and the pilot. That was the team. We owed everything to them. And not only them but those pretty little WAAFs that used to pack our parachutes too. We owed a hell of a lot to them.

WOMEN'S AUXILIARY AIR FORCE

Members of the Women's Auxiliary Air Force, formed in June 1939, performed essential jobs of a non-fighting nature, allowing men to be released into combat roles. During the Battle of Britain, WAAFs worked as plotters, RDF operators, drivers, parachute packers, administrative clerks, flight debriefers, barrage balloon operators and in a multitude of other jobs.

Marian Orley
Women's Auxiliary Air Force
When the Women's Auxiliary Air Force was created, companies of fifty women were formed. Each company had a company commander with the rank of Flight Officer, a junior officer and a sergeant. There were only five trades at the beginning – equipment assistants, mess and kitchen, cooks, drivers and clerks.

Vera King
Women's Auxiliary Air Force, served as NCO
You used to see women in uniform, and it all seemed rather glamorous – but my father was very service-oriented and his memory of the women's services from the First World War was that they had bad reputations. His theme was, if you go into the services, no decent man will want to marry you.

Marian Orley
Women's Auxiliary Air Force
When war broke out, we were all mobilised. We had no uniforms but we converged at Castle Bromwich. That night, we slept on straw palliases in a warrant officer's house and the girl who was put in with me tried to strangle me. She had a nightmare and I ended up grappling with her on the floor. After that, I was posted to Hednesford. The main training was drilling. We were trained by an RAF flight sergeant who treated us as though we were Girl Guides. I think they thought we were in it for fun.

Alison Hancock
Women's Auxiliary Air Force
We had a male sergeant-major taking us for drill. To get in formation, he put us in order of size. There was a tiny little soul who'd joined up and he yelled at her, 'Get to the bottom, duck's disease!' The poor little thing waddled to the bottom and I thought, 'How humiliating! How cruel! How beastly you are!'

Pat Pleasants
Women's Auxiliary Air Force
I went to West Drayton for two weeks' initial training but I couldn't do it because those horrible shoes they gave me made my feet come up in blisters so I couldn't walk. They were really hard leather and you had to wear the nearest size to what they'd got. So I got out of all the training. It was brilliant.

Vera King
Women's Auxiliary Air Force, served as NCO
My original idea had been to join the Wrens. I went into the recruiting office where they had a sample Wren uniform on display. The hat was like a smaller version of a school felt hat and when I tried it on, I looked like the village idiot. So I thought, 'No, this is not for me,' and I went next door into the WAAF recruiting section where they took me on.

A WAAF arriving at her station, kit-bag on shoulder.

Felicity Ashbee
Women's Auxiliary Air Force, served as plotter at Fighter Command HQ
A lot of girls simply joined the WAAFs because they liked the colour of the uniform. I had to read the riot act one day to a mutinous mass of women and I really rode into them. I said, 'Look! You chose this service because of the colour of the uniform and now you can stay in it and like it!'

Marian Orley
Women's Auxiliary Air Force
The uniform was important. We all thought that blue would suit us better than khaki.

Alison Hancock
Women's Auxiliary Air Force
I liked the blue shirts with the neck-tie. And we had separate Van Heusen collars. It was a very nice uniform to wear. The grey stockings weren't all that attractive to enhance one's limbs but we got over that.

Marian Orley
Women's Auxiliary Air Force
The shirts had pockets in them and I stopped at one woman I was inspecting and said, 'Empty your pockets!' but there was nothing in them – she just had the most enormous bust.

Mary Harrison
Women's Auxiliary Air Force, served as plotter
The uniform didn't do anything for you unless you were tall and slim. I wasn't. I did all sorts of little alterations. The knickers were called 'passion crushers'. If you didn't get a good fit, they could drop down below your knees. I've got plump legs so mine held up.

Marian Orley
Women's Auxiliary Air Force
Hair had to kept off the collar. No jewellery was allowed except a wedding ring. And no one plastered their faces with make-up.

Alison Hancock
Women's Auxiliary Air Force
I bought a lot of Elizabeth Arden make-up and it was stolen. I reported it to the officer in charge. I went in and said, 'Ma'am . . . ' and she shouted, 'Go out of the room! And take that lipstick off!' 'Oh my God!' I thought.

Marian Orley
Women's Auxiliary Air Force
At the start, there were a whole lot of titled people in the WAAFs. It was the upper strata of society. But a lot of them couldn't take it. Out of 60 of us, about 30 didn't come back after a week's leave at Christmas. I had to parcel up all their effects and send them back.

Fanny Jones
Women's Auxiliary Air Force, served with Y Service
After a while, WAAFs became all sorts. One girl was rather smelly. Somebody said, 'We've got to explain to her that she's got to have a bath. Who's going to do it?' I did it because I was a bit older than the others and I explained as tactfully as possible that there were very nice bathrooms here and the water was always hot and she should try it. She wasn't quite so smelly after that. I don't think she'd ever had a bath.

Mary Harrison
Women's Auxiliary Air Force, served as plotter
We were a broad social mix. The dustman's daughter and the duke's daughter had to muck out the toilets together. One of my closest friends' father was a road sweeper. You learned to take people for what they were and you all got on.

Marian Orley
Women's Auxiliary Air Force
One of my girls had been absent without leave for 69 days and I was sent up to Glasgow to get her. I had to take one of her own rank and an NCO with me. We rushed to the station with our railway warrants and said to the guard, 'Which is the Glasgow train?' and he pointed. So we hopped in this train which set off and then we saw the Lake District going past. I said to someone, 'Where's this train going?' 'London, first stop Crewe.' We were going the wrong way. We got out at Crewe and we spent most of the night playing cards with army officers because there were no trains that night. We arrived in Glasgow the next morning and we went to a tenement block of flats. You can

A WAAF cricket team.

imagine what it was like. The sergeant stood at the bottom of the stairs and the other rank and I went to the top of the stairs and knocked on the door. The absentee opened the door. 'Oh, come in ma'am,' she said, 'my mother's ill – that's why I've had to stay at home. Would you like to see her?' 'Yes, certainly I would,' I said. I've never seen such poverty in my life. It was a filthy room with a large double bed with stale bread and a scrape of margarine and a very dirty elderly woman lying in filthy sheets. I started talking to the mother and as I talked to her, the absentee slipped down the back staircase and disappeared. I had to go back without her and I was told that I ought really to be court-martialled for losing a prisoner. The girl finally came back and she was given 14 days confined to camp.

Alison Hancock
Women's Auxiliary Air Force
I was surprised at the girls from the poor families who couldn't sew. A lot of them had no idea how to use a needle. It seemed rather sad – and you'd think they'd be the ones who knew, wouldn't you?

Winifred Ivy Button
Women's Auxiliary Air Force, served as parachute packer
After my training, they asked me what I wanted to do. I was a machinist and I'd always done sewing so I trained to mend and pack the parachutes. We had long tables and we had to untangle the rigging lines, fold them in a certain way and then fold them into a pack and tie them up. If they weren't packed properly, the rigging lines would get tangled and they wouldn't work and that was it. When someone was suddenly posted off this kind of work, we imagined they must have made a mistake.

Igraine Hamilton
Women's Auxiliary Air Force
On duty one night, in charge of some huts, I thought there was something wrong in one of them and I went in and found one of the girls hanging. I cut her down and got help immediately but she was dead. The story was that she'd started to unpack parachutes because she'd become paranoid that she'd packed them wrong. She'd heard stories of pilots coming down and the parachutes not opening and she kept thinking that it was her fault. I had tried to get her leave for a fortnight just to let her unwind and get herself together but they said that they couldn't possibly spare her for two weeks. Once that happened, they had to spare her forever.

Alison Hancock
Women's Auxiliary Air Force

I was at a station where you had to suck up to the sergeant because he'd decide where you where going to be posted. I remember sitting on a bench and letting him kiss me because I wanted to go to Fighter Command to be a plotter.

Mary Harrison
Women's Auxiliary Air Force, served as plotter

I was a plotter but I became bored of it after the Battle of Britain. There wasn't much to do and I didn't want to do it for the rest of the war. I wanted to do something more active. One of my colleagues said to me, 'There's something I think you ought to try. They're asking for people who've been to art college.' I applied and I was sent on a model-making course at Newnham Courtney. I ended up making models for aerial bombing, commando raids, all sorts of things.

Felicity Ashbee
Women's Auxiliary Air Force, served as plotter at Fighter Command HQ

I had been a plotter but I was taken off special duties. I suspect that a Catholic colleague reported on me that I was pro-Russian. In the rooms at night – when somebody said, 'Oh those terrible Russians,' I might have said, 'I don't know, there's always two sides to everything.' That looked dangerous – there were a lot of people in high places who preferred Hitler to Stalin.

Pat Pleasants
Women's Auxiliary Air Force

I worked for the intelligence department that used to interview the pilots when they came back from a sortie. They had to interview them while their memories were still very fresh. I was a very fast shorthand typist and I got the job of taking it down and transcribing it.

Alison Hancock
Women's Auxiliary Air Force

I gave lectures to other WAAFs on poison gas. Sometimes senior officers from the Air Ministry would sit in on the lectures. I got wise to this and when they came in, everybody stood up and I'd say, 'Sir, now I'm lecturing on gasses. Actually, I'm just asking questions.' I'd look at his rank and see that he was an Air Vice Marshal and I'd say to somebody, 'If you're walking down Piccadilly with an Air Vice Marshal and you were sprayed with mustard gas, what would you do?' To which the answer was, 'Oh, I'd take my clothes off.' That used to relax the atmosphere.

Marian Orley
Women's Auxiliary Air Force

An RAF officer had been killed and his wife wanted a military funeral. They wanted a WAAF escorting party so we drilled up. As we were lining the route for the funeral cortege, an RAF sergeant scurried over and said, 'You're the senior NCO on parade. You'll have to call the parade to attention and salute the firing party.' So there we were, rows of RAF, rows of WAAF, and there was my tiny voice, 'Royal Air Force! Women's Auxiliary Air Force!' That was quite intimidating.

Alison Hancock
Women's Auxiliary Air Force

I was put in charge of discipline – although I needed some myself. One girl came to me, terribly upset, and told me that she had venereal disease. If a girl was thought to have venereal disease, she was sent to Evesham and it was put on her record sheet. Some girls would feel suicidal in her situation. I said, 'Don't worry! You're only being sent there as a precaution. A lot of girls have discharges.' She went to Evesham and one day the telephone rang and I was told that she hadn't had venereal disease after all and she was being sent back to the station. I was thanked for being so kind to her. It showed me how careful you have to be when handling people. You've got to be broad-minded, tolerant and kind.

Marian Orley
Women's Auxiliary Air Force

I began to get a bee in my bonnet about equal pay. I was posted to Leighton Buzzard which was Air Ministry Signals – the nerve centre for signals for the whole country. There were about twenty telephone operators on one switchboard – men and women. The NCO in charge of the watch was a woman sergeant and she was paid less than an ordinary airman on the switchboard. That got under my skin a little. But I was too disciplined to do anything about it.

AIR TRANSPORT AUXILIARY

The men and women of the Air Transport Auxiliary ferried aircraft from factories and maintenance units to the squadrons. The first eight female pilots were accepted into the ATA in January 1940. The women were initially not allowed to fly operational aircraft until they were given permission to fly army co-operation Lysanders. It was only in May 1941 that they were given the go-ahead to fly Hurricanes and Spitfires.

First Officer Jackie Moggridge
Female South African pilot with Air Transport Auxiliary
I joined the ATA on July 29, 1940. At first, I was so scared of all these very glamorous-looking women, and they were you know, mostly sort of socialites who could afford to fly for pleasure, and they all looked absolutely gorgeous, all beautifully sophisticated and beautiful long tapered finger nails and beautiful make-up, and poor timid little ugly me, I felt terribly out of it.

Marie Agazarian
Female pilot with Air Transport Auxiliary
I went up for my wings check with a flight captain. I had been told how nice he was but when he took me on the test, I didn't get a smile out of him – he had a face like an old boot all the way through. The test took two hours and by the end, I was so dejected but when he got out he turned to me and said, 'You were very good.' He went in to see my commanding officer and came out again smiling. Then I went in to see the CO and he said, 'Well, you have passed, you have got your wings, but I'll tell you in all fairness, I didn't think you should be passed because I didn't think you were serious, you're always laughing, but the flight captain tells me you did well...'.

First Officer Jackie Moggridge
Female South African pilot with Air Transport Auxiliary
We were taking aeroplanes from the factories to the aerodromes and to the operational units. We were also taking them away from the operational units when they weren't in very good condition back to get things or mended or altered. I was not a bit confident. I was terrified really. The most terrifying thing was when you had to collect an aeroplane that you'd never seen before. When I started, I'd only flown single-engine Tiger Moths, little aeroplanes which cruised at 80 mph. We were given a notebook a few inches thick, and

each page of that notebook consisted of an aircraft and how to fly it the simplest way and which knobs to pull and which not to pull. If we'd lost the notebooks, we couldn't fly the areoplanes because every one was different. We also had a piece of paper which said we had the authority to fly any aircraft that was stated on that book.

Marie Agazarian
Female pilot with Air Transport Auxiliary
There was a terrific sort of line shooting which was underplaying what you did. The chaps would say, 'What did you bring in?' Perhaps an undercarriage had stuck or something so you'd say, 'Oh it was all right. It will be needing repair . . . ' But you didn't say anything much about it and they'd look at you. Great fun.

First Officer Jackie Moggridge
Female South African pilot with Air Transport Auxiliary
The day after I joined the ATA, I went to Scotland. Five of us had to take five aeroplanes up and we had one map between the five of us. I was told that I was the fifth one and I had to watch where the fourth one was going and do whatever she did. So we took off but we only had two hours' flying time so our first landing was at Ternhill where we refueled, took off again and landed at another place two hours later. I was the fifth one to go each time in our gaggle of five. When we got to Carlisle, which is the last stop before Prestwick in Scotland, it was very misty and you could hardly see the airfield.

However I knew that all the others had landed so I came in last, and just as I was taxiing, out of the mist, I saw the four aeroplanes taxiing out again to take off. I'd just undone my straps and I looked at my petrol tank. 'We haven't got much petrol left,' I thought, 'what are they doing?' So I hurriedly strapped myself up as best I could and hastily took off to follow. We followed a railway line and then a river. There were hills on either side, absolutely nowhere to land and my petrol was registering pretty nearly empty. I couldn't understand why they'd taken off again. But then I saw a runway and I landed and never thought about the others. They came in and landed after me. I had about one and a half gallons of petrol left which would have lasted a few minutes. However, when the other four people got out of their aeroplanes, they were four entirely different girls from the ones I'd started with. They said, 'What are you doing here, Jackie?' I said, 'I was following Rosemary Reece and all that lot,' and they said, 'They landed at Carlisle!' I said, 'Well where did you come from?' and they said, 'We just took off from Carlisle. We've been stuck there for a week in bad weather, and we took off hoping that we could get to Prestwick before we lost the daylight.' So I went home with these girls on the night sleeper and the girls that I'd originally been flying with were stuck at Carlisle for four more days because of the weather.

Marie Agazarian
Female pilot with Air Transport Auxiliary
We used to get very tired. One night, I fell asleep in my Spitfire. I don't know for how long but when I woke up I was still flying straight and level. Later that night, I went to a party with an air force bloke and when we arrived I put my head on his shoulder and I woke up at six o'clock. 'That was a lovely party,' he said and brought me home again.

First Officer Jackie Moggridge
Female South African pilot with Air Transport Auxiliary
You didn't have to be physically strong. If you were the type that needs to use brute force, then you wouldn't be good at the job because aeroplanes don't need brute force. They need a delicate touch. I only weighed seven stone and I'm five foot three and I used to put my parachute under me and I carried a great big cushion which I used to shove behind me. I also used to sit on my log books. Very often I couldn't strap myself in because I had to be so far forward to reach the rudder pedals that the straps wouldn't reach. Some of the American aeroplanes were built for six foot-plus people and people of my size weren't allowed to fly them but I did, anyway, because there was no one else to do it.

Marie Agazarian
Female pilot with Air Transport Auxiliary
In an aeroplane, to go slower, you pull the stick back to alter the attitude so that it slows. One day, I drove a car and when I got to the first crossroads and I tried to pull the steering wheel back . . . and we sailed across the crossroads. My passenger looked at me. I told her that I'd never driven before. 'Oh my God!' she said and after that I learnt how to drive.

First Officer Jackie Moggridge
Female South African pilot with Air Transport Auxiliary
I was more terrified of having an accident than I was of killing myself. I used to pray that if I had an accident, I'd rather die because I didn't want to damage an aeroplane. If you had an accident and you lived, you went before a court.

They decide whether it's your fault. I went before a court; I was bringing a Spitfire into Eastleigh. I was told that I should be careful with this Spitfire because some things might not be working. So I was bringing it in to land when suddenly all the balloons went up – which meant that even if I'd wanted to, I couldn't have gone round again. As I came down, I found that the flaps didn't work. A Spitfire is just like a bullet without flaps. Eastleigh was just a little field with great guns, manned by soldiers, at the end of the runway so to miss the guns, I steered but the brakes weren't working so I went into the fence. I had either to do that or raise the undercarriage which would have ruined the aeroplane. The boys manning the gun saw the Spitfire coming towards them at terrible speed before I steered away at the last minute. They were shattered as they watched me climb out of the Spitfire. So I had to go before a court to decide whether it was my fault. The court asked me why I didn't go round again. I said, 'Well, for one thing, I didn't know that the flaps weren't going to work and for another, the ballons went up just as I was coming in to land. What should I have done?' Naturally, I was cleared.

We lost about 30 women out of 130 – which wasn't bad. Conditions could be very difficult. I once had to pick up army officers from Scotland and take them down to Warmwell. There was a major, a captain, a lieutenant and a sergeant. We were in an Anson, a medium bomber that was used as transport. It was just solid cloud. I was praying that it would clear but the officers were getting very worried – especially the young lieutenant. The major was sitting in one of the seats at the back and suddenly the window blew in, shattering glass everywhere. Eventually the clouds cleared and I descended and brought them in safely.

Once, later in the war, I went to pick up a Mosquito from a station and the engineering officer flatly refused to let me have it. He wasn't having any schoolgirl flying the aeroplane that he'd worked so hard on, thank you very much. He just wouldn't let me have it. I showed him my authorisation card but that wasn't enough. He rang everybody up from the Air Ministry down to the station commander, but he had to give it to me in the end. He'd been abroad and he didn't realise women were doing this sort of job. That's the sort of thing we had to contend with.

The Second Phase:
Radar and Airfield Attacks

I was worried about the amount of blood that I was losing but it didn't seem to be coming out very fast and I thought there'd be enough to last.

The attacks on the Channel convoys had failed to draw the British fighters into the air in sufficient numbers to eliminate them, which had been the prerequisite for an invasion. On July 31, Hitler issued Führer Directive No. 17, which gave instructions to 'overpower the English Air Force . . . in the shortest possible time . . . primarily against flying units, their ground installations and their supply organisations, also against their aircraft industry'. Thus began the next phase of the Battle of Britain. Hermann Goering, the Commander-in-Chief of the Luftwaffe, now assumed direct control of the battle. A First World War flying ace, Goering had been a close ally of Hitler since the early days of the Nazi party. He was overweight, vain and ostentatious but his buffoonish image belied a ruthless ambition. At a meeting with his commanders on August 6, Goering decided that an attack would be mounted which would destroy the RAF within four days. The attack would begin with a concentrated blow on a day to be referred to as *Adler Tag* (*Eagle Day*). This attack was eventually launched on August 13 and over the following weeks, attacks were consistently made on Fighter Command airfields. On the day before the assault began, RDF stations were attacked.

Edward Fennessy
Radar expert with Air Ministry
General Martini, the Luftwaffe Chief Signals Officer, had by this time a pretty

shrewd idea that we had an RDF system operational and he had to argue very forcibly with Goering to allow the Luftwaffe to attack the RDF stations. Goering's attitude was that the Luftwaffe was an offensive air force and it was not going to bother with any new-fangled defensive devices. He wanted to get on with the air war. However, Martini persuaded him to allow some attacks.

The first we knew of this was on the morning of the August 12, when they attacked a station named Dunkirk (not the Dunkirk in France) near Canterbury. They did a moderate amount of damage. A 1,000-pound bomb nearly wiped out the transmitter building. A half hour later, they attacked the Dover station. Then they attacked Rye and Pevensey. But it wasn't until the afternoon when they attacked Ventnor with 16 dive-bombing Stukas, that they really did damage. They set most of the buildings on fire and that station was out of action for many weeks afterwards. But all the other stations were back on the air by midnight.

Ernest Clark
Wireless Operator working at RDF Stations
It's very difficult to do damage to an RDF site. The lattice masts can't be seen from the air and they were so designed that they could stand up on any two of their gimbals. And the blast used to go through them.

Pilot Officer Richard Leoline Jones
64 and 19 Squadrons, RAF
We were at readiness at Hawkinge and my aircraft just would not start. Everybody else took off and suddenly the German aircraft came low over the aerodrome and started to bomb it. I nipped out of the aircraft very smartly and found a small bomb shelter. There must have been about twenty of us trying to get inside it. I got inside but then I was pushed out of the door at the other end so I had to run round the front to get back in again. That happened three times in a row. I laugh now but it wasn't funny at the time.

Leading Aircraftman Joe Roddis
Flight mechanic with 234 Squadron, RAF
We left St Eval on August 13 for Middle Wallop. We left in a Handley Page Harrow. When we got over Middle Wallop, we saw the ground was erupting. There was a raid on and there were German aeroplanes everywhere. The pilot went straight down to the deck, hedge hopping to get away. He flew around for about half an hour until he got word that the raid was over and then he went and landed where he could. We were told, 'Right. Go and get a meal and

then come straight back.' 609 Squadron was already there and they were the big aces. We were the newcomers and we took some stick from the ground crew in the dining room when we walked in. We were given a mug full of hot, sweet tea and as many slices of bread and butter and plum jam as we wanted. Then the siren went and the place emptied like mad and we thought, 'What have we got here?' We never used to run at St Eval when the siren went but they'd all gone and we sat talking and the next thing, bombs were dropping everywhere. Lumps of masonry were flying about, tables were erupting – we were right in the middle of it. So we shot outside as quick as we could, mug of tea in one hand, bread and jam in the other. We didn't know where the shelters were but running round the cookhouse, we saw the heating pipes with the slabs taken off so we dived down there with our cups of tea. The Germans knocked hell out of the place.

Josephine Fairclough
Women's Auxiliary Air Force
On August 13 we were bombed terribly at Detling. It started off as a perfectly normal day. I was doing a spell in the parachute section and we heard some aircraft coming and a fellow went out to have a look and he came back and said, 'Move! Those aren't ours! Those are Jerry's!' We went like hell into the nearest shelter and there was a terrific wallop just as we came down the steps and a lot of smoke and dust came up. The other end of the shelter had been hit. After an age, we heard the all-clear. When we came up, there was dust everywhere. You were rather disorientated. Everything seemed to be a long way off. Things had flown about – there was a terrible mess. We did a bit of digging and got some people out. A message came through to report to Flight Officer Cope. She started to count us up and some of the officers were missing. The back part of the officers' mess had been knocked down, the operations block had had a direct hit, some of the hangars were damaged and the commanding officer had been killed. The whole place seemed to be strewn with wreckage. It was remarkable that they got the runways going again through sheer dogged determination.

Ernest Wedding
German Heinkel 111 bomber pilot
We were briefed in the morning to fly sorties against airfields and each squadron was given a specific airfield. I was in what they called Luftflotte 2. We flew into the sector of 11 Group on the airfields Manston, Brighton, West Malling, Biggin Hill. One of them was North Weald and as it so happened I

had to fly to North Weald. It was the first time that I attacked the airfield on a low-level raid. The heaviest bomb we were carrying would be 50 kilograms and we had a lot of machine gun ammunition, more than usual. Normally on a Heinkel 111 you had 750 rounds per gun, but on that day we had 1,500 rounds per gun. So we could do damage with the machine guns. As we got to North Weald, we turned the runway over. The runway was out of use. All right that wouldn't have made any difference to the fighters, they could take off on grass, but heavier aircrafts couldn't use the runway for quite some time. I was stationed at Chartres – it is quite a long flying time and back. The further you were away the less missions you flew because of the time. The closer you were to the Channel the more missions you flew.

Leading Aircraftman Joe Roddis
Flight mechanic with 234 Squadron, RAF
At Middle Wallop, a string of bombs came through a hangar and lifted the hangar door and dropped it on a crowd of airmen and WAAFs who were running past. We ran down to see if we could do anything. We couldn't but I saw a WAAF's arm sticking out with a wristwatch on. Still going.

Pilot Officer Dennis Armitage
266 Squadron, RAF
It was about seven o'clock in the morning at Eastchurch when the Germans arrived and plastered us with 50-pounder bombs. The Isle of Sheppey tends to be a bit boggy and these bombs fell in, hit the ground and threw up a little mound of earth. The whole place shook but they did no damage except for a direct hit on one of the airmen's huts which killed several of the lads and a hit on our hangar. The aircraft were all dispersed but our spare ammunition was in there so it went up like a firework display. Of course, we needed a new supply of ammunition boxes but the telephone lines were all out and we had no communication at all. I climbed into an aeroplane and went off to Biggin Hill and got on a telephone.

The first people I phoned were 11 Group headquarters because we were in the 11 Group area. It was difficult to get through. You had to convince everybody that yours was a priority call and it took half an hour just to get through. I told them our sad little story and said, 'Could we have some more ammunition boxes, please?' They said, 'Just a moment.' And there was a lot of muttering. I could just hear it and chattering in the background. And after a minute or two of this they came back and they said, well, they were very sorry but we were not in 11 Group. We had been posted to Coastal Command for the particular operation we were on and we weren't in 11 Group. And so they were very sorry but they couldn't let us have any ammunition boxes.

Next I tried Fighter Command. After a lot of mucking about I got through to them. And I told them the same story and they said, well, they're sorry but they couldn't do anything for us but they suggested I should ring Coastal Command. So I rang Coastal Command and told them the story and again there was a bit of muttering and they came back and said, yes, we are with them and they would love to supply us with ammunition boxes but unfortunately they just hadn't got any. And they said, 'If there's anything else we can do for you just let us know.'

By now, I was getting a bit fed up and I was tired. So I rang through to 12 Group at Wittering, which we were nothing to do with at all. And they immediately put me through to Harry Broadhurst, who was in charge there. Broadhurst, whom I knew, said, 'OK, Tage, leave it to me.' And about midnight, I was walking round with our CO when three big Humbers suddenly drove up laden with ammunition boxes from top to bottom. Broadhurst had fixed it for us. He'd cut through the red tape, bless him.

Flight Lieutenant Charles MacLean
602 Squadron, RAF and Sector Controller
On August 13, 1940, I went south with the squadron to Westhampnett which is two miles west of Tangmere. There was an air battle going on when we arrived but we landed and we went to the officer's mess which was in a little farmhouse. As we approached, Paul Webb came out of the front door and said, 'Come in and meet 145 Squadron! Great chaps! Both of them!' And we went in to find the two survivors of 145 Squadron sitting rather disconsolate on the stairs, waiting for their transport to get away. They'd been at it since the start of August and in two weeks they'd been practically wiped out. It was quite a shock.

Pilot Officer Dennis Armitage
266 Squadron, RAF
On August 14, we started our Battle of Britain routine where we flew off from Hornchurch to Manston each morning and operated from there. Manston was as near as we could possibly be to occupied France and Belgium and the idea was that we'd catch the Germans before they got inland. But I'm not sure that it really worked that way because we always lacked height. You wanted to be above them and preferably up in the sun because then you had a darned good chance but we were trying to get the height as quickly as we could and

Pilots of 19 Squadron confer after a sortie.

very often we went into battle below them. So I don't know that being at Manston was really much of an advantage and we very quickly got into trouble. The day after we arrived, we lost both the CO, who was killed and the other flight commander, who was badly singed. The CO was seen to bail out but according to the report I got, he was shot up on the way down in his parachute. The description was, 'His body was as full of holes as a sieve'. Whether that was true, I don't know but I found myself in charge of the squadron.

Flying Officer Jeffrey Quill
Vickers Chief Test Pilot and 65 Squadron, RAF

When we used to take off from Manston, we had to turn inland. It would have been folly to climb straight out to sea – we'd have been vulnerable to the Germans because we wouldn't have had enough height. So we used to climb inland to get a bit of height and then turn back.

Pilot Officer Dennis Armitage
266 Squadron, RAF

Poor old Manston was catching it several times a day. On one occasion, three lads who'd just landed got shot up by six 109s as they were climbing out of their aircraft. One made it safely to the side of the airfield but the number two tripped and fell as he ran to the dispersal hut. He started rolling on the ground and the 109 came in, trying to get its sights on him and shot the ground to the side of him. The lad got one bullet in his arm but it wasn't a serious wound. The third chap – a big New Zealander – hadn't got a chance of getting clear so he kneeled down in a sort of Muslim prayer position with his parachute covering his bottom. He wasn't hurt at all but when they came to repack his parachute, they picked three bullets out of it.

Ulrich Steinhilper
German Messerschmitt 109 pilot

In a raid on Manston, for the first time I realised my guns were mowing down human beings. I was going down so closely, firstly I was hitting two Spitfires, I was moving from the Spitfires very low to a lorry, and the man holding the rubber hose connecting it was hit. I was very much touched – so far, I'd been shooting at machines, but this time I was fully aware that I had hit and probably killed a human person.

Leading Aircraftman Joe Roddis
Flight mechanic with 234 Squadron, RAF

The Stukas started knocking hell out of Middle Wallop. We were short of fuel and the flight sergeant, the bloke in charge of the ground crew, said to me, 'We need some fuel. Go and get some!' I jumped into the tractor that was towing the fuel bowser and off I went across the airfield. With all hell going on. It didn't worry me. I never thought for one minute that anything would kill me. I got to the petrol dump but there was nobody about so I went into the office, found the key, filled up and I started trundling back across the airfield in the tractor with a full bowser of fuel behind me. I looked up and I saw a Heinkel 111 above me and I could see the bombs leaving it. The tractor wasn't going fast enough so I jumped off and ran and ran until I couldn't run another inch. Then I had to run back to catch the tractor up and drive it back to dispersal.

Pilot Officer Ronald Brown
111 Squadron, RAF

When Croydon was bombed on August 15, they killed the old squadron pet. He was a Staffordshire bull terrier called Butcher. He was badly injured and we couldn't get him out from under the stonework. I'll always remember Johnnie Walker, a Canadian, had the unfortunate job of crawling underneath and shooting him to put him out of his misery. There were also two or three chaps killed and a young telephonist who was lying there with half her head blown off.

Edith Kup
Women's Auxiliary Air Force, served as plotter

My friend Winifred and I were extremely annoyed. We'd come off duty at Duxford, gone home and cleaned our house from top to bottom. It had to be inspected by the sergeant before you were allowed to go out and if there was any dust you had to do it all again. Anyway, we got ours passed first time, and off we went into town. We decided to change into mufti, which you weren't allowed to do, but we did, and we had our day and enjoyed it, and when we arrived back at camp, the sergeant was waiting for us. 'Your house has been bombed,' she said, 'you'll have to come and sleep on my floor. *And what are you doing in mufti?*' So we got ticked off for that. But we were livid because we'd spent all that time cleaning the house for nothing.

Flying Officer William David
87 and 213 Squadrons

I landed at Tangmere on the day that the Stukas caught the whole WAAF contingent changing from one watch to another. They killed a lot of girls. After that attack, a captured German was seen to smirk and the RAF commander hit him very hard to stop him laughing.

Flight Lieutenant Arthur Banham
264 Squadron, RAF

It was decided that we had our feet right in the Channel at Tangmere, so to speak, and we knew that the Huns were building these barges for the invasion. So all the members of the station were told to get a WAAF or someone to sew a square yellow band on to their left arm. It was an indication to the guards at Tangmere that you were friendly in case of an invasion. Of course, if the Germans had known about the yellow bands, they could have sewn on yellow bands too. It was just so stupid, really.

Pilot Officer Thomas Neil
249 Squadron, RAF

On August 16, 249 Squadron gained the only Victoria Cross awarded in the Battle of Britain. It was won by my good friend Nicolson and it was also the day that I lost my aeroplane which I loved like a brother. On that day, Nicolson – who was my Flight Commander – forbade me to fly because I'd been on duty the night before. This irritated me no end, because it meant lending my aeroplane to somebody else. I had to loan it to a 19-year-old chap called King.

The squadron took off and intercepted a large group of aircraft over Southampton. Probably due to their inexperience, Nicolson's formation of three were bounced and Nicolson was set on fire. He was overtaken by the German who'd shot him and he stayed in his cockpit while it was burning and shot the bloke down. This was his famous VC act. Then he baled out and on reaching the ground, he was shot by the army and peppered with bullets. Fortunately, he had his back turned to the gunner so he collected most of the things in his rump. King, who was flying my aeroplane, P3616, was also shot down and came down by parachute. The army shot him too and destroyed his parachute and he fell in somebody's garden and was killed. Many of the army on the ground were Home Guard and they were lunatics. They fired at everything they saw in the air.

Flight Lieutenant Charles MacLean
602 Squadron, RAF and Sector Controller
On August 16, we got involved in a battle over Ford aerodrome. We arrived, as usual a bit too late, but by this time there were streams of Stuka dive-bombers peeling off from their formation and diving on to the aerodrome, one after the other. We tried to latch in behind them but we could only really finger our way in from the side. While we were engaged in that, Messerschmitt 109s latched on to our tails and a number of fellows were hit. My Flight Commander was riddled with bullets but he struggled back to Westhampnett with shrapnel through his body. In the end, we destroyed six Stukas and shortly after that, the Germans gave up attacking aerodromes with the Stukas. It became too expensive for them.

Pilot Officer Dennis Armitage
266 Squadron, RAF
We'd been having a scrap and we got mixed up with a lot of German fighters. I went round in a tight circle with three of them and eventually got my sights on the rear one and had a squirt. A bit of smoke came out so I must have hit him and they all turned down and dived away. I didn't follow because the 109 was known to be quicker in the dive. I couldn't catch it and there was always the danger that there'd be another one above who would catch me as I dived. On this particular occasion, there was one up in the sun above me. I don't know how he got on my tail – but I got hit. A cannon shell hit the fuselage and exploded behind my seat. It blew the canopy clean off so that the cockpit was open. There was a colossal noise of rushing air as I wondered what the hell was happening. The spent head of the shell had gone underneath the armour plating of my pilot's seat and hit the back of my leg. My leg went completely numb and I remember reaching down with my left hand and thinking, 'Is my foot still there?' It was and I pulled myself together and started turning. I saw the aircraft that had got me, diving away, several thousand feet below. Off I went home and I landed without any trouble but we found that the aileron control wires were hanging by a single thread. A second shell had gone through the starboard wing, leaving a great gaping hole. My aircraft was pretty much scrap.

Ernest Clark
Wireless Operator working at Poling RDF Station
During the week before August 18, a Stuka was brought down on Angmering Golf Course. We all went over to the Stuka and found a map inside it. On this

map was the whole of the south coast with circles on it. On these circles, there were numbers. An Air Ministry warden looked at them and said, 'That's funny! These are dates!' Every RDF station on the coast had been ringed for an attack. As a result, Poling was cleared of all non-operational staff on August 18.

Aircraftman Wilfred Slack
Engineer working at Poling RDF Station
On August 18, Poling RDF station was dive-bombed by 31 Stukas who dropped 80 bombs. The CH long-range warning equipment was put off the air because the receiving aerials on one of the wooden masts was blown away. I'd come off duty at eight in the morning and gone back to my billet to sleep. At 2.30 in the afternoon, I was awoken by the noise of bombs. I hurriedly put on some clothes and went into the shelter until the raid was over. After that, I went to the station to find utter chaos. There were bomb craters everywhere and the top of a wooden mast was missing – but none of the personnel operating the radar was hurt in any way.

Ernest Clark
Wireless Operator working at Poling RDF Station
I went up to the site and was told to clear off because there were too many delayed action bombs about. But I heard a voice saying, 'Click! Got you, you bastard! Click! Got you, you bastard!' On top of the building was one of the Green Howards who had been shell-shocked as the bombs dropped around him.

Aircraftman Wilfred Slack
Engineer working at Poling RDF Station
The shell-shocked soldier had to be carried off the roof to ground level. Most of the bombs had been at the receiver end of the compound. At the other end, there were no craters at all. About halfway down the compound, there was a CH Low installation which was not damaged in any way.

Ernest Clark
Wireless Operator working at Poling RDF Station
Poling was knocked off the air but that night, they brought down an MB1 transmitter and put it up in Angmering Park. It sent out a similar signal to the RDF transmitter and it deceived Jerry into thinking that he hadn't put us off the air. It was very effective. We were only off the air for two or three days.

Edward Fennessy
Radar expert with Air Ministry
Goering summoned all his fighter chiefs to a conference in East Prussia after the attacks on the RDF stations. At that conference, Goering told Martini that the Luftwaffe had wasted its time trying to knock out the radar stations. They were already operating again. He ordered that there would be no more attacks on RDF stations. Had he attacked the other stations with the effectiveness that he'd attacked Ventnor, then RDF would have been out of action for weeks, if not months and during that period, Fighter Command would have been completely blind to what the Luftwaffe was doing. Goering would have been able to thrown his fighters and bombers across the Channel and done what he wished. He would have wiped Fighter Command out as an effective fighter unit. And that would have given the Wehrmacht and the navy what they wanted for an invasion. That conference marked the day that Goering lost the Battle of Britain.

Flight Lieutenant Charles MacLean
602 Squadron, RAF and Sector Controller
On August 18, the phone went in the little hut at Westhampnett from which we were operating. The phone connection was a cable draped over hedges. I answered and a distant voice said, 'Wing Commander somebody-or-other from White Waltham.' He wanted to speak to our CO and I knew that he wasn't around, so I said, 'I'm the Flight Commander of A flight. Will I do?' 'Yes,' he said, 'how are you off for aircraft?' 'Oh,' I said, 'very bad. I'm looking out of the window of this hut and I can see daylight through one of them and quite a lot of others are in that state.' 'How many of them do you want?' he asked. I drew breath and said, 'Six.' 'I'll have them there within the hour,' he said. And sure enough, they arrived. The CO came back to find six brand-new Spitfires hurtling around Westhampnett.

Pilot Officer Ronald Brown
111 Squadron, RAF
When they did the big Dornier low-level raid on Kenley on August 18, they scrambled us to get us off the airfield. When we were airborne, we were vectored to intercept these Dorniers. We picked them up about ten miles from Kenley. I'd just about got into firing range and I got a long-range burst in at the leader of one of their sections when he broke formation and pulled up. I was damn certain that I must have hit him but just at that moment, as we were about to cross the airfield, the airfield defence system went into action.

Rockets fired wires and parachutes into the air. I'd heard of these things but I'd never seen them before and I damn near hit them. I went up very fast to avoid them. In the meantime, bombs were bursting below us. I got over the other side of the airfield and picked up another Dornier which was right down in the valley. I got in a good long burst on his starboard quarter and down he went. He burnt up in a field. I saw another one going over a housing estate. I was about to fire at him but at that moment I visualised a woman and kids in a kitchen cooking the Sunday lunch so I sat behind this fellow for quite a long time while his rear gunner popped off at me. When he was clear of the estate, I took a burst at him but that was my third attack and by now I was out of ammo. I don't know if he got home. Not many of them did.

Gerhard Schöpfel
German Messerschmitt 109 pilot
On August 18, my comrades and I were flying over south-west England when I spotted a large English formation heading inland so we communicated with hand signals and put ourselves into the sun. My comrades flew on but I descended and moved in behind the English formation. I knew I had good ammunition and good accuracy. They didn't notice that I was there and I shot three down and but then I noticed I had some damage and there was oil everywhere, so I had to break off. My squadron commander came down to help me and he shot two planes down. Then we went home.

Hans-Ekkehard Bob
German Messerschmitt 109 pilot
Our bomber formations were supposed to fly in close proximity to each other but they used to fly too spread out, contravening their instructions. This meant that we in the 109s were unable to protect them. Goering ordered us to adapt to the bombers speed and fly alongside them. This meant throwing away the fighters advantage. The whole point of a fighter is the fact that it's fast. And now we were ordered to give up our speed and to fly alongside the bombers. In this situation, when the English arrived and were flying towards us from high altitudes and at great speed, we didn't have the slightest chance and we started to incur heavy losses.

Flying Officer Christopher Foxley-Norris
3 Squadron, RAF
When Goering insisted that a large proportion of the fighters should actually fly with the bombers, this more or less destroyed their effectiveness. The

correct tactic would have been to send in high flying sweeps of 109s ahead of the bombers. And then the fighters would be entirely their own masters as to tactics, keeping up in the sun and threatening our aircraft from above. So a great number of the 109s were completely wasted.

Flying Officer Douglas Grice
32 Squadron, RAF

I heard over the RT, 'Don't land at Hawkinge, the airfield has been bombed.' So, of course, being very curious, I flew straight to Hawkinge where there were considerable signs of bomb damage and the airfield seemed to have molehills on it. 'This looks interesting,' I thought and seeing a path between the molehills, I landed and taxied between them to where I'd taken off from. A flight sergeant came up and said, 'I think you'd better take off again very quickly, sir!' 'Why?' 'You see all those molehills? They're unexploded bombs!' How innocent we were. I hadn't realised this. So I weaved my way through the molehills, found the same avenue between them, took off rather smartly and flew on to Biggin Hill.

Pilot Officer Dennis Armitage
266 Squadron, RAF

The fact that the Germans were always outnumbering us was starting to make things a bit desperate. 266 Squadron had started off with a full complement of pilots – about 20. But by the time we were sent back to Wittering on August 21, we were down to five. This meant that all five of us had to go on every patrol and it wasn't much of a squadron, really. I clearly remember our last patrol. We were waiting for the relief squadron to arrive at midday when we were called at eleven to be told by operations that a large German formation of 200-plus was approaching. We were to go and try to break them up. But immediately the five of us had climbed through the cloud, operations told us that this 200-plus had turned away and we were to descend through the cloud again and land. And as we landed, I saw the relief squadron coming in ahead.

Sergeant Ronald Dalton
Observer with 604 Squadron, RAF

When I arrived at Middle Wallop in late August, I went to the sergeants' mess when the siren went. I heard some aircraft overhead and then – whistle, crunch, whistle, crunch. Two hangars went up within a hundred yards of me and Spits and Hurricanes were tossed into the air like toys. I dived into a ditch, pulled my hat over my head and thought, 'Christ! What a welcome!' My heart was racing but it wasn't fear. It was excitement.

Flight Lieutenant Frederick Rosier
Commanding officer 229 Squadron, RAF
At Northolt, I was on my way to the aeroplane in dispersal, when I heard the noise of incendiaries coming down. I promptly lay on the ground. Nothing happened. Rather sheepishly, I got up again to walk. The noise I'd heard was a pig snoring.

Flight Lieutenant Duncan Stuart MacDonald
213 Squadron, RAF
The Hun got to know that the RAF always sat down to lunch between twelve and one. They seemed to attack at that time.

Edith Kup
Women's Auxiliary Air Force, served as plotter
I was going on duty at Debden for the eight o'clock changeover when the sirens went. So we all took to our heels as if mad dogs were after us and shot into the Ops Room, just before the door shut – it was a steel door that was kept shut whatever happened. We carried on plotting like mad but there was quite a lot of damage done. There was a direct hit on one of the shelters and people were killed in there. The station was a bit of a mess when we came out.

Flight Lieutenant Frederick Rosier
Commanding officer 229 Squadron, RAF
At Northolt, there was civilian labour rebuilding things and mending runways. As soon as the civil air raid alarm would go, they would retire to their trenches or dugouts. Whereas we would continue. That used to annoy us.

Edith Kup
Women's Auxiliary Air Force, served as plotter
One girl had hysterics while we were being bombed – which we took a pretty poor view of. She was a silly girl in any case. Another girl just sat there as if she was dumb. She went on leave and never came back. But that was all. Everybody else was fantastic.

Mary Harrison
Women's Auxiliary Air Force, served as plotter
I was flaked out from plotting when the sirens went. The corporal in the next bed said, 'Come on, get up!' I said, 'If Hitler's going to get me, he can get me in bed.' So the corporal plonked a tin hat on my head and left.

Pilot Officer Alec Ingle
605 Squadron, RAF
One night the Germans dropped a stick of bombs right across our particular dispersal and I slept right through it, as I think most people did. You just got accustomed to it.

Flight Lieutenant Charles MacLean
602 Squadron, RAF and Sector Controller
On August 26, there was a heavy attack on Portsmouth. I was leading A flight and we attacked but we didn't seem to do much damage. I followed the formation back over the Channel and was engaged in doing head-on attacks on the leading aircraft of this big wave of bombers. I had two head-on attacks and on the second one, I'd slowed down to about 160 mph to increase the amount of time for shooting – when you're coming at something head on, you don't get much time to shoot. Suddenly there was a frightful bang and a searing pain in my right leg about six inches above the ankle. I looked down to find my right foot hanging loose, all messed up with blood and sinews. I was at 16,000 feet, the pain was fiendish and I thought I'd have to bail out. I threw back the hood, took off my mask and looked down at the sea. It looked beautiful – blue and inviting. Then I tried my throttle and the engine was answering. I thought to myself, 'My Gosh! If you can get this thing back to Tangmere, you can spend the rest of your life on an artificial leg!' So with that in view, I flew back to Tangmere as fast as I could. I was worried about the amount of blood that I was losing but it didn't seem to be coming out very fast and I thought there'd be enough to last. Indeed there was and I landed back at Tangmere with the wheels up. That was because you can fly an aeroplane without rudder but you need the rudder to steer on the ground or else you charge about all over the place, knocking into people and killing them. And as I hadn't got a foot to work the rudder, I thought it best to land with the wheels up. Which I did. I retired to hospital after that where it was the usual old story. They tried to pretend that they hadn't taken the leg off but it was pretty obvious that they had. About four or five days later, the hospital was evacuated from Chichester and we were all taken on a hospital train to

Leamington. It was a fiendish experience. We were travelling from four in the morning until eight at night and when we got to Leamington, I said, 'I've got to have some morphia!' 'You can't!' said the nurses. 'Why not?' 'It's habit forming!' they said. They told me I'd have to see a doctor to get some. So a doctor was produced – a wee Japanese girl. And she said that she couldn't give me morphia without the permission of Mr Taylor, the chief doctor. 'Well get *him* then!' 'He's gone for the day.' 'Oh, goodness . . . ' Finally, about an hour later, I got the morphia. By jiminy, I needed it.

Jean Mills
Women's Auxiliary Air Force, served as plotter at RAF Duxford
We WAAFs arrived at the little railway station at Whittlesford in the last week of August. We were arriving at Duxford to become plotters, replacing men who were being sent out to Singapore. We lugged our tin hats and gas masks behind us up the platform. There was an openbacked lorry waiting. The driver said, 'Shove the kit bags up here, girls', and there we were, about a dozen of us, clinging on to the side, laughing and talking. We were quite excited because we were pretty young – eighteen or nineteen I suppose and most of us hadn't been away from home before and life was a great big adventure. We were feeling very hyper, I imagine. We bounced over these country roads and suddenly we reached the brow of a hill and we could see Duxford stretched out before us. Planes seemed to be landing from all directions and as we looked, one of them appeared to hover for a moment and then it nosedived straight down into the ground with smoke trails rising. We looked at each other shocked and the mood changed. We were all very much sobered up and we all realised that this wasn't a great lark. It was a serious business. We were reminded of this because the pilot who was killed owned a large Alsatian dog which just seemed to roam the camp looking for him for the next few days until somebody else took him over.

Patricia Crampton
Civilian in Beaconsfield
I was at Beaconsfield Post Office one Sunday afternoon when I recognised the sound of a German aircraft. Down he came – and I was the only thing moving. The blighter saw me and I flung myself to the ground and he peppered the Post Office wall. The marks were there to prove it until the end of the war. I rushed back and said to my mother, 'I say! Did you hear that German aircraft going over? It shot at me!' My poor mother. I had no sensitivity to the fact that she might faint – but she was too much of a memsahib to do that. She did feel rather dreadful though.

Sergeant Cyril 'Bam' Bamberger
610 and 41 Squadrons, RAF

On August 28, I rejoined 610 Squadron at Biggin Hill having been away at Flying Training School and an Operational Training Unit. Not many of the auxiliary pilots that I'd known pre-war were left. They'd been in operations since the evacuation from Dunkirk and they'd lost three COs. Morale was not particularly high. I went down to the dispersal hut and prepared to take on the German Air Force. The squadron had been landed away somewhere – as they often were. The air raid sounded and I was scrambled on my own for airfield defence. That was my first fight. I took off and I was told by control to climb to 15,000 feet. There was me on my 'Jack Jones' and all I could see was Biggin Hill below me and I was being told that plots of bombers were coming in to bomb the airfield. I was no longer the confident aviator – I hadn't the slightest idea what to expect or what to do and fortunately the raid was diverted to some other airfield and I was told to land.

Squadron Leader Alan Deere
New Zealand pilot, 54 Squadron, RAF

I was caught and blown up while I was taking off from Hornchurch airfield. We were told to get to readiness, then we were told to go to standby and then we were told to return to readiness so we got out of our cockpits and started walking back to dispersal when the phone rang and we were told to scramble as quickly as possible. So we had to get back to the aircraft, strap in and we were caught taking off. The Germans were already overhead and dropping their bombs. I was held up by a new pilot who got himself in the take-off lane and didn't know where to go. By the time I'd got him sorted out, I was last off and I caught the bombs. I was blown sky high – three of us were. I was pretty badly concussed and my Spitfire was blown up and I finished up on the airfield in a heap. My number two finished on the airfield with his wing blown off and the number three wasn't seen for two hours until he reappeared at dispersal, carrying his parachute, having been blown in his aircraft about a mile away. He'd landed the right way up, got out and walked back to the airfield. I was pretty badly concussed. I had all the hair grazed off the top of my scalp – that's why I haven't much hair now. A doctor plastered me up, bandaged me and said, 'Forty-eight hours and report back.'

Squadron Leader Roger Frankland
Sector Controller at RAF Biggin Hill

They attacked us at Biggin Hill at the same time as they attacked Kenley and

Sergeant Cyril 'Bam' Bamberger, pictured after the war.

North Weald. They came in from a direction we didn't expect and we had a lookout on top of the officer's mess. I asked him if he could tell me what type of aircraft were being so rude. 'I don't rightly know, sir,' he said, 'I'm being attacked by a swarm of bees . . . '. His bees were an immediate problem but the German aircraft made pretty good hay on the airfield and destroyed nearly every hangar. One bomb lobbed into the Operations Room just behind me which put paid to any form of fighter control. The Operations Room was full of dust and debris. Afterwards it had to move into other quarters – a butcher's shop in the village, which was rather original. We had miniscule control in the butcher's shop. We could talk to the squadrons but we were reliant on the work done by the Post Office engineers who were mending the landlines 24 hours a day so that we could get the radar information.

Squadron Leader Thomas Gleave
Commanding Officer 253 Squadron, RAF

August 30 – that was a very busy day. Goering was sending in enormous strings of fighters. There must have been 85 aircraft at least. They did a huge sweep, over Rochester, east of Maidstone, out just west of Dover and back. The idea was that we'd look up and see these fighters and have the life scared out of us. Total nonsense.

Sergeant Leslie Batt
238 Squadron, RAF

The Germans pulled a bit of a fast one on us. They sent over a mass of fighters without any bombers. I went to attack one and I thought a steam roller had hit me. I opened the hood and did all that was necessary to bail out – but suddenly I couldn't open my eyes. They were gummed shut. I hadn't been wearing my goggles because I could see better without them. I had to lift my eyelids to be able to see and when I did I saw a dirty great conglomeration of oil hanging off the windscreen and flicking into my eyes. I was at about 20,000 feet and it was getting damn cold so I shut the hood again and the mass of oil landed in my lap. I glided like a brick because my engine had gone and the Hurricane doesn't glide very well. Fortunately, I was over land and when I broke cloud, I was at about 2,000 feet over Selsey Bill. There was no field bigger than a postage stamp so I thought the best thing to do was to land as near as possible to a farmhouse so I could be extricated if I made a cod's head of it. I landed with wheels up in a barley field and I thought I was going to bash my brains out on the reflector sight as my head went forward and hit the head rest as it went back. When I came to a standstill, I unbuckled very fast and ran along the wing and fell, apex over base, into the dry barley. I ran away in case the aircraft blew up and the Home Guard came running across the field with their rifles. Having been covered in oil and landing in the bone-dry earth, I was more the colour of a German pilot than an RAF one so I put my hands in the air as a precaution. They took me to Tangmere where I cleaned myself up with toilet paper as best I could and I made my way to the control tower where the station warrant officer saw me and said, 'Sergeant! Where's your hat?' I told him bluntly where my hat was and I left him absolutely speechless. I was eventually picked up by another member of the squadron and taken back to base. I took the precaution of telling my CO of my comments to the warrant officer. He just smiled.

Squadron Leader Thomas Gleave
Commanding Officer 253 Squadron, RAF
I bought it on August 31. I was looking forward very much to another chance to prove my firing skill. I was always very proud of my firing skill. Unfortunately, that morning, Starr, the commanding officer, had bailed out and was shot in his parachute and he was dead when he landed. I was very angry. I took over the squadron again and we raised seven aircraft that afternoon and we stood by, with myself as the squadron leader.

At 1230 hours, we were ordered off and told to climb to 2,000 feet to await orders and to join up with a squadron from Croydon. When we reached 1,000 feet, this other squadron came flying south in an extraordinary inverted J formation. So I joined up on the shorter side to make a sort of inverted U and off we went. When we got to about 15,000 feet, near Biggin Hill, I looked up and sighted a huge formation of Junkers 88s, flying in several parallel lines, 1,000 feet above us and closing rapidly. We flew within machine gun range of the bombers but the rest of my formation forged ahead, doing nothing about them.

I decided to attack the Junkers 88s from underneath before they could open fire or drop a bomb. So I rocked my wings and pulled up, and I raked number five in the line of 88s. I faked a stall at the top and dived, and I repeated the process on number three. As I turned over at the top of the climb, I saw clouds of white smoke pouring from the port engine of number three. But as I dived to attack number one, I received an incendiary in my starboard tank. My aircraft burst into flames and I attempted to locate the fire, at the same time skidding and losing speed, but the fire increased and I tried to get out. I was unable to move due to burns but then the aeroplane blew up and I was blown clear. Which is why I'm still here.

Lieutenant Arthur Curtis
7th Field Company, Royal Engineers

As I was driving near Tangmere, I could see a Heinkel in trouble with two Spitfires on its tail. The trouble was that the Spitfires were above the Heinkel and when they missed it, they were spreading their bullets down the road where I was driving my small car. So I stopped the car and jumped hastily into a ditch. Fortunately I managed to get away with that, otherwise I would have been shot by the RAF.

Squadron Leader Alan Deere
New Zealand pilot, 54 Squadron, RAF

As August turned into September, we were desperately short of pilots. The aircraft had started coming in again but we were getting pilots who had not flown Spitfires before. They were coming straight to the squadron from their training establishments. We got two young New Zealanders in my flight. Chatting to them I found they'd been six weeks at sea coming over. They were trained on some very outdated aircraft out in New Zealand and they'd been given two trips in a Hurricane before they arrived at the squadron. We were pretty busy, so one of the pilots took them up to see the handling on the Spitfire. Then they went for one solo flight and circuit and after that they were into battle. The answer, of course, is that they didn't last. Those two lasted two trips and they both finished up in Dover hospital. One was pulled out of the Channel, the other landed by parachute.

Pilot Officer Roger Hall
152 Squadron, RAF

In August 1940, they were badly in need of fighter pilots. I was in the army but I had been trained to fly by the RAF and when they asked for people to transfer to fighters, I volunteered. The following day, I was posted to an operational training unit near Chester to train on Spitfires. I was given four days and then I went off to the squadron at RAF Warmwell. I didn't feel very proficient at all. All that I could do was take off, fly and land again.

Flying Officer William David
87 and 213 Squadrons

On the night of August 24, a German bomber had got lost and jettisoned its bombs on London by mistake. Churchill was furious and gave permission for bomber command to bomb Berlin. That made Hitler furious and he ordered Goering to stop bombing our airfields and start bombing London instead. At that time, the Germans had been starting to win. They had realised that the way to attack Fighter Command was to hit them at their bases. So it was very bad luck on the Londoners – but it saved England. It gave the fighter fields a chance to regroup.

Flying Officer Christopher Foxley-Norris
3 Squadron, RAF
If they had continued to attack airfields, communication stations, sector headquarters and so on, for a matter of days, I'm fairly certain we should have lost.

Hans-Ekkehard Bob
German Messerschmitt 109 pilot
There were days when the British air force didn't have a single fighter aircraft that was capable of flying a mission but the German side hadn't realised this. *We had air superiority* – only it wasn't noticed.

Ernest Wedding
German Heinkel 111 bomber pilot
If we had kept on as we started the RAF would have been beaten, but we changed the plan and through that we lost the Battle of Britain. Pure and simple.

Squadron Leader Alan Deere
New Zealand pilot, 54 Squadron, RAF
I think the Germans, so to speak, 'lost their cool'.

The Beginning of the Blitz

To watch London burning from 25,000 feet is a sight one shall never forget.

German intelligence reports in late August were suggesting that British fighter resistance was almost eradicated. The time available for an invasion of Britain was growing short and Hitler wanted to intensify his efforts. For some days, German bombers had been attacking economic targets in major cities and the time had now come to launch a massive attack at Britain's political heart. Such an attack would force Fighter Command to send up all remaining fighters and would irreparably harm civilian morale. The British raid on Berlin had removed any moral obstacle to a devastating strike and on the afternoon of September 7, 1940, 350 German bombers delivered a raid on the docks of East London. The attack took Fighter Command by surprise. The Luftwaffe had been able to fly almost unmolested over the capital and by the end of the day 28 British fighters had been lost. Once night fell, the bombers returned and further destruction was inflicted on the docklands.

Horace Davy
Civilian in London
The Blitz really began on September 7. That was the Saturday afternoon when there was the first heavy daylight raid on London.

Walter Blanchard
Civilian in Barking

I was on duty as an air raid messenger. The red alert had gone and the distant sirens were sounding. You could hear the sound of anti-aircraft fire and the hum of a lot of aircraft engines. And I do mean a lot. My father, a senior warden, said to me, 'Get on your bike, go down to the footbridge, climb up and see if you can see them coming.' I went and looked and for the first time, I had a feeling of cold fear. There were, by my count, more than 600 aircraft in the formation of a huge letter 'I'. These were the German bombers coming by daylight – Heinkels and Dorniers and above them the German fighter escort reeling about.

Hans-Ekkehard Bob
German Messerschmitt 109 pilot

As we approached Greater London, we came across the balloons and then there was the concentration of anti-aircraft weapons. This was simpler for us fighter pilots than for the bombers because we could fly either around or over them. But the bombers had to get right into it, and so you would say to yourself, 'My goodness, that takes some doing, flying into that anti-aircraft fire when the entire sky is black from the detonations!' They had to doggedly head into it and you really did think, 'My goodness, that is really a tough job and these people who fly into these defences are truly worthy of admiration.'

Horace Davy
Civilian in London

The sirens went and we went to a local air raid wardens' post to shelter. I can remember looking up in the sky to see the German bombers and seeing some of our aircraft, the puffs of smoke from the anti-aircraft guns and the barrage balloons which seemed to be pretty useless. I climbed up an exterior fire escape to get a better view and I clearly remember some pinging noises. It was the shrapnel from exploding shells that was beginning to fly around. Then my father shouted at me to get down.

Ballard Berkeley
Special Constable in London

It was a beautiful September evening round about teatime. I was in Park Lane. The sirens had gone and I looked to the east. There was a huge formation of German bombers surrounded by fighters dashing in and out. It was hard to tell if any of our fighters were about. I'm sure they were. That night we were drafted down to the docks to assist. When we arrived – it was chaos. We didn't know where we were and there was nothing we could do. The place was in flames – streets were gone. We wandered around, seeing if we could help. Suddenly there was the most tremendous screaming noise – I didn't know what it was – and I dived into a building damn quick and everybody dived in behind me. We were lying there and somebody started to laugh. I said, 'What the hell are you laughing at, at a time like this?' He said, 'Look up there!' We looked up and realised we'd taken shelter under a huge glass roof. We all bolted out again.

Walter Marshall
Metropolitan Police War Reserve

We looked up and saw these massive aircraft, beginning to manoeuvre, turning in formation over central London. I went back to my police station and the sergeant said, 'You, you and you! There's a van outside. Get in the van!' So we were transferred down to Plaistow. I'd never been there before – and organisation simply didn't exist. There were coppers who had been brought in from other stations, not knowing their way around and not knowing what to do. *No one* knew what to do. All night, we were coming in and going out as directed but nothing like this had ever happened before. At six o'clock the next morning, the sun tried to come out but it couldn't. The intensity of the smoke over the docks wouldn't allow it. It was the nearest I'd ever seen to hell. I couldn't imagine hell being any different.

Kathleen Clayden
Auxiliary Fire Service in London

We got a call to send two pumps to Surrey Docks. Then we had to send two more – and that was how it went on all night. We could do nothing much back at the station so we sat round the table and played cards all night. We waited and waited and waited but the men didn't return and we got worried. We'd sent them out at nine o'clock in the evening and they didn't come back till five o'clock the following afternoon. When they came in, they were soaked to the skin, they smelt terrible and they hadn't even had a cup of tea, some of them. We made them some sandwiches but they were too tired to even eat. One fireman just sat by the fire and he looked at me and said, 'I never thought I'd see you again.' I put this man to bed but then after only two or three hours sleep, they were sent out again.

Flight Lieutenant Duncan Stuart MacDonald
213 Squadron, RAF
To watch London burning from 25,000 feet is a sight one will never forget. The smoke was rising from the docks of London up to about 5,000 feet, and it was following the Thames, right down to the mouth of the Thames, this huge billow of brown smoke, and it was still dense as it sailed slowly across the Channel to France, where it dispersed. It was quite uncanny, to say the least.

Stan Jarvis
Civilian in Plaistow
I saw people walking through Plaistow in refugee columns very similar to those you saw when the Germans invaded the Continent. It's the only time I ever saw that in this country.

Teresa Wilkinson
Air raid warden in West Ham
The people who had been bombed out began walking in our direction down the road. That affected me very much. We took about 30 of them and we put them in the shelter overnight and found them food the next morning. I went round the houses to see if anyone had an article of clothing to spare because all that these people had was what they stood up in. After a while, they began to get very cross because no one was around to do anything for them. I rang the council people but it was a weekend and no one was there. The bombed-out people said, 'If you don't get us away from here, we're coming down to smash your air raid post up!' I notified the police but that evening, we looked out from the post to see these people striding along towards us. I told them, 'It won't do any good to anybody, damaging our equipment. It only means we won't be able to help anybody else.' Just then, the siren went and they all turned tail and went into the shelter. On Monday, thank goodness, we found some help and buses came to take them away. It might seem an ungrateful reaction but they were terrified; they'd lost everything and they didn't know what to do.

William Gray
Milkman in London
I'd got as far as Stratford Broadway and all I could see was smoke. Queen Mary's Hospital was in ruins. There were planes by the hundreds up there. I went to my house but there was nobody there. My mother got home after the

THE BATTLE OF BRITAIN

raid stopped and she said, 'I don't know where your father is.' A little later a copper came and said, 'Your father's been killed. He was in the heavy rescue and that's received a direct hit. I'm sorry but he's gone.' Then, about a fortnight later, another copper came to the door and said, 'We've found your father. He's in a hospital at Watford with a crushed back.' He'd had no identification on him and they'd taken him to Watford. He was in hospital for a few months.

Horace Davy
Civilian in London
When the all-clear sounded, we came out of the shelter. It was still early evening but we looked across Mitre Square towards the east and the sky was blood red. We went home for a while but the sirens sounded again that night. From then until May 1941, there was bombing most of the time.

Pilot Officer Roger Hall
152 Squadron, RAF
The fatal thing that Goering did was to start to bomb London. It had been touch and go whether Fighter Command could carry on existing, never mind hacking the Germans down. But when the Germans started to bomb London, they desisted from bombing the airfields. And this really, from Fighter Command's point of view, was an absolute miracle.

Hans-Ekkehard Bob
German Messerschmitt 109 pilot
We had been bombing the airfields. In terms of warfare it was both understandable and important. But once London was being attacked, we told ourselves that this was something that we wanted to have less to do with.

Flight Sergeant George Unwin
19 Squadron, RAF
I spotted a lone Dornier going home that afternoon so I went after him. He had a rear gunner in a dustbin hanging below the fuselage and you had to fix him first and then close in for the aircraft. I could see him shooting at me and I gave him a burst and shut him up. At least I thought I had. As I closed right in again, I suddenly saw the rear gunner shooting back at me with little red sparks. I carried on firing for quite a long burst, leaning forward to the gun-sight which was in the middle of a piece of bullet resistant glass. Suddenly a hole appeared in this glass directly in front of my face. I thought, 'Good God.

I must be dead!' but there was no blood. I was covered in smoke and I thought I was on fire. So I whipped the hood back, undid my straps and started to get out. I was halfway out of the cockpit when I suddenly saw that the smoke wasn't black and I could smell that it was glycol. So I strapped myself back in again, left the hood open and started looking for a field to land in. I got down to a thousand feet, dropped the undercarriage and did a forced landing in a field with a few cows in it. I hadn't even got out of the cockpit before an army jeep with a young subaltern and two soldiers with fixed bayonets came roaring through the gate in a jeep. When I got back to Duxford, they found a bullet at the bottom of the cockpit. It had gone through the glass before my eyes and just dropped to the floor.

Big Wing

It all seemed a lot of organisation and not a lot of result.

The assault on London marked not only the beginning of the Blitz – night raids continued almost every night for the next eight months – but also the beginning of Fighter Command's recovery. The relentless attacks on airfields had ended and Dowding's fighter squadrons were able to regroup. In the days after September 7, the Luftwaffe mounted further daylight raids on London. The raids consisted of 300–400 aircraft in two to three waves and in response, Keith Park, commander of 11 Group, began sending up his squadrons in pairs. The Luftwaffe, believing Fighter Command to be on the point of collapse, was astonished to find itself confronted by more aircraft than ever before. During this period, controversy raged over Douglas Bader's 'Big Wing' theory. Bader, flying from Duxford with 12 Group – away from the main 'battlefield' – had come up with the idea of sending huge formations of fighters up to meet the enemy. The idea, vehemently opposed by Park, was put into practice by Leigh-Mallory, commander of 12 Group.

Group Captain Frederick Winterbotham
Deputy to Chief of Secret Intelligence Service with special responsibility for the security of Ultra messages
There was a very strong faction in the air force led by the commander of 12 Group, Leigh-Mallory, who began complaining to the government and to the Secretary of State for Air, that Dowding was carrying on the Battle of Britain

all wrong. Leigh-Mallory wanted us to send up enormous formations to tackle the Germans but Leigh-Mallory did not get Ultra, and he did not know that the object of Goering's raids was to get us all up into the air.

Flight Lieutenant Frederick Rosier
Commanding officer 229 Squadron, RAF
The main problem was the conflict between Leigh-Mallory and Keith Park. And Dowding's reluctance to do anything about it. I think Dowding should have banged their heads together or got rid of one of them. And I know who I would have got rid of. Leigh Mallory. He was quite wrong and Park was right.

Flying Officer Jeffrey Quill
Vickers Chief Test Pilot and 65 Squadron, RAF
To get a wing airborne was a hell of a business. A wing was two or three squadrons – 36 aircraft. It took a long time to taxi out and get formed up in the air. It was rather a ponderous business. The point is that in 11 Group, during August and September 1940, there was no time for that sort of thing. It was alright for 12 Group further north. They had a little time to form up and they'd come down with their big wings of Hurricanes in support of 11 Group, but 11 Group was the frontline of defence and we had no time so we never operated as wings. We were quite lucky to get a whole squadron airborne in time.

Flight Sergeant George Unwin
19 Squadron, RAF
In 12 Group, we were perfectly situated for the Big Wing. We had Duxford and Fowlmere three miles to the west. Three squadrons of Hurricanes took off from Duxford and as they went past us at Fowlmere, our two squadrons took off. Then we did a 90° turn to the left and we were on course for London, in perfect position.

Pilot Officer Dennis Armitage
266 Squadron, RAF
I flew on the 12 Group fighter wings from Duxford under Dougie Bader. There was plenty of organisation and leadership but not enough enemy. The leading squadron might well get into action but very often the other squadrons would do very little. Personally I was not in favour of the idea; the first problem was that we took so long to get to the job. By the time five squadrons had got off from Duxford and got down into the battle area, all we usually saw was the

back end of the enemy disappearing over the Channel. So it was only Dougie Bader and the Poles in front who really got stuck into them if at all. It all seemed a lot of organisation and not a lot of result.

Fred Roberts
NCO *served as armourer with 19 Squadron, RAF*
Even some of the pilots involved in the Big Wing didn't like it. They felt they were losing their individuality. They didn't like it at all.

Flight Sergeant George Unwin
19 Squadron, RAF
As part of the Wing, we really *did* make a difference. Apart from the number of aircraft we shot down, the effect on the moral of the German pilots was tremendous. They had been told that we didn't have many aircraft left – and suddenly they came across 60 aircraft in one gaggle, coming to meet them. But the number of times we weren't alerted soon enough was fantastic. Whether that was due to the rivalry . . . I don't know.

The Luftwaffe Resisted – September 15, 1940

On September 15, 1940, we knew there'd been a monumental battle but it wasn't at all clear that we had won.

At a meeting of his commanders-in-chief in Berlin on September 14, Hitler accepted that air superiority had not yet been achieved – due to bad weather – but he stressed that it must still be won before invasion was attempted. Preparation for *Operation Sealion* would continue but a new date would be set. This was Goering's cue for a final great effort. After eleven o'clock on the next morning, massive German formations crossed the Kent coast. As they flew towards London, they were engaged by numerous British squadrons, including a Big Wing of five squadrons from Duxford. The bombers scattered and their bombs fell aimlessly. A second attack of almost 600 aircraft arrived over Kent and Sussex in the afternoon. Twenty-eight squadrons came up to meet them. Some of the squadrons engaged with the bombers as they flew on, two or three squadrons at a time; the majority of the squadrons were waiting for the bombers as they reached London, by which time the escorting 109s were running out of fuel. On arrival over London, cloud prevented the bombers from finding their targets and once again their bombs caused little significant damage. By the end of the day, 56 German aircraft had been shot down, as against 29 British fighters. Fighter Command had not been defeated. On September 17, Hitler postponed the invasion indefinitely. The plans were never revived.

Group Captain Frederick Winterbotham
Deputy to Chief of Secret Intelligence Service with special responsibility for the security of Ultra messages

On September 15, Goering was going to have his final whack at London. He ordered practically the whole of the bombers that were left in France to come over and bomb London. Ultra had good advance information about that. Churchill was told about it and he went down to the headquarters of 11 Group to watch the battle and when this vast German formation came over in the daytime, Dowding sent up every Spitfire that he'd got. This time, he hadn't got to bother about keeping the air force intact. They completely shocked the vast German air fleet and the Germans just turned round, dropped their bombs and fled. The Ultra which came from Goering almost burnt the paper. He ordered them to turn round, refuel their aeroplanes and go back and bomb London. Churchill, seeing the enormous formations that were coming over on the plotting, turned to Keith Park and said, 'What reserves have you got?' Park said, 'Perhaps you'd better ask the Commander-in-Chief, sir.' So Dowding was telephoned at Stanmore and asked, 'What reserves have you got?' Dowding's remark, 'I have no reserves, sir, every aeroplane is in the sky,' put old Churchill in his place.

Flight Lieutenant Gerald Edge
605 and 253 Squadrons, RAF

We took off and climbed up and we saw this huge formation coming in. We were ideally placed to take them head-on. We got into position and turned into attack. We dived in and opened fire. When you had a bit of experience, it was amazing how close you could get and still get away. I opened on the third one away from the centre. He swung away. I don't think he could believe I was coming at him, straight out of the sun. I then shot at three or four on the line, rolled off and went down. As I was pulling out, the bombers jettisoned their bombs and turned for home. One bomb went slowly past my wingtip, feet away. It was going slowly because I was going down at nearly 400 miles and hour and the bomb hadn't got its speed up yet.

Sergeant Charlton Haw
504 Squadron, RAF

It was such a busy day – it went on all day long. That was their biggest effort to try and bomb London into submission. 504 Squadron lost seven that day. Ray Holmes shot a Dornier down – which crashed in the grounds of Buckingham Palace – before he was shot down and bailed out. His parachute wrapped round the chimney pot of a house and he fell off the roof and landed in a dustbin. Fortunately the lid was off. Basil Bush had a cannon shell in his windscreen and his face was covered with glass. Pilot Officers Frisby, Wendle and Gurteen were all killed that day. There were more Germans about and we seemed to get into them more than we had done in the past. I tried to go up on my own – somebody had brought a Hurricane back but he'd pulled the quick release off the harness so I couldn't take it up. I had to wait till they all came back and then we all went off again in the afternoon.

Flight Sergeant George Unwin
19 Squadron, RAF
I got lost from my squadron and when I looked, there was not a soul in the sky. Then in the distance, I saw some ack-ack and I went towards it and I saw these waves upon waves of German bombers coming in. It was a fascinating sight. There seemed to be hundreds of them and I forgot about anything else. Suddenly, I found aeroplanes whizzing all around me. I'd flown smack into the middle of the fighter escort. Without thinking. Damn fool. I went into a tight turn and shot at several 109s as they went through my sights – and I actually shot two of them down. I got the first one and he bailed out. When I went to sight the next one, the light in my reflector sight failed. The bloody bulb failed. I was still in a tight turn and I shot the second one down without a sight. His petrol tank went up. It was probably the turn that saved me – the Messerschmitt couldn't turn like a Spitfire. It frightened me – I was all on my own in the middle of I don't know how many Messerschmitts but I didn't get a hole in me. I must have had a guardian angel with me.

Flying Officer Hugh Dundas
616 Squadron, RAF
We got in amongst this very large number of 109s. It was the biggest clash of fighters that I ever saw, before or since. It was a real whirlaround and the squadron claimed three or four.

Pilot Officer Thomas Neil
249 Squadron, RAF
September 15 was a very special day. 249 Squadron, North Weald, had taken off in the morning and we'd intercepted about 30 Dorniers over Maidstone but we hadn't done very well. I certainly didn't do well. I shot at something but nothing happened. Then at about three o'clock in the afternoon, we were sent off again. We intercepted another group of Dorniers over Maidstone and

this time everything went swimmingly. I found myself behind a Dornier and as I was firing at it, the crew suddenly bailed out. I was so close behind it that as one of the bodies came out, I ducked in the aeroplane, thinking, 'My God, he's going to hit me.' Their parachutes were undeveloped, they fell out. And then I remember breaking away and being attacked by some German fighters. They set about me furiously and I defended myself. And then, as so often happened in combat, you're surrounded by aeroplanes like bees round a honey pot, and suddenly everything is quiet and there are no aeroplanes. It happens instantaneously.

Then I saw another Dornier flying across my bows, about a mile away, which I immediately followed. It was going down the estuary, by this time we'd got up roughly over Gravesend. It took some time for me to catch it up because it was going in a slight dive. Eventually I caught it up and I suddenly found that a Spitfire was to my left. And thereafter it was fairly straightforward, a single aeroplane, on its own, two of us, we took it in turns to fire, it went down and down and down, out to sea, across a convoy of ships, because there were masses of convoys in those days, out to sea. I thought, 'Oh God, we're going to lose this one, he's going to get home.' The Spitfire and I had run out of ammunition but we flew alongside it. I could read all the letters on the cockpit, and I could see the damage that had been done. And then it got slower and slower and slower and the nose came up and up and up, and suddenly the tail hit the sea and it splashed down. I felt satisfaction – total satisfaction. The pair of us flew around and usually when an aeroplane hits the sea, it goes down and then comes to the surface. We flew around and nobody surfaced. As we flew back over the convoy, the ships all blew their whistles – I could see steam coming from the whistles. I flew back to North Weald and gave my report in and that was that.

Three days later, a couple of senior officers arrived and my squadron commander, John Grandy called me forward and said, 'These blokes want to talk to you.' They said that the chap in the Spitfire said that two of the 109s that I'd shot at were destroyed. They said that the incident had so much publicity value, would I like to do a broadcast? So I said, 'Of course.' The Spitfire pilot turned out to be a chap called Pilot Officer Eric Locke. He was a tiny fellow from Shropshire. So we were invited down to the BBC on October 25 to make our broadcast, and we disappeared in the bowels of the place. We had a bit of a script but the director said couldn't we ham it up a bit because the 40 million people listening didn't want to be told something that sounded like the stock prices. At which point Eric Locke just went into shock because he suddenly realised what he was doing. He could hardly get the words out.

Anyway, we made the broadcast. Then we were asked to stay on in the evening and make another broadcast for the overseas programme and then I didn't get out of the BBC until twelve o'clock at night. When I got out I found somebody had pinched my car. I didn't know what the heck to do. Eventually I went to Scotland Yard and I learned that they had taken it. I said, 'Why mine? There must be millions of cars, why did you pinch mine?' When I eventually got back to the squadron, I said, 'Anybody listen to it?' And nobody had. Such was fame.

Many, many years later, when my grandsons were saying, 'What did you do in the war, grandfather?' I rang up the BBC and said, 'Please could I have a tape of my broadcast?' And I got a very nice letter back saying that they only kept things which were worthwhile and they destroyed all the others . . .

Pilot Officer Tony Bartley
92 Squadron, RAF
September 15, I was flying. I did five sorties on that day when Goering just gave up. They said, 'We just can't beat them.' They gave up the huge onslaught because their losses were so terrific. Then they called off the invasion.

Group Captain Frederick Winterbotham
Deputy to Chief of Secret Intelligence Service with special responsibility for the security of Ultra messages
Through Ultra, we got a signal from Hitler giving permission to dismantle the air loading bays in Holland. Now that seemed a fairly harmless sort of operation, but as we knew exactly how the invasion was going to take place and we knew that they wouldn't invade unless they had all this proper air support, it was tantamount to saying the invasion was off. I sent that signal sent straight through to Churchill and that very evening Churchill ordered a conference down in the room under the Foreign Office. And I was commanded to go along with my boss to explain it to the chiefs of staff. It was one of the most extraordinary moments of my life.

Down there were all the chiefs of staff, a few secretaries, the Prime Minister, General Ismay, my chief and myself. Churchill said, 'Well, gentlemen we'd like to know what this signal really means.' I was called upon because I'd studied the whole thing. I pointed out that if these loading bays were dismantled it meant that they would not have their proper air support and that in fact Hitler had given up the idea of invasion. So Churchill looked at me, and then he turned to the Chief of Air Staff. 'May I have your views?' he asked and Cyril Newall said, 'That is entirely our view. With the dismantling of these, the invasion is off.' Churchill sat back, smiled, pulled out a big cigar and lit it. He said, 'Well gentlemen, let's go and see what is happening upstairs.' There was a terrific blitz going on upstairs. The whole of Carlton House Terrace was in flames, and the bombs were dropping all around. Churchill came up smoking his cigar and put on his tin hat. In front of the door of the underground offices was a concrete screen, and everybody tried to prevent him walking out because there was so much metal flying about but he went out and I can see him today with his hands on his stick, smoking his cigar. 'My God,' he said, 'we'll get the buggers for this.'

Ernest Wedding
German Heinkel 111 bomber pilot
September 15 was the biggest onslaught where we lost a hell of a lot of aircraft. That was the pinnacle of the Battle of Britain. After that everything tailed off and units were withdrawn to be made ready for the invasion of Russia. It was a feather in the cap of the RAF and especially of the high command of the RAF, of Dowding and of Churchill because they hadn't lost their nerve.

Ronald Melville
Private Secretary to Chief of Air Staff at the Air Ministry
Nowadays we celebrate September 15 as Battle of Britain Day but when the Battle of Waterloo was fought, Wellington knew at once he had won. On September 15, 1940, we knew there'd been a monumental battle but it wasn't at all clear that we had won. That only gradually filtered through.

Hans-Ekkehard Bob
German Messerschmitt 109 pilot
I do not consider that Germany lost the Battle of Britain, I think that the end result was neutral. Nobody won. We Germans didn't manage to maintain our air superiority over Great Britain but giving every due recognition to the bravery on both sides and to the strategic possibilities which existed – one could not speak of a victory. *Unless* you want to say that the British won because the Germans did not carry out a landing in England.

One could argue about *why* this landing was not carried out. Some people say that Hitler had a soft spot for England, that he was an admirer of England and that he didn't want to humiliate the English. The Germans and the

English are a related people, and when kinsfolk fight with one another, there can never be a happy ending, all that will ensue is ill will.

For me, the Battle of Britain was a battle which arose as a result of the situation for which both countries should take a heavy burden of responsibility. Taking everything into account, it is my opinion that in that battle there were neither victors nor vanquished – only losers. We both lost. England lost its vast dominions, its world supremacy, and Germany lost its dignity and its national identity.

Ernest Wedding
German Heinkel 111 bomber pilot
The Battle of Britain was a complete loss to the German air force. It was a victory for the RAF.

The Battle Plays Out

*When we were flying the 109s with bombs on board, when the bomb
had been set to 'live', if there were any technical errors, it meant that
the plane would suddenly explode right there in the air.*

As autumn drew on, the daylight bombing raids petered out. A few
were still launched – 58 Heinkel 111 bombers attacked the Bristol
Aeroplane Company factory at Filton, Bristol on September 25 – but the
Luftwaffe could no longer afford the substantial losses. New tactics were
introduced. Large formations of Messerschmitt 109s were sent over
southern England at high altitude in an attempt to lure British fighters into
the air. Other 109s were adapted to fly as fighter bombers with a 250kg
bomb slung underneath the fuselage. Neither of these measures troubled
Fighter Command unduly. Germany had failed to win air superiority.
Hitler had been successfully resisted for the first time and the battlefield
moved to the night skies.

Pilot Officer Percival Leggett
615, 245 and 46 Squadrons, RAF
At the same time that Hitler began the night blitz on London, he also went in
for a policy of formations of 12 to 15 Messerschmitt 109s, many of them
carrying a single bomb. These formations were sent over very high – at least
30,000 feet and they'd come across, drop their bombs almost anywhere and
then turn round and scurry off for home in the hope of picking off an RAF
aircraft on the way. The bombs weren't aimed at anything. The object was
simply to make sure that we went up to get at them. The bombs were just a bit
of bait.

Heinz Lange
German Messerschmitt 109 pilot
I made 30 missions in a Messerschmitt 109E with bombs, a new weapon. We didn't like transporting bombs at all. We had no exact instrument in order to take aim when dropping the bomb – we only had a line at the cabin window at 45° and when this was horizontal, we dropped the bombs. We couldn't exactly aim and I'm sure that mostly we hit fields and no military targets.

Hans-Ekkehard Bob
German Messerschmitt 109 pilot
When we were flying the 109s with bombs on board, when the bomb had been set to 'live', if there were any technical errors, it meant that the plane would suddenly explode right there in the air. A situation like that is terrifying. You can imagine it, you have a comrade or a friend flying alongside you, and then suddenly his plane dissolves into bits – if you witness that, it shakes you to the core. A crazy situation. Those are situations that really get to you.

Pilot Officer Percival Leggett
615, 245 and 46 Squadrons, RAF
On my third scramble, I encountered a formation of 109s with bombs. At the time, the policy was that Hurricanes would operate at about 15,000 feet and in the absence of any particular incoming raid, we'd be put on the Maidstone patrol line with the object of intercepting any bomber raids that did come through. We flew in a tight formation of 12 aircraft in vics of three aircraft, line astern. We'd climb up in that formation to the patrol line whereupon the two tail aircraft would climb up and watch our tails from two or three thousand feet above. We relied on them to give warning of attack. That's exactly what happened on my third sortie. We'd been on the patrol line for ten minutes when the controller announced that there were enemy aircraft in the vicinity. At that moment, one of our formation called 'Aircraft above at twelve o'clock!' At the same moment, one of our tail-end Charlies called out that there were 'Snappers astern!' Snappers was the code word for enemy fighters. They dived down on us and the flight commander called, 'Break port!' which meant that we had to pull the aircraft into a tight turn into the incoming attack on the port side. I hadn't got my oxygen mask properly tightened and when I turned, the mask pulled away from my face. I'd had my goggles up on my forehead and they pulled down over my eyes. It was all a bit hectic. The next thing I saw was an aircraft going down in flames. I couldn't

see who or what it was. After a bit, the flight commander called, 'Reform!' which we did until we were told by control to 'Pancake!' which meant return to base and land. That was my first encounter with front line warfare. It seemed like several hours – in fact I daresay it was several seconds. Exciting enough.

Pilot Officer Roger Hall
152 Squadron, RAF

The Germans more or less put the Filton Aircraft Factory out of action on September 25. We were rather taken by surprise on that day. I was part of B flight and we were sitting on the ground, waiting for the scramble when we looked up and saw a massive, great phalanx of aircraft coming over us. We'd had absolutely no warning but we took off regardless. This was the first occasion that I was in action and there were just four of us against 80 or 90 bombers with an escort of about 20 fighters. We caught up with them round about Yeovil and all we could do was to attack them head-on and hope for the best. The bombers were round about 15,000 feet and we got up to them quite quickly, wheeled round and attacked. We were closing on them head-on at a combined speed of 600 miles an hour and then we'd break away underneath and come round again and have another shot. The German fighter escort didn't interfere at all. You see, they'd come all the way from Cherbourg and they didn't want to use up any more fuel than they had to and they saw just four Spitfires and didn't think it was worth wading into us.

When we turned in, we formed an echelon and I was watching the leader to see what he was going to do. I had my goggles on to prevent splinters from the Perspex hitting me as I attacked. My goggles were a bit misty and I couldn't see very well and so I put the goggles up and I saw my numbers one, two and three going down but by then it was too late for me to go down. I couldn't get down quick enough – I'd have hit the Heinkel 111. So I pulled the stick back very sharply and went up over it. When you exert a lot of pressure on the control, you black out. All the blood goes from your head and you can't see anything at all. All your faculties are there but you can't see. Well, as I went up, I couldn't see and the aircraft stalled and spun and I was in a state because I was still depressing my firing button and the bullets were going into the ground. I took my finger off the button and tried to get out of the spin. I had a lot of trouble because I wasn't 'all there' quite frankly.

By the time I was out of the spin, there was nothing else in the sky. This is what happens. One minute the sky's full of aeroplanes, the next minute there's nothing there except you. I was on my own. So I flew back to the aerodrome and by that time most of the others had come back and that was that. By that time, A flight had taken off as well. They reached the German formation after they had bombed Filton and killed a lot of people but they chivvied the Germans on the way back and I believe they shot down five. We lost two. One was a New Zealand pilot called Sergeant Holland who shot a Junkers 88 down and followed it to watch it crash but shortly before it hit the ground, the rear gunner took a shot at him and shot him down. They both crashed in the same place.

Sergeant Charlton Haw
504 *Squadron, RAF*

The Germans came back to Filton on September 27 but this time, we were waiting for them. They got the shock of their lives. There was a clear blue sky and they came in below us and I picked one off, came in behind it and shot it in the wing root. It went down in flames and I started looking for something else when I smelt burning. A bullet had hit the oil tank and the engine seized up. There were forty 110s still around so I thought I'd better make it look as though I'd had it and I put the Hurricane into a spin. I kept it in a spin until I was sure that they'd leave me alone. When I was low enough, I left the wheels up and put the flaps down and landed in a field. There was a chap doing his farm work and he was quite cross because he didn't know if I was English or not. Then I put my parachute on my back and walked to the road where I met a commercial traveller who took me to the nearest pub. I couldn't phone the squadron because all the lines were down with the bombing. I was entertained royally with lots of beer and sandwiches and I didn't get back to Temple Mead Station in Bristol until half past eleven that night, having been shot down at ten in the morning.

Flight Lieutenant Duncan Stuart MacDonald
213 *Squadron, RAF*

In October, our Hurricanes were moved out of Tangmere to make way for Spitfires – we weren't considered quite fast enough. But before that, we were doing a patrol very high up and we got into a dogfight with some 109s. My whole squadron got split up and I chased a 109, but not close enough to fire at him. He went scuttling off and I scuttled off after him, trying to catch him, trying to catch him, trying to catch him – never did. There was a solid cloud layer below at 5,000 feet, and I thought, I'd better get down and see where I am. We had started somewhere around Beachy Head. So I came down below cloud level, and I couldn't recognise where I was, couldn't recognise the terrain at all. And then I suddenly realised the transport was driving along the right-hand side of the road. There had been a tremendous high wind from the north and I'd crossed the Channel. It was as simple as that. It just goes to show how narrow the Channel is.

Pilot Officer James Goodson
American pilot, 43 Squadron, RAF
Some pundits have decided that the end of October was the end of the Battle of Britain. Nobody told us about it and we didn't notice that it had finished. We kept right on flying. But as the Germans switched to night bombing, we didn't have so much to do in the day time. And then we went back to convoy patrols and then gradually to fighter sweeps over the Pas de Calais area.

Aftermath

I don't think we were conscious of making history until
Mr Churchill made his speech about 'The Few'.

Towards the end of November, Dowding and Park were removed from their posts. Dowding had been due to retire for some time but the manner of his dismissal distressed his supporters. He received a telephone call informing him that 'The Air Council has no further work for you.' His opposition to Leigh-Mallory's Big Wings and his alleged lack of time for the pilots were cited as reasons for his dismissal. He was replaced by the Deputy Chief of Air Staff, Sholto Douglas. Park was replaced by his old adversary Leigh-Mallory.

Flying Officer William David
87 and 213 Squadrons
Dowding and Park were both sacked in a very nasty way. Dowding's office was taken over by Sholto Douglas before he had time to clear his books out. We were livid. We couldn't believe it happened because we loved Dowding and Park. They won the Battle of Britain. The others were hangers-on. Leigh-Mallory was a very dangerous piece of work.

Flight Lieutenant Hugh Ironside
Personal Assistant to Air Chief Marshal Sir Hugh Dowding
It was a sad day when 'Stuffy' left Fighter Command. That's about all you can say. I left too, at my own request. The fellow that took over – Sholto Douglas – I didn't like him anyway.

Pilot Officer Thomas Neil
249 Squadron, RAF

Sholto Douglas was somebody I didn't really care for – he was very much a politician. I remember him coming to see us at North Weald, and in the course of our discussion he said, 'What do you think about flying a Spitfire?' I thought I'd misheard him. I said, 'What?' He said, 'How do you like flying a Spitfire?' We weren't flying Spitfires at all and I thought, 'This man's mad, he really is.'

Pilot Officer Antony Thompson
85 and 249 Squadrons, RAF

Air Vice Marshal Sholto Douglas was a pig of a man. At least I thought so. I'd had a quick burst at a Dornier one day before it went back into cloud and I never saw it again. Unfortunately, it had jettisoned its bombs right down Clacton High Street. The upshot was that I got the most imperial bloody rocket from Sholto Douglas. He gave me a terrible raspberry on the telephone for allowing the Dornier to drop his bombs on Clacton High Street. 'Well sir, I'm afraid I can't find him in cloud,' I said. 'It doesn't matter! You should have shot him down!' 'I did shoot him but he went straight back into cloud.' 'Nonsense!' he said, 'You should have stopped him!' What a pig of a bloody man, I thought. I carried him as a passenger years later when I was a pilot with BOAC. I went to the back to speak to him. He was with his wife, who was very pleasant. I said, 'The last time we spoke, sir, you pulled rank on me!' 'Hmm,' he grunted. 'You were an Air Vice Marshal and I was a Pilot Officer.' He grunted again. His wife said, 'Sholto! The captain's trying to be pleasant. At least try and talk to him decently!' I'd won a point at last.

Flying Officer Roland Beamont
87 Squadron, RAF

The Battle of Britain was a battle *for* Britain. We were young fighter pilots – scarcely schoolboys – but the cockpits of our fighter aeroplanes were all that stood between invasion of this country by the Germans. We'd seen what they'd done to the nationals abroad. We lived in this country and some of us lived within sight of our airfields. I used to fly often to Portsmouth and look down on my home, where my family was, in Chichester. Tangmere was being bombed ten miles away. It was all a very personal thing. When you got into your aeroplane, you felt the fears that everybody fears when going off to fight but overpowering all that was this feeling that if you and all your chaps didn't do your damnedest on every operation then all these Germans were going to be flooding over your country, your homes and destroying everything that was worth preserving. That was what it was all about.

Flying Officer Hugh Dundas
616 Squadron, RAF

I don't think we were conscious of making history until Mr Churchill made his speech about 'The Few'. We all puffed our chests out a bit then and thought how important we were but until then I don't think we'd thought about it.

Flight Sergeant George Unwin
19 Squadron, RAF

When Churchill said, 'Never has so much been owed by so many to so few,' my Commanding Officer reckoned he was referring to our unpaid mess bills.

Flight Lieutenant Duncan Stuart MacDonald
213 Squadron, RAF

I once asked Brian Kingcome, a very famous fighter pilot from Biggin Hill, what he thought about the whole affair. And he said, 'Well, looking back on it, if I'd known we were making history, I'd have fought much harder . . . '.

Pilot Officer Irving Smith
New Zealand pilot with 151 Squadron, RAF

About 10 or 15 years ago, I asked an RAF doctor whether he had ever identified any physical factors common in people who did superlatively well in fighters and he said that there were two. One was exceptional long sight and the second was a very high tolerance of G forces. Both those things were true in my case.

Flying Officer Peter Matthews
1 Squadron RAF

During the Battle of Britain, I shot down an Me110 over Sussex. The pilot and gunner both got out and they were all right. They both live in America now and I had a letter from someone who said, 'Would you like to get in touch with them?' I wrote back and said no, thank you. I do go to America fairly frequently but I couldn't see any point. We haven't got anything in common any more.

Ulrich Steinhilper
German Messerschmitt 109 pilot

Very recently a young English man wanted to present me with the remains of a Hurricane, which most probably I had shot down in September 1940. I said,

'Young man, I don't want to keep it. In that same raid I killed one of your pilots.' And he said, 'The man from this Hurricane, he bailed out.' But I said, 'Maybe you do not understand, but I'm very aware that in this war I killed a few people.'

Pilot Officer James Goodson
American pilot, 43 Squadron, RAF
After the war a reunion of Luftwaffe pilots was held and Adolf Galland asked Bob Stanford Tuck, Douglas Bader and myself to attend. Doug Bader refused. For him the Hun were still the Hun. Eventually he agreed, saying, 'All right, I'll come over but don't ask me to be polite to the bastards.' So I said to Galland, 'He'll come but I'm not sure you'll really want him because he said he's not going to be polite.' Galland said, 'Tell him we don't want him to be polite. We just want him to come.' So we went over. It was held at the Hofbrauhaus in Munich and we arrived at this beer cellar and Doug waddled up to a balcony and looked down over a beer cellar and there were at least a thousand ex-Luftwaffe pilots below him. Doug looked down and said, 'My God. I had no idea we left so many of the bastards alive.'

Richard Seddon
Official War Artist
The idea for Paul Nash's famous painting, *The Battle of Britain* came from a little nineteenth-century French lithograph of a storm over Paris. In the lithograph, Paris was laid out below with the Seine winding away into the horizon just as Paul had laid out London with the Thames winding away to the sea. And in the sky, which occupied most of the French lithograph, was a thunderstorm with clouds and flashes of lightning. All Paul had done was to take this literally and put smoke trails where the thunderstorm was. And of course, he'd done it much bigger in oils.

The first time I saw it, Paul said, What do you think about that?' I duly admired it and he said 'I've got one puzzle and that is about these smoke trails. Are they always white? Have you seen any?' 'Yes,' I said, 'I've seen a lot of smoke trails.' He had seen them in photographs, perhaps, but he'd never seen them himself. 'What colour are they?' he asked. 'White, usually,' I said. 'Are they always white?' 'No, sometimes they're white against a blue sky. Sometimes they're dark against a blue sky. And sometimes they're dark against a cloud. It depends what the trail is – a plane might be giving out vapour or it might be giving out smoke.' So he said, 'Show me!' And I did a little trail. I carefully mixed the colour and painted a greyish trail. And when I saw the picture on exhibition in London, there was my trail still there.

Robert Grant-Ferris
Member of Parliament for North St Pancras and Fighter Pilot

One day in the autumn of 1940, when I was at group headquarters at Preston, I received a great privilege. It was a telegram from the Prime Minister and it was worded like this, 'Request you make first speech Thursday.' And that was his invitation to me to move the loyal address at the opening of the new session of Parliament six weeks after the termination of the Battle of Britain. I happened to tell the ADC and he said, 'Well you must go at once!' So there I was, trying to put my speech together and as I was walking about the House of Commons scratching my head, I ran into Harold Nicolson who is known nowadays as a great writer and diplomat. And he said to me, 'I've got the best peroration you could possibly have to finish your speech tomorrow because I hear you're going to move the address.' And I said, 'Well thank you very much I've been trying to make my own but I'm very glad to have somebody who can do one very much better.' And he said he'd give it to me the next day. Well, when the next day came, he told me he couldn't find it. So I said, 'Oh well, never mind,' and I had to go on and make my own conclusion to the speech which wasn't very good. At least I didn't think so. And then the next day just as I was leaving for my unit, Nicolson came to me and he said, 'I've found it, here it is!' And he passed a slip of paper into my hands. I have that slip of paper now – I've always kept it because when I read it, it was quite the most incredible thing. It was written in 1737 – over 200 years before the Battle of Britain – by Thomas Gray, famous for the elegy and the translation from the Latin goes like this:

The day will come when thou shalt lift thine eyes
To watch a long drawn battle of the skies
And aged peasants too amazed for words,
Stare at the flying fleets of wondrous birds.

And England, so long mistress of the seas
Where winds and waves confess her sovereignty,
Her ancient triumphs yet on high shall bear
And reign the sovereign of the conquered air.

Well, if I could have stood up and said that at the time, it would have been electric and of course Churchill would have been absolutely delighted. Everybody would have been delighted. But it wasn't to be. It is surely the best peroration that never was made.

Part Three
THE BLITZ

The Battle of Britain and the Blitz were distinct events in the minds of the British public but for Hitler, there was no such distinction. They were part of his concerted effort to bring Britain to heel – whether by invasion, negotiation or popular uprising. The Blitz, he believed, would have such a terrible effect on civilian morale that the government would be forced to sue for peace before collapsing under the weight of revolution. At the start of the Blitz, therefore, the bombs fell predominantly on London. From September 7, the capital was attacked on 57 consecutive nights. In November, when Hitler realised that Britain was not about to concede defeat, his strategy changed. He began to plan for an invasion of the Soviet Union – which he believed would result in victory by the spring of 1941. In the meantime, he ordered the Blitz to be widened to target the major industrial and port cities. His intention was to shatter Britain's economy so that when he returned his full attention to Britain, the country would offer little resistance. This phase of the Blitz began with the horrifying attack on Coventry on the night of November 14, 1940, when 568 people were killed and the entire city centre was eradicated. Attacks followed on Southampton, Birmingham, Liverpool, Manchester and Sheffield, amongst others. On the night of December 29, London received its most ferocious raid yet. From February onwards, the attacks on the ports intensified, with huge raids on Swansea, Plymouth, Portsmouth, Bristol, Belfast, Clydebank and Hull.

The Night Skies

The anti-aircraft fire gave the civilian population a feeling that something was being done.

At the beginning of the Blitz, the Germans were flying the same heavy bombers that they had flown during the Battle of Britain; the Dornier 17, the Heinkel 111 and the Junkers 88. The outdated Dornier was phased out at the end of 1940 and Messerschmitt Bf-110s and Stuka dive-bombers flew only occasional sorties. In addition, the Italian air force flew Fiat BR 20 medium bombers on raids over Britain from airfields in Belgium. These raids began in October 1940 but were not a success and the Italians headed home after only three months. The Germans would locate their targets using the *knickebein* radio beams which were transmitted from occupied Europe. The *knickebein* was subsequently jammed by the British using transmitters known as *aspirins*.

At the beginning of the Blitz, British night fighters were achieving almost no success against the bombers. Hurricanes, Spitfires and Defiants were sent up at night without radar and achieved little. The Bristol Blenheim was fitted with Mark I airborne interception (AI) radar but the radar was unreliable and the aircraft was old and very slow. The situation improved when the Bristol Beaufighter entered service. It was well armed, fast and it was fitted with the upgraded AI Mark IV radar. By the time Ground Control Interception radar came into use at the end of 1940, allowing a ground controller to vector a pilot accurately on to an enemy aircraft, an effective system of night fighting was evolving.

Anti-Aircraft Command, under General Sir Frederick Pile, was equipped with 3.7 inch and 4.5 inch guns at the start of the Blitz but they rarely found their target. Under pressure to be seen to be doing something about the raids, Pile ordered his gunners to fire continuously, even if they were aiming at nothing. This 'tactic' had two results. It boosted civilian morale and it forced the German bombers to fly higher. As the Blitz drew on, developments in radar significantly improved the accuracy of Britain's anti-aircraft guns.

Erik Sommers
German Bomber Pilot

After we had established our superiority over the Continent, we went into training in a very remote field in Pomerania, and it was very encouraging, because we found that we could bomb any target within 250 kilometres with an accuracy of about 150 metres. On our early raids, the beam would ensure that we would hit the exact target.

Group Captain Frederick Winterbotham
Deputy to Chief of Secret Intelligence Service with special responsibility for the security of Ultra messages

The German beam consisted of one beam sending out dots all the time and another beam some miles away, at a different angle, sending out dashes. So the bomber pilot flew his aeroplane along and heard dots on one side and dashes on the other. But when they came together and he heard one note, he knew he was over the target.

Robert Cockburn
Scientist with Royal Aircraft Establishment, Farnborough

My job was to find out how to jam – or if you like, bend – the German beam. These beams were such an obvious device for the Germans to use but it took no account of the possibility of countermeasures. It was a fairly straightforward job. They used a dot dash Lorenz beam and all I had to do was radiate additional dots. Initially, we did it in synchronism – in other words we received the dots down at Worth Matravers and transmitted them by telephone line to Beacon Hill near Salisbury where we had a jammer. But I very soon realised that it didn't matter a damn whether they were synchronised or not. They just had to be at the same time because when the German pilot got on to the signal beam, he would still hear these extra dots coming through which would make him go off to one side. We were being too meticulous for the rough and tumble of war.

Erik Sommers
German Bomber Pilot
There was no bending of the X beam but the British tried to lay beams in a different direction or to mess it up. The young bomber crews lost their bearings with it, but I personally know that experienced old crews always got through – although without the concentration of bombing experienced over Coventry. We had very little loss from anti-aircraft guns or night fighters over the British Isles. All our losses were through mismanagement, bad navigation, bad weather and by other accidents like wireless failures, bad landings and so on. Sometimes we observed collisions in heavy concentrations of German aircraft. Night fighter opposition was no opposition at all. We were all the time aware that something could be in the air behind us, and there was a lot of panic action against night fighters, but we had not proof of one loss from night fighters up to May 1941.

Flying Officer William David
87 and 213 Squadrons, RAF
There was a tremendous political pull to get the RAF to tackle the night bombing menace because the Germans were really doing a lot of damage at night. The public were saying, 'Where are our fighters?' So in September 1940, we went through a spell of doing night fighting in Hurricanes. It was very tiring and the idea of a Hurricane fighting at night in 1940 was an absolute waste of time. The approaching speeds of six miles a minute just didn't work at night. You couldn't see anything. You needed the AI radar to compete with the bombers.

Pilot Officer Irving Smith
New Zealand pilot with 151 Squadron, RAF
We had Hurricanes and painted them black. We had a very high accident rate and we were 100 per cent ineffective.

Sergeant Richard Mitchell
229 Squadron, RAF
On the night Coventry was bombed, my commanding officer sent for me. He said that he'd received permission to night fly. He said, 'I'm going off now. You take off in three-quarters of an hour's time.' It was a moonlit night and I duly went off. The air was full of bombers but without a radar set-up, it was like looking for a needle in a haystack. I never saw one. I flew all the way to the south coast with a bomber allegedly off my starboard wing tip. I never saw it.

When it was time to land, I got back over Northolt but I couldn't see the airfield. I was circling like mad. I said, 'You'll have to put on the Chance light.' That's a huge light at the end of the runway. 'We can't!' they said, 'The bombers are going over!' Eventually they put the light on but I was facing in the wrong direction and by the time I'd turned, the light was off again. But they put it on a second time and I landed. After that, the CO decided that it was a waste of time and we didn't do it again.

Flight Lieutenant John Cunningham
604 Squadron, RAF
Chaps who had just learnt to fly, suddenly faced with instrument flying, were not instrument pilots. An awful lot of accidents happened at night.

Sergeant Stanley Wright
NCO served on aircraft interception radar work
I flew in the deadbeat old Blenheim. It leaked like a basket. If you went through a cloud, you were wet. If the gunner decided to transfer his turret, he kicked the radar operator in the back of the neck. But they put a tray of .303 Browning guns underneath it, shoved a Mark IV AI airborne interception set into it and turned it into an 'up-to-date, modern, wonderful night fighter'.

Sergeant Ronald Dalton
Observer with 604 Squadron, RAF
I remember going up in a Blenheim for two and a half hours during the winter of 1940. There was no heating and we'd been up at 15,000 feet for two hours. I was the air gunner and there was plenty of fresh air coming straight into the gun turret. I wore three pairs of gloves but when we got down to about 2,000 feet, the pain in my hands was incredible – and I was very fit. On the ground, I sat in front of a stove for half an hour before they thawed.

Corporal Jack Clabburn
Armourer with 25 Squadron, RAF
My Blenheim was fitted with air interception radar. That's where they carried the gunner who used to sit in the back and look into a screen and he would get a blip when he picked up the target. Which he didn't do very often. He picked up blips from everywhere except the target.

A pilot and gunner of 29 Squadron climb aboard their Bristol Blenheim Mark IF for a night sortie.

Sergeant Stanley Wright
NCO *served on aircraft interception radar work*
We managed to hack some enemy aircraft down here and there in our Blenheims but it wasn't until we got the Beaufighters that life became difficult for the Germans. Any Junkers 88 could outrun a Blenheim.

Flight Lieutenant John Cunningham
604 Squadron, RAF
The Bristol Beaufighters appeared at the end of August 1940. The Beaufighter was the first real successful war machine that the air force had for night fighting. It had lots of power, four 20 millimetre cannon, radar and adequate performance to deal with the Heinkel 111 and Junkers 88.

Sergeant Albert Gregory
Air gunner with 219 Squadron
Our Beaufighter had AI radar. Initially the equipment was poor, but I was responsible for operating it. We'd be directed by the ground section to go to a specific area at a certain height. Then we were left to ourselves to find the enemy aircraft. The AI radar looked like a small television screen fixed at chest height. There was a line in the middle of the screen and a blip would appear. If the blip was over to the left, the aircraft I was being guided to would be to port so I'd tell my pilot to move that way to get the blip into a central position. If the blip was below the centre of the screen, the aircraft that we were chasing was below us and I'd tell the pilot to decrease his height. As we got nearer to the aircraft, the blip would get bigger and bigger until the pilot could see the aircraft. In November we claimed a Heinkel 111 over Sussex. We saw sufficient to claim it as being destroyed and it was later confirmed.

Flight Lieutenant John Cunningham
604 Squadron, RAF
My first night success; it was not very nice weather, there was a certain amount of cloud. My radar operator said, 'I have a radar contact and its ahead about two miles and it's going to the right.' I turned and thought, 'That's what those searchlights are probably trying to find.' So we closed in and the range reduced and got to some thousand feet ahead and slightly above. I saw exhaust flames which were blueish. I was still unsure – ground would only tell you, 'We think this aircraft is hostile.' Very often it would be another sector's night fighter or a Wellington bomber. IFF [*Identification, Friend or Foe*] was nominally fitted but it was totally unreliable. So I would have to get close

enough to make a visual identification, which I could do by closing in and getting underneath the aircraft so I could see the plan form of the wing. And while you were underneath, the bomber's gunners were less likely to see you than if you were above them. Now I could see it was in fact a Junkers 88 and I began to climb to its height very slowly and gently. We had to be very nearly at the same height and pointing at the enemy to use the gun sight and get the cannons to bear. We had a very primitive gun sight – a ring and a bead which was illuminated electrically with a rheostat beside one's left hand to adjust the light intensity. Well, it was a very dark cloudy night and when I came up to the level of the Junkers to shoot at it, looking through this sight which was far too bright even turned down to its dimmest – it wasn't very accurate shooting. But I hit it and the whole thing went down suddenly beneath me and then we lost radar contact. Of course, if you hit it and didn't pull out of the way very quickly, as often as not, you would get damaged by quite a number of bits of the aircraft. So when you had four cannon into a target, it was a few rounds and there was a big flash and you stopped firing and pulled away.

Pilot Officer Irving Smith
New Zealand pilot with 151 Squadron, RAF
It was very difficult to identify an aeroplane unless there was some background against which to silhouette it – light or fires or whatever. You couldn't hear another aircraft. I sat underneath a Wellington's tail and I could actually see the gunner in his turret and he didn't see me. I had to get in that close before I could identify that it was a Wellington by the shape of the gun turret.

Flight Lieutenant John Cunningham
604 Squadron, RAF
By May 1941, I had 12 successful combats in my Beaufighter. I was given the nickname, 'Cat's Eyes' by the Air Ministry to cover up the fact that we were flying aircraft with radar because there was never any mention of radar at that period. So by the time I had had two or three successes, the Air Ministry felt they would have to explain that I had very good vision by night. I actually had very good vision by day and average by night. Night vision was highly overrated in the actual success of an interception and shooting down of an aircraft. Even if the pilot's night vision wasn't particularly good, he had only to go into the minimum range that the radar would allow – between 800 and 900 feet – and anyone could see exhaust flames then.

A crashed Junkers 88, inspected by the New Zealand High Commissioner.

Dore Silverman
Ministry of Information
The idea that night fighter pilots ate a lot of carrots to give them better sight in the dark was nonsense. It was a ploy to get people to eat more carrots. They were nutritious and they didn't have to be imported.

Sergeant Ronald Dalton
Observer with 604 Squadron, RAF
I remember chasing a German aircraft across London at night. We never caught him but the ack-ack was coming up. We were a bit blasé, thinking, 'The ack-ack will never hit us,' and it never did. It didn't frighten us all that much because we didn't think they were very good.

Ernest Wedding
German Heinkel 111 bomber pilot
The worst thing at night is when you're flying through flak. After I had dropped my bomb load and I was heading for home, I personally would screw myself up as high as I could get with the aircraft because the anti-aircraft predictors were aiming at the lowest flying aircraft. Another thing is I had sufficient height and I could afford then to put the nose slightly down and gain speed. In flying, speed is safety.

Erik Sommers
German Bomber Pilot
Anti-aircraft guns didn't bother us except in very concentrated areas like Plymouth and Bristol.

Betty Cuthbert
Auxiliary Fire Service in London
The anti-aircraft fire gave the civilian population a feeling that something was being done.

Second Lieutenant Cyril Sherwood
91st Heavy Anti-Aircraft Regiment, Royal Artillery
The 3.7inch anti-aircraft guns had ten to a dozen people on the crew. There was a gun position officer in charge. There was a range finder which worked out the range and a predictor which followed the course of the plane and predicted where the plane would be when the shell reached a particular point. There were people on the gun traversing and elevating the gun, setting the

315

fuse on the shell, loading the shell on the tray, ramming it home and firing.

The range finder works in the same way that your eyes work. If you focus on a point, you can recognise if it's ten yards or a hundred yards away by the amount that your eyes have to diverge – and it's exactly the same with the range finder. You have two mirrors at either end and the amount that they have to diverge towards each other, indicates the range. We also had very simple radar. It had an enormous mechanism – almost the size of a small caravan. It had enormous aerial arrays. It worked like a cathode ray tube. It sent out a pulse and if it hit an aircraft, it came back. At the moment it was sent out, a blip went across the cathode ray tube. If the pulse came back, it would create another blip and the time it took to get to the plane and back would determine the length between the blips on the cathode ray tube. You'd measure that off and you got the range.

The predictor told us the right point to fire. If a bomber is weaving about, there's not a hope in hell of being able to hit it but there's a period when it has to do a run-up – it flies at the same height, the same speed and in the same direction so that the bomb aimer can drop his bombs accurately. That run-up was the period when you could perhaps hit the plane and that was the period when the predictor used to follow the plane through telescopes and according to the rate of change of the bearing, you could get an idea of where the plane would be when a shell exploded. The shell had a fuse at the front which was set to a particular time, for example six seconds, and it would explode at a particular height. Theoretically, the plane and the shell would be at the same point. It was an almost impossible job. The best you could hope to do was to get the shells near enough to deter the plane so it moved off, making the bomb aiming less accurate.

Marguerite Crowther
Ambulance driver in London
A mobile bath unit was erected near one of the big anti-aircraft guns and one day, nothing was happening so the gun crew came across for a quick bath. Whilst they were all in there, singing their heads off in the cubicles, the sirens went and I shall never forget because the eight cubicle doors flew open and these pink bodies shot out. All they had on was their battle bowlers but they leapt on the gun and started firing away.

A battery of 3.7 inch anti-aircraft guns fires at German aircraft.

The reflection of an anti-aircraft gunner in his searchlight reflector.

Theresa Bothwell
Civilian in Birmingham
We heard that a shell had gone up and it had fallen back down on to a church hall where there was a wedding reception going on. The bride lost the bottom half of both her legs and the husband was killed. But we heard no more about that, because they weren't allowed to print anything in the papers.

Thomas Parkinson
Civilian in Kentish Town
One young fellow was going with a nice-looking girlfriend. He walked her home to her house in Camden Town and he was sitting in the kitchen having a cup of tea with her when an anti-aircraft shell that had gone up and didn't explode, came straight through the house, hit her and killed her stone dead. While he was sitting there.

Stanley Clark
Civilian in London
The mood round our way was – why can't we hit back at the bombers? So they brought anti-aircraft guns up Gray's Inn Road for a couple of nights. But it was just morale boosting – it didn't do any good.

William Gray
Milkman in London
We were always glad to hear our ack-ack opening up. I understand since that they weren't very successful. It was just so we could hear that somebody was hitting back.

Bombs and Sappers

I can remember saying to my mother, 'Go a bit further!
Drop the bombs on anybody else but don't drop them on me!'

Many different kinds of bombs were dropped on Britain during the Blitz. Incendiary bombs – known as firebombs – were only nine inches long but they were made from a magnesium alloy so that when ignited by a small fuse, they burned for ten minutes at a staggeringly high temperature. They were feared for the amount of fire damage they caused. As the Blitz progressed, exploding incendiary bombs were introduced which blew up once they had caught fire. High explosive bombs ranged from the most common 50kg and 250kg bombs to the massive 'Max' which weighed 2500kg. Landmines were actually magnetic shipping mines with an adapted detonator which were dropped by parachute and caused colossal damage. In May 1940, 25 sections of Royal Engineers were formed to deal with the disposal of bombs. Each section consisted of an officer, a sergeant and 14 sappers. Within two months, the number of sections had increased to 220. Most officers arrived directly from the Officer Cadet Training Units. In the early days, their expertise was limited.

William Gray
Milkman in London
Every night was the same. They came over and every morning you'd go out and find another building gone down or another row of shops destroyed. You got used to it. After about three months, if Jerry didn't come over, you thought he was on holiday. You got a night's sleep.

Ivor Leverton
Undertaker in London, served with Auxiliary Fire Service
We'd all heard the rumour of the 'big bomb' that was going to be dropped in the middle of London and destroy most of it. We thought we were all going to be wiped out. We lived from day to day.

Hugh Varah
Auxiliary Fire Service in Hull
The most terrifying part of a raid was the sound of bombs coming down. When bombs are released from a plane, they travel in the same direction and at the same speed as the plane. As they begin to lose speed, they start to fall earthwards, tracing a large curved trajectory, picking up speed as they fall and the dreadful noise made by the air rushing past the tail fins herald their coming. That means that there's just time to dive for cover. We quickly learned that if the sound was rising in pitch, they were coming our way. But if the note got deeper, they were heading in someone else's direction.

Betty Brown
Civilian in Chingford
We'd hear these planes coming over and I can remember saying to my mother, 'Go a bit further! Drop the bombs on anybody else but don't drop them on me!'

Albert Prior
Stretcher bearer with West Ham Civil Defence
I watched a bomb drop. One house collapsed under it and as it did, three or four houses folded on to it just as though they were a pack of cards.

Hugh Varah
Auxiliary Fire Service in Hull
When bombs were falling, I have seen big men become rooted to the spot, transfixed by terror beyond their control. I have seen others set off and run blindly in sheer panic, in no particular direction. I have seen people of all ages and [both] sexes cover their heads with a coat in an effort to ward off a bomb. They could not imagine any escape so their minds turn inwards and blotted out any threat of danger.

Alan Bryett
Civilian in Brockley
I wasn't really nervous. I never thought it would happen to me. I had the innocence of youth which told me that I was going to survive when all these other people were going to die.

Francis Goddard
Auxiliary Fire Service in Tottenham
To deal with the incendiary bombs, you had a bucket of sand and a shovel. The idea was that either you scooped up the bomb before it went off and put it in the bucket of sand or if it had gone off and it wasn't too dangerous, you tipped the sand over it to put it out.

Joan Varley
Civilian in London
The morning after they first dropped incendiaries, we went into the bank and discovered one on the upper floor. We'd never seen one before. It wasn't very big but it was plainly a device and there was a hole in the wall where it had entered. It was found by one of the bank cashiers, rather a stately, stiff kind of man and we were saying, 'Pick it up! Get rid of it!' so he picked it up and put it in a fire bucket full of water. He was taking it to the lift but we said, 'No! No! You mustn't go in the lift! If you blow up the lift, *we* won't be able to get out!' So we made the poor man walk down the stairs where he handed it to an air raid warden. We found out afterwards that the last thing you should do with an incendiary is to put it in a bucket of water.

Stan Jarvis
Civilian in Plaistow
There was no point using water on an incendiary bomb because the bomb contained magnesium and water wouldn't extinguish it. We had stirrup pumps but these were to deal with fires caused by incendiary bombs, not to deal with the incendiary bombs themselves.

Marie Price
Civilian in Liverpool
The two old people who lived next door, an incendiary bomb went into their bedroom. My brother and I were determined to save their home for them so we dashed up their stairs with a stirrup pump. Their mattress was on fire so I said to my brother, 'We have to throw it out of the window!' and my brother

said, 'No! We'll put water on it with the stirrup pump!' The argument turned into a fight and the old lady who lived in the house started shouting, 'Stop fighting! Stop fighting you two! Just put this fire out!'

William McEvoy
Civilian in Birkenhead
An incendiary bomb went through the roof of a house so this bloke and I ran into the house, up the stairs and into the bedroom. The idea was to put something over the incendiary to kill the supply of oxygen to it and the first thing we found was the pot under the bed. There were a lot of kids in this house and I can still remember the smell today.

Vera King
Civilian living in the Wirral
We had incendiaries in the garden, and we all rallied round and put sandbags on them. When we had no sandbags left, the air raid wardens started digging up our garden desperately trying to douse the flames, and my poor mummy was distracted, 'Oh, my poor hollyhocks!' The warden said, 'Bugger your hollyhocks missus, we've got to put the fire out.'

Stan Poole
Auxiliary Fire Service in London
Incendiary bombs were dropped onto the outfitters Charles Baker's on the corner of Tottenham Court Road and Euston Road. Two of us went upstairs and there was fire everywhere, flames flickering, and on the landing there were all these mirrors and in front of them we could see an air raid warden trying on suits by the light of the flames. We went past him up on to the roof and there were incendiary bombs lying about. We didn't have a bucket, we didn't have sand, no stirrup pump, nothing. So we got hold of a shovel and we started shoving all these blazing incendiary bombs off the roof down on to Tottenham Court Road. A voice shouted up from the street, 'Stop that!' I couldn't believe it. What did they want? For the place to burn down?

Walter Blanchard
Civilian in Barking
After a while, the Germans started fitting incendiary bombs with an anti-personnel device so that while you were dealing with the bomb, it would explode and spray you with flaming magnesium. One of those landed in the roof of our own house and father and I tackled it. It did indeed explode but it

Demonstrating the use of a stirrup pump.

blew out through the roof. It didn't come down inside and set the house afire.

Walter Marshall
Metropolitan Police War Reserve

I remember one PC approaching an exploding incendiary in the middle of the roadway. It was spluttering away full tilt. Holding a dustbin lid in one hand as a shield and a bucket of sand in the other, he made a pantomime display. It was the first firebomb I'd seen and it exploded as he approached. The explosion hit the dustbin lid and the PC finished up on his behind about ten yards back.

Alexander Flett
Metropolitan Police in Southwark

I stopped a little boy and stuffed up his jersey he had two live incendiary bombs that hadn't gone off. He said, 'Oh don't take them, guv'nor, don't take them! I haven't got a souvenir and my mates have got some of these!'

John Lodge
London Fire Brigade

The worst bombs were the landmines – parachute mines with enormous explosive power. They caused terrible destruction.

Hugh Varah
Auxiliary Fire Service in Hull

I arrived at London Road Station in Manchester in the middle of a raid. It became known as 'the silent raid' because the bombs were coming down on parachutes and you couldn't hear them come down. The idea was that these great cylinders of explosive – landmines – would land in a street, roll over and detonate and cause a great deal more damage than ordinary bombs that buried themselves 20 feet below the ground before they exploded.

Joan Varley
Civilian in London

Opposite the bank where I worked was a news cinema. It showed Pathé News and British Movietone News and it lasted about an hour. We knew the manager very well and he gave us some passes so we could go in for free. One morning, I looked out of the window and saw him arriving at the cinema and I waved and he waved back and disappeared inside. A few minutes later, he

A landmine, with parachute attached, which fell in a field in Essex.

Police and bomb disposal officers with a 1000-kg landmine in Glasgow.

came out in a state of great trauma. He was waving his arms about – it looked like a Charlie Chaplin film. When he'd gone into the auditorium, he'd been faced by a landmine that hadn't gone off. Later in the morning, along came a lorry and we all stood at the windows and watched as this lethal thing was very gently loaded on to the lorry for disposal.

Francis Goddard
Auxiliary Fire Service in Tottenham
I'd got home early and I was out in the garden and there was a raid. By that time we didn't bother about going into the shelter but we were near the shelter and suddenly this object came floating along the top of our house. It came down low enough and I could only see a parachute and a rope hanging below it. I jumped up and went to grab the rope but it drifted up and it went over the embankment and carried on down to the marshes. Where it blew up. I'd nearly grabbed hold of a ruddy landmine.

John 'Chick' Fowles
Civilian in London
One of my duties in the Boy Scouts was to locate unexploded bombs on Hackney Marsh and report them to the police station in Clapton. I had to look for little softenings and flutings in the ground. I only ever found one. When I look back, they really shouldn't have been asking young people to do that – but it was quite exciting.

James Lawrence
Trimley St Martin Home Guard
I saw the first bomb that dropped in Ipswich. I saw it leave the plane and I threw myself down but there was no bang because the bomb had been sabotaged.

Second Lieutenant John Edmund Emlyn Jones
Royal Engineers
Before there were any bomb disposal units, I went out as a Royal Engineers subaltern with some gun cotton to deal with a bomb in a field, knowing nothing at all about German bombs. It was shortly after that that I received my first instruction at RAF Manby in Lincolnshire by which time the War Office had set up a number of bomb disposal sections.

Sapper Walter Fielding
22nd Bomb Disposal Company, Royal Engineers
I was called up and marched to a bomb disposal training centre. That was the
first that I knew I had anything to do with bomb disposal. We were all hit by it
but we took it calmly. There was no panic. The country could be taken over at
any moment by the Germans – that's why we took it calmly. We had very little
training at all. You picked it up as you went along. And a lot, of course, didn't.

Lieutenant Stuart Archer
105 Bomb Disposal Section, Royal Engineers
The average life of a bomb disposal officer was about ten weeks before he was
blown up.

Sapper George Ingram
22 Bomb Disposal and 89 Bomb Disposal Companies, Royal Engineers
In the early days, it was all trial and error – we didn't even know that some of
these bombs were magnetic and any metal would set them off. So it wasn't for
a while that our tools were bronze alloy and not steel.

Lieutenant Stuart Archer
105 Bomb Disposal Section, Royal Engineers
When an unexploded bomb was found by the police, it would be reported to
the regional headquarters who told us where the bombs were and what had to
be done. The bomb we found most often was the 250-kg bomb. It would
completely collapse two houses side by side and take the roofs off over 100
yards diameter. A lot would depend on how deep they were. A bomb on the
surface would blow the roof off, the one fairly deep would break up all the
drains and the foundations.

Sapper Len Jeacock
Royal Engineers
The bomb would be given a category. Category A – you would have to dig the
bomb up immediately. Category B – you could wait four days. Category C –
you could wait more than four days.

Lieutenant Stuart Archer
105 Bomb Disposal Section, Royal Engineers
Category A was subdivided into A1 and A2. An A1 might be a bomb next
door to a telephone exchange – it had to be dealt with immediately and it had

to be prevented from exploding. An A2 would be by the side of the railway – it had to be dealt with immediately but it didn't damn well matter if we blew the damn thing up to get rid of it. It was the job of the sergeants and their men to dig down and get to the bomb.

Sapper Len Jeacock
Royal Engineers
We would start digging. It might take days. If it was in the road you had mechanical tools but it was in the houses, ordinary shovels. And you dug down until you found the thing.

Sapper Walter Fielding
22nd Bomb Disposal Coy, Royal Engineers
I remember banging my shovel onto what I thought was a very big stone. I put my hand down and I felt cold steel. It was the end of the bomb.

Lieutenant Stuart Archer
105 Bomb Disposal Section, Royal Engineers
Some of these bombs would go down five, ten, 15 feet and the sides of the excavation had to be shored up. At first, we would simply lift the bombs out of the hole but then we started finding delayed-action fuses all round the country.

Sapper Leslie Clarke
245 Field Company, Royal Engineers
The Germans used impact fuses – bombs that were meant to go off on impact and delayed fuses – bombs which were delayed up to 96 hours before going off. They were marked so that different numbers denoted a different fuse.

Sapper Len Jeacock
Royal Engineers
German bombs had numbers stamped on the bottom. Impact fuses had a number that would finish with a five and once you'd seen that you knew jolly well that it should have gone off but didn't. Anything finishing with a seven would be a delay. Simple as that. They'd got to know what to put in the bomb so the armourer knew what he was doing.

Lieutenant Stuart Archer
105 Bomb Disposal Section, Royal Engineers
A 17 fuse was a clockwork delay fuse that was set for anything up to four days by the armourer who put the bomb in the plane. The Germans realised that delayed action really disturbed the area that they were bombing because people had to move out and stay out until the bomb was gone. A delayed-action fuse could put a factory out of action for days or weeks. We started endeavouring to remove these fuses and at first we would simply take it out by hand.

Sapper Leslie Clarke
245 Field Company, Royal Engineers
There was a fixing ring that held the fuse into the sleeve so we unscrewed the fixing ring and then we could withdraw the fuse. Once the fuse was out of the bomb, the filling was safe.

Lieutenant Stuart Archer
105 Bomb Disposal Section, Royal Engineers
After a while, we started removing the fuse using the Crabtree discharger. We would undo the fixing ring and then we would tie some cord to the discharger. The Crabtree discharger was about an inch and a quarter in diameter with two little spikes sticking out the side of it which pressed down two little electrical connections and at the same time it had a sidescrew which held it on to the fuse itself. Putting the discharger on the bomb shorted the fuse. The cord went to a pulley and from a distance, we would pull the cord so that the fuse would come out. Now, the bomb was, in effect safe. The explosive in the bomb without the fuse was completely inert. It was no problem whatsoever so we could take our time, dig it out and blow it up somewhere else.

Sapper Joseph Gibbs
Royal Engineers
In London, we used to collect the bombs and take them over Hackney Marshes, put them in a hole, set the charge, push the plunger and blow them up.

Lieutenant Stuart Archer
105 Bomb Disposal Section, Royal Engineers
When the Germans discovered that we were getting the bombs, putting them on lorries and taking them away before they could blow up, they started

adding a second fuse pocket with an anti-handling fuse. The 17 delay fuse would be sitting in one fuse pocket, whilst six to eight inches away another fuse pocket would contain a 50 anti-handling fuse to stop us taking the bomb away. This fuse had a tolerance of one millimetre before it would go off. Somebody managed to get these fuses out – for some reason they were faulty – and they were sent to the War Office who discovered how they operated and they told us how to deal with them. They discovered that the clock could be stopped with a magnetic clock stopper – a large length of electric cable which would be placed over and around the fuse and then switched on to several very strong batteries. They then found the means of dealing with the 50 anti-handling fuse – you would very gently put something over the fuse that sucked the air out of it with a little pump and then you turned a tap on which would push a liquid right inside the fuse which destroyed the electric current within the batteries.

Sapper Leslie Clarke
245 Field Company, Royal Engineers
We used doctors' stethoscopes to listen to the bomb to see if the clock had started up.

Sapper Leslie Clarke
245 Field Company, Royal Engineers
Another method we used for stopping a clock – apart from a magnet – was a solution of water and sugar mixed. We forced it into a fuse with a bicycle pump. But the sugar started running low because some of the lads were taking it for their tea. When the authorities heard about this, they sent us a brown treacly fluid to use instead of sugar. It was no good for tea – the lads tried it.

Lieutenant Stuart Archer
105 Bomb Disposal Section, Royal Engineers
I had once removed a 50 anti-handling fuse with a pickhead. I had tried to get it out by putting the Crabtree discharger on it and pulling but it was partly jammed into the fuse pocket so I pressed gently with the curve of the pickhead to pull it out. It should have gone off but it didn't – luck, luck, luck. It was quite clearly faulty. A lot of my friends did the same and they were blown up. I was lucky and they weren't.

Sapper George Ingram
22 Bomb Disposal and 89 Bomb Disposal Companies, Royal Engineers

We were sat about 100 yards from a bomb in a children's playground in Grays, having our coffee break, when suddenly it exploded. The blast hit me – it was real hot, like when you open a furnace door and it sears your face. Big clods of earth fell on us and my ears started to bleed. People in the houses nearby came out and they were very angry, because they thought we should let them know when we were going to explode the bomb. Well, we didn't know – it exploded itself. We were very fortunate that we were sat away from it but later on, it sent me deaf.

Sapper Joseph Gibbs
Royal Engineers

It was a very dangerous job. I was glad when I got off of it – I tell you that.

Lieutenant Stuart Archer
105 Bomb Disposal Section, Royal Engineers

We got a call to go to the oil refinery north of Swansea. There were four unexploded bombs in a line, a couple of hundred yards from each other. I looked at them and decided that the one to tackle was beside a big oil tanker. There were flames 50 yards away to our left and we began to dig, two men digging at any one time. While we were doing this, one of the other four bombs went off – on a delayed-action fuse. Then another one went off and then the third – all while we were still digging. When I got down to see the face of the fuse, it had been torn off on impact so I couldn't see what the fuse was.

I did the most unusual thing – I unscrewed the base plate at the back of the bomb and exposed the inside of the casing. I found that the explosive was a powdered explosive. I reached down with a trowel and dug out the whole of the powdered explosive from the back of the bomb until there was no explosive at the back. It took about half an hour and it exposed the fuse pocket running from side to side. I grabbed hold of this and with brute force and bloody ignorance, I managed to get the whole of the fuse pocket out of the back of the bomb complete with its clockwork fuse and all the booster charges. I was able to take the fuse pocket away and have a look at it. I got a pair of pliers and pulled the innards of the fuse out of the pocket. As I was doing it, I heard a little something going off. It was a booby trap to prevent the clockwork fuse from being withdrawn – called a Zus 40. As luck would have it, I had pulled that out as well. I think the reason it didn't explode was that there was some water in the hole and because the head of the fuse had been damaged, some water got itself into the fuse pocket, preventing the Zus 40 from working.

We were then able to dig the bomb out and move it away to another part of the refinery where it was blown up for us. All the other bombs had gone off while we were dealing with this bomb. One went off at twelve o'clock, another at two o'clock, the third at three o'clock. We finished the whole operation at four. That made it a bit scary. There were four bombs and the one I chose was the one set to go off last. It went off – just a little fuse cap – at half past six that evening. Luck, luck, luck.

It was mainly for this incident that I won the George Cross. The King wanted to award the Victoria Cross for things like I had done but he discovered that within the conditions of the Victoria Cross, the act of valour has to be in the face of the enemy. And I wasn't facing the enemy unless you count the bomb as such. So he invented the George Cross and it was given for this sort of thing. Somebody read of my award in *The Times* and telephoned me. I wrote a little note to my wife and sent it by dispatch rider. The investiture took place in November 1941. My mother went to the Palace with me because my wife was about to have my son and it was not appropriate.

Sapper George Ingram
22 Bomb Disposal and 89 Bomb Disposal Companies, Royal Engineers
We were shown this new equipment for steaming the TNT out of the bomb. It was a portable boiler on wheels and you had to put sandbags round it. There was a platform that you sat on and a really good mechanism with wheels and gears that sent two drills into the metal of the bomb and into the TNT. There were gauges on the boiler measuring the pressure and it sent steam through a metallic hose into the holes made by the drill. There were clamps like long arms that went round the bomb. When it was drilling, you could hear it from a distance whining. When we were at Ipswich, this sergeant was using the steaming equipment on a bomb. It was pushing the metallic hose into the bomb but it started howling – it couldn't penetrate any further so he called for a dispatch rider to bring up a new section of metallic hose. While he was waiting, he sat there smoking and when the dispatch rider came up with the metallic hose, he was just about to hand it to him when the bomb exploded and killed both of them.

Sapper Walter Fielding
22nd Bomb Disposal Company, Royal Engineers
Ack-ack shells were very dangerous. The noses of the shells would be damaged by passing through the ground and they could go down to 15 feet. On a farm near Brentwood, we began to dig down to what we thought was a 50-kg bomb but when we got down to 15 feet, it turned out to be an ack-ack shell.

Sapper Joseph Gibbs
Royal Engineers
At Maidstone, an ack-ack shell had come down and cracked the pavement. We started digging under the pavement but we couldn't find anything and all of a sudden, a woman came out and said, 'There's a bomb in my roof!' and there it was. It had bounced up into her thatched roof.

Sapper Leslie Clarke
245 Field Company, Royal Engineers
A bomb had dropped in a residential area towards Aintree in Liverpool and it had come through the roof of a house and landed in the cellar. Everybody was evacuated and we went down to deal with the bomb. In the room above the cellar was a piano and one of my squad was a pianist and while we dealt with the bomb, he sat upstairs and played the piano.

Sapper George Ingram
22 Bomb Disposal and 89 Bomb Disposal Companies, Royal Engineers
We were working on a bomb in the centre of Lowestoft when we heard a loud explosion. We couldn't leave our job and go investigate, so we carried on but when we finished we were told that a bomb had exploded in a back garden, killing a young officer and a corporal who was nearby. It blew the corporal over a row of houses, across the road, and into the garden of the house opposite. I was detailed to try to find any trace of the officer. People showed us the exact spot where he'd been and we worked on this site from early morning to about half past four, but we never found any flesh at all, nothing. Absolute smithereens. I was picked to go to his funeral, at Norwich Cathedral and I bet they put sandbags in his coffin.

Sapper Leslie Clarke
245 Field Company, Royal Engineers
We lost lads but there wasn't a lot said about it. They were with you one minute and gone the next. It played on my mind that I was doing a dangerous job. But we were well liked. If we went into a pub, people would see the flash on our arm and we would be bought beer. On the tram, they only had to see our flash and it never cost us anything.

Sapper George Ingram
22 Bomb Disposal and 89 Bomb Disposal Companies, Royal Engineers
We worked on a big 1,000-pound bomb that fell on Ipswich. We worked every day for several weeks and after we had got it out, we were entertained by the Lord Mayor and all the civic heads of Ipswich at a dinner. When we were shown into the banqueting hall, they all stood up to attention. I remember having champagne and a lovely dinner and there were speeches by the mayor and our commanding officer.

Sapper Walter Fielding
22nd Bomb Disposal Company, Royal Engineers
When we finished a job at a big house in Leiston, the sergeant went to the house and told them that the ground was clear and he was handed a pound note. There were 20 of us so we each got our shilling.

Sapper Len Jeacock
Royal Engineers
In May 1941, we cleared five bombs from Victoria Station. I was working there for three or four days and then I received permission to go to Bournemouth to see a girlfriend. I took a train on an indirect line and when I got out at Bournemouth and gave the bloke my ticket, he said, 'One and ninepence excess fare, sir, you've come the loop line.' So I said, 'I've just spent three days digging bombs off your Victoria Station!' 'Pay the one and nine, sir . . .'

Sapper Leslie Clarke
245 Field Company, Royal Engineers
We'd been working for a few days in Liverpool and we couldn't find the bomb we were looking for. There were crowds that used to watch us working at a distance so we got a bomb that we'd got out previously and during the night, we stuck it down the hole. The next day, we produced this bomb and the

crowd started cheering. One of my squad went round and made a collection and we took all the money down to the first pub we could find.

Sapper Len Jeacock
Royal Engineers
Bomb Disposal people were unique really. They were great friends and they lived dangerously and they lived very well together. It was a strange business but I've never found any camaraderie similar to it anywhere. You'd have little batches of 30 chaps together in a house with one officer and you'd go about your business together, four or five on each bomb and the officer would be circulated. The spirit was great.

Lieutenant Stuart Archer
105 Bomb Disposal Section, Royal Engineers
I was there to do a job and it was no use saying, 'I don't like the sound of that.' You just got on with it. I'm glad to say that I didn't suffer from nerves.

Sapper George Ingram
22 Bomb Disposal and 89 Bomb Disposal Companies, Royal Engineers
I remember one sapper who was an absolute nervous wreck. He was courting and she was a very nice young woman but he committed suicide by putting his head in a gas oven. He was always a bit on the nervous side, even when he wasn't working on bombs.

Sapper Walter Fielding
22nd Bomb Disposal Company, Royal Engineers
I had pains in my chest and I went to the Medical Officer and he referred me to Colchester Military Hospital where they examined me and X-rayed me. The sister came round and mentioned a word which made it sound as though she thought I was 'swinging the lead'. I told her that I wasn't and that my pains were real and she said, 'Oh no, you're all right!' But then I was sent in front of what I thought was a regimental officer. I didn't know anything about psychology and he asked me if I believed the doctors. I said, 'I have to believe the doctors because they're cleverer than what I am.' Then he said, 'Do you believe there's nothing wrong with you?' I said, 'How do you account for the pains that I'm getting?'

A fortnight later, there was notice for me to go to Mill Hill Emergency Hospital in London where I was seen by Dr Hans Eysenck, a big authority on psychology. I was there for about three months. While I was there, I did a bit of

A bomb defused.

military training and I did an engineering course at Hendon Technical College. I was sent for and asked if I wanted to go back to bomb disposal or would I like to be retrained. I didn't like the idea of going back to my unit and spending all my days in the billet so I said I wanted to be retrained as an engineer. I went on a vehicles course at Gainsborough and when I was there, I had a terrible nightmare. I could hear bombs falling and I was really frightened. I woke up and the noise I could hear was a goods train going through the station. Even lately, I've had dreams of working down a bomb hole and I've had a really intense feeling of working on this bomb and wondering if it goes off, will I survive?

Sapper George Ingram
22 Bomb Disposal and 89 Bomb Disposal Companies, Royal Engineers
I used to drink quite a lot. Bomb disposal work made you drink a lot more than you should. I used to say to tell civilians: 'Join the Army and see the world. Join bomb disposal and see the next one . . . '

Taking Shelter

You got old men, old women, with their faces next to babies' bums.
Everybody was crowded in like sardines and it smelled.

A ir raid shelters came in various forms. Anderson shelters – named after Sir John Anderson, Lord Privy Seal before the war and Home Secretary from September 1939 to October 1940 – consisted of curved, corregated steel walls. They were supplied free to two and a half million families with gardens. Also supplied free were steel fittings which could be used to reinforce basements. Surface shelters were built on streets to provide protection for anybody caught outdoors during a raid and Morrison shelters – named after Herbert Morrison who replaced Anderson as Home Secretary – consisted of a six foot long rectangular steel cage to be used indoors. These began to come into use at the end of the Blitz. Many buildings with basements and cellars were turned over for use as public shelters and communal shelters were built to serve rows of houses and blocks of flats. A move began to make deep shelters available – which led to London Underground stations being made available.

There might be ten air raid wardens' posts per square mile in a city and each post was staffed by six wardens who were responsible for about 500 members of the general public. The warden would make nightly rounds, providing a 'presence' to reassure the public. During a raid, the warden would be expected to know the whereabouts of the people in their area. If a bomb dropped, the warden would report the incident and request the assistance of the services. He or she would then assist at the scene of the incident until the services arrived.

Thomas Parkinson
Civilian in Kentish Town
The worst part of the bombing was when the siren went. It would send a chill down your spine.

Ivor Leverton
Undertaker in London, served with Auxiliary Fire Service
I've only got to hear an air raid siren on an old film to get butterflies in the stomach.

Ruth Tanner
Child in Walthamstow
We had a dog and his name was Spot, and he used to hear the sirens before they went off. We'd be in the house and Spot would go absolutely potty, running round the kitchen and my mother used to say, 'Come on kids, down the shelter.' When we were down there, the sirens would go off. I think Spot used to hear the sirens somewhere further out and he didn't like the noise so he'd create hell.

Sylvia Clark 20305
Post Office worker in London
I'd get home from work and I'd just want to go to bed but my sister would say, 'Don't you know the siren's gone off?' and I'd have to go down into the damp shelter.

Walter Blanchard
Civilian in Barking
My father was an air raid warden and it wasn't his policy to take cover. He believed that people would take heart from him being about. He used to call out to them in the lulls – 'Everything all right?' and people would take confidence from that. I was scared stiff . . . but reassured by my father.

Teresa Wilkinson
Air raid warden in West Ham
I was out one day with a friend who was beginning her training as an air raid warden. Even though I was a bit hazy as to what wardens did, I came home and said to my father, 'I'm going to be an air raid warden!' At the time, I didn't like getting up in the morning and the next day, I found a cartoon my father had drawn attached to the outside of my bedroom door. It showed

people in the street shouting, 'We want the warden!' with explosions in the background and you could see my father and brother with their heads out of my bedroom window shouting, 'All right! All right! We're trying to wake her!' I thought, 'Damn them! I will be an air raid warden!'

The training was one night a week and it went on for about six weeks. We were told we had to parade around and see that people were all right. Every house in the post area was supposed to give us a list of the people in the house and where they slept. And they were supposed – though they never did it very well – to come around and tell us if they were going away for the weekend so we didn't go on digging for them.

We were shown how to fit gas masks. When I went round to one lady to fit her child's gas mask, she was downright rude to me. She shouted and carried on that I was interfering. I fitted the gas mask and withdrew hastily. During the first air raid, the same woman came running across the road to me and said, 'You mustn't let anything happen because I'm not going away till Thursday.' I wanted to say, 'Yes, I'll give Hitler a ring when I get home.'

Stanley Clark
Civilian in London
Air raid wardens worked in pairs. The younger men were with older chaps and we'd go out to do our two hours and we'd go round all the shelters to see that people were inside.

Teresa Wilkinson
Air raid warden in West Ham
Air raid wardens had no authority to make people take shelter. One night, we were passing a block of flats and this man was standing outside. 'You should get into a shelter!' we said – and he told *us* what to do in no uncertain terms. So we left him standing there and walked on. When we came back, he was still outside the block of flats. His head was about four steps further along.

Stanley Parker-Bird
Chief Shelter Officer for Marylebone
My first duty as Chief Shelter Officer in 1939 had been to inspect the main streets in Marylebone to see which basement accommodation could be made into air raid shelters. Those that I recommended were then inspected by the architects department. In due course, shelters were made in the basements of many of the big shops and church crypts. Some places – such as Madame Tussauds – were not sufficiently well constructed to be made into shelters.

Teresa Wilkinson on the telephone at her warden's post in West Ham.

A sand-bagged shelter in Woolworth's basement, London.

Alda Ravera
Secretary in London
After a few severe bombings, we were told that we must never sleep in the house at night. So for six months, we slept in the shelter in the park. We'd come home from work and we'd each have a bowl of coffee and some French bread to dunk in it. Then we'd go in the shelter. The bunks were all full up and I can remember getting an *Evening Standard*, putting it on the floor and lying on it. For six months, that was my bed.

George Frankland
Civilian in Lambeth
We used a shelter built on the play area of our council flats in Lambeth. They dug a hole in the ground and built a brick wall and a roof over the top but it was very dangerous because it was only just below ground and the brick wall was above ground.

Alda Ravera
Secretary in London
My godfather was running a restaurant in Jermyn Street so for a while we slept in the kitchen below the restaurant. One morning, I woke up and I had a cockroach on my face. Everyone was laughing. I wasn't.

Teresa Wilkinson
Air raid warden in West Ham
I had a friend who'd just got engaged and she went to spend the weekend with her fiancé's family. They had a shelter in their cellar and when she was there, a water main burst and the cellar filled with water and they all drowned. I used to think of them standing there and the water coming up.

Phil Piratin
Communist councillor in Stepney
There was a need for proper deep air raid shelters. In 1938, I had produced a pamphlet on deep shelters, which I presented to the Civil Defence Committee. It was rejected out of hand. And that was that. When the bombing began in 1940, we decided to go all out on a campaign to open the Underground stations as shelters. We documented it all but no notice was taken. So we started our 'pressure stunts'.

In the first place, we thought we must get into the headlines and we decided to occupy the shelter of the Savoy Hotel. I put my best suit on and

A couple shelters in a basement.

A Sikh family shelters in a church crypt.

spoke in my best voice and I went along to the hotel and explained that some friends were coming over from the United States and they were concerned about the shelters, so could I please see them? One of the officials showed me around and I memorised the layout. I went back to Stepney where I was a councillor and I asked our four best group leaders to bring along ten people to the Savoy Hotel on the Saturday night. Then I found four tough boys – I wasn't untough myself – and I explained that we would do the 'breakthrough'. So at about eight o'clock on the Saturday night, when the siren had gone, these four chaps and myself went down to the Savoy shelter's back entrance, where we found one member of the staff standing outside. He said something to me and I said, 'No, it's all right . . . ' We gently pushed the man aside and we were in the shelter. After we came in, the other Stepney groups came in at ten-second intervals. In all, 78 people turned up. Among them were a number of children and a couple of dogs. That – as you will agree – is typically English. Nothing is good enough for the English dog.

People came forward to protest but I told one of the waiters to get me a wooden chair and I stood up and made a speech. I explained what we were doing and why we were doing it. The senior Savoy man – an Italian type who spoke in broken English – tried to intervene and I said, 'I'm taking no interest in you! I will only discuss this matter with English people!' Now that might be wrong – but on the other hand, we were feeling very bitter.

Then a police inspector came in with about 12 or 15 police. He asked if I was in charge. Then he said, 'You're not worried about shelters, are you, Mr Piratin?' 'No,' I said, ' *I'm* not worried about shelters. I'm only waiting for my call-up. But what would *you* do if your wife were put in the position of that women over there. Her husband's in the army. She's got four children. What would *you* do?' The inspector said to me, 'You're right, guv, you're right. Well, what do you intend to do here?' I said, 'We don't really want this place. We want the tubes opened!' He said, 'Oh, quite right!' But his duty was to take names and addresses because we were now occupying a place where we had no right to be. Meanwhile, a number of the English waiters got together. One of them came over and said, 'Can we do anything for you?' I said, 'Yes, everyone's tired. They want tea. And the little ones want milk. What's your price?' The waiters laughed. I said, 'We'll pay you the price of a cup of tea in a Lyons restaurant. We'll pay you tuppence,' and they agreed. So they came in with silverware trays, serving teas and providing milk for ladies with babies. The Inspector said, 'When do you intend to leave?' 'When the all-clear sounds, we'll go,' I said. So when it did, that was that. Everyone left, elated and there was publicity in the Sunday papers.

On the Tuesday, it was arranged that when the sirens went, some comrades would break open the gates at Goodge Street Underground station. A couple of crowbars were waiting there for us and it happened – the gates were broken open. We had a megaphone, and it was announced that shelter was available down in the tube station. The police didn't know what was happening.

A few days later, the Home Secretary stood up in the House of Commons and announced, 'After due consideration, the shelters will be fitted for occupation . . . ' He announced that all arrangements would be made. So that was done. And when the Cabinet papers for 1940 were revealed under the 30-year rule, the Cabinet meeting was recorded where Mr Churchill expressed concern about the Savoy Hotel incident. He said, 'Something must be done. Or we'll have the people from other areas of London besides East London coming into the West End. And that would be fatal . . . '

George Frankland
Civilian in Lambeth
We used to sleep on the platform at Lambeth North Station. We'd go down in our pyjamas with a blanket and we'd take sandwiches and tea in a flask. We stayed down there all night and came up at dawn and walked home.

Oliver Bernard
Child in London
The tube platforms were quite transformed. Instead of being hard, shiny circles covered in white tiles, they became lined with softness and grey brown colours. They became rather friendly and nice. People were laughing, singing and telling stories, almost like a party was going on. It was very cosy.

Christabel Leighton-Porter
Model for Daily Mirror cartoon character 'Jane'
People would come down to the tube platforms with their bundles and they'd have their little places marked out. There were people playing accordions and the youngsters could hop on a train and go round the Circle Line and have a wonderful time. I can remember seeing new twin babies down there and really watching them grow up.

Dore Silverman
Ministry of Information
You had children coming from school, waiting outside the Underground station at 4.30, admitted at 6.30, sleeping the night and getting home at six

the next morning. As they grew up, this was their life. They had no home life, no play time, no study time, no normal life.

Elizabeth Quayle
Women's Auxiliary Air Force, served as plotter at Fighter Command HQ
There were rows of people with their belongings, cats and dogs and children. They were as good tempered as it was possible to be. You would have thought nothing of leaving your bags or your suitcase there. Nobody would have taken anything.

Gioya Steinke
Welfare Adviser with London County Council Rest Centre Service
One night, I said to a perfect stranger how I would give anything to have a bath. This stranger handed me her keys, told me her address and said, 'Go to my house tomorrow and have a bath and leave the keys under the mat.' She said that if I could take my own soap and towel, she'd be pleased but if I couldn't, that was all right.

Ellen Harris
Reporter with Reuters News Agency in London
I wakened one morning to find a great big black man sleeping next to me. I was horrified to say the least. But my father was with me on the other side so all was well. But the question of colour, class, type of person – it all went by the board.

Alan Bryett
Civilian in Brockley
The spirit in the Underground was remarkably good. There was a feeling that the bombing wasn't going to win the war – we are Londoners and we're going to see this through. It was a grim determination.

Gioya Steinke
Welfare Adviser with London County Council Rest Centre Service
When the trains were running, you could hop on and off a train and go to another station, say hello to your friends who were sleeping there and come back again.

Christabel Leighton-Porter
Model for Daily Mirror cartoon character 'Jane'
When a train stopped one had to be very careful when one got out because the people were lying close by and only allowed you about a foot to get out of your train to walk along to the exit.

George Frankland
Civilian in Lambeth
It was crowded and claustrophobic. It was so packed that everyone had their own designated place and the people who were there for the odd night would have to sit on the staircase.

Mary Warschauer
Civilian working for Air Ministry in London
You got old men, old women, with their faces next to babies' bums. Everybody was crowded in like sardines and it smelled.

Christabel Leighton-Porter
Model for Daily Mirror cartoon character 'Jane'
The smell hit one very hard. The Salvation Army and other groups used to make cocoa and cook sausages down there for the people and of course there was no real means of letting the odour out. It wasn't a bad smell but I remember it very distinctly.

Stanley Parker-Bird
Chief Shelter Officer for Marylebone
The shelters on the platforms had to be adapted because they were below the levels of the sewers. Latrines had to be prepared on the platforms with buckets which had to be dealt with by the sewage staff and taken away.

Stan Poole
Home Guard in London
There were as many packed in as possible but everybody made room for someone else to come in. There were men, women, girls, kids and there were outbreaks of scabies. There were accidents with kids peeing on the line – 50,000 volts and that would be it. But there was a jolly atmosphere.

Men and women bedded down for the night on a staircase at Elephant & Castle Underground Station.

The platform at Elephant & Castle Underground Station.

Christabel Leighton-Porter
Model for Daily Mirror cartoon character 'Jane'
When the war was ending, a lot of old people were terribly distressed wondering what they were going to do with their evenings. They'd thoroughly enjoyed their nights down the tube stations.

Dore Silverman
Ministry of Information
People from poorer homes suffered more greatly than the middle classes. Middle-class people probably had an Anderson shelter.

Teresa Wilkinson
Air raid warden in West Ham
The Anderson shelter was made of corrugated metal. It came straight up and curved over at the top. There was a section which closed off the back and the front had a door in it. You dug a deep hole, put the shelter in and then covered it with all the earth you dug out. They were very, very effective. They stood up to a lot of punishment.

Alan Bryett
Civilian in Brockley
Inside the Anderson shelter, it was cold and damp and uncomfortable. The only light was a torch that you took down and people didn't really like going into them. Some families rigged up beds in them but they were damp.

Ruth Tanner
Child in Walthamstow
Our dad built an Anderson shelter in our garden, and being as he was a builder, it was done properly and had a floor in it. It didn't get water in it and the inside of it was painted a beautiful pink with sawdust thrown all on it to absorb any condensation. Our beds were fixed on the side so that my mum could fold them up and let them down as necessary.

Theresa Bothwell
Civilian in Birmingham
Mother was the handywoman. Dad was useless with a hammer and nail so she put up the Anderson shelter and erected two bunks on the left-hand side of the shelter. On the other side she put a bench for us to sit on, and a shelf for putting tins and packets of food. We'd got a paraffin heater and a bucket for toilet use.

Two children step into their family Anderson shelter.

Betty Brown
Civilian in Chingford
Dad built a turreted bit on top, like a castle and he put a notice over the door, saying, 'SAIFA ERE'. That was the shelter's name – 'Safer here'. He thought that was great fun.

Arthur Dales
Bicycle messenger with ARP in Hull
My mother filled a small suitcase with important documents such as ration cards and insurance policies. When the air raid warning sounded the suitcase was brought down into the shelter with us.

Theresa Bothwell
Civilian in Birmingham
Mother got us into a particular routine every night. We'd put our coat on the back of a chair and put a hat, scarf and gloves in the pockets. Then we'd take our clothes off, fold them up and put them in a pillow slip, keeping our vest, knickers and socks on. Then we'd put our shoes at the side of the bed with the laces loosely tied so we could slip our feet into them and walk to the shelter without tripping.

Thomas Parkinson
Civilian in Kentish Town
We didn't have an Anderson shelter but there was one over the wall from our house. We had very heavy bombing one night and I climbed over the wall and cleared all the cats mess out of the shelter and I went back to my house and went through the house telling everyone that the shelter was clear. By the time I went back to the shelter, it was full so I had to stand outside while they were dropping bombs at the end of the street.

Teresa Wilkinson
Air raid warden in West Ham
The Anderson shelters were very good. They would stand up to everything – except a direct hit. There were four people in one particular house and three of them used the Anderson shelter but one of them – an elderly man – refused point blank to enter the shelter. So he was sleeping in his own bed in the house when a bomb fell on top of the shelter and made an unholy mess, leaving him without his family.

James Oates
Dagenham Home Guard
The people next door used to take the mickey out of us for going down into our shelter. They used to laugh. They'd stay in their bedrooms saying, 'Hitler can do what he likes!' That was all right until Hitler started dropping incendiary bombs. As the incendiaries fell and the anti-aircraft fired away and shrapnel pinged on the roof, our brave neighbours rushed down the stairs and slammed their back door.

John 'Chick' Fowles
Civilian in London
We had an Anderson shelter in the garden but we felt that we stood just as much chance in the house. It might have been the wrong thing to do but that's what the old man wanted. And he'd been in the First World War . . .

Francis Goddard
Auxiliary Fire Service in Tottenham
Halfway through the Blitz, people became fed up going down the little shelters and used to go back to bed. You'd hear shrapnel – 'tap, tap, tap' on the roof or you'd hear a bomb whizzing down, going off somewhere.

Betty Brown
Civilian in Chingford
A lot of the shelters got waterlogged and after a while, we decided that we'd sleep inside. My Dad managed to get hold of lots of very heavy timbers and made a false ceiling in the front room a bit like a wooden canopy so that if the house had come down, the false ceiling would have taken quite a lot of the pressure. We put our beds in there.

Walter Miller
Civilian in London
We had a Morrison shelter – the indoor shelter with the flat top. It was a heavy steel structure which was intended to withstand a house actually falling on it. We put a mattress inside it and all four of us slept in it for quite a few nights. It was intended to be an improvement on being under the stairs, which is where we first used to shelter.

Joan Seaman
Civilian in London
My aunt was saved by a Morrison shelter. Three of them were sleeping in it. The roof came in and they crawled out dusty but all right.

Thomas Parkinson
Civilian in Kentish Town
My friend didn't have a Morrison shelter but he had a big kitchen table. He kept a piece of pipe under there so that if the house collapsed on the table, he'd have something to breathe through.

Walter Marshall
Metropolitan Police War Reserve
When the bombing was heavy, they started building surface shelters.

William Gray
Milkman in London
I don't think surface shelters would have stopped a lot. They were just two rows of brick on the street with a concrete roof. Kids used them for toilets. You used to put your sleeping bag on the concrete floor.

John Cooper
Fire Service in Hull
The roofs of the surface shelters in Hull were not tied into the walls at the top so they weren't effective against lateral blast. The walls would be blown in or in some cases outwards and the whole roof would come down in one solid piece

Walter Marshall
Metropolitan Police War Reserve
Surface shelters were mostly used by ladies of easy virtue or by people needing to relieve themselves. You had to be careful what you trod in. I think they were there more for morale boosting than anything else. In fact, during a rain of incendiaries, an officer dived into a surface shelter and an incendiary bomb came through a hole in the roof. They hadn't even finished building it.

Edward Ardizzone
Official War Artist
Most people in the shelters weren't frightened – or they didn't show it. But

The Morrison shelter could be used as a table by day and a shelter by night.

you occasionally got somebody who was trembling with fear. When the bombs came pretty close, very often an elderly man would sort of break down and that was horrid because he made everybody else frightened. Fear's catching.

Leslie Hyland
Civilian in Liverpool
Mother used to scream and shout during the raids. She felt that every explosion was coming towards her. I remember trying to reassure her that most of the explosions were our own anti-aircraft shells exploding in the sky.

Arthur Dales
Bicycle messenger with ARP in Hull
My uncle had been a professional boxer and he was a shelter warden in Hull. On one of the heavy bombing raids, there were 50 people in his shelter when his 16-year-old daughter became hysterical. My uncle realised that it would be very difficult if all the women and children in the shelter became hysterical so he took his own daughter, picked her up and knocked her out with a blow under the chin.

Winifred Harding
Nurse at Hull Royal Infirmary
I remember seeing people catching the last bus out of Hull and taking their young children and sleeping under hedges on the outskirts and going back on the first bus in the morning because they daren't sleep in the centre of town.

Ernest Beavor
Conscientious objector imprisoned in Wormwood Scrubs
During an air raid, all of us prisoners in Wormwood Scrubs were hammering on our doors wanting to get out. We were all locked in. It was very frightening.

The Human Cost

*I saw what I took to be a piece of rag. I moved the light to one side
and I saw a child's arm.*

Private Albert Dance
Rifle Brigade
When Maisie and I married, I was given four days' special leave. We were
married in the garrison church at Woolwich and then I went back to my unit
and I'd been there for just over two weeks when Lieutenant Alexander came
into my billet at night time and said, 'Don't make a noise. Get dressed and
come back to my billet.' I did this and when we got to his billet, he poured me
a whisky and said, 'Drink that.' I wondered what was coming. He said, 'I'm
sorry but your wife has been very badly injured in a bombing raid over
London. I've got a pass and travel documents here. You go home.'

She'd been at her electronics factory. The air raid warning had sounded and
the foreman told them to go down in the shelter. Maisie and her sister were
the last couple to go in. A bomb came down and exploded in the entrance to
the shelter. Maisie caught the full blast. It was an oil bomb, intended to burn
afterwards.

I got out of the train at Woolwich Arsenal station and her father had been
waiting there for me for the best part of a day. He took me straight to St
Nicholas's Hospital in Plumstead. Maisie was there – and I couldn't believe it.
She was a beautiful girl with lovely hair. Her hair was all matted with oil, her
face was bashed, stones were embedded in her cheeks. She was crying with
pain because her back was shattered and her arm was shattered. It was awful. I
went home that night to my mother's. After about four days, Maisie started to
cheer up a little. But they couldn't deal with the wounds and they just encased

her in plaster from her neck down. It started to smell and I took in some lavender for her so she wouldn't smell it. Then they moved her to a hospital in Dartford. They said to me that they didn't know what she'd be like when she came out. I had to go back to my unit and I'd been back three days when I got another telegram that I had to go home immediately. I went straight to the hospital and I could see she was terribly ill. She'd developed tetanus. Her whole body was rigid. Her face was locked. I don't think she even knew I was there. I stayed with her and then – I make no bones about it – I dropped on my knees and I prayed to God that she would not suffer any more. I walked out to get a nurse and a doctor and as I walked back in, she died.

Harvey Bennette
Messenger boy in Croydon
Attending on an air raid in Croydon was the first time I saw a dead body. I heard the bombers coming over and I saw big clouds of smoke rising, followed very quickly by the noise of an explosion. Very shortly afterwards, we were notified to send ambulances from the first-aid post and they asked me as a messenger to go along in case I was needed to bring back messages. We went down to a scent factory where the tanks that held the cosmetic substances had burst – and the smell was quite, quite appalling. Some people, thinking it was gas, put on their gas masks. I saw some legs under a machine. I thought, 'Oh, must get that fellow out ...' and he was pulled from under the machine, covered in dust and debris. There was no blood. He hadn't been cut at all. But he was dead.

Stanley Clark
Civilian in London
Before the war, when Great Aunt Fanny died, they had her in the parlour, laid out in her coffin and everybody came to have a look and say goodbye. That was all very tranquil. Well, the next time I saw dead people, six of them were propped up along the wall of a blazing estate near us and I thought, 'That's funny. They look just like guys on firework night.'

Albert Prior
Stretcher bearer with West Ham Civil Defence
A public house used to have stacks of wood in the yard from other bombed houses that people used to take and use as firewood. One day, a bomb dropped on the yard and I went down there with my squad. A man came up to me and said, 'Have you found a little girl?' 'Did she have pink knickers on?' I said.

Private Albert Dance. Pictured in 1943 as staff sergeant in Glider Pilot Regiment.

'Yes.' 'Just come with me . . . ' I took him into a house that we'd used to lay out those who were dead. I uncovered this particular girl on a stretcher. The man looked down and walked away very sad. During the afternoon, the same man came up to me and said, 'I've just found out that my little boy was with my little girl. Have you found a little boy?' 'Did he have a green jersey on?' I said. 'Yes.' 'You'll have to come with me again . . . ' On the way to the house, we passed the Salvation Army tea hut and I said, 'Have a cup of tea before you go in there with me.' He had a cup of tea. Then we went into the house. Before I uncovered the boy, I said, 'You're in for a shock. This body's got no head on.' He looked down, bent over and stroked the body. 'So that's how you went, Jimmy?' he said. I took him outside and he put his hand out and he said, 'Thank you for that cup of tea.'

James Oates
Dagenham Home Guard
After a landmine had hit a shelter, a young child walked up to me, gave me a paper bag, and said, 'Mummy said I should give this to you.' When I opened the bag, there was a woman's thumb inside.

Hugh Varah
Auxiliary Fire Service in Hull
I arrived at London Road Station in Manchester in the middle of a raid. We were told to take cover. I thought the best thing to do was to marshal the other passengers and keep them alongside the thick brick wall. I got them nicely settled, some sitting, some crouching – but one man dashed down the slope. He was trying to cross the road to reach an air raid shelter that he said was up a side street. He arrived at the bottom of the slope at the same time as a falling bomb. If I close my eyes, I can still see his head come bowling back up the slope, like a hairy football.

Francis Goddard
Auxiliary Fire Service in Tottenham
After a raid in the early hours of the morning, my wife and I went looking to see if there was any damage nearby. On the Tottenham High Road, a bomb had blown all the shop windows out and people were lying injured. We were the first ones there and I ran over to a man with no arm. He was a shop dummy. They all were. From the tailor's window.

Shop dummies from John Lewis department store lie on the gutter after a raid on Oxford Street.

Marie Price
Civilian in Liverpool
As I walked up the street, I watched something attractive floating down from the sky like a parachute. It landed right at the bottom of Great Mersey Street and wiped out the whole street. I went up there with my friend who lived further along the road and she ran to look for her mother. She started to scream because her mother had beautiful white hair, and she saw her lying there. I just thrust her into somebody's arms and ran home as fast as I could. It was just awful, it was just unbelievable.

Ivor Leverton
Undertaker in London, served with Auxiliary Fire Service
Our flat was bombed when we weren't there but our neighbour was never found. She must have disintegrated. There were quite a lot of trees in Oakley Square and there were bits of clothing and rubbish up there for a long time afterwards and we sometimes used to look up and wonder.

Hugh Varah
Auxiliary Fire Service in Hull
I went to a shelter that was standing intact apart from some very deep score marks gouged out by pieces of the bomb casing. I was relieved to discover that there was no one inside the shelter – but as I came out I heard a dog whimper. Dogs often gave us an indication that someone was trapped so I went back to the rescue chaps and borrowed their torch to look for the animal. I found him in a building a little further down the street. His nose was thrust in among some fallen timber which had been part of the staircase. I took hold of his collar and pulled him back a little so that I could shine the beam under the timber. At first, I couldn't see anything but then I saw what I took to be a piece of rag. I moved the light to one side and I saw a child's arm and I realised that the rag was part of her dress. I tore frantically at the timbers and I crawled to where the child was. I pushed my arm beneath her and cradled her in my arms. Then I realised that she was holding the hand of another child. That's as far as my memory will allow me to go. I can't say what happened next – whatever it was has been blotted from my memory. I came to – so to speak – in a first-aid post. A first-aid worker was washing my face and hands which were liberally covered in blood and dirt. She couldn't find any wounds except for torn nails, cuts and scratches as though I'd been tearing at rubble with my bare hands. My tunic was splattered with blood. I asked how I came to be in the first-aid post and I was told that a policeman had found me wandering

A reconstruction of a dog searching amid the rubble for signs of life.

around. I'd been carrying the decapitated body of a little boy over my shoulder and the lifeless form of a little girl under my right arm. With some difficulty, they had persuaded me to let them take the little girl away on the understanding that they did not wake her as she was asleep.

Alfred Senchell
Auxiliary Fire Service in London
They turned the ground floor of a block of tenements into a shelter. There were about a 150 casualties. They were all so badly damaged that the only way they could tell the sex was to feel them.

Francis Goddard
Auxiliary Fire Service in Tottenham
There was a wardens' post at the back of where they later built the Broadwater Farm estate in Tottenham. There'd been a very bad raid in the area and they weren't getting any answer from the wardens' post and a couple of us were sent down to have a look. The other fellow went into the post first and he came out quickly. I went down and saw the wardens playing cards round the table. They were sitting round the table, holding their cards. Dead.

Clara Thompson
Nurse at Hull Royal Infirmary
Blasts used to do peculiar things to people. People could look perfectly normal but the blast would take their oxygen away and they would die.

Private Herbert Anderson
Pioneer Corps
I remember specially a big factory that had been bombed – Hartley's – which was quite well known as makers of marmalade and jam. And the situation there was indescribable, because the dead were covered in marmalade.

Doreen Kluczynska
Nurse in Luton
A lot of women from a hat factory came into the hospital full of needles. The needles had been blown out of the machines into their bodies.

Gioya Steinke
Welfare Adviser with London County Council Rest Centre Service
One of the welfare advisers at Newington Green rest centre was a young

married women who was expecting and she used to knit little bootees for her baby while she was on duty. When the centre received a direct hit, she was killed outright and a firemen brought the bootees with the needles in them out of the rubble. There was a young man at the centre who was very much in love with her, even though he knew she was married. He used to write poetry for her and he couldn't stop crying every time he thought of these little bootees coming out of the rubble.

Ivor Leverton
Undertaker in London, served with Auxiliary Fire Service
I can remember one case of a man being decapitated and his mother just went and sat with his head on her lap for three hours.

Sergeant Charles Lyons
Royal Army Medical Corps
I went to Coronation Avenue, a five or six storey block of flats in Stoke Newington with shops underneath. A bomb had pierced through the floors and exploded at shop level. Underneath the shops was a big shelter and the water mains burst and more than a hundred people were just drowned. The civil defence authorities put up hoarding all the way round the outside so that it was completely hidden from view and the water had to be pumped out before we could get in. There was no question of digging. Once the entrances were open, we were just getting them out – some of them without a mark. There were young children, women, elderly people, all dead. We looked to see if they had any identification and most people at that stage did have some – a wrist bracelet, a name tag or something. We put them all into ambulances and took them to various different mortuaries. I still occasionally dream about it. I was to see many bad things in Japanese prisoner of war camps but nothing to compare to that.

Dorothy Rothwell
Women's Land Army in Kent
Elsie and I went upstairs to our bedroom to get ready to go out and we heard gunfire. We both did what we'd been told not to do – we ran to the window to see the anti-aircraft fire and the next thing was an almighty bang and everything went black. I was buried under the debris. The bomb had fallen directly on the house. It weighed 50 pounds and it had gone through our bedroom and burst in the room below. The daughter of the house died next day in hospital and the lady next door was killed as well. Elsie caught the full blast of the glass and she had 45 stitches in her face.

I was unconscious at first but then I came to. I was upside down with my watch in my right hand and I tightened my grasp on it but apart from that I couldn't move at all. I was completely buried. I prayed to God that they'd find me. After a couple of hours, they dug down and they got my right leg out up to the knee and I felt a morphine injection go in. They kept digging until I just smelt fresh air. They said my left arm was behind my back with a beam through it so they had to saw through the beam before they could pull me out and they didn't want anything else to fall on my face. I had one ankle broken and I injured the other knee and I had a shrapnel wound on the shoulders and shrapnel in my neck and a piece of brick in my chest. But my feelings were just relief.

I was put into an ambulance and taken to a first-aid depot where they cut off what clothes I had on. One of the ambulance men was only a young lad so I waited to the last piece of clothing and then I told him I had nothing on underneath and he said I could keep that one on. Then they put another injection in my arm and another ambulance took me to the hospital with the back open and the canvas all flapping. I could see a lot of fires burning out of the back. We stopped on the way and the nurse said to me, 'We've stopped because the road's closed but it's all right, you're an emergency and they'll let us through.' Then they gave me yet another injection in the arm and I went to the operating theatre. I ended up with both legs in plaster from my thighs to my toes. I had a plaster across my chest, one across my forehead, one across my leg and my father came in and stood at the end of my bed and tutted. I was just glad to be alive.

I didn't start work again for over a year. My hand wouldn't open and they said the best thing for it was knitting. They said it was the severe bruising of the muscles that was stopping it opening. When I was getting better, the doctor told me to ride my bicycle – and to ride uphill standing on the pedals. But after that, I was very nervous when an air raid was on.

Gabrielle Davy
Child in London

The night that our house went, we were all sitting in our family room. The siren had gone and we were all aware that we would have to go into our shelter rather quickly, but suddenly the whole window behind us caved in. There was a very loud explosion and the clothes fell on to the fire, causing a fire that had to be put out straight away. The lights went out and we had to find torches. My youngest brother, who was about five, had been on the settee. Now, we couldn't find him for a while because the settee was covered

Children in Mill Hill, London who have been orphaned or made homeless by the Blitz.

in rubble. My mother eventually found him but he couldn't speak. It would appear that he was struck dumb and that lasted for almost a week. He wasn't hurt but something had happened to this little boy that had severely shocked him. Gradually his voice came back, particularly as we then went off to Oxford and at that time, there was no sign of the war there. Once he got playing and had friends, he was able to become quite normal again.

William Ryder
Worker at Woolwich Arsenal
One lunchtime, I went round to see my mother and father. I said to Mum, 'Where's Dad?' She said, 'We haven't seen him since he went to work Saturday morning.' He wasn't found till the Monday morning. He was buried upside down in an air raid shelter. He said he was trying to make a sound and he heard someone saying, 'Over here! There's someone alive over here!' They started digging and they dug him out. After that, he had facial injuries. There was something wrong with his jaw and he couldn't speak until his jaw was in the right place.

Alexander Flett
Metropolitan Police in Southwark
A bomb fell on the flats opposite our police station and Bill Carey, a PC at Southwark, burrowed into the wreckage and rescued somebody. When he dug this chap out, he recognised him. Bill had arrested him and got him three months a while back. He got a medal this time.

Joan Varley
Civilian in London
I was woken in the middle of the night by the sound of a stick of bombs coming down. I could hear that it was going to be very near. I reckoned it was going to be more or less a direct hit. I can remember saying the Lord's Prayer before it came down. It fell through the conservatory of the next-door house and I waited for the explosion. It seemed an eternity but it didn't come and I went off to sleep again. That may sound surprising but we learnt to sleep through the Blitz. At breakfast, I told my parents that an unexploded bomb had gone through the next door conservatory but they didn't really believe me because it hadn't woken them. However, I went next door and knocked and a very ancient man with a blanket round his shoulders came to the door. I said, 'Excuse me but I think you have an unexploded bomb in your conservatory.' To which he looked at me angrily and said, 'We have nothing

like that here!' and shut the door in my face. So I went off to work. When I came back, round our houses were the barricades with the notice 'Unexploded Bomb'. They came and took it away the next day. Had it exploded, I wouldn't be here, telling this story.

Alfred Baker
Home Guard in Plymouth

Something came through the roof of the house opposite us. I was called by the neighbour who asked me what it was. There was a hole in her roof going down through her front bedroom and through the ceiling of her hallway. There was a hole in the floor of the hallway and her piano was halfway out the window. I shone a torch at it – it looked metallic. It was a bomb. I immediately got in touch with the police who didn't want to know. I didn't blame them. Bomb disposal were too busy to do anything at all and I was given the job of guarding this bomb. Why I don't know – I'm sure no one wanted to pinch it. I had to stop people coming through the area and there was another guy at the other end doing the same. We were doing it for three days until eventually, the bomb went up – and it took three houses with it. Fortunately, I was not on duty at the time. I'd been relieved by a regular soldier.

Marie Agazarian
Voluntary Aid Detachment

My little sister was sleeping in the next bed and we were next to these huge windows, 11 feet high. In my sleep, I heard these sticks of bombs whistling down and I must have got out of bed and lain on top of my sister. That woke us both up and we went into the corridor. Our brother Jack was up and together we decided to go out and walk round London. It was the most extraordinary night. We helped to pull people out in Jermyn Street. We were climbing over rubble up to the first floor. Christie's was on fire and those wonderful firemen were right up at the top on these ladders with their huge hoses. When we got back at dawn, after the all-clear had gone, the whole of the flat was full of glass and right through the middle of my pillow was a shard of glass. Sometimes you were meant to catch it and sometimes you weren't. If I hadn't got up and lain on top of Yvonne, the glass would have gone through my head. It's amazing isn't it, really?

Sergeant Charles Lyons
Royal Army Medical Corps
I think that most people really got tired but it didn't stop them going to work in the morning, it didn't stop the shops opening and it didn't stop the firefighters.

Stan Poole
Auxiliary Fire Service in London
I was only a messenger with the Auxiliary Fire Service but I used to help on fires. We were in the West End in the thick of it. I'd get home from work, have something to eat, put on my gumboots and go and patrol the streets. I was thinner in those days and one night we saw a house on fire with people in it and they lowered me down into the coal cellar with a rope around me to see if anyone was left down there. There was no arguing about safety – if someone was in trouble, that was it. My mates were standing by with a hose pipe. Up the stairs and in the back, there were three women. They didn't have any clothes on. Whether they'd been blown off them or they'd got up in a panic, I don't know. 'Come on, out!' I said – my language was a bit stronger than that – but they wouldn't move. They were terrified. I got hold of a couple of them by the hair and marched them out and I kicked the other one out with my gumboots.

Alfred Senchell
Auxiliary Fire Service in London
At first the regular fire service didn't care for us in the Auxiliary Fire Service. They thought that we were going to be 'cut price firemen'. There was needle. The regulars used to cook their own dinner in the kitchen and one day they burnt our instructor's dinner because he was training auxiliaries. But once the Blitz started, everything was all right. We were all matey.

Kathleen Clayden
Auxiliary Fire Service in London
In the Auxiliary Fire Service, there was a mixture of the classes. We used to get people with very posh voices and we used to get cockneys and they used to challenge each other to snooker competitions and they used to be pals.

Robert Stepney
London Fire Brigade
One of my auxiliaries at the Knightsbridge station had a double-barrelled name. When it was raining, his butler would come to the station with an umbrella to see him home.

Hugh Varah
Auxiliary Fire Service in Hull

I think of the firemen as the unsung heroes. They were mostly volunteers, working by day and fighting fires by night. At the time of Dunkirk, before the Blitz started, people used to shout at us, 'Army Dodgers!' But when the Blitz started, they couldn't do enough for us.

Alfred Senchell
Auxiliary Fire Service in London

When you're fighting a big fire, it's very hot and wet. Sometimes the atmosphere is choking, depending on the substance that's burning. You don't just put water on the fire, you knock it out with the force of the jet. You try and find the seat of the fire. It's no good tackling a fire at the top because it will keep spreading up from the bottom. Outside London, firemen used to take 'potshots'. They'd stand in the road and operate their hoses through windows. We preferred to go inside and knock the fire out.

John Cooper
Fire Service in Hull

We didn't use the same scientific approach to fires as we did in peacetime. In peacetime, the idea was to extinguish the fire in any one particular room or building with no water damage but during the Blitz it was just a case of getting the fires out before the next night. And we had the assistance of the Auxiliary Fire Service – provided they could hold a pump, use a nozzle, and soak a building, that was fine.

John Lodge
London Fire Brigade

We had problems with access, getting into a street when other buildings had fallen down. We also had problems finding our way into parts of London with which we were not familiar – they'd taken all the signs down to confuse the invaders.

Brian Rust
Auxiliary Fire Service in London

There was a lot of running down roads full of rubble trying not to fall over them. It was like an obstacle race in almost total darkness.

Auxiliary firemen work together to control a hose.

Fires raging at Eastcheap in London.

Ivor Leverton
Undertaker in London, served with Auxiliary Fire Service
When you got a really big raid, there was no possibility of getting enough water to deal adequately with it.

John Lodge
London Fire Brigade
Very often the Germans mounted their raids when the Thames was at low tide so one couldn't draw water from the river. So someone had the good idea of sinking borehole pumps from several of the Thames bridges. They could start these electrically and they would pump water up to iron pipes laid on the surface of the street. There was another set of pumps in the Serpentine in Hyde Park. We had all these water sources listed in a book that we carried on our fire truck. It was a very effective system.

Ivor Leverton
Undertaker in London, served with Auxiliary Fire Service
There were emergency water tanks all over the show. Every corner had one of these whacking great tanks which lasted quite a time as long as you were conveniently placed.

John Cooper
Fire Service in Hull
One night, when there was no water in the mains, we lifted a manhole from the sewers and pumped the sewage. That extinguished the fire in one ward of the infirmary. We used basket strainers in addition to the usual copper strainers. Now and again, we heaved it up to wash the basket.

Flying Officer Basil Stapleton
South African Pilot, 603 Squadron, RAF
When London was being bombed, four of us from the squadron drove in to see if we could help with anything. We saw a fireman who couldn't hold his hose straight because there was a chap in a Rolls-Royce driving over his hosepipe. The onlookers were doing nothing so we went over, stopped the car and with the help of some other people, we turned the Rolls-Royce over.

Alfred Senchell
Auxiliary Fire Service in London
When St Katharine's Dock caught fire, the whole East Basin was alight. We had 500 pumps on that fire. After the fire had been burning for three hours, I lit a cigarette and I felt a tap on the shoulder. It was a policeman. 'Sorry chum, no smoking in the docks,' he said.

Sylvia Clark
Post Office worker in London
I remember watching firemen attending to a building that was on fire, coming down the ladders wearing mink coats, mink capes and fur hats. They were singing like mad as the bombers were still coming over. It was about the only time I had a good giggle during the war.

Robert Stepney
London Fire Brigade
When I was the station officer at Marylebone, I was left with two fires on my hands, each of which required at least 15 pumps. One was at Marble Arch and the other was on the Edgware Road. We got both fires out eventually but the front of a public house had been blown out and the landlord came out and said, 'Can I give your chaps a drink?' 'Not at the moment,' I said, 'but I'll get them relieved and if you want to give them a beer, you can . . . ' A couple of hours later, I was still tramping round and I passed the same pub. The landlord said, 'You haven't had a drink yet,' and he put a glass of beer in my hand. I drank it down. It wasn't beer. It was neat whisky. When I got back to the station, my sub-officer took a look at me and told me to get to bed.

Oliver Bernard
Child in London
Early one morning, I saw a fireman so exhausted that he was asleep on the outer cover of a fire pump's diesel engine while it was actually running.

Marguerite Crowther
Ambulance driver in London
At dawn we used to wait while they were pulling people out of wrecked places. There were people wandering around in their nightshifts not knowing where they were, blood streaming down their faces. We tried to comfort them as best we could. One old man said he was looking for his false teeth. He'd lost his mind and he didn't know where he was. Then, as we were waiting for a girl

that the rescue party was getting out, we turned round to see the King and Queen behind us.

Dora Falconer
Doctor with Emergency Medical Service
They didn't bring too many Blitz victims to the hospitals at once, fortunately, because they had to dig them out. They would collect one houseful and bring them along and then the ambulance would go back and bring another load.

Sergeant Charles Lyons
Royal Army Medical Corps
I was told that there was a group of people who had been injured in the docks at Rotherhithe but we couldn't get near them with our whole team. I was asked to go over a bridge with three ambulances to bring them away. The first two ambulances went over the bridge. I was in the last ambulance with a load of badly injured people when the police stopped us and told us that we couldn't go over the bridge because a bomb had landed right in the middle of it. The bridge was still holding but there was a massive hole through it. Our ambulance would make it collapse. At first, I said, 'Right, we'll wait . . .' But then I realised that these people were too badly injured to wait so I asked the ambulance driver whether we could take a chance. He got out and looked at the bridge and the hole. 'Yes, we can,' he said so I said to the policeman, 'We must take a chance and go over!' 'No!' said the policeman, 'it will be impossible!' 'There's no alternative,' I said, 'we've got to go otherwise these people will die!' So the driver backed up the ambulance and the policemen told him to take it slowly but the driver said, 'No! I'm going to take it at speed!' He got up speed and went over to the bridge. Our back wheels literally dropped into the hole as we crossed but we managed to get over. As we reached the other side, the whole bridge collapsed but we got those people safe.

Marguerite Crowther
Ambulance driver in London
It started to become difficult to find a hospital that would take people. We had to go further and further out but on one occasion I had a woman in the ambulance who was having a baby. So I *had* to go to the nearest hospital and I went to Great Ormond Street. As I got there, a building was burning and the firemen were in the road, saying, 'Don't come up here! This building is coming down!' I drove past them and managed to get the woman to hospital

An injured woman is helped from a first-aid post in Liverpool.

in time but I'd driven over a lot of rubble and I'd got a puncture. We'd been told that whatever happened, we were not to damage an ambulance so we had to do something. I started to change the wheel but a fireman was shouting, 'Get out of it! This building's coming down!' I said to him, 'Don't stand there shouting at us, come and help!' And he did but by the time we'd put two screws on, the whole building started coming down and we got in and drove backwards into Theobalds Road. It was too late and the ambulance was blasted and I lost control and it spun round. Everything stopped and the building came down on top of us. It didn't come through the roof. I don't know why but it didn't. Then I heard a bang underneath the ambulance. I got out and looked underneath and saw the top of a policeman's helmet. A policeman had been blown under the ambulance.

Gladys Smith
First-aid worker with Civil Defence
You did what you could to help as people were being transported to hospital. You could stop bleeding – you had to know your pressure points – and you could immobilise a broken limb. I don't mean attempt to set it but if a leg was broken you could strap the legs together.

Marguerite Crowther
Ambulance driver in London
There was always a joke from the injured. There was no screaming and yelling. Everybody was controlled and very determined not to give way. People I carried in the ambulance were so quiet, so determined – so British.

Clara Thompson
Nurse at Hull Royal Infirmary
We couldn't do anything for some of the patients except give them morphia and leave them to die. I remember a pretty young girl who was brought in on a stretcher. The whole of her back had been taken off – her kidneys were exposed. There was nothing you could do for her. She was going to die.

Dora Falconer
Doctor with Emergency Medical Service
The Blitz injuries were mostly blast injuries. The worst of it was the dirt. They were all covered with dust, rubble and plasterwork which had to be cleaned away before you got down to what was really wrong. In the films, they're all so clean and tidy.

Winifred Harding
Nurse at Hull Royal Infirmary
The injured . . . their skin was so black . . . they were like coal miners. The dirt was pitted right into the skin with the force of the blast.

Gladys Smith
First-aid worker with Civil Defence
You might get them cleaned up and find that they'd got no injuries – they were just suffering from shock.

Dora Falconer
Doctor with Emergency Medical Service
We didn't do anything to prevent shock – we didn't know enough about it. We only had saline and plasma to give them.

Doreen Kluczynska
Nurse in Luton
A very badly injured lady was brought into the hospital with a two-year-old child. In those days, the children had to go to the children's ward. They couldn't stay with the mothers. The mother wasn't expected to live but even though the child didn't have a scratch on her, she just sat in the corner of the cot, in a heap. She wouldn't eat, wouldn't look at us, wouldn't do anything. After three days, she just died. And the mother lived. I never forgot that. It upset me and it still does – even though it's just one thing amongst many. The verdict was delayed shock.

Robert Wager
Civilian in Croydon
Although she wasn't injured, I do say that the war killed my wife. She had some heart trouble and on one occasion, a bomb was falling and I threw her on the floor in the kitchen. She was carrying my second child. She suffered a shock and she died a year later.

Marie Agazarian
Voluntary Aid Detachment
I remember a chap in hospital with half his face blown away. He was dying and he was making this awful rattle. In the next ward, a woman started shouting, 'Can't somebody stop that man making that noise?' The man was her husband but she didn't know it.

Teresa Wilkinson
Air raid warden in West Ham

During a heavy raid, a warden gave me a torch and a piece of paper and said, 'You're wanted in the school shelter!' I looked at the piece of paper and it had printed details on how to deliver a baby. I dashed down and among the crowd of people inside was a woman lying on the floor about to give birth. An ambulance had been sent for and I've never prayed more fervently in my life that it would get arrive soon. The man who'd sent me down came in with a screw-topped jar with two bits of string inside. He said, 'We've put them in boiling water.' I waited and waited and then the baby came out. As I was unscrewing the jar, I was thinking, 'Suppose I don't tie it up tightly enough? Suppose I tie it too tightly and they both die?' Just then a nurse came and she took over. I was never more relieved in my life.

Clara Thompson
Nurse at Hull Royal Infirmary

A woman who was eight months pregnant had been brought into Swansea General Hospital with her legs broken. She was taken up to a ward on the top floor and then a bomb hit the hospital. Matron said to me, 'There's only you and me with midwifery training. One of us ought to be with that woman.' So I went up to stay with her. They started trying to get everybody down off the top floors but then a second bomb hit and all the windows went. Everywhere was covered with rubble and smoke. The electricity went and the lifts wouldn't work. Myself and another little nurse were left on the top floor with eight male medical cases and this woman, eight months pregnant with two broken legs. We thought we couldn't possibly survive. We got one or two of the men and pulled them underneath the beds for safety. One dear old man was very ill and I went and sat on his bed and he said, 'I'm an old man and I've had a good life and I'm quite prepared to die . . . but you're so young and it's wrong that you should have to die as well.' 'What are you talking about?' I said, 'I'm not going to die and neither are you!' Nobody came near us until the all-clear went. The porters just disappeared. I never forgave them for that.

Katharine Day
Cvilian in Whitstable, Kent

At about nine o'clock one night, it was jet black outside. My daughter, Olga came running and she said, 'Mother! An aeroplane's coming down and it's going through the butt!' It swished along and the end of it went into the trees.

It didn't touch our house. It was a miracle. It was a great big bomber and its wings had been cut off by the trees. It had just come back from Germany and it went straight into a wall – crash, bang, wallop. I jumped on my bike and I said to my son, 'Run down and get the ambulance!' He was only ten and he got on his bike and went three miles to Chipping Norton. I pulled on my pinafore and I put the torch on the front of the bike and I rode a quarter of a mile to a place called Hill Barn.

When I got there, I could see all bodies lying about and I tied the torch round my neck and I tried to make a way for all these men. They were on their knees, on their backs, there was one stuck up a tree, one hanging over a wall. I didn't know where to start. I managed to lay seven of them all in a row. They were all dead. But not the man hanging on the wall. I went over to him and said, 'Are you all right?' and he said, 'Fag! Fag!' I had two Woodbines and my lighter in my pocket. I gave him a fag and he kind of revived and smoked it and then all of a sudden, he fell back, knocked me flying and fell on top of me. I got hurt but not like him – he died. So I laid him out and covered them all up with the sheet that I brought.

I turned round and nobody had come yet. I thought, 'Wherever have they got to?' I was petrified. It was a haunted place and just over the wall was a barn full of bats and they were all flying round me, in the air, everywhere. I was hitting them to get out of the way. I tell you, it was terrible. Suddenly, I heard a groaning. I thought, 'What's that?' It was a man screaming all of a sudden. He'd come to. He was sitting in the cockpit of the aeroplane and I said, 'Are you all right?' I thought, 'How am I going to get up there?' I was big and fat, I was a huge woman, 12 stone.

Suddenly my husband arrived and he brought my friend's husband Frank Tanner with him and I said, 'There's a man in the cockpit and he can't move or get out!' His leg was almost gone – one of his legs was caught. I said, 'He'll have to have some morphia. I haven't got none, what can you do?' So my husband said, 'Well send somebody over the manor. There's a nurse over there that looks after an old man. She'll have morphia.' So the nurse arrived and put the morphia in him and the lad went quiet and my husband and Frank Tanner stood on top of the fuselage and they lifted him up by his arms and they got him out and just at that moment, the ambulance came. I looked around and I saw two other men from the aeroplane and they were in an alcove of trees and they were on top of one another and their faces were smashed in. Then, the old army doctor came up from Chipping Norton and he certified the dead. By this time, most of the village people were rushing up because I had the bike and they'd all walked.

In the end, they gave the nurse the George Medal and they should have given it to me as well. I didn't tell them what I'd done but they all knew. The Reverend Spencer, the vicar, used to say that he would give me something later. After a couple of years, he honoured me with a community centre – a big hut – in a field opposite Daisy's Pub. He said, 'I know you never got a medal but you deserved ten!'

Leslie Stark
Civilian in Sussex

A large bomb demolished a farm at Wadhurst Park. There were two women in the house and several children. A bomb landed on the side of the house and one of the women was killed and the other one was blown out through the wall. The story was that Vic Dunk, who fired the engine at the sawmill, was staggering home from the pub when the bomb blew him over. He picked himself up, heard the babies crying in the house and scrambled inside. He managed to get upstairs and he got the babies out. The girl who usually looked after the children had had a night off and she came home just then and Vic handed the youngsters to her and off he went home. As far as Vic was concerned, that was the end of it. Later on, *she* was awarded the George Medal. The official citation said, 'For crawling upstairs under incessant enemy activity . . . ' Everybody knew that Vic saved the children but there was nothing we could do about it. But Vic didn't care. He was a nice old stick who liked his beer.

Harry Errington
Auxiliary Fire Service, awarded George Cross for rescue of colleagues

We were down in the basement of Jackson's Garage and we were all asleep when a bomb hit us. I was blown right across the basement floor. I got up in a daze and threw a blanket over my head. I started running for the exit when I heard John Holinshead shouting and screaming. I didn't think. If I'd thought, I probably wouldn't have turned back. The flames were near him and his back was burning and I started digging his legs out from under a pile of rubble. Every time I touched him, he was in agony. As I carried him out to the stairway, I saw John Terry, pinned to the ground by a radiator. He had a lump the size of an orange on his head. I carried Holinshead up the stairs and then I went back to get Terry. By now the flames were worse and by the time I'd lifted the radiator off him, the stairs were blocked. I dragged him out another way and got him outside where I left him propped up against a wall. Then I picked up Holinshead and half dragged him to the Women's Hospital in Soho

Square. He wasn't screaming any more – he'd gone into shock. As we struggled on, I heard a whistling sound. It was a bomb coming down. 'John! Duck!' I screamed, as though that would make any difference. I pushed him to the ground and we felt the full force of the bomb. I carried him on to the hospital and I found out later that the first-aid people had taken John Terry to the Middlesex Hospital. They both survived. They're both dead now, of course, but I'm still in contact with Terry's wife. She once said to me, 'Because of you, my two children were born.' I was very touched by that.

Ivor Leverton
Undertaker in London, served with Auxiliary Fire Service
Three of us were standing beside a metal-lined coffin at the National Temperance Hospital when a bomb came down the lift shaft and exploded. It tore a woman on the other side of the doorway to pieces. One of us was behind a wall and he was badly shocked but the blast missed him. The second one was badly cut by the glass from the door. I was sent up twenty stairs. I flew through the air, presumably with the greatest of ease. The metal coffin had been split right down the middle. How we weren't split down the middle, I don't know. I'd lost my glasses and my first reaction was to look for them. The chance of finding anything in all the debris was pretty remote but people did daft things.

Brian Rust
Auxiliary Fire Service in London
I was trying to cope with a fire as these people came out of a dance hall. They didn't have the sense they were born with. One girl in a flowing evening gown bent down to pick up a bit of bomb. 'Oh, it's hot!' she said. I nearly turned the hose on her. What did she expect?

Ronald Oates
Civilian in London
My grandfather was as deaf as could be and when he saw two people lying on the pavement, he bent down to help them up. They'd thrown themselves down because the bombs were falling all around but he didn't know that. They grabbed him and pulled him down, and that's when he realised he had a problem.

Walter Marshall
Metropolitan Police War Reserve
A whole ruddy row of slums had been blasted and there was fear of fire from gas leaks. As myself and another officer were patrolling, trying to find out if anyone needed help, we saw a flickering light inside one of the houses. We clambered over the rubble to look inside and we heard a voice. An old man came stumbling towards us with a candle in his hand. 'Who's knocking at the door at this time of night?' he muttered. He was stone deaf. He didn't know anything about any bombs.

Doreen Kluczynska
Nurse in Luton
I remember a lady coming in who'd been suspended in her bath when her house had come down. She was sitting in her bath and the firefighters got her out but all she was concerned about was that she was naked.

Stanley Parker-Bird
Chief Shelter Officer for Marylebone
When the front of a building was blown out in Lisson Grove, the rescue party went up a ladder to the bedrooms above where they found an old lady, still in her bed, and they tried to take her out. 'Yes, I'll go,' she said, 'but I want what's under my pillow.' They fetched out a bottle of brandy. 'Yes,' she said, 'I keep that in case of accidents.'

Francis Goddard
Auxiliary Fire Service in Tottenham
A bomb sliced the corner off some houses in Lordship Lane and I remember looking up and seeing a gentleman sitting up on the top floor lav with his trousers down. He was going to the toilet when a bomb split his house in half and there he was on the loo.

Stanley Parker-Bird
Chief Shelter Officer for Marylebone
When I was on duty in the control centre in Marylebone Road, I went out one morning and on the running board of one of the parked cars was a pigeon's egg which had been laid during the night. The bombs had that effect on the pigeons.

Joan Seaman
Civilian in London
When my uncle's house was bombed, all he was really concerned about was his goldfish.

Francis Goddard
Auxiliary Fire Service in Tottenham
After a raid, we heard a lot of chickens kicking up a fuss. I went round to have a look what was going on. It was a chicken run with a couple of dozen chickens in it and the blast had blown all the feathers off some of them. We saw these chickens running around without a feather left on them. We all had chicken dinners the next day – and we didn't even have to pluck them.

Eileen Livett
Civil Nursing Reserve
As we stood at the entrance to our Anderson shelter, my father said, 'Funny! I can smell onions frying! Would you believe it, someone's frying onions, with a raid on!' I was hungry and they smelled marvellous. After a few minutes, I said, 'Daddy, it's coming from next door's garden!' What had happened, the incendiaries had set light to our neighbour's allotment garden, where he'd got a bed of onions. Those were our fried onions.

John Lodge
London Fire Brigade
My first big fire was in an East End warehouse where the floors had collapsed and there was a huge amount of debris – largely consisting of tea. You could smell tea being made by hot water running across it. It was a very pleasant smell but very sad that all this rationed tea was being destroyed.

Francis Goddard
Auxiliary Fire Service in Tottenham
One night, they hit a tyre factory. I was on the fire tender and you can imagine the smell of thousands of burning tyres. Then suddenly, we heard this dreadful 'crack, crack, crack' noise and we were given the order to take cover. We thought it was an aeroplane firing at us but then someone realised that the Tizer factory next door had caught alight and we were hearing the Tizer bottles exploding. It was the blooming caps blowing off.

Albert Prior
Stretcher bearer with West Ham Civil Defence

I got home late and I made myself a cup of cocoa and a cheese sandwich. Just then a bomb dropped a fair distance away and my table with my cocoa and sandwich on it disappeared through a set of sliding doors into the next room.

Captain Charles Drake (RN)
Naval Intelligence Division

Winston Churchill often watched the bombing from the roof of the Board of Trade building in which our offices were situated. One evening he was up there in the cold. And one of the others asked him if he would like his overcoat as it was getting so cold. Churchill said, 'No, no, don't fuss me! I'm perfectly warm. In fact, rather too warm.' Later, a little man came up and looked nervously round and disappeared again. A few minutes later, he appeared again. And then a third time. Churchill turned on him and said, 'My man, I know you are probably only doing your duty up here but what is it?' 'Please, sir,' said the man, 'you are sitting on the smoke escape shaft and they're complaining down below that the building is filling up with smoke.' No wonder Churchill was warm . . .

Glenys Branson
Civilian in Sussex

We had a father and son sent to us in Sussex from Leeds as directed labour. We had a three bedroom cottage and we took them in. The old man used to dress himself up properly every night – collar and tie – and then him and the son used to walk two miles to the pub. One night, my parents, our evacuee and myself were sitting playing cards when the old man came down, all dressed up and ready. He shouted up to his son, 'Come on boy! Hurry up or the pub'll be shut!' He went over to the back door and as he took hold of the knob, there was a tremendous explosion. The door came off and he landed in a corner off the room with the door on top of him. We were all blown on to the floor. The son came down the stairs and fell down the bottom. The old man got up and dusted himself down. 'Come on boy, the pub'll be shut,' he said and off they went.

Elsie Foreman
Civilian in Battersea

Our windows were blown in and my younger sister came outside and started sweeping the glass into the kerb while the raid was still going on. Then my older sister came out and they had a terrific row because the younger sister was wearing a pair of the older sister's high-heeled shoes. She made her take them off. Bombs were dropping around them and they were having a row over a pair of shoes.

Teresa Wilkinson
Air raid warden in West Ham
I went into a house which was damaged but still standing and a very old lady was inside, shaking like mad. She was alone. She'd hurt her feet and the ambulance man came in and removed her boots by cutting the laces. 'Oh what are you doing?' she asked sadly, 'I had such a job tying those up tonight . . . ' She was shaking with cold and hanging on the hook in the hall was a coat so I put it over her shoulders. Well, the next day, the people who lived in that house came in and said to me, 'How dare you take one of our coats!' 'If you go to the hospital,' I said, 'you can get it back again. I think it was very mean of you to leave an old lady on her own in the house!' They were very disgruntled. I don't know if they got their coat back or not and frankly, I don't much care.

Thomas Cunningham-Boothe
Civilian in Coventry
In spite of having served as an infantry soldier on the Rhine and in Malaya and Korea, I saw more devastation on the night of November 14, 1940 in Coventry than during any of my military experiences.

Dilwyn Evans
Red Cross in Coventry
The Coventry raid lasted from about seven o'clock at night until half-past five the next morning. First of all, they sent a wave of planes over with incendiary bombs which they dropped on the city, lighting it up. As soon as the city was alight, over came the heavy bombers, and they just dropped everything that they'd got. I was at home and as soon as I realised how serious things were – at about nine o'clock – I got on my bike and went into the city centre. And when I got there, I had to carry my bike over rubble on the roads. The amount of damage to armament factories outside the city centre was very limited compared to the damage to the cathedral and the commercial buildings in the centre.

Thomas Cunningham-Boothe
Civilian in Coventry
The centre of Coventry was absolutely destroyed. Firemen were so badly affected by the flames that women were leading them away because they couldn't see.

Dilwyn Evans
Red Cross in Coventry
That night was dramatic. I can remember walking past the council housing in the centre. Everything was burning away, debris all around. A lot of people were going about trying to find relatives, friends, goodness knows what. The fire-fighting service was getting through but once the mains were out of action, all the firemen could do was stand by and watch it burn itself out.

Thomas Cunningham-Boothe
Civilian in Coventry
When the sirens sounded on the night of November 14, my mother told me to go to the shelter as usual. But she and my youngest sister stayed behind because my mother was doing some ironing. But my mother was a very intuitive person and she felt there was danger. She called to my sister and they both went under the stairway where there was a large chest. My mother went to put her arm around my sister – and it was all over. The walls of the house went out, the roof came down and my mother got trapped in the house. My sister should have been buried alongside her but she finished up stark naked on the roof of the house. God knows how that happened. She never spoke for four days. My mother survived. She'd had an artificial leg since she was a baby and she was trapped by this leg and she had to work the harness free to release her body from the leg. She crawled out of a hole that a rat couldn't get out of.

Dilwyn Evans
Red Cross in Coventry
When it was realised how devastating the raids on Coventry had been, we in the Red Cross were were told to go and see what we could do. We went to areas that had got the brunt of it. There was smoke everywhere but the fires were burning themselves out and for about three days, we worked night and day. We were absolutely shattered. Having seen a particular person trapped, it was a case of removing the debris by hand. There were always people willing to help but in a lot of instances, they did more harm than good – you had to evaluate the position that the injured person was in and to try and make them

The scene in the centre of Coventry after the raid of November 14, 1940.

as comfortable as you could. Once a person saw that your main factor was to help them and get them free, they were prepared to just lay back and let you do what you wanted. There were times when I felt like getting up and walking away – thinking I've had enough. The hardest experience was when we evaluated the condition of a body and realised there was no life but you'd still got to get the body out. That happened in the High Street and as we were recovering this body, I was on my hands and knees and I felt a tap on my shoulder. I turned round – it was the Mayor of Coventry. He said, 'Excuse me, I've got someone here who would like to have a word with you.' I got up and looked and there was King George VI in full field marshal's uniform. He just put his hand out and thanked me very much for what we were doing. That repaid me for everything I'd done.

Thomas Cunningham-Boothe
Civilian in Coventry
I would rate Coventry folk as being a shining example to the nation during the war. People who'd lost their homes continued turning up for work in the factories.

Hugh Varah
Auxiliary Fire Service
I was in Manchester on the terrible night of December 23, 1940 and I grabbed the first opportunity to join a rescue team. Someone fitted me with an axe, a jemmy and a torch and we were ordered to the hospital as fast as possible. It had received a direct hit and when we got there, the patients and staff were being evacuated. Part of the building was a shambles and the bulk of its roof was blown to pieces. Two nurses in that wing had been killed and a roll-call had left three others unaccounted for. There was a possibility that they had gone in an ambulance with the evacuated patients but a porter who had been dug out of the ruins said that he thought that they were still on the top floor.

A large bomb had dropped straight down the lift shaft, bringing the lifts and cables crashing down and the stairs crashing down with them. There was just a deep and empty abyss with a tangle of cables all the way down to the basement. There was no way either up or down and it was impossible to get a turntable ladder near the building. Before we had a chance to work anything out, there was a shout of 'Take cover! Bomb coming down!' Crouched down in the rubble, I looked up into the blackness of the sky and I could see nothing unusual. Then I noticed what appeared to be a dark tent-like canopy – a parachute. Then I saw that there were two of them, so close that they were touching one another. As they came lower, I could make out a long black oil drum suspended between them. It was the first view I ever had of a landmine. A swirling gust of wind blew the parachutes sideways, wrapping them around a chimney stack. It was fortunate that they did because I'd left diving for cover a little bit late. The landmine came to rest with a thump against the chimney where it hung swaying on its lines, making a grating noise as it scraped to and fro against the brickwork. I'd been told by a bomb disposal chap that these landmines had to roll over to set them off, so if the canopy held, it would be safe but there was no guarantee that the lines wouldn't tear under the strain. There was a sudden scurrying as everyone made frantic efforts to move away. I was left all on my tod. Someone signalled frantically for me to take cover but for some strange reason, I ignored him and turned to my left, looking up at the building. If the porter was correct and nurses were trapped up there, I was going to climb the face of the building.

I ignored the cries of the bloke calling me – a policeman – and I crunched over the rubble and started to climb. It was a dodgy business. Almost every movement I made dislodged a bit of rubble. About halfway up, I found that a large area of the face of the building had been blown out. I peered into the gaping hole but decided that it would be far too risky to enter at this point. The only way to proceed would be to travel horizontally until I came to a section where I could once more start climbing. The climb looked straightforward to the right but that would have taken me nearer to the landmine so I had to go to the left and I came to a tangle of metal at the end of the building that had been the external fire escape. I grabbed hold of it and began to climb. The higher I got, the easier it became. I reached the top platform and looked through the jagged hole where the escape door had been. The ceiling of the corridor had completely gone and I could see stars and the searchlights through the rafters. I shone the beam of my torch along the floor and saw long cracks like a large spider's web. I came to a large ward. There was plaster, soot, bricks and rubble over everything. The place was a shambles. I called out, 'Anybody there?' A faint sound came from the far end of the ward and I went across. 'Anybody there?' I repeated and a creaking sound came from under one of the beds. I went down on all fours and shone my torch under the bed and there – sure enough – lay a nurse.

Her uniform was badly torn, one of her shoes was missing and she was covered from head to foot in grime. Her left arm was trapped under a large piece of heavy timber which held her down. She had struggled to free herself without success. Her eyes were open and there were little streaks down her cheeks where her tears had washed little runnels in the dirt. 'Hold on a minute lass!' I said, 'I'll soon have you out of there!' I pulled the bed away and with a bit of an effort, heaved the beam away from her arm. As gently as I could, I lifted her on to one of the beds. She could only whisper because her mouth and throat were bunged up with dirt and dust. Shining my torch around, I spotted a water dispenser at the end of the ward. I filled a cardboard beaker and told her to wash her mouth out and spit it on the floor. Then I let her have a drink and I wiped her face. She told me she was a staff nurse and her name was Sally. She'd damaged her knee and her arm – it looked broken – and she was in some considerable pain. I asked her if there was any morphine on this floor and she said that if I could get into sister's room, there was some in the medicine cabinet but it was always kept locked and she didn't have the key. I didn't intend that anything as trivial as a locked door would prevent me from doing what I wanted.

I went to find sister's room. There was a huge pile of timber and debris in the hallway – too much of it to shift. So I scrambled up the heap of junk and as the ceiling now lay on the floor, I could poke my head over the top of the wall and look down into sister's room. The light from my torch showed up two people in the room. One was sitting at a desk, holding her head in her hands. The other was laid on the floor. The porter had been quite right. There were three of them up here. I climbed up and dropped into the room.

The girl sitting at the desk looked at me but when I spoke to her, she only shook her head and pointed to her ears. She had been deafened by the explosion and robbed of the power of speech. I noticed a cupboard hanging on the wall, containing all kinds of bottles. It didn't matter whether it was locked or not as any glass it had possessed was shattered. I found a small metal container with a syringe inside and a dark green bottle with 'MORPHINE' printed on the label. I put them in my pocket and turning to the girl, I mimed to her to stand on the desk and then on my shoulders so that she could scramble up through the ceiling joists. She nodded and up she went. I heard her making her way across the pile of rubbish as I knelt beside the nurse who was laid on the floor. She was a much older woman and from the gash on her head, she looked as though she'd received a fairly heavy whack. As I couldn't detect any breathing, I assumed that she was dead. There was an odd smell about and I remember thinking, 'What an odd scent she uses . . .'

With some effort, I retraced my steps over the ceiling joists and slid down the pile of rubble to find the deaf nurse standing at the bottom, waiting for me. Taking her by the hand, I led her through the debris and into the ward where Sally lay. 'Poor girl,' said Sally, 'her name's Joan and she only joined us this week. She must be scared to death, poor lass.' Following Sally's instructions, I inserted the needle through the rubber membrane of the bottle and drew morphine into the syringe. I had to clean a patch of her skin but there was no more water in the dispenser so I licked and sucked a place above her elbow until it was clean. Soot mixed with plaster is not a taste I recommend but there was no other way. I made sure there were no air bubbles in the syringe and I took a portion of the cleaned area between my thumb and finger, inserted the needle and pushed the plunger home.

As I was waiting for the drug to take effect, I had Joan knotting some sheets together to make a rope to make our descent. I found two pieces of wood which would serve as splints and as gently as I could, I placed the splints either side of Sally's broken arm and proceeded to bind it into place. Joan could see what I was doing and she came across and took over the task. I had no way of knowing how much damage her knee had sustained and I didn't want to make it any worse when I moved her so I tied her legs together with a piece of timber between them to act as a splint. By this time, the morphia was taking effect and killing the pain. Sally managed a little smile and said, 'Trussed me up good and proper, haven't you?' I returned her smile and said, 'So that I can have my wicked way with you!' I gave her a little kiss and that brought a proper smile.

I carried Sally to the far end of the building and Joan carried the knotted sheets. I thought it would be harder going down than coming up – this time I'd be carrying Sally. I fastened one end of our escape rope to the fire escape, making sure that it was secure and I flung it clear so that it hung down to the ground with a little to spare. I signalled to Joan that she was to tie Sally on to my back. When I was satisfied that Sally was secure, I made Joan understand that I would return for her and she nodded. It was much easier going down the rope than I had anticipated – even with the dead weight of Sally on my back. As we got lower, people on the ground steadied us over the last few feet. They untied Sally and we lowered her on to a stretcher. Stretcher bearers carried a stock of tie-on labels so that all relevant information could be written down to inform the medics at the hospital. I wrote Sally's name and the details of her arm, her knee and the morphine. On the back of the label, I wrote, 'Gave her a little kiss'. I know it was a silly thing to write but I thought when someone told her, it might cheer her up. As I was tying the label on, she put her good hand over mine and asked, 'Who are you?' I only managed to say, 'A stranger . . . ' before the stretcher bearers shot off at the double and all she had a chance to do was wave and call, 'Thanks, stranger.'

The next move was to fetch Joan but when I looked up, she was already halfway down the rope of sheets so I caught hold of it to stop it swinging and steadied her as soon as she came within reach. She clung to me and began to shake all over. I held her firmly and shouted for another stretcher. Immediately, two more chaps came bounding over the rubble and laid a stretcher down. We lowered her on to it and as gently as I could, I freed myself from her tight embrace. I wrote another label for her, tied it to her and gave her a little kiss also. The stretcher bearers shot off.

Only then did I allow myself to think of the landmine. I was all right – but silly ass that I am, I went and looked at it again. It was quite light now and I could see the thing clearly. It looked menacing and I thought of the woman on the floor in sister's woman and I began asking myself if she was really dead. Could I have been mistaken? I knew that question would haunt me as long as I lived. I turned to look at the building and I started to climb again. It was much easier climbing up a second time. I passed through the junk and lowered myself down again into the sister's room. I pulled open the top drawer of the desk and there was a stethoscope inside. I ripped open the top of the nurse's uniform and listened for a heartbeat. At first, I couldn't detect any sound. I moved it nearer her left breast and then I heard her heartbeat. 'Thank God I went back,' I said aloud.

I went into the ward to get some blankets to make a sling – but I couldn't tear them and I started to panic. I was getting to the end of my tether. Something inside me was screaming, 'Run, you idiot!' I swore at myself, I swore at the blanket but before I lost all self-control, I heard footsteps. I looked up and there was a policeman. He said, 'I saw you look at the bomb and start to climb again so I knew someone else must be trapped. I came to see if I could help.' My mind cleared. Together, we tried to haul the nurse over the ceiling joists. I could see that he was as scared as I was and I said to him – I don't know why – 'Let's pretend we're a couple of storks carrying a baby.' He grinned at me, the tension was broken and we guided her between the joists and carried her to the fire escape platform, before lowering her to the ground. The policeman and I followed down the rope – for the last time I hoped. I went so fast that I actually burnt my hand with the friction. As I wrote out her label, I asked an ambulance man, 'Who is the top man at Manchester Royal?' 'Dr McDonald,' he said. I signed that name on the label. By way of explanation, I said, 'If I sign my own name, it wouldn't carry any weight. I know this woman is alive and I don't want some clever dick of an intern saying different! Do you think I would be playing silly buggers under that damn bomb if she was dead?' My voice had raised several notches. I was very near to breaking point. Just then, it came to me what her problem was. That curious smell. It wasn't perfume. It was diabetes. She had sugar diabetes and she was in a coma. I recognised the smell from an infirmary where I'd spent time in my younger days. I told the stretcher men and they looked at me, 'Don't you worry, doc! We'll see that they take notice.' And off they went.

Walter Marshall
Metropolitan Police War Reserve

At the end of 1940, Lord Haw-Haw declared over the radio that there'd be a ceasefire for the Christmas period. But in the afternoon of Sunday, December 29, I'd been for a walk up the West End with my roommate. At about five o'clock, it was dark, and the first incendiaries started to fall. My mate said, 'I think London's getting a hiding tonight.' He was right. That was the night they set the city on fire. It was the big fire that St Paul's managed to escape – but not much else did. We were in Hoxton Street and we could see it getting nearer and nearer to us.

Leslie Mitchell
Broadcaster with BBC and British Movietone News

I was working at Bush House on the night of December 29, down by the Strand and we were told that there was a tremendous Blitz on and we'd better not go out but we managed to persuade the man to let us on to the roof and the whole of the vista outside was fire. St Paul's appeared to be on fire. The line along the Thames was on fire – that was the warehouses. The City was well ablaze. It was a very frightening sight because one really believed, 'Now, we've had it . . . '

Stanley Baron
Reporter for News Chronicle

As soon as the all-clear went that night, I decided to walk round London. It was on fire. The Guildhall was on fire. Wherever one looked up the narrow alleys of the City, you saw what looked like red snowstorms. Great showers of sparks were coming from the burning buildings. I managed to get inside the entrance of the Guildhall while it was still on fire. Firemen told me that Gog and Magog were burning. And looking up from outside the building, I saw the quite extraordinary picture of the silhouette of a fireman on a high water tower and his jet illuminated by the flames from the building. What struck me most about that night was the extraordinary beauty of it. It sounds fantastic but it really was a very beautiful scene. The colours were fantastic. The dome of St Paul's was to be seen against a background of yellow and green and red with great billows of smoke coming across it. And at the Guildhall, the silhouette of this fireman was black against the extraordinary glowing sky. Before the war, I had walked around most of the City. I loved the City and I knew its buildings. And there I was, simply watching the whole thing burn.

Mary Warschauer
Civilian working for Air Ministry in London
My boyfriend and I went on to Westminster Bridge and although it was pitch black, everything was silhouetted in red. But the bit that got me was the river. Everything was reflected in that river, and it wasn't a river of water, it was a river of fire and it was alive. It was a combination of horrendous and beautiful and magnificent.

Walter Marshall
Metropolitan Police War Reserve
After the December raid, warehouses were turned into makeshift mortuaries in Golden Lane. Certain police officers – thank God it wasn't me – had to arrange the bodies as they were dug out. They had to put them together for identification purposes. A casualty list came out on the teleprinter. It would be rattling away for an hour sometimes. Name after name after name. Lots and lots of them were unidentified. Whole families disappeared, never to be heard of again.

Horace Davy
Civilian in London
I went to explore the area after the raid and I remember the stench from the burnt out buildings and trying to pick my way through streets littered with glass and debris with fire hoses all over the place looking like strips of spaghetti.

Walter Marshall
Metropolitan Police War Reserve
During the day of December 30, I was sent down to stop sightseers. I was told just to allow in essential vehicles and firefighters. A lot of the roads around St Paul's were wooden block streets, and I looked up one street and the wooden blocks were on fire. The ruddy road was still on fire.

Leslie Mitchell
Broadcaster with BBC and British Movietone News
The next morning, the firemen were still working and things were still possible. Very difficult – but still possible. One thought, 'Thank God for that'.

Ballard Berkeley
Special Constable in London
The most horrifying sight I saw was the bombing of the Café de Paris in London in March 1941. By this time, one was accustomed to continuous night bombing. You'd seen as many horrors as you'd expected to see; buildings down, trying to get people out who were buried, complete horror all round – but this was something that was so different. The reason it was such a horror was because the Café de Paris was reckoned to be a safe place. It's underground. And it was registered in some kind of way by Westminster Borough Council as being safe. But they were dead unlucky in that the bomb that struck entered a ventilator shaft at the top of the building and it came right down the shaft and it burst on the dancefloor in front of the band led by Ken 'Snakehips' Johnson, a wonderful coloured musician. The explosion within this confined space was tremendous. It blew legs off people, heads off people and it exploded their lungs so that when I went into this place, I saw people sitting at tables quite naturally – dead. Dressed beautifully without a mark on them. Dead. It was like looking at waxworks. It was a horrifying sight. I remember speaking to a sergeant friend of mine who looked terrible. He said he had tripped over something and when he bent down to pick it up, it was a girl's head. And then he saw her sitting at her table without a head. And he was sick.

Alda Ravera
Secretary in London
We knew the cashier at the Café de Paris. She was caught in the bombing. She wasn't hurt but a thing you often hear, 'it makes my hair stand on end' – well, I'd never seen that happen but I saw it with her. Her hair stood up. She was talking but I wasn't listening – I was just looking at her hair.

Ruth Wittmann
Civilian in London
At nine o'clock, I was dancing with my husband at the Café de Paris. The place was packed and I stopped right in front of 'Snakehips' when something

told me to get off the dance floor. I said, 'Let's have something to eat. We have all night to dance.' As we sat down, the bomb fell right in front of the band, literally where I'd been standing. 'Snakehips' lost his head. I was blown back and I was struck across my nose and eye.

My first reaction – ridiculous – was that someone had thrown a bottle in my face. There was a big blue flash and I realised that it was a bomb. I heard my husband calling my name and he clambered over heaps of bodies and he carried me up the stairs. A soldier gave me a pad and told me to keep it pressed to my eye until I got to a first-aid station. My husband said, 'Let me have a look at your eye!' and when he saw it, he fainted. So when the first-aid man got to us, he thought that my husband was the casualty. My husband said, 'At least we didn't pay for our dinner!' He was recovering by then. A morbid crowd had gathered and they cheered that comment.

I was put in the ambulance with my husband and another couple. I'll always remember this lovely girl wearing what had been a white satin dress. She was sobbing her heart out and on a stretcher was her young man in uniform. I thought he was dead. He was so white and I could hear the 'drip, drip' of the blood from his head. Then in 1988 I was introduced to a man who still had a terrible hole in his head from the Café de Paris. I was talking to him and then we were joined a lady who had been with him on that night in the Café de Paris. And it turned out that these were the people who had been in the ambulance with me and my husband. The man had been married a couple of times and I heard him say to the woman, 'You're as lovely as ever!' Very nostalgic.

The Westminster Hospital was wonderful. They let my husband stay in the room opposite and they lay on a day and night nurse. I was in terrible pain and they had to operate without anaesthetic – just a little morphia. They couldn't use anaesthetic because I was suffering from shock. As the surgeon was picking little bits of metal out of my eye, I was counting the little drops of sweat running down his nose on to me. I was in bed for about two months after that. They had hoped to save a little bit of sight but some months later, they had to remove the eye.

Ballard Berkeley
Special Constable in London

There was looting going on that night at the Café de Paris. This was one of the most awful things. One hears a lot about the bravery and the good things that happened during the war but there were also some very nasty people and some very nasty things that happened. Some of the looters in the Café de

Paris cut the people's fingers off to get the rings. That, to me, was the most awful thing. It was impossible with the dead, the injured, the firemen and wardens and police everywhere, it was impossible to know who was who and it was very easy to cut away a finger here, snap off a necklace there.

Marguerite Crowther
Ambulance driver in London
Every night, after dawn and the all-clear, we used to have to go back and clean up our ambulances. Wash out the blood. And then we had to try and get home but the tubes were full of people sleeping down there so I bought a bicycle. On the way to work, I used to come whizzing down from Hampstead to St Martin's Lane but on the way back in the morning I had to carry it because the rubble was everywhere.

Norman Smith
Civilian in London
The thing that sticks out more in my mind than anything about the Blitz is the smell of burning and of people sweeping broken glass.

Alan Bryett
Civilian in Brockley
When I came out of the shelter in the morning, my first reaction was to look round and see where the bombs had fallen.

Derek Haycock
Child in London
It used to look as though a giant fist had come out of nowhere and smashed the buildings. Rubble, ruin, water everywhere. The firemen kept pushing us back and you could see odd bodies under the rubble where the firemen were pulling them out. It was so unreal.

Doreen Kluczynska
Nurse in Luton
I was on a double-decker bus in Luton one morning when it suddenly pulled up with a screech. A car had driven straight into a huge crater in the middle of the road, a second car was halfway in and our bus was next along.

Joan Varley
Civilian in London
I'd always noticed that the pavement in front of the shops on Brixton Hill was very wide but I'd never understood why. Well, on one of my morning journeys, I saw that a bomb had gone through the pavement and it revealed the River Effra which was running underneath the pavement. That answered my question.

Francis Goddard
Auxiliary Fire Service in Tottenham
If you can think of walking up to your ankles in water, hoses criss-crossed over the road so that you could hardly walk between them, damaged houses with people trying to rescue what they could of furniture. You'd hear people: 'Well, you know, Annie, I'm living with so-and-so, I got bombed out yesterday. The bastards knocked the whole lot down.'

Leslie Hyland
Civilian in Liverpool
We came back from the shelter to find our house severely damaged. I can recall pushing a handcart through Liverpool to my sister's house with pieces of furniture that we'd managed to salvage.

Teresa Wilkinson
Air raid warden in West Ham
I was walking down a road where the whole row of houses were bombed and a man was sitting in the gutter. He laughed as we went by and said, 'I'm better off than you!' 'Why?' we asked. 'Because you're all worrying about your house and your belongings. I haven't got anything to worry about. I haven't got anything left.'

Gioya Steinke
Welfare Adviser with London County Council Rest Centre Service
I sat at a desk in the rest centre and interviewed a steady stream of people who had crawled out from their bombed houses. I tried to rehouse them. They only had the clothes they stood up in and we set up a room for the children to use while the mothers went out to get clothes and contact relatives. Sometimes, they went back to the bombsite to see if they could find anything. It was very distressing. There was a lot of grief and crying. At first, I used to burst into tears with the person I was interviewing but I was told I must try and learn not to. It was difficult.

Theresa Bothwell
Civilian in Birmingham

The morning after a heavy raid, a policeman came to our door about seven o'clock and said, 'You've all got to be evacuated. Last night, the Germans dropped delay bombs all over this estate, and nobody will be allowed into the houses until the army can spare the men to make sure there are no bombs left.' Mum said to Dad, 'Where can we go? We don't know anybody.' They decided to go to Dudley where Mum had two cousins who owned a large pub. 'We'll take a chance that they'll be able to help us,' she said and we got the tram to Dudley. Mum and Dad went into the pub and left us in the side entrance where the beer was delivered. They came back out with Auntie Kitty, who said, 'You've got a cheek coming here!' Mum said, 'We'd got nowhere else to go, Kitty!' Kitty said, 'You'd better wait here, I'll go and discuss it with my husband and my sister.' She went into the private quarters at the back and then she came back and said, 'You can stay, on the understanding that you return to where you came from as soon as possible!' Mother said, 'Don't worry Kitty, we won't burden you any longer than we have to . . .'

Auntie Kitty took us through to the sitting room where her three sons were sitting and she introduced us all. We were taken upstairs and given the smallest bedroom and we were treated like lepers. Auntie Kitty just wasn't interested. Come the night time, as we were preparing for bed, she said, 'I hope that you haven't brought the German planes with you.' Mother said, 'That's very unlikely, don't you think, Kitty?' Kitty said, 'I don't know.' We went up to bed but we'd only been in bed an hour when the air raid warning sounded. Auntie Kitty said, 'This is the first warning we've had. What did I say to you, Molly, about bringing the planes over?' Mother said, 'Oh, don't be stupid, Kitty!'

We got our things together, and we all trooped down to the beer cellar. The barrels were on a brick plinth around the outside walls. Auntie Kitty told us to get up on the plinth and try to keep the central floor as clear as possible. We'd no sooner made ourselves comfortable, there was one almighty bang, and the earth in the cellar shook. The look on Auntie Kitty's face, you'd have to see it to believe it. Shock horror. Mum said, 'Don't say anything Kitty! How could I possibly influence what the German air force does?' Kitty looked at her. 'The sooner you find somewhere else to live, the better.'

Bernard Nicholls
Conscientious objector involved in social work in London

We realised that there would be distress and homelessness as a result of the bombing and we were aware that down Hungerford Lane, underneath the arches of Charing Cross Station, was a congregation of what were called 'down and outs'. People slept rough all over the floor of this arch. Under the leadership of the chief shelter warden in Westminster, we requisitioned the arch and equipped it as a special shelter. We took people from the 'submerged' thousands of Westminster's population – people who had lived out of sight of the population, in the parks and round the backs of the hotels, sitting over the air extractors which belched out warm air, ferreting round dustbins for their food. A slight grade above – if that is the right way to put it – were the people who inhabited the worst of the lodging houses. Many of these rackety buildings were being blitzed and the amount of accommodation had been much reduced. In our shelter, Westminster Council installed bathrooms, a canteen, a medical centre and accommodation in three-tier shelter bunks for about 120 men and women. And they provided a central open space as a social area. The final touch was an enormous baronial castle style fireplace which would be something very familiar and attractive to these 'down and outs'.

Sylvia Clark
Post Office worker in London

One night, my aunt let a young man, about 16 years old, into our shelter. We sat talking and he seemed like a nice boy. He carried on coming to the shelter and my aunt told him that if he had nowhere else to go, he could come home at the weekend and have a Sunday lunch and then come back to the shelter at night. Well, the next night, the boy didn't show up and my aunt showed me a photograph of him that he'd given her. I looked at it and said, 'This isn't a picture of a boy! This is a girl! That's a girl's arms and she's wearing a school blouse!' My aunt showed the picture to a policemen – at that time you suspected any strange person. A little later, we were told that the boy had been found. He was the son of wealthy parents and he'd run away from home. The picture was his sister's passport photograph.

Gioya Steinke
Welfare Adviser with London County Council Rest Centre Service

A lot of the old people who were brought into the rest centre were rather pitiful. They had had very hard lives, most of them. Some had lost their families in the First World War or even the Boer War and they were beyond tears. In those days, people were much older at 50 or 60 than they are today They would come into the rest centre and for a lot of them, that was the first decent, hot meal they had for a long time. Some of them had been living on bread and butter and tea. We usually had to put them into an old people's home. They couldn't be rehoused on their own.

Bernard Nicholls
Conscientious objector involved in social work in London
I found a man leaning up against a wall, absolutely exhausted and possibly dying. Colleagues and I took him to St Stephen's Hospital. We carried him into the casualty department, in a sort of hammock of blankets and deposited him on the floor. The male orderly looked at him and got a can of disinfectant and he ran a ring of disinfectant all the way round the man. He said, 'This man is so lousy that I can't have his lice walking all round the place!' The casualty sister said, 'Take this man away! We can't cope!' So I said that we would stand within the circle of disinfectant, undress him and wrap him in clean blankets. When we got to the man's skin, I was absolutely horrified. All the outside skin on his back had gone. The whole of his back from his neck to his buttocks was a wet pusy mass. The staff now recognised the seriousness of his condition and they were only too anxious to deal with him. They saved his life. He was in hospital for months. He was mentally feeble and he had been living in St James Park for months and had just become weaker and weaker and lousier and lousier. We sent his clothing to the School of Hygiene and Tropical Medecine and they did what to an outsider would be considered a most extraordinary thing. They meticulously went over every square inch of the clothing and they picked off the dead lice and registered every one on a counter. They counted over 15,000 lice on his clothing.

Ivor Leverton
Undertaker in London, served with Auxiliary Fire Service
My father was one of the area organisers for the mortuaries. They were largely in schools. Possibly the most effective mortuary was in Hampstead where they took over the baths. Mortuary attendants came from all sources. I remember one particular man – he was a toastmaster and that work finished completely with the Blitz and he was only too glad to get £3 a week as a mortuary attendant. He'd never had anything to do with death at all and he was handling these casualties. And they were terribly upsetting, some of them. Identification was a great problem. Quite often, a family had gone and there

was nobody left to identify the body but the remains had to be kept until identification was either definite or impossible. I can remember one woman identifying her daughter by a mole behind her right knee. That was after a couple of weeks but some funerals didn't take place until three or four weeks after death and there was no way of refrigerating such large numbers. I can remember the smell now. I take my hat off to the completely inexperienced men who were handling these bodies. There were mass graves. I knew quite a number of cemeteries that had so many deaths in their particular area that there was no other way. It wasn't the sort of thing that was publicised.

Leslie Hyland
Civilian in Liverpool
Forty to 50 people had been killed by a landmine on Index Street and most of them were buried in a mass grave. There was a mass funeral and a great pit into which the coffins were placed.

Marie Price
Civilian in Liverpool
I had a friend whose father was an undertaker, and he was taken to court for putting sandbags in coffins and taking them to be buried. And he said, 'What's worse, telling people that I couldn't find any bodies or pretending that the bodies were in these coffins?' The courts saw the sense of that.

Blitz Spirit

There were no class distinctions at all. I mean you were all in the same position. You were all in danger.

Joan Varley
Civilian in London
I was travelling on a bus at nine o'clock at night. There weren't many people on the buses at that time. I'd formed a bad teenage habit of smoking and you could only smoke on the top deck so I went up there and sat at the back. There was only one other passenger – a man at the very front. We were driving down Great Smith Street in Westminster when we heard a stick of bombs coming down and we knew that they were just a bit ahead of us. The bus driver, very sensibly, took a right-hand turn to avoid the bombs. As he weaved through various streets, we heard the bombs explode and then he returned to his route. But as we were driving towards the bombs, not knowing that the driver was going to be able to avoid them, the man at the front of the bus walked down the bus, sat next to me and we held hands. Neither of us spoke a word and once we were through the bomb area and were back on to the route, he moved back to the front seat without a word being said.

Mary Warschauer
Civilian working for Air Ministry in London
I went to the National Gallery with this laddie that I was engaged to, one of the air force boys, and we looked at a picture. 'Is that supposed to be a sunrise?' I asked. 'No,' he said, 'that's gunfire from the deck of the ship.' He asked me whether I'd ever seen gunfire up close. I said I hadn't. So he said, 'When there's next a raid, we'll go off to Hyde Park and watch the guns.' We did.

Idiots. We sat on a bench opposite the Grosvenor Hotel, with one tin hat between two of us, and the guns blazed away at the back of us. There'd be a quiet spell and then suddenly, you've never heard such a racket in your life. Shrapnel – large lumps, small lumps, all hailing down on the roofs. A piece fell between our feet. It was very hot. We walked up to Marble Arch and there wasn't a soul around, not a vehicle or a person anywhere. So we did the polka down the middle of Oxford Street as far as Bond Street and then we danced hand in hand, singing our heads off towards Piccadilly. Who else in the world has done that?

Alfred Senchell
Auxiliary Fire Service in London
The Blitz brought an air of excitement that nobody experienced in everyday life. Everyday life is humdrum; you go to work, you come home. To me, it was out of this world.

Marie Agazarian
Voluntary Aid Detachment
People would turn up for work and start talking and everybody's bomb was a bigger bomb than anyone else's bomb – 'Oh, we had a bomb. *So many* people killed!'

George Frankland
Civilian in Lambeth
As kids, we tried to find shrapnel. We'd find nose cones from shells and take them into school next morning like they were prizes. Even the teachers got excited – 'Where did you find that?' It was an adventure.

Gioya Steinke
Welfare Adviser with London County Council Rest Centre Service
I was firewatching with two lorry drivers who told me that I had to learn to distinguish the smells of the different bombs and the easiest way to do that was by smoking a special cigarette that they would roll for me. I wasn't a smoker and they made me a cigarette and I smoked it all the way through. I nearly choked to death – but they were rolling on the floor with laughter. I really thought I was being trained to spot the different bomb smells. After that, I was accepted and I was allowed to join their darts team.

A Union Jack flag displayed among the rubble.

Christabel Leighton-Porter
Model for Daily Mirror cartoon character 'Jane'
There were no class distinctions at all. I mean you were all in the same position. You were all in danger.

Gioya Steinke
Welfare Adviser with London County Council Rest Centre Service
As soon as the all-clear went you had the wardens and the firemen bringing all these people into the rest centres and they were in a pretty terrible state, covered in bomb dust. Everyone was reduced to the same level. You didn't know who was a street market person and who was from the posh flats. They were all reduced down and this I think was the reason for the wonderful camaraderie of the Blitz.

Gioya Steinke
Welfare Adviser with London County Council Rest Centre Service
I remember the terrific friendliness. People were talking to each other who didn't know each other and it was a sort of, 'Hello mate!' as if they were friends.

Joan Varley
Civilian in London
I used to travel to Bank each day from Streatham by bus and it was very heartening to see the outward expression made by the commercial people. I passed a draper's shop where they had big plate glass windows that had been shattered by a bomb blast and the draper had put up a big notice, saying, 'Goering may break our windows but he can't break our hearts.'

Albert Prior
Stretcher bearer with West Ham Civil Defence
Outside Stratford Town Hall, they used to put a list of casualties for London for the previous 24 hours. Many a time, I'd had more casualties through my hands alone than were supposed to have come through the whole of London but the official figures were designed to keep the morale of the public up. If people had seen the real numbers of casualties, there'd have been trouble.

Second Lieutenant Arthur Binnie
7th Battalion, King's Regiment
Public morale started to get a bit dicey before the end of the Blitz. I regret to say that there were occasions when we had to fix bayonets to prevent people

entering bank vaults that were opened by the bombing. I was getting the feeling that some people wouldn't stand the Blitz for much longer.

Marie Price
Civilian in Liverpool

Churchill was telling us how brave we all were and that we would never surrender. I tell you something – the people of Liverpool would have surrendered overnight if they could have. It's all right for people in authority, down in their steel-lined dugouts but we were there and it was just too awful. People were walking out of the town to escape the bombing.

Private Herbert Anderson
Pioneer Corps

Liverpool was the only place during the war where I witnessed a demonstration for peace and negotiations with the enemy. There were small groups marching with banners indicating that they wanted an end to the war.

James Kelbrick
Civilian in Liverpool

Liverpool – because of the docks and its strategic importance – was well and truly hammered. The people that got it worst were in Bootle but the destruction in the centre of Liverpool was almost unbelievable. There were so many buildings just smashed to pieces – but the spirit in Liverpool was so good. There was such togetherness and sharing. And when there was a fatality, everybody wanted to take part in the funeral. A personal grief was taken as a personal grief by everybody.

Joan Seaman
Civilian in London

As far as morale was concerned, the government posters weren't really important. They were a laugh. I don't think propaganda was important.

Betty Brown
Civilian in Chingford

All around us were these notices, 'Careless talk costs lives', and while I was on a weekend for young people, the warden in charge started asking us questions that people didn't normally ask – 'Where do you work? What sort of work is that? What do you do?' It made my bristles go but one youngster started answering his questions. The warden asked him about the factory where he worked. He asked him how near it was to where he lived, whether he could get a bus to the factory and I calculated that, from his questions, he could almost pinpoint where this blessed factory was. I was very perturbed by this, and I came home and told my dad, who telephoned Chingford police, and they came and interviewed me in my lunch hour.

Captain Charles Drake (RN)
Naval Intelligence Division
When the Ministry of Information wanted a new head of the propaganda service, they found a candidate named Pick. Mr Pick was the managing director of the London Passenger Transport Board and he'd been doing a tremendous job keeping London transport going. He was brought in and given the job in charge of propaganda. Churchill heard of this and asked to meet him. Sir Kenneth Clark brought him to see Churchill. 'Tell me, Mr Pick,' said Churchill, 'What is going to be your policy as regards the propaganda machine?' 'Well, Mr Churchill, I think in general my propaganda would be based entirely on the truth.' 'Oh, Mr Pick,' said Churchill, 'in that case, I don't think I have anything further to say to you. Good morning.' With that Mr Pick was shown out. The bell was rung and Sir Kenneth Clark arrived. 'Never again,' said Churchill, 'are you to let that sanctimonious bus conductor come within my purview.'

Oliver Bernard
Child in London
One regretted a bit that George VI was so much less powerful a speaker than Churchill and he had a slight impediment with his speech which made him seem even more feeble when one listened to him but I don't think people doubted his genuineness and sincerity. The feeling was pretty friendly towards the Royal Family, even among left-wing people. They were grudgingly admired for being bombed and for visiting the houses of people who had been bombed – and getting there quite quickly. And for staying in London. The Blitz was very good for the Royal Family.

Marguerite Crowther
Ambulance driver in London
One woman who'd been bombed – she was shattered. 'Never mind, ducks,' the rescue man said, 'Buckingham Palace has just been bombed.' And this woman flew into a rage and shook her fist up at the sky and shouted, 'You bastards! You can do what you like to us but leave our Liz alone!'

Francis Goddard
Auxiliary Fire Service in Tottenham
A German plane came down in Enfield and I saw a parachute come floating down with the pilot under it. Women came out of some nearby houses, some with brooms, and they surrounded him and started dragging him along until a policeman arrived and took charge. Afterwards, I heard the poor little bugger thought the women were going to tear him to pieces. They were so wild.

Joan Batt
Civilian in Coventry
I still feel hatred for the Germans. They took everything off me.

James Oates
Dagenham Home Guard
Often a German plane would be shot, and some parachutes would drop down. I used to say to my father-in-law, 'I've got a good mind to get my rifle and shoot the bastards as they come down!' And he looked at me sternly and he said, 'Jim, one day you'll be sorry you said that.' I looked at him with surprise, because he still had a terrific shoulder wound from the First World War and I'd have thought he would have hated the Germans.

Ethel Clarke
Civilian in London
My boy who was killed in a raid was ever such a happy boy. He was scared of the raids but the Lord took him in one. My daughter used to say, 'Mum, if you see a German, spit at him!' I used to say, 'Ethel, don't be silly. They didn't ask for war. They lost their sons, we lost our sons.' That's right, isn't it?

Oliver Bernard
Child in London
You used to hear, 'Bloody Jerry!' or 'Old Adolf's having another go at us!' but it was half-jokingly said and felt. It was as though this was the 1914–18 war when there was less to choose between the two sides. Very few people realised how incredibly horrible the Nazis were. I already knew that from my Jewish friends but it hadn't got to most people what their true character was. They were just our adversaries.

Alda Ravera
Secretary in London

An Italian cousin came over to London and my mother took care of her. She started working in a delicatessen and she spoke very little English. One night after a very severe raid, she fell in a hole and she couldn't get out again. Someone said to her, 'It's the fault of your bloody Mussolini!' and she said, 'I no see Mussolini! I no know Mussolini!' She was crying but we were laughing so much.

Joan Varley
Civilian in London

There was an ice cream parlour called *R Marco Antonio* which was obviously Italian and the owner put up a sign, saying, 'R Marco Antonio, naturalised British citizen. All my business and interests are in this country.' I was always pleased that whenever I passed it, no one had broken his window.

Percy North
Norwich Red Cross

Conscientious objectors were one of my pet aversions, I might tell you. They were cowards. When I was in charge of stretcher parties for the hospital, there was one of them – a big fellow – and I said to him, 'Next time we have any wounded in, I shall see you get hold of one and have some wet, warm, sticky blood flow through your hands.' 'Oh no, don't!' he said, 'I shall swoon!' so I said, 'I'll put you on that grass in front of the hospital and keep you there whatever the weather!'

Gioya Steinke
Welfare Adviser with London County Council Rest Centre Service

Newington Green rest centre was run by the Quakers. They had a pretty rough time because they spoke nicely and they were conscientious objectors. I can remember how they won me over by their lovely quiet manners. There was no question they were conscientious objectors because they were afraid, it was just they did not wish to kill. I remember they also made me think because I had never come across this difference before. I think they were very brave men most of them, very brave indeed because they did everything that was required.

Paul Eddington
Conscientious Objector worked as entertainer with ENSA

My opposition towards Nazism was as keen as anyone's but I felt it ought to be expressed in a different way. I didn't know what that was. I don't know all the

A session of the tribunal for conscientious objectors.

answers and I don't know the answer to that one. I take refuge in admitting it frankly. I really don't know. All I do feel, as I felt then, is that no matter how extreme the circumstances, another way has to be found.

Stan Poole
Home Guard in London

Two of my mates joined the army under age and they came back as local heroes. 'How did you manage to do it?' and they told us. They didn't change their birth certificates, they changed their baptism certificates – which weren't legal documents. So they couldn't be done. So in May 1941, when I was just 16, I did that and went down to join up with the East Surreys. They knew but they weren't bothered. I got the King's Shilling and I had to explain to my mother what I'd done. She took it well – she didn't start bawling and howling and I was sent to the barracks at Canterbury.

William Gray
Milkman in London

I was 16 years old when I came home from work to find that all my family had been evacuated. There was an old dear in the flat opposite ours and she told me that they'd come down in lorries and taken them all away. They finished up in Norfolk somewhere and they just left me here. I thought, 'Well ... I'll go in the navy.' So I went along and asked the navy and they said, 'Sorry. Not till you're 17 and a half.' So I went to Romford and tried the army. I went and he said, 'How old are you?' and I said '18.' He said, 'Have you got a birth certificate?' I said, 'No. Lost in the Blitz.' He said, 'Sign here.' And that was it. I was in. And I couldn't believe the food we were given in the army. Porridge for breakfast. Bacon and mash. I'd never had anything like that in my life. Beautiful dinners and better afters. It was smashing. I'd never been so well off in my life. I loved it.

Francis Goddard
Auxiliary Fire Service in Tottenham

I went up to Tottenham Town Hall for a medical examination with about 200 others. We were lined up in rows in the big hall. Two hundred men, lined up, stripped naked. We had medical officers coming round and examining everybody. Mine was a female doctor and she had a little cane and she came along and lifted up my John Thomas to see if I had any disease. It didn't matter if you were shy or weren't shy, you all got the same treatment. Then I went to another officer, who was sitting at a desk with a sergeant and a corporal. I was asked various questions – what I'd done in civvy life, was there anything I wanted to volunteer for. If you wanted the navy or the air force, you were sent to one side. I put down for the RAF. I was told I'd be sent for another medical and away I went. This time, I came up before six different medical officers. One was a colonel. They told me they'd be in touch and the next thing I had a card turning me down – Medically Unfit, Grade Three, Tuberculosis. They'd gone through my old medical records and found out I'd had TB as a child. After that, I joined the fire service.

Horace Davy
Civilian in London
Throughout the Blitz, everyone listened quite a bit to the wireless. I have a very strong recollection of the nine o'clock news on a Sunday night. It was the focal point of the week.

Leslie Stark
Civilian in Sussex
I used to listen to William Joyce on the wireless. Sometimes, Joyce came out with more things than the BBC. After a big raid he came on the next night and said, 'The glorious Luftwaffe have dropped a number of bombs on oil refineries in Batts Wood, Sussex.' He had everything tapped. He knew exactly where the bombs had been dropped.

William Joyce, better known as 'Lord Haw-Haw', had been the deputy leader of the British Union of Fascists until he was sacked by Sir Oswald Mosley in 1937. He fled to Germany just before the outbreak of war and broadcast to the British people from Berlin. 'Claims' attributed to Joyce were often the pure invention of his listeners but they spread quickly around a rumour-hungry British public.

Dorothy Hont
Civilian in Liverpool
In Knotty Ash, we put sticky tape on our windows to stop the glass showering and cutting people if it was blown out. One night, Lord Haw-Haw came on the radio and said, 'Don't think I've forgotten you people in Knotty Ash with your kisses on the window.' That made you feel creepy to think he was sitting in Germany and he actually knew about Knotty Ash, an insignificant little area.

Stanley Clark
Civilian in London
We heard Haw-Haw's latest – 'We have sunk the *Ark Royal*,' while it was sitting in Portsmouth harbour.

Brian Rust
Auxiliary Fire Service in London
I used to listen to jazz and no other kind of music. Anything I regarded as commercial was 'out'. I didn't want to know. Records were 3s 8d each including purchase tax which was a seventh of what I earned in a week. It was monstrous – I had money of my own but I couldn't afford to buy the records because some fathead had started a war and put the price up.

Joan Seaman
Civilian in London
I kept very quiet about Vera Lynn. Now I realise what a difference she made to so many people but as a young person in my early twenties, she was not my sort of music.

Brian Rust
Auxiliary Fire Service in London
There was a big number that 'Snakehips' Johnson made popular – 'Tuxedo Junction'. It was more popular than Glenn Miller's version of the same song. Orchestrated jazz was at its height during the Blitz.

Betty Brown
Civilian in Chingford
My mother and I used to go to the pictures a lot. If I saw a very romantic film, I'd come home and be just like the heroine. It would take me a long time to calm down. My Mum would ask, 'Would you like a cup of cocoa?' And I'd think, 'Cocoa? That's far too mundane . . . '

Ballard Berkeley
Special Constable in London
During the Blitz, the theatres would have a matinee at one o'clock in the afternoon and then open at five o'clock and close as it got dark.

Christabel Leighton-Porter
Actress, appeared as 'Jane' on stage
Our revue might open with a troop of dancers doing a kicking routine. Then you'd have members of the company in a little sketch. Then a singer. Then you might have a beautiful scene on a wild island, or something like that, with Hawaiian singers and dancers and perhaps I'd come up and do a Hawaiian dance in the middle. Then you'd have a comic – someone like Jimmy Jewell or Ben Warris. And we used to have bits from the Jane cartoon – there was one cartoon called Jane's Gym and we had all the girls dressed up in little short skirts and little sweaters and we went through the Jane's Gym routines. That wasn't easy to do.

Emily Clare
Waitress in London
I used to go to the London Palladium for the 6.30 show. An air raid alert light used to come up next to the number of the turn. Some people would leave – but not many. The turns used to carry on and I stayed because I wanted my money's worth.

Christabel Leighton-Porter
Actress, appeared as 'Jane' on stage
We played the Bedford Theatre, Camden Town. It's a lovely little old theatre but the back of the theatre was corrugated iron. And the week I was there we had raids every single night. It was quite frightening, the shrapnel on that corrugated iron was deafening. And remember one night, it was so bad that, people really couldn't go out and couldn't go home. So they stayed in the theatre and the orchestra played. They came up on the stage and danced and had a bit of a knees-up. The artists went back on and got a sing-song going and we got a few of the people up from audience who'd got a bit of talent to give a little song. And we kept this going well into the night. Some people were dozing off to sleep in their chairs but the whole company had to stay there. And the all-clear went some long time later and we were able to go.

Betty Brown
Civilian in Chingford
We went to the Regal, Edmonton. They had an organ which came up from the floor and it was called 'Sidney Torch and his Illuminated Organ'. If the warning sounded while you were there, a notice would flash on the screen

that the air raid siren has sounded outside and you are welcome to stay because the show will go on but if you leave to take shelter, that's OK.

Christabel Leighton-Porter
Actress, appeared as 'Jane' on stage

I appeared nude on stage which was very daring for those days but really and truly it meant absolutely nothing because the lighting was so subdued. When we were touring in Hull, we became friendly with the crew of an air-sea rescue boat. One night, I was doing the daring part of my act. There was a crucial moment when I was supposed to drop my robes and immediately after that there was a cued blackout. Now these boys from the air-sea rescue boat all came in one night and they'd all got the big ship's telescopes and they all focused on me on stage as the lights went out. Oh, the house was in a roar, it really was.

Gunner Derek Erridge
234 Battery, 89th Heavy Anti-Aircraft Regiment, Royal Artillery

I went out one night in Birkenhead to a pub where the landlady said that soldiers weren't welcome in her pub. When we heard that, everybody walked out – the locals and all. I don't know what she objected to.

Christabel Leighton-Porter
Actress, appeared as 'Jane' on stage

Nine times out of ten when we were in Bristol, we'd finish our show and on the way home, the air raid warning would go. And the whole company would bail into a little pub and the publican would lock the door and lock us all in. We didn't have a lot to drink because whisky and the short drinks were very few and far between and the beer had probably run out ages ago. But it was a haven. We spent nearly every night in there and went back home in the early hours.

Sylvia Clark
Post Office worker in London

I belonged to the YWCA in Tottenham Court Road and we used to have dances. There was often a decent band and all sorts of service chaps used to come in and I was asked if I would be a hostess. Although I'm rather shy, because we wanted the boys to enjoy their dancing and chatter for an evening, I agreed. I used to see six or ten fellows standing all together and I used to go up to them and say, 'Good evening! I'm on duty tonight as the hostess and if you boys want to dance, we've got a jolly nice band. I've got ten WAAFs over there who want to dance. Please come over with me!' They were always very good until one chap said, 'No! I'm not going to come over with you! I want to *dance* with you!' So I said, 'As an extra special favour, I'll give you ten minutes of my very busy time!' And I enjoyed it very much.

Marie Agazarian
Voluntary Aid Detachment

We'd go out dancing. We went to the Mayfair – it was underground and at midnight, they'd always play 'God Save The King' and everybody would be standing all round the dance floor, ladies and gentlemen in their dressing gowns with an eiderdown and a pillow. And as soon as 'God Save The King' was over, they'd clear the dance floor and they'd lie down to sleep. It was quite extraordinary.

Francis Goddard
Auxiliary Fire Service in Tottenham

John Brown was a barman and we used to go round to his flat and he used to have his own bar fixed up in the lounge and he used to knock us up all kinds of cocktails. He'd try the cocktails out on us that he was going to sell in his bar. I'd get real 'sausaged' and drive home. Luckily, in those days the police weren't running around in cars. They were walking on the beat and there was hardly any traffic about so no one used to take much notice of you.

Dorothy West
Woman Police Constable with Metropolitan Police Force

I was posted to Hyde Park for two months and that was interesting, I can tell you. I was there with a very nice WPC and we spent a lot of time looking around. If we saw a couple on the floor under a blanket – 'Hey! Hey!' We turfed them out. We couldn't have things like that going on, could we?

Betty Brown
Civilian in Chingford

My friend Valerie and I were in Kensington Gardens, and we picked up with this couple of Canadian soldiers and we made a date with them to go to the pictures. Mine was a very nice man, very proper, didn't try to do anything improper in the cinema, but hers was an older man and she was quite offended because I think he was poking around.

Dorothy Hont
Civilian in Liverpool

I had a Victorian grandmother. She was a truly Victorian woman. From the day I was born, she overruled my parents. You wouldn't dare to sit and show your knees. You had to pull your skirt down. You wouldn't dare go out and not say where you were going or come back later than nine o'clock. You didn't have a key to the door until you were 21. And so with this upbringing, I may have been just a little bit different than the average. I had a cousin who used to go roller skating and she had a very easy-going mother and many nights she didn't come home because she spent the night in an air raid shelter. My father thought that was outrageous. You could have come up against anybody. As soon as the war finished, I had quite a few boyfriends but as soon as they became a bit cheeky, they didn't get any change out of me. Only harlots go with men before they're married and that's why I'm still a virgin.

Betty Brown
Civilian in Chingford

When my sister gave birth to a son, I said, 'Have you got a big scar?' She said, 'I don't know what you mean.' I said, 'Where they cut your tummy and lifted the baby out.' She said, 'You don't have a baby like that!' 'Well, how do you have a baby?' I asked. 'The same way you go to the lavatory,' she said. Which was very off-putting.

Vera King
Civilian in the Wirral

I had no idea how babies were formed. That seems extraordinary being the eldest of five. I suppose it was quite common in those days for girls to get married . . . and 'learn' when they were married. You could have got into all sorts of trouble. I think people depended on a natural modesty to keep you on the straight and narrow.

Betty Brown
Civilian in Chingford

One fellow tried to put his hand down my blouse which I thought was very shocking. But my sister didn't think it was as shocking as I did. She was five years older than me and I think things were beginning to change because the war was on.

Gioya Steinke
Welfare Adviser with London County Council Rest Centre Service

We had a supervisor who was probably in his thirties but he looked older. He was married to a teacher 20 years older than himself and she had been evacuated away with her school. He took a great fancy to me. I'd had rather a sheltered life and I wasn't used to a mature man making advances to me. While I was counting blankets in the store room with him, I was very aware that he was breathing heavily down my neck. I absolutely froze. Then he started to put his arms round me and started to kiss and cuddle. I went home that night, thinking, 'Oh No! He's in love with me! What do I do?' But then I was told by someone else that he was already having an affair with his deputy. I told the deputy what had happened and the next day, he came in with scratches down his face. After that, she made sure that I wasn't on duty with him too often. There was an awful lot of sleeping together going on all over the place, but my ignorance protected me.

Betty Brown
Civilian in Chingford

I used to hitchhike a lot. On one occasion, a fellow gave me a lift and he got out and he said something about injuring his arm and would I help him do his trousers up? 'Certainly not!' I said, 'You're quite capable of doing your own trousers up!' I was quite offended. He got back in the car and said, 'When can I see you again?' and I said, 'You can't!'

Doreen Kluczynska
Nurse in Luton

I worked with a probationary nurse who told me that her mother had left home when she was a baby and her father had brought her up. A bit later, when I moved to Luton, the same girl wrote to me and said that she'd been taken advantage of by an airman at a party; she was pregnant and her father had thrown her out, saying she was just like her mother. She said she had been with these airmen at a party somewhere in Leeds and they'd had drinks and she didn't remember much about it except that one boy took her into a bedroom and she found herself pregnant. After her father threw her out, she'd gone to live with somebody and she was just stealing potatoes and cabbages from the allotments to stay alive. After the child was born, it was adopted and she came down to Luton and she had to go into digs while she looked for a job. She asked me to write her a reference. Well, I didn't tell any lies. I just said that I'd worked with her and she was honest, clean and bright. She got the job – as a conductress on the Green Line [bus] route from Luton to London. I had to help her out with her first week's rent because even when she started the job, she didn't get paid till the second week and she had no money for food. Eventually, she got married and had another child. After that, I lost touch with her.

Walter Marshall
Metropolitan Police War Reserve

One night, I was on duty at the Highbury and Islington tube station. It was a quarter past four and I was regulating the queues to get down into the station. Normally the bombing would start later but that night, the sirens went when people were still queuing. There was a panic and a young lady left the queue to go home. I got talking to her and I advised her to stay where she was and let the panic settle down a bit. I've been married to that lady for over 60 years now.

Private David Elliott
Stretcher bearer with Royal Army Medical Corps

I found myself attracted to a girl named Margaret who'd been evacuated from Liverpool. She was my tennis partner and it wasn't long before we fell in love. I was very fond of her but one was still conditioned by the First World War and by the fact that one might not get through it. I didn't know what the future was and something told me that I shouldn't get married at that stage. When I was commissioned, she joined the ATS in order to follow me. But I managed to cool it off. Perhaps I shouldn't have done. After the war, I was invited to a blind date at a hunt ball. I was asked to partner an ex-ATS girl called Margaret who'd had rather a sad time. So I went along thinking I was being set up with the girl from 1940 – but it was wasn't the same girl at all. It was a different ATS girl called Margaret who became my wife . . .

Patricia Crampton
Civilian in Beaconsfield

I was very young to have somebody but we had definite plans together. He was the older brother of a friend. His name was Bob Cosgrave and he was learning to fly Wellington bombers. He actually came and waggled his wings over our school which was a moment of tremendous pride for me. I knitted him dreadful air force scarves – I was no needlewoman. When he was killed, I was young and my parents had no desire to regard him as somebody of special importance in my life. To them he was just somebody I went swimming with and played tennis with. But when I went up to Oxford three years later, it still overshadowed my life. I suppose my mother had – quite rightly – more important things to think about . . .

Sylvia Clark
Post Office worker in London
My brother said to my mother, 'Mum, are there any single girls round here? Because I feel I should be getting serious with a girl.' Mum said, 'There's only one girl left. Her name is Hilda Williams.' 'I remember her,' said my brother, 'is she still single?' 'Yes,' said Mum, 'and she's a jolly nice girl.' Without more ado, he had a wash and called at Hilda's mother's house. Hilda's father came to the door and my brother said, 'If you don't mind, can I have few words with Hilda?' So Hilda came to the door and said, 'Hello! What are you doing round here?' 'Well,' said my brother, 'I'm a bit fed up and a bit lonely. Mother said you're the only single girl around here. Are you doing anything tonight?' 'Well, no,' said Hilda, 'but Mum and Dad are here and Gran's over the road and I'm not very keen on leaving.' 'I'll tell you what,' said my brother, 'we'll go out for an hour.' So they went out for an hour . . . and my brother married her.

Marian Orley
Women's Auxiliary Air Force
My fiancé rang me up and said, 'I've been posted overseas and we could get married tomorrow!' So we went and got married. You could get a special licence to get married in a day. It was the thing to do. It was rather like saying, 'Let's go out to dinner.' That was the war. After we married, he went off to the Middle East and I didn't see him for five years.

Betty Brown
Civilian in Chingford
My sister had a romance which failed and she got talking to a woman on the bus, the girl took her home for tea and my sister met the girl's brother. She was on the rebound and she married the following year. She had a white wedding and I had a blue taffeta bridesmaid's dress with bouquets. We catered at home, because everything was on rations.

Francis Goddard
Auxiliary Fire Service in Tottenham
I'll never forget Bill and Ivy Brown's wedding. After the service, as they came

out of the church – I was always mucking around – I grabbed hold of Ivy in all her wedding finery and stuck her in the back of my three-wheeler car and cleared off with her. Bill chased behind the car because I'd nicked his bride. I think he'd laid on a horse and cart to take them off but I disappeared round the block. Eventually, I came back and deposited her but he was flaming mad. In the evening, I went down to the wedding reception. My wife was already there and I set off to join her and I saw a party taking place and I thought, 'Oh, this must be it,' so I stopped, went in and yeah, it was a wedding. I had a few drinks and I thought, 'I don't know some of these people here. Oh well. They know so many people . . . ' Then some feller came up to me and said, 'Have you seen the bride?' and I said, 'Not yet,' and he said, 'You must come and have a drink with the bride,' so he took me to the bride and bridegroom. Bill and Ivy hadn't half changed their looks because these were two complete strangers. I said, 'I don't know you!' and I was classified as a gatecrasher and there was nearly a fight and I just happened to say, 'It's Ivy Brown I'm looking for!' 'Oh! Ivy Brown! She's further down the road! Oh that's all right, mate! Have another drink! We understand.' Apparently, Ivy Brown and the bride at this wedding were friends and a couple of them escorted me down to Ivy's reception and everyone had a damn good laugh at what I'd done. So later, at Ivy's, there was a conga and I got the head of the conga and I led the crowd up the road, into the house where the first wedding was on, up the stairs, around the different rooms and we came out, we had the other bride and bridegroom attached and we took them back to our reception. It was about two or three o'clock in the morning when we finished.

Gioya Steinke
Welfare Adviser with London County Council Rest Centre Service
Some of the lorry drivers I was on duty with were very rough. We had a kitchen with a little hatch and we'd open the hatch to hear what the lorry drivers were saying. Some of their talk was so coarse, I couldn't repeat it but I remember one of them – a huge, fat, ugly, sweaty man – talking about his marriage and he was asking the finance officer whether he thought it was alright to go with his wife twice every night. The finance officer asked, 'What does your wife say about this?' 'What's it got to do with her?' replied the lorry driver.

Brave New World

The children changed – they became quite different. They sat at the table, and became better – no, I shouldn't say that, should I?

The British people took pride and comfort in their ability to maintain a stable way of life, unaffected as far as possible by bombing and wartime restrictions. Yet evacuation, blackout, rationing and the ever-present sense of danger could not fail to transform social attitudes and day-to-day lives.

Derek Haycock
Evacuated to Wales

I packed a few clothes and took them to school one day. I thought that the idea was to leave them at school in case our house got bombed. But when I got to school, there was no morning prayers and we were given a badge to wear with a number. We were told to sit in a class, everyone was looking at each other but no one told us anything. We were told to go to these old-fashioned Ford coaches and we got on them. Our parents were waiting outside and when we got on the coach, your mother got on the coach as well. We were being evacuated. We were billeted with a family in a little village in Wales. I'd never been to the country before. We went to a little village school. It was like a dream.

Lionel Levine
Evacuated to Biggleswade, Bedfordshire

About fifteen boys and girls with the adult supervisor walked up a wide street in Biggleswade. We stayed on the right side which seemed to have more

Evacuees from London learning Welsh in a schoolroom in Wales.

gentrified homes and the supervisor asked each woman who came to the door to take one of us. The woman would come into the middle of the pack and look for the neatest and sweetest little girl. The pattern became obvious and not wishing to cause embarrassment I stayed at the back knowing that I was not in contention. After all the girls had gone, the women expressed resentment that only boys were left. But eventually all the single boys were housed and only my brother and I were left. The supervisor explained that we were brothers and shouldn't be separated. No one wanted us. I remember a burning resentment and a secret hope that no one in Biggleswade would take us and we would have to be sent home to die in London to the embarrassment of the government because no one in the country would take us. But that was not to be. Near the end of the street, a lady took us – tempted no doubt by the financial inducement of a double allowance.

Joyce Barrett
Evacuated to Dunstable, Bedfordshire
I can't remember all that much about the first two weeks I was at Dunstable. We were told to be brave, We were wrenched away from our parents with strangers, and our only link was with our teachers.

Hilda Cripps
Civilian in Great Wakering, Essex
My next-door neighbour took in two little boys and their little sister from London, and as soon as she started to prepare a meal, they would go and sit on the doorstep. They weren't accustomed to sitting around a table. Tremendous change in those children's lives. When they went for a walk down on the farm, one of the boys was horrified – 'eughh' – he didn't like seeing milk coming out of dirty cows. After a while, the parents came down to visit with another baby, and they'd have liked to leave that one as well, they'd got such a good home. The children changed – they became quite different. They sat at the table, and became better – no, I shouldn't say that, should I?

Stan Poole
Evacuated to Dunstable, Bedfordshire
We used to have a visiting dentist where we were evacuated and one day all us kids were queuing up to see him we heard the most awful noise going on inside, 'Oh! Leave me alone!' Suddenly the door burst open and a kid leapt out with his apron on being chased by the dentist with his pliers in his hand. By the time they caught the boy, there wasn't a kid to be seen in the queue.

We were all rounded up again and the boy was sent back in. But exactly the same thing happened and they couldn't find the kids to queue up a third time.

Betty Brown
Evacuated to Southend, Essex
I was 14 when I was evacuated. My periods hadn't started then but I'd had a bit of sickness and tummy upset and I think these country people were very worried for me. So they had bought a packet of sanitary towels and a sanitary belt, and they left it on the table for me to pick up. But they couldn't bring themselves to talk to me about it.

Arthur Dales
Evacuated to Bridlington, East Riding of Yorkshire
There was a scare when one of the evacuated boys contracted typhoid fever. The boy went off to hospital and we were all put into quarantine. Quarantine meant fourteen days when we couldn't go to school. Every morning we went down to the sands and played football or went for a walk in the country. It was like being on holiday – very free and easy. Our parents were worried but somehow we all escaped contracting the fever.

Doreen Kluczynska
Nurse at TB sanitorium at Knaresborough
I worked at a TB sanatorium with children who'd been evacuated from Hull. Emergency huts were put up to accommodate us and the children. It was very hard work and the children were heartbreaking. They had orthopaedic TB and they were curved with feet down and head down. There were three lovely-looking girls, aged 17, 18, and they were all going to die. These girls had terribly ulcerated limbs and backs where the flesh was eaten away right down to the bone. I thought I must be very careful with these three girls when I was going on dates or going dancing, because these were things that these girls would never know. But whenever I was on night duty on their ward, they used to call me across and say, 'Where are you going on your night off?', 'Are you having a date?' and they seemed to want to know. They even wanted to know what I was going to wear – 'Oh show us your dress! Bring it in tomorrow night!' They seemed to want to live through what I was doing. And they did die.

Derek Haycock
Evacuated to Wales
A lot of kids were lucky. They went to Canada and America and Australia and New Zealand. They stayed there and made a completely new life. They weren't like me. I came back from Wales, left school and got jobs working on the railway and odd jobs in factories. They started a new life.

Oliver Bernard
Evacuated to Lancing College, Sussex
Westminster School was evacuated to Lancing College which was next to Brighton. It wasn't a jingoistic school. It was a bit exceptional among public schools in that people got reputations not for being captain of the cricket team but for being 'learned' as the boys used to say. Tony Benn was in the year above me and I remember when he was told to stand as the Labour candidate in a mock election. I can remember him standing up, looking very pink and naïve and saying nervously to the assembled boys and male schoolmasters, 'Ladies and gentlemen . . .' to which a shocking, amusing boy with a reputation for being a homosexual, said, 'I'm glad you've discovered my sex . . .'

Gabrielle Davy
Evacuated to Devizes, Wiltshire
When we were evacuated, I was nine years old and I was used as a skivvy. The family fed me and looked after me but in return they expected me to do the washing and look after the house. I can remember vividly doing all the dusting and carrying buckets of water around from the well. In the meantime, my brothers couldn't do anything wrong. The youngest one was four and the next one was six and the family had one son of their own and they were more into boys than girls. They thought girls were put on the earth to work.

Alan Bryett
Bank Worker in London
I'd only been working at Barclays Bank in the Brompton Road for six or eight months and I suddenly found that instead of sticking on stamps and doing all the menial jobs, I was jockeyed into one of the more senior jobs like writing entries in ledgers and doing clerical work, which I normally wouldn't have touched for three, four or five years. I was covering for all these fellows who'd gone into the army. After that, instead of having a new junior fellow in the bank every six months, they had a girl. These were really the first girls who

came into the bank. Up to that stage, we had typists who were young ladies but no clerks. From then on, lady clerks started coming in and replacing the boys. They fitted in extremely well.

Gioya Steinke
Welfare Adviser with London County Council Rest Centre Service
Women were suddenly going out to work. A lot of them worked in munitions factories. But my boss's secretary had been to university which was something in those days. And she never wore stockings! Summer or winter, bare legs! She was an out and out Labour person with very socialistic ideas. She was very friendly and she told me that everything on the earth should belong to the people. I'd never heard this! Politics? I didn't even know what politics were. She said that water, electricity, gas, all of this should belong to the people. She was so passionate and I was in awe.

Joan Reeves
Nurse at Fountain Hospital, London
Women became very independent. And I don't think it did us any favours. The idea of equality of men and women is a stupid one. We were never meant to be equal. We have two completely different roles in the world. I should be able to do and think things that my husband doesn't do and think.

Winifred Harding
Nurse at Hull Royal Infirmary
Nowadays, if you walked out in a blackout, you would be afraid of being attacked but it was blackout all the time then and you could walk the streets and people would only help you. They wouldn't attack you. There was nothing like that going on.

Sylvia Clark
Post Office worker in London
One night, I passed this doorway near my house and before I knew where I was, I had a chap's arm round my neck. I swung round and I don't swear but I used every foul word I'd ever heard. I said, 'If you don't leave me alone, I will scream and scream and somebody will come and help me!' He was rather short and I called him a short-arsed something. His hands dropped and I ran like the wind round the next road to my home. I was so frightened. I turned the key in the door as this chap was coming down from upstairs and I suppose I must have fallen into him. I said, 'Oh, John, somebody's got hold of me in

Tollet Street,' and he said, 'Can you remember how tall he was?' and I said, 'He was a bit shorter than me. Had black hair. Very slim build,' and he got straight on his bike and rode around for hours but couldn't see anybody.

Mary Warschauer
Civilian working for Air Ministry in London

I was walking along Victoria Street and on the other side of the road was a French sailor. He crossed over and there wasn't anybody else in sight and he came over and he started trying to get off with me. I just said, 'No! No!' and he shoved me into a doorway. I was pretty strong in those days, and without any compunction, I gave him the hardest slap on his face you've ever seen. I felt instantly, 'God! What's he going to do?' And it was the weirdest thing – you know how a cat spits? That's what he did. Then he took me by both shoulders and shook me and shook me and shook me until my plaits which were pinned up round my head fell down my back, and then he went off.

Dilwyn Evans
Worker at Armstrong-Siddeley factory in Coventry

The blackout; I got so used to it that I just accepted it. You had to draw your curtains at home and if you showed a glimmer of light, a warden would shout, 'Put that light out!' If you had a motor car, a motorcycle, even a bicycle, you had to have a device fitted to the headlamps that shone them directly at the ground and not in front. Of course in those days, there wasn't the volume of cars there is today and you couldn't attain the speeds you can today. It would be pretty dangerous driving a car in those conditions nowadays.

Theresa Bothwell
Civilian in Birmingham

I don't know if you've ever tried walking out in pitch black holding a torch with the top of the glass blacked out and a little mask over the top so that no light shines upwards? My mother told my sister and I to go down to the chemist to get a jar of Vicks because my little sister was poorly with bronchitis. On the way, I dropped the torch and we spent about fifteen minutes on our knees, feeling with our hands trying to find it. I eventually found it and we went on but there was a man hanging round in the car park and as we walked past, he followed us. We got to the shops and tried the chemist's door. It was locked up with no lights on but we heard someone inside so we banged on the door. The chemist said, 'I've just locked up.' I said, 'Our baby sister's very ill and mummy can't afford to send for the doctor.' So

White bands painted on the trees along the Albert Embankment, London, to assist drivers during the blackout.

he put the lights out, opened the door, let us in and gave us the Vicks.

When we got outside again, I put the torch on – and the battery had gone. We heard someone shuffling round and my sister said, 'That man's here again! He's following us!' We hurried on and his footsteps eventually faded and we walked and walked and walked until we hadn't a clue where we were. It was pitch dark, we had no torch and we heard some footsteps coming towards us. By this time, I was crying with fear and I started screaming. I sat down on the ground and I couldn't move. The footsteps stopped and I heard a voice saying, 'Frances? Theresa? Is that you? Is that my girls?' It was our father. 'Daddy! Daddy! I'm so frightened!' I got up and he came towards us and I jumped up at him and he put his arms round me and he said, 'Shhh. You'll be all right. Where on earth have you been?' We'd left to go down to the chemist at about quarter to five and it was now half past seven.

Edward Stevens
Taxi driver in London
A few taxi drivers drove at night because they had to continue earning a living and also because they could help people in the raids. I had bought a cab just before the Blitz started and I decided to go on night work just to see what it was like and I found I could get around satisfactorily so I kept to it until the raids finished in 1941. Very often, one had to take detours because of bomb craters but one could follow tram lines, which made it a little easier. Generally speaking, things were very quiet. The few vehicles were spread out so far that you could go quite a few miles without seeing another vehicle. It was a risky business. You couldn't see much at all. It was better on moonlit nights.

Theresa Bothwell
Civilian in Birmingham
We saw a man staggering about in the blackout. Mum said to my sister and I, 'You stay here, girls. I'll go across and see what's wrong with him – he might be ill.' She went over to him and stood with him for a little while before she came back to us. She said, 'He's drunk. He reeks of whisky.' As she was talking, I looked up and I saw him walking along the tramlines. Mum went up to him and said, 'No! You mustn't! There'll be a tram along in a minute and you'll get run over!' 'Leave me alone!' he said, 'I know what I want to do!' and he pushed Mum so hard that he knocked her over. He carried on and after a while we heard a tram driver put the brakes on and there was a screech and the tram driver jumped down and he was shouting, 'I didn't see him! I didn't see him!' A bobby came up and asked my mother if she'd witnessed it and she

said yes. The bobby said there'd be a coroner's inquest and Mum would be required to attend.

So Mum got a letter, asking her to report to the court three days before the inquest. She went along and when she came home she was as white as a sheet. Dad asked her what was wrong and she wouldn't tell him and she never said a word to us girls. After the inquest, Mum came home at six o'clock and she was shaking from head to foot. Dad said, 'What on earth's the matter, Molly?' and she just shook her head. Before we went to bed, she said, 'I want to say something to you girls. When you go to and from school from now on, keep your eyes open. If you see any strangers hanging around and they're rough, burly types, possibly wearing cloth caps, you're to come indoors, and if Dad and I aren't here, lock the back and front doors.' We said, 'What's wrong, Mum?' She said, 'Just do as I ask! Please!'

Weeks later she told us what had happened. The first time she went to the court, the widow and the family of the dead man had followed her outside, surrounded her and threatened her, saying that if the inquest went against them, they would come looking for her and her family. At the actual inquest, Mum was called to give her evidence. She told the coroner that the man had been drunk and he had a small bottle of whisky in his pocket. The widow stood up and shouted, 'That's a lie! My husband's never drunk! He's a member of the Temperance League and he's got an insurance policy with the League! If the result is suicide, I don't get a penny and we'll be thrown out on the street! You're lying! You change your testament!' And then – in front of the coroner – the widow said, 'If you don't change your testament, we know where you live and we'll come looking for you and your daughters!' The coroner warned her that if she made any more threats she'd be arrested for threatening violence. In the end, despite all this, the coroner gave the verdict in the widow's favour. A man from Birmingham Tramways Committee had admitted that the lights on the tram were not adequate for the blackout. The coroner decided that the man had been walking away from the tram and the driver hadn't seen him. But Mum knew that he had been walking towards the tram. It was suicide. Definitely.

Francis Goddard
Auxiliary Fire Service in Tottenham

I was bringing my wife home from her work, one night and I was on Tower Bridge. It was early hours of the morning and two of her colleagues were with us. I had this little three-wheeler car and four of us were crammed in, one of the girls on my wife's lap. I dropped one girl off and then a thunderstorm broke and I must have driven into the kerb and knocked part of the exhaust pipe off. This was in the blackout and I got out and got underneath the car to fix the blinking exhaust back on. I'd had quite a lot to drink and I must have been under the car 15 or 20 minutes and eventually my wife got out and started tugging at my leg. I'd fallen asleep under the car and I was lying in the gutter. For fifteen minutes, water had been flowing down my neck and out through my trouser bottoms. Right the way through me. The exhaust pipe was lying across me and my wife and her friend were standing over me, laughing.

Theresa Bothwell
Civilian in Birmingham

If you lit a cigarette out in the street, you had to mask it under your coat or with your hand. Who would see a cigarette lighter hundreds of feet up in the sky? Ludicrous – but those were the regulations.

Stanley Brand
Middlesbrough Home Guard

Everything that wasn't done and didn't work during the Blitz was accompanied by the statement, 'Don't you know there's a war on?' If your works' bus didn't turn up – 'Don't you know there's a war on?' If your rations weren't there – 'Don't you know there's a war on?' If you asked for a set of batteries for your torch – 'Don't you know there's a war on?' Of course we knew there was a war on. We were sick of hearing about it.

Christabel Leighton-Porter
Actress, appeared as 'Jane' on stage

My memories of touring with our theatre company at this time was of terribly cold trains, always late, always crowded, no food on the trains, poor digs, the landladies had got no heating, coal was short, electricity was cut off, gas was short, food was very tight.

Vera King
Civilian in the Wirral

When the water mains were hit, they used to send little water carts round. There was a form of bush telegraph – somebody would see it and it was a case of follow that cart. We all queued up, all the family and the children with buckets and bowls and kettles. It was most difficult with small children, because you couldn't really spare the water to wash them.

Alan Bryett
Civilian in Brockley
Rationing was quite devastating for the women who were doing the housekeeping. You began to notice that things were disappearing. You had a very limited amount of meat and cheese and eggs. Fruit began to disappear. Bananas completely disappeared and you got very few oranges. When you went into a restaurant, items of food were starred. Television stopped once the war started but on the radio, they had programmes on how to make the best of a pound of sausages and that type of thing. There was a great move to turn local parks into allotments.

Christabel Leighton-Porter
Actress, appeared as 'Jane' on stage
I went to a dance in Brighton where they auctioned things for charity that had been donated by people. I remember getting about £100 for a lemon. I don't know where it came from because I never saw another lemon all the way through the war.

Elsie Foreman
Civilian in Battersea
Nylons! We used to tramp miles to find a pair of nylons. One Saturday, we heard a rumour that a shop in Camberwell had nylons from America so we got up at six o'clock in the morning to get there by seven. And we got a pair of nylons from America. It was very unusual. You could only get one pair and you couldn't get silk stockings at all.

Mary Sawyer
Civilian in London
You got half a pound of meat a week. Sausages, offal, anything you could get. An ounce of cheese a week. An egg a week. Two ounces of sugar. Two ounces of margarine. We did all sorts of things with potatoes. We made cakes with potatoes. They tasted quite nice.

Ruth Tanner
Child in Walthamstow
You didn't have fridges, so you couldn't hoard things in your fridge. Food just went into everybody's oven. And you didn't scrape food into the bin. Nothing was wasted. You kept the wrapper the butter came in to grease a tin for something you might be making. And for us kids, toast and dripping with a bit

of salt and pepper on it was lovely. But kids today would just be absolutely disgusted by it.

Derek Haycock
Child in London
My staple diet was dripping sandwiches and dripping on toast.

Eileen Livett
Civil Nursing Reserve
The meal at Barnet General Hospital would be a tiny little bit of meat and potato and a bread and butter pudding for the sweet which was some watery, greyish-looking milky fluid with a couple of bread crusts floating in it. We were all getting a bit run down, working like mad and half starved. I developed acute sciatica. I didn't take much notice – the pain was spasmodic but one day I was walking down the ward of my hospital with a tray of thermometers and my leg went and I nearly fell over, which would have been a tragedy, not for my leg, but for the thermometers. So, I told the staff nurse, and she told me to report to sister who told me I'd have to go sick.

Ruth Tanner
Child in Walthamstow
When my father came home from the brickfields, he left his lorry outside the house. And when it got dark, he went out with my brother and moved the bricks away, and between them they brought in a pig, a great big pig, obviously dead. They put it on the kitchen table and my mother started ranting and raving. My father said he'd been out in the country in the middle of the road and he hit it. So for a while, everybody around us done quite well for pig. It didn't fall off the back of a lorry – it got hit and ended up *on* the back of a lorry.

Francis Goddard
Auxiliary Fire Service in Tottenham
I was coming down the Angel one day and I saw a queue outside a butcher's shop. I stopped to ask because I knew it wasn't the day for meat. Somebody said it was a ration-free meat. So I queued up for it. I bought about a pound – what the butcher would allow us and carted it round with me all day long. I brought it home at night and we had it next day for our meal. It was quite a dark brown colour meat with a deep yellow fat. It was horse flesh. Afterwards, I spoke to somebody about it and they said it was horse meat. Apparently, the

butcher had a horse that had been injured so he slaughtered it, brought it in and sold it in his own shop.

Ruth Tanner
Child in Walthamstow
In Wood Street, there was a vegetable stall. But every so often the word used to go round that he would be having rabbits, which weren't on the ration. Queuing would start at the crack of dawn. My mother would start in the queue and she'd set the alarm for my elder brother and when it went off, he'd come down and join the queue and she'd go back home to get my younger brother up. And then she'd go back and join the queue. And you got the rabbit with the skin and everything else. And I can see my mum now, quite adeptly taking the head off and peeling the skin off very carefully. She used to have a frame out the back – four nails and a piece of wood – and the skin used to go on there and she'd rub the side with salt and leave it up there. And we'd have a smashing pair of slippers.

Gioya Steinke
Welfare Adviser with London County Council Rest Centre Service
We actually started school dinners in the Rest Centre Service; White Lion Street was one of the first schools to serve school dinners to the school children who had remained in London but they didn't like our food. The children were used to a bag of chips or whatever they had at home and one day when we served up salad, they said, 'We're not rabbits!' and we got pelted with food.

Alison Hancock
Women's Auxiliary Air Force
In the services, we weren't rationed for anything and I used to be so ashamed when I went home and found that my parents had saved up the tea ration. There we were in the service, having all we wanted. Very spoiled.

Kathleen Clayden
Auxiliary Fire Service in London
In the fire service, we got more rations than other people did because we only used our ration book on our days off so it only had to last us for three days. We got our food when we were on duty. So we were luckier than most of the public.

Elizabeth Jones
Wife of RAF fighter pilot

As a young mother, I was very well off from the rationing point of view. My husband had double rations because he was a fighter pilot and we had good allowances of milk, orange juice, blackcurrant juice and cod liver oil.

Phil Piratin
Communist Councillor in Stepney

There was always ill feeling towards people who had all they wanted to eat. In London you depended on your rations but in a restaurant, your lunch had nothing to do with your coupons. But as a worker only got £2.10s a week, a restaurant lunch wouldn't be a worker's lunch.

Mary Warschauer
Civilian working for Air Ministry in London

I went to the Lyons Corner House in the Strand. They always put four people at a table and there was myself, a Canadian serviceman, a city gentleman and a woman you couldn't describe as anything more than a fading tart. We were all complete strangers. When the gentleman had finished, he put some money under his plate as a tip and he left the table. The woman sort of edged a bit and edged a bit, and she took the money from under the plate as if it were her own. The soldier said to her, 'Do you mind if I smoke?' and she said 'I couldn't care if you ruddy well went up in flames!'

Ronald Melville
Private Secretary to Chief of Air Staff at the Air Ministry

I remember the Churchill Club. This was a very elegant and rather exclusive luncheon club which was restricted to people from the Cabinet Office, the private offices and there were certain Americans connected with it. It was situated in the buildings of Westminster School just by the Abbey, the school having been evacuated. Lunch was on a cafeteria basis, and your meals were offered to you by distinguished and beautiful high-born ladies. My identical twin brother and I were both members – so he would have lunch at one o'clock wearing his uniform and sure enough he would have lunch again, half an hour later, not wearing uniform. And the ladies used to say, how hungry that man must be.

Gordon Knowles
Civilian in Whitstable

A market gardener asked if I wanted to buy some geese. At that time, I'd buy anything so I bought six geese and four ducks. I didn't have a van so I put them all on the back seat of my old Morris Oxford and I drove them home to Whitstable. When I got home it was late at night and I wondered what to do with them. I decided to let them run loose in the back yard and I put banana boxes across the alleyway to stop them getting out. I went to bed but at about three o'clock in the morning, I heard 'Bang, bang, bang' on the back door. It was Sergeant Sells of the Whitstable police. He said, 'Have you got some geese?' 'Yes.' 'They're out in the road!' The wind had got up and blown the banana boxes away. So we tried to round them up and chase them down the alley, which we eventually did. The next day, I decided to sell them. I bumped into Fred Gann, a JP. 'Mr Gann,' I said, 'I've got just the thing for you!' 'What's that?' he said. 'Do you want to buy a goose for Christmas dinner?' 'I'll buy it!' he said. 'Matter of fact, I'll buy two! I'm going to my daughter's for Christmas and I'll take one for her.' I didn't care what he did with them as long as I sold them. Anyway, Christmas came and he went to his daughter's in Reading. He told me afterwards that he hadn't known how to kill it so he shot its head off with a shotgun. Then he wrapped it up in a parcel and took it on the train. He put it on the rack above the seats and the blood started to drip onto the passenger next to him. All over the chap's coat and hat. The only thing that saved him was that the chap had to get off at the next stop and he didn't have time to exchange details. When he got to his daughter's, she cooked it and it was so tough that they couldn't get a knife into it and they never had a Christmas dinner. When he told me this, I apologised and I found out later that the man who sold these geese to me had been exhibiting them in shows for years. He said, 'You should have looked closer. You'd have seen 1914 stamped under his wing.'

Francis Goddard
Auxiliary Fire Service in Tottenham

Everybody had their crafty ways of getting extra food. Black market food. It was the only way you could survive. My wife used to bring food home in her knickers. She was working in a restaurant that had really good food – salmon, pheasants, turkeys, steaks, roasts – and whenever they got the chance, the staff brought things away. I got luxury food during the war, that I'd never had before. Fresh salmon, steaks, kippers – and she brought it all back in her knickers. When she was serving, she'd slide food into the extra pair of knickers she'd put on. I had some fine meals at three o'clock in the morning. I'd be in bed and she'd come home and wake me up. I'd be under the sheets and she was on top of the bed and she'd empty her purse out and pour out the tips and say, 'Cor, I've had a good night, tonight, I've collected over £3, and out would come a piece of tissue paper and she'd undo it and there'd be two nice pieces of cold cooked steak and we'd sit there and eat them. Or it might be a piece of salmon or some tasty sweet. She might even bring out a great big piece of chocolate. We'd laugh and I'd say, 'I hope you haven't worked too hard and sweated too much . . . '

Horace Davy
Civilian in London
Everyone tried to find ways of making their coupons stretch a bit further than they were supposed to. The sorts of things that were in short supply – cigarettes, radios, clothing, drink, petrol – these things were being sold on the black market.

Ruth Tanner
Child in Walthamstow
Someone would have a box of butter, and the word got round, you know, 'Are you interested?' That was a silly question to ask during the war when you were getting an ounce of butter with your rations. Whatever came along, people shared in it. If my mum got a bag of tea, Aunt Floss and Aunt Maud would get some as well. I don't think anybody thought of it as blatantly criminal. It was just the way we lived.

Alexander Flett
Metropolitan Police in Southwark
A lot of barter went on, I think that could be a better name sometimes than black market. It was illegal because you were only supposed to have your ration and that was it.

Stanley Brand
Middlesbrough Home Guard
After my son was born, the butcher gave my wife some extra butter. I made her take it back. Dad would have had fits if I'd accepted it and it was drummed into us as a family – get your ration and be thankful. Black marketers were beyond the pale.

Dilwyn Evans
Worker at Armstrong-Siddeley factory in Coventry
In one of the side streets, there was a little shop kept by two ladies. Now I don't know why, but I could go into that shop, and one of the ladies would say, 'We've got sweets!' And she'd give me sweets and chocolates. Or she'd put her hand out and give me a packet of butter. I could go in there sometimes, and she'd say, 'We've got some cigarettes' – Player's, Park Drive, Gold Flake – and I used to take them back to the factory for the lads. Don't ask me why these ladies picked on me. I didn't even know them.

Mary Sawyer
Civilian in London
I never saw the black market. I heard about a man that used to live next door to the police station. He used to give the police so much meat a week and one week he didn't give them any so he was in trouble.

Christabel Leighton-Porter
Actress, appeared as 'Jane' on stage
The spivvy type got spivvier. You mostly found them in markets and they had watches, nylons, food, all sorts of things. I remember one who made a hissing noise to attract my attention and he was selling bottles of whisky at £10 a bottle. I can't tell you how many bottles he sold. They were cold tea.

Ronald Oates
Civilian in London
I escorted my mother to Romford market and we saw a group of people standing round two spivs. 'Oh, look!' said my mother, 'they've got stockings!' This spiv stood on a box, and said, 'I've got stockings here, lovely stockings, four stockings for £1.' And I said to mother, 'Pick the ones he's holding, all the others will be rubbish!' I pushed her forward quickly and mother, taken by surprise, stepped forward and said, 'I'll have them!' 'All right missus,' and she turned round to me and handed me the stockings. I walked away and left her to it. When she came out of the crowd, I said to her, 'What's the matter?' She said, 'Do you know, that spiv wanted a whole book of clothing coupons for those stockings. I had my £1 but he wanted a book of coupons. No way was I going to give him a book of coupons! I'm not going to have the stockings.' 'But look!' I said, 'I've got them here! You gave them to me!' 'Ooh,' she said, 'I forgot! We'll have to give them back!' 'No fear!' I said – and it was the only time we got one up on the spivs.

Ronald Walsh
Seaman served aboard HMS Bulldog

I was a sailor on *HMS Bulldog* and we'd been up in Scapa Flow and I hadn't had any leave for a year. One day, they broadcast that we were going to Liverpool to have a boiler clean which meant that a part of the ship's company would be given five days' leave. My mate, Spike Ellis and I were given leave and we were really looking forward to it. So we got into Liverpool and Spike and I went to a place called the Blue Rooms in the middle of the city. We sat there having a few pints – nothing much happening, when Spike turned to me and said, 'Look at those blokes in the corner. Over there. One of them keeps looking at you.' I looked round but I didn't recognise him so we carried on drinking. Then the bloke got up and came over. He said, 'Are you Ron Walsh?' 'Yeah,' I said, 'Why?' 'Were you on the *Glasgow*?' he asked. 'Yeah.' 'Ah,' he said, 'I was on there with you. I did a runner in Canada. My name's Gibbons.' He said he was doing fine outside the navy and that he had a few mates here in Liverpool so I wished him the best of luck and that was it. Spike and I carried on drinking but just before closing time, Gibbons came back to our table and said, 'How would you like to go to a nightclub?' 'Sounds good to me,' I said so we went off to this place – 10 Hanover Street. It had a door with a little peephole in and Gibbons tapped on the door and the peephole slid back and the door opened and we were ushered into a room with a big bar.

There were lots of girls and we were quite thrilled. After about half an hour, Gibbons said, 'How would you two like to earn a fiver each? If you come with us on a little thing we've gotta do, we'll give you a fiver each.' I asked Spike what he thought. He said, 'We're on leave again tomorrow. We could do with a fiver.' So we went off with Gibbons and his mates and we walked up Lime Street. We got to this big shop and Gibbons said, 'Right. You two – stand in this doorway. Don't let anyone come past you. Push them on. That's all you've got to do.' So we just stood there and suddenly we hear a bang. They had broken their way through the glass door and into the shop. 'Oh Christ!' we thought. They came back out several times and dumped stuff next to us. Then they came out and told us to put our arms straight out. We did and they loaded us up with fur coats. Gibbons said, 'Right! You're two sailors. Sailors get up to all sorts of things. No one'll take notice of you. All you've gotta do is walk behind us and carry these coats.' So we followed him all the way down Lime Street with this big pile of coats until we got back to the nightclub.

About five minutes later, Gibbons gave us a fiver each. By then, we'd been drinking most of the evening and we were in a state where nothing really mattered. We were having a good time but then Gibbons came over again and he said, 'Right! We're gonna do another job!' 'I don't think so,' I said, 'We're gonna get back to the ship . . . so we'll just have this drink and then we'll push off.' 'No, you won't!' he said, 'because if you leave this door, without our sanction, you won't get much further than the end of the street! You'll have had it! So you'll just do this job and then we'll let you go!' There was no use arguing so I said to Spike, 'We're in this, mate, but there *is* an answer. We'll follow them but when we get there and they've gone inside the shop, we'll beat it, get a taxi and go back to the ship.' 'Yeah,' said Spike, 'that's a good idea.'

So we followed them again and we went back to the same shop which seemed like rather a foolish thing. Spike and I were stood in the doorway when suddenly all hell broke loose. Whistles blew, police cars charged up, a Black Maria arrived and we were grabbed. They'd been watching us. We were shoved in the Black Maria and taken to the police station and kept there overnight. The next morning, an officer from our ship came to see us. 'Look lads,' he said, 'you were only in Liverpool a few hours and you find yourselves in this state. The point is, the police are rounding up a gang of looters. Now they've got the ringleaders but they still want to get the others and take them all to the assizes at Manchester. Unfortunately, you were there at the time, so you're witnesses and you'll have to be there when the case comes up. So, you're not coming back to the ship – you'll either be remanded on bail or in custody. If you're on bail, you'll go to Liverpool's base ship for the navy and stay there until the case comes up. If you're in custody, you'll go to Walton Jail until the trial. And you'll have two lawyers that the navy's employing to look after you.' They remanded us into Walton Prison.

Because we were on remand, we couldn't join the other prisoners in the recreation rooms – we were restricted to our cell from half past six in the morning to half past seven at night. After about two weeks, they'd caught all the other looters so we were taken to Strangeways prison for the Manchester assizes. At the assizes, nine or ten men were lined up, charged with looting, and Spike and I were in the middle, dressed in uniform. One of our lawyers was Rose Heilbron, who later became the first female judge at the Old Bailey. The judge, Mr Justice Hallett, came in and said, 'First of all, I want those two sailors out of the dock. To my mind, they're not criminals. They're heroes!' So we came out of the dock and we sat and watched as the judge gave all the others eight years, nine years, whatever. Gibbons got nine years, I think. Afterwards, Rose Heilbron told us that it was over. We were clear and the next day we were on our way to Portsmouth barracks.

Horace Davy
Civilian in London
The first committee I was allowed to sit in on as part of my training was to do with pilfering. We all trooped out into a Black Maria – a police van – that had been sent up by the Port of London Authority and we were shown items of clothing, goods and bales of cloth that were being pilfered from the docks. I remember being quite shattered that pilfering in the docks should be a problem during the war.

John Dorgan
Civilian in London
Our house lost its roof and windows and we couldn't lock the door when we went out. We could only put a brick behind it and the house was open to anyone who wanted to go in and we lost a lot of possessions, including the diary I'd kept in the trenches during the First World War. What good that would be to anyone, I don't know.

Walter Marshall
Metropolitan Police War Reserve
Most of what they called 'looting' during the Blitz took place when they were clearing places and they came across the contents of a shop. A tobacconist, for example, where you could immediately pick something up and disappear. To my mind, it seemed ridiculous to charge somebody with taking something that they could use. The same thing if he hadn't taken it would have been thrown away as rubbish.

Teresa Wilkinson
Air raid warden in West Ham
To be perfectly honest, I was guilty of looting. One house had come down and we were going through it and there was a book called *A Mountain Daisy*, a very old Victorian book. I'd had a copy when I was young but somehow my copy had got lost. I looked round this house – and all the people who'd lived there were dead – and I thought, 'No one will miss that!' We did get notices round from the council saying, 'If you pick things up, you'll be looting!' so I felt a bit guilty but I didn't think anyone else would mind.

Leslie Hyland
Civilian in Liverpool
As we were walking from the shelter after a raid, we crunched through all this jewellery on the ground outside a shattered jeweller's shop and we took not the slightest bit of notice of it. All these gold articles – and we walked over them.

William Ryder
Worker at Woolwich Arsenal
I heard a bomb drop on the road where my mother and father lived, just off Woolwich Common, and thought I'd nip round to see how they were. When I got there, their house was practically demolished and looters were sorting out the silver, the knives and forks and they were even killing the rabbits and chickens that dad kept. When I showed up, they just ran off.

Derek Haycock
Child in London
My dad was in the fire service. He was on his way to a fire one night when he came across a woman in the middle of the road, pulling her stockings up. The fire engine stopped in front of her and they told her to get out of the way but she just carried on. She'd nicked these stockings from a shop which had been bombed and she'd never had the luxury of good nylon stockings before. She was fascinated just to stand there and keep pulling them up and down her legs.

Walter Marshall
Metropolitan Police War Reserve
The City Road Police Station had a visit from George VI. His Majesty was introduced to a PC who'd received a medal for rescuing two people. That PC was later done for flogging batteries that his son had nicked from the Ever Ready factory in Dagenham and he spent six months inside.

Stan Poole
Home Guard in London
There was a rumour about the black market people at King's Cross who were robbing the trains. We were told to keep our eyes open because a railway copper had gone down there and vanished. Years later, a dying bloke – one of the thieves – admitted that they'd thrown this copper in the fire box of one of the trains.

Ernest Beavor
Conscientious objector imprisoned in Wormwood Scrubs

When I was in the cells below the court waiting to be called, there was a soldier in the next cell. He said, 'What are you in here for, mate?' I said, 'I'm a Jehovah's Witness and I can't engage in warfare.' He said, 'Have you been up before?' 'Yes.' 'What did you get?' 'A year.' 'You'll get two years this time.' I asked him what he was in for. He said, 'I robbed a church. But I'll get off.' While I was waiting for my case, I listened to his case. His commanding officer was in the witness box, declaring that he was a very good soldier and a very gallant man. Consequently, the case was dismissed. When my case came up, the judge said to me, 'I think you're the worst of your kind and I have no hesitation in asking the jury to return the verdict: Two years with hard labour.' When I got back downstairs again, the soldier said, 'There you are mate! I told you so!'

William Heard
Conscientious objector imprisoned in Feltham Borstal

There were quite a few people who committed crimes in order to end up in prison rather than serve in the armed forces.

Private John Graham
Argyll and Sutherland Highlanders

I was up in Perth, serving in a Highland regiment. A large proportion of the recruits came from Glasgow and some of them used to sew razor blades behind the regimental badge on their hat. In my innocence, I asked a corporal if I should be doing this too. 'No, no, you don't do that,' he said. They did it because in the area of Perth was the Polish Cavalry Division. The officers of this Polish unit had pretty saucy uniforms and the girls went for them in a big way. The theory of the razor blade exercise was that my Glaswegian colleagues would go out on a Saturday night with their pay in their pockets and eventually they would find a Polish officer with a girl on his arm walking down the street. Being an officer, they would have to salute him. But the plot was to raise their hand in the position of a salute but not to complete it. Instead, they whipped their hat off and brought the edge of the razor blade down across the wretched Pole's cheek. They sent him to hospital and walked off with the girl.

Dorothy West
Woman Police Constable with Metropolitan Police Force
There were plenty of drunk women who used to come into the police station. Sometimes it took as many as six of us to hold these women down. They were really revolting – and the strength of them! We had a desk in the hall and this woman put her hand down on to it and out came the inkwell. Terrific strength. They used to lie about in the parks and drink meths. They were pulled in by the van. We didn't often walk them in.

Marian Orley
Women's Auxiliary Air Force
One of my WAAFs was a corporal who was getting married. Her husband was an army officer and he had 14 days' embarkation leave. They were going to spend their honeymoon in Newcastle. So I signed her pass and she went off for her honeymoon. A fortnight later, I was duty officer on the Sunday morning, and the police rang up and said, 'You've got to identify a body of a woman. We've got reason to believe she's one of yours.' I had to go and look at this body. She'd seen her husband off on the midnight train and she'd walked home. She'd been set upon and raped by a young man. I had the very unpleasant task of dealing with her effects. The police told her family. They got the man. He was a 19-year-old merchant seaman. Drunk. He was hanged.

Ivy Warwick
Women's Auxiliary Air Force
One day I was walking to Didcot Station. No one came along to give me a lift – and I would never put my hand out for a lift. If they wanted to stop, all well and good. Then two men stopped. They had a trailer at the back for a horse. They said, 'Do you want a lift? Where are you going?' 'Reading.' 'Oh we're going to Reading! We haven't any room at the front but there's room where the horses usually go! It's comfortable and you can look out!' I was exhausted so I said, 'All right then thank you very much.' So I sat in the horse's seat, looking out the back and off they went. In the corner, there were these beautiful apples. I was tempted but I thought, 'No! You mustn't! Don't be naughty!' On the other side were these huge logs. We got as far as Reading and I'd told them where I lived and where they could drop me. I saw my house – and it disappeared. We carried on driving through Reading and I got panicky. I got one of the logs and started banging it on the thin partition between me and the men. They were sitting with their back against it. No way could they not have heard me. I was frantic – they were taking me

451

somewhere. We drove through a little village and I was standing up shouting, 'Help! Help!' Nobody took any notice. We then came to a crossroads in another village and I jumped out. I could have broken my neck. I got on a bus to Reading and when got home, I told mother. She said, 'What a silly girl you are! They could have done anything with you and nobody would have been any the wiser!' I never did anything like that again.

Sylvia Clark
Post Office worker in London

I applied to go on the switchboard at the Gerrard Exchange between six and ten. Life was exciting there. Gerrard Street was right in the middle of Piccadilly and it was used by the prostitutes. One night, a blonde came up to me and said, 'You work in the telephone exchange, don't you?' 'Yes,' I said. 'Can you do us a favour?' she asked. I knew that she was a prostitute, so I said, 'Look. I have a job with the Post Office during the day and I'm doing this exchange duty because I want some money to go into digs. I want this job and I don't want to lose my ordinary job. So be very truthful about whatever you want me to do for you.' She said, 'My mate is ill and they've taken her to some hospital out of town. I want to speak to her for longer than three minutes. What I want you to do is not to cut me off when I'm talking to her.' 'You realise,' I said, 'that I'm on that switchboard and I have a supervisor at the main desk who can see everything I do and even listens in to our conversations because I mustn't hold conversations with casual callers.' 'I promise you,' she said, 'I won't say anything out of place, as long as you don't cut me off.' So I took a chance. Instead of saying, 'Caller, your time is up. If you require further time, please put your money in the box,' I just said, 'Carry on . . . ' and I left the line but I listened to the conversation. At one point, she said to the girl at the other end, 'She's in bed with flu!' and the other girl said, 'In bed with Lou?'

The Climax of the Blitz

A prostitute came up from Piccadilly, up from the Empire cinema.
It was a warm, clear evening and as the incendiary bombs came down,
she put her umbrella up and started singing, 'I'm singin' in the rain'.

May 10, 1941 was the most devastating night of the London Blitz. In a final great raid, intended to divert attention away from Hitler's preparations for the invasion of the Soviet Union, the Luftwaffe took advantage of a full moon and a low tide to start almost 2,500 fires in the capital. Nearly 1,500 people lost their lives and 5,000 houses were destroyed. The British Museum lost 250,000 books and the House of Commons burnt to the ground. Damage was caused to the War Office, Westminster School, the Royal Courts of Justice, St James's Palace, Westminster Abbey, St Thomas's Hospital and other institutions. And though no one in Britain realised it that night, it marked the end of the Blitz.

Ballard Berkeley
Special Constable in London
We hadn't had a big raid for some time and suddenly on May 10, this really big raid happened. The biggest raid on London. It was a beautiful night and I was up on Coventry Street. Lyons Corner House was always busy and full of people – good and bad. When I was on duty, the sirens had gone and the City was being bombed. The city was getting well lit up. We knew the pattern – the incendiaries would light up the target and then the bombers would come in and bomb. So we heard the screech and down came the incendiaries. This

was the first thing then you knew the raid was going to spread. It was a strange night. People were not frightened. They were still going in and out of the Lyons Corner House and I remember one man putting a steel helmet over an incendiary bomb. God know why. It was absolutely hopeless. The helmet just went red hot, then white hot and disintegrated. But it was the night of the Cup Final and as the bombs came down, the newspaper seller just stood there shouting 'Star, News, Standard, Cup Final Result'. And then a prostitute came up from Piccadilly, up from the Empire cinema. It was a warm, clear evening and as the incendiary bombs came down, she put her umbrella up and started singing, 'I'm singin' in the rain'. I remember thinking at the time, 'I wish Hitler and Goering could have a look at this.' The bombers were right over blooming head.

After a while, it looked as though the north side of Old Compton Street from Dean Street to Wardour Street was going to be burned down. The Fire Service was so over-extended, they couldn't possibly cope so they evacuated Old Compton Street. As we were evacuating the shops, carrying the food and wines out, people were trying to buy it off us. At the time, I had a six foot four drunken Canadian fellow following me around and I was trying to shake him off. He had a large bottle of whisky in his pocket and he kept calling me 'Captain'. He insisted on coming down to Old Compton Street with me and he joined in, picking up cases and moving them, and suddenly I saw one of our chaps flying out of a door. 'What are you doing?' I asked. 'I've just been hit!' he said. 'Hit?' 'Yes! By some Canadian bastard who's looting in there! He's smashing the place up!' It was my Canadian friend and he had a greatcoat on full of cheese, wines, whisky, cigarettes and by now he was raving drunk. We didn't know how to tackle him. In the end, we attracted his attention while two policemen came up behind him and put a cloth over his head. As he went to get the cloth off, two men got each arm and we subdued him. He sobered up and I chatted to him. I said, 'You think you're helping? The only people you're helping are the Germans! Now for God's sake go away!' We didn't have time to arrest anybody.

Suddenly, it happened. I'd heard bombs, been near bombs – but when a bomb hits so close, you don't hear it. It was the most extraordinary thing. Everything stopped and there was complete and utter silence. It was so quiet, it was unbelievable. Perhaps the explosion had deafened the eardrums. I don't know but everything was silent. Nobody moved. The whole place was filled with grey mist. It was like a theatrical scene with a gauze stage cloth in front of it. After a few seconds, everything came to life – except the people who were dead. This was a 2,000lb bomb. I couldn't move. I was standing up but I couldn't move. I thought my legs had gone but in fact, I was up to my knees in rubble and bricks. That's why I couldn't move. As I was clearing the rubble, I was thinking, 'Am I all right?' I thought I was, but then the most extraordinary thing happened. A tremendous panic came over me. I was suddenly scared out of my life. I had to get away. I had to run. And I did. I ran. After a few yards running, I was suddenly outside of my body, looking down at myself and talking to myself. I said, 'Why are you running? Why are you frightened? This is your job. You're supposed to do something here!' And then I seemed to re-enter my body again and I became calm and cool and collected. I stopped running and I went back. I will never forget that night.

Then I saw a poor devil lying on the ground like a rag doll. It was my Canadian friend again. He couldn't move. He must have broken his back. I asked him if he was all right. 'I'm all right,' he said and then he looked up and asked, 'Can you give me a cigarette, guv?' I thought, 'No! No! I've heard this in the films and laughed at it too many times! This doesn't happen in real life!' But it *was* happening in real life.

What surprised me about that night more than anything else was the fact that one accepted it. One was not as scared and frightened as one thought one was going to be. You had the scary moments – but you knew you had to do a job. I think the whole country knew that we knew we had to go through this period. We knew it was going to be awful but we knew that we would bloody well win. It would all end one day and we would win. There was never any question.

Katharine Elliot
Wife of Walter Elliot, MP

My husband was a Member of Parliament. On the night of May 10, he went back to his house after Parliament rose but a heavy raid was starting and he went back to the Houses of Parliament where he saw that the House of Commons was on fire. He got inside and realised that it would be impossible to save the House of Commons but that Westminster Hall – the greatest medieval hall in this country – was just about to catch fire. The roof is entirely made of wood and it was right next door to the House of Commons. The fire brigade engines were some way away from where the fire was catching and the water was never going to reach that height. So he led the fire brigade into Westminster Palace Yard, which is just outside Westminster Hall. There was a policeman standing outside the great door. My husband said, 'We've got to get in here!' The policeman said, 'Well Mr Elliot, the keys are in the central lobby,' but the central lobby was by this time burning. So my husband asked one of the fireman for an axe and he crashed the door open, rushed the water from all the engines in at the bottom and soaked the roof before the fire could reach it. They poured so much water into Westminster Hall that night, that when he left three or four hours later, he was up to his knees in water.

The next day, I went into the House of Commons chamber and it was completely burned out. It was still smoking and there was an extraordinary hissing noise from the burnt wood. It was a mass of tangled wood, iron and there was no roof left. You could see right to the sky. The whole thing was a disaster. The House of Commons wasn't rebuilt until after the war.

Horace Davy
Civilian in London

On the night of May 10, my mother and I went into the deep shelter, below the civil defence post, in Fenchurch Street which we shared with about five other people. Our building was hit by high explosive and incendiary bombs. I remember a great 'Whumph' and the emergency lighting in the shelter came on. My mother and I got out of our bunks and put on our shoes. I looked down at the floor and I saw liquid of some sort running along the floor. I said, 'Hurry up! It looks like we're going to be flooded!' In fact it was wine from a wine cellar in the room next door. Someone else in the building later told me that he'd had a telling off from his wife because he'd arrived home that night, exhausted, went to bed, muttered something, and when he got up the next morning, his wife accused him of being drunk. She said she could smell it on his clothes. Anyway, my mother and I made our way up to the warden's post. We didn't know it then but we were the only ones to come out of our room alive.

By the time we got to the next ground level, the building was on fire down to that level. We wandered around for a while and somebody opened the doors to another building and we spent the night there. When we came out in the morning, we began to make our way home. We were told that we could not go the direct route because of damage and so we began to make our way via the network of air raid wardens' posts and that's how we heard that our own home had been destroyed. We were not allowed to go anywhere near it. So my mother and I were literally walking the streets. Nowhere to go.

Everything was very quiet. There was no panic – it was a numbness. At one point, I wanted to spend a penny. I went down the public conveniences near the Monument and I can remember standing there in front of the stalls when suddenly there was an explosion and the set of stalls in front of me dropped down a foot. I scampered out – I don't know if I finished what I went there to do.

Eventually a message came to us that Mr McDonald, the housekeeper for the Chamber of Shipping, knew of our plight and he invited us to share his shelter. We did this until the Wednesday. We still weren't allowed to go home. We'd been wandering around in the clothes in which we stood – I was in my Boy Scout's uniform. On the Thursday we found a flat in one of the City Corporation estates. It had been arranged that I was to start work at a scientific instrument manufacturer's firm in the city but that place had been destroyed on the same night so my first job went up in flames with my house. What to do with me? Mr McDonald said that someone on the staff of the Chamber of Shipping had been injured and they needed an office boy for a few weeks. So I had an interview on the Thursday and they agreed to take me on for six weeks. I started at the Chamber of Shipping on May 19, 1941 and I retired from the same company as Secretary and one of the Deputy Directors General in September 1989.

Ellen Harris
Reporter with Reuters News Agency in London
It was the night London was set afire. I'd been in a dug-out under Liberty's in Regent Street which my father felt safe in. And I went with him. My husband was on duty in Fleet Street. And I left early enough to get home, wash and change and get back on duty in Fleet Street by eight o'clock. So this was fairly early but the raid was all finished and over. And I think I must have had to walk it and it's a good long distance from Oxford Circus to where I lived in Islington. I was walking over hosepipes, dozens and dozens. No bus could have run, there were hosepipes everywhere and the firemen were fighting the blazes still.

A middle-aged man, almost in tears, who had been taking cover in a shelter in Lincoln's Inn Fields, stopped me and said, 'What are we going to do? We can't go on like this! We've got to seek peace! We've got to say we must have peace! We can't go on this way!' He was really very panicky and I said to him, 'Do you realise that you're playing right into Hitler's hands? This is just what he's setting out to do. If he can do this to you and you start on me and I join in with you and I go up the road and tell somebody then you'd get people in the state of mind and their morale goes. You've got to remember you're in the front line as if you were in the trenches in the last war! Buck up! We're going to be very sad when we see what happened last night but you take it upon yourself to boost other people! We've got to keep going!' And he said, 'Thank you! Thank you very much!' He was bucked up and he went off.

Continuing that journey home, I went past Mount Pleasant post office.

Fires everywhere. I came up past Sadler's Wells theatre and what brought me to tears was when I saw people pushing children's prams which they'd filled with little things they'd rescued from their homes. There were no tears, nothing whatsoever, just the firmness – 'we'll rescue what we can'. What brought me to tears was a birdcage hanging in a window with a little, dead canary inside. Can you understand that? I just burst into tears going up the road.

My home and all around there was alright, except the gas mains and the water mains so you couldn't have a cup of tea or anything locally. But there was a local butcher and he had some oil arrangement down in his basement. He set the stoves going and he set up a stall outside. He cooked sausages and whatever he'd got in his shop, he cooked and he put out there for the people to come along and help themselves. He wasn't that kind of man at all but he said, 'Poor devils. There was no gas or water or anything. But I had the stove . . . what sort of person would I have been?' I said, 'How much did you charge them?' He said, 'Oh, I didn't charge them. They couldn't even get themselves a cup of tea.'

Then I went up on duty. We were all very distressed, coming through the City, fires still raging. I saw firemen flung across the fronts of their motors where they were so exhausted, having gone all through the night, they just threw themselves across it for ten minutes' sleep.

When it came time for me to go out to lunch, there was a Lyons on the corner but there was no gas or water. Everywhere, there was not even a cup of tea. But various vans had come along and I don't know whether it was the Salvation Army but you could get yourself a cup of tea from these various vans. Nothing else was available anywhere.

I got back to the office and I burst into tears and I said, 'God, this is terrible.' 'What's the matter? What is it?' said the editor. 'I've just been out,' I said, 'and the firemen are still fighting the fires and half the firemen are dead on their feet. You can't get anything to eat and there's not a drop of water.' And then it was his turn to push morale into me. 'You, of all people!' he said, 'I'm ashamed of you! Pull yourself together! We're looking to the likes of you to keep everybody going!' He gave me a jolly good lecture. 'I'm OK, now. I'm OK, I'll be all right,' I said and never once after that did I falter.

Robert Stepney
London Fire Brigade
On the night of May 10, I was dealing with fires from end to end. I saw a fire in one warehouse that burned down. There was nothing I could do about it –

we didn't have enough equipment and there was no water. At one point, I intercepted a peacetime fire appliance. They said that they'd driven down from Witney in Oxfordshire and they were going to report to the control room. 'Never mind that!' I said, 'I want you here!' I got them to work. But they were only using half-inch nozzles – which would have been ideal in the country but not in the middle of London. We had not got our fires under control by the time the all-clear came. This was most unusual. We were at the extreme range of our capabilities and if the Germans had come back the following night, we certainly would have been finished.

Teresa Wilkinson
Air raid warden in West Ham
After May 10, 1941, we didn't get a bad raid again. The worst of the Blitz was over and air raid wardens went back to £3 a week for doing nothing and I got bored.

Joan Seaman
Civilian in London
In May, when it suddenly stopped, we couldn't believe it. We thought, 'My goodness! What's happening?' And life gradually went back. We went back upstairs to bed again.

Group Captain Frederick Winterbotham
Deputy to Chief of Secret Intelligence Service with special responsibility for the security of Ultra messages
We knew to the day when the invasion of Russia was going to take place and we knew where most of the German forces were. Somebody made up a report which was handed to the Russian mission, giving an outline of what we knew, but in no way giving away that we got it from intercepted material. It was a summary of the information which we would have had from other sources, telling the Russians what the Germans were trying to do. I don't think the Russians believed a word of it.

Walter Blanchard
Civilian in Barking
The Blitz had been an exhausting, trying time. A terrible yet exhilarating time to grow up in.

Patricia Crampton
Civilian in Beaconsfield

In 1942, I can remember lying awake, listening with great pride to the seemingly unending roar of the British planes setting out on their thousand bomber raids over Germany. It was just fantastic. I expect it sounds bloodthirsty now, but after the Blitz in which we had been in great danger – it was marvellous.

Albert Prior
Stretcher bearer with West Ham Civil Defence

You've only got to look round nowadays to see the tower blocks and new buildings – nearly every one's been built on a bomb site from the Blitz.

Joan Seaman
Civilian in London

One or two things happen nowadays when I think back to the Blitz. I was on a bus recently during a tube strike and this little tiny bus came along to go to Brixton and we all piled in together, absolutely squashed and someone shouted, 'This is like being in the Blitz!'

Gioya Steinke
Welfare Adviser with London County Council Rest Centre Service

My family have no idea what I did in the Blitz. When I tried to tell them, they thought it was just Mum boasting. It wasn't. I had adventures they'll never have.

Over 43,000 people lost their lives in the bombing. Many more were made homeless. The raids would not disappear completely until the end of the war, but as the *All Clear* sounded on the morning of May 11 1941, the Blitz was at an end. Over the course of the previous year, forces of social change had been set in motion that would drastically alter the face of modern Britain. The events of 1940 and 1941 had brought people of different classes and social groupings together. They were eating the same food, wearing the same clothes, buying the same furniture. They were working in the same factories, taking shelter together and firewatching side by side. Poor children were evacuated to middle-class homes where understanding replaced mistrust. Legislation was passed ensuring factory workers a guaranteed wage and a right to appeal against unfair dismissal. Women were taking jobs long considered the preserve of men. Whilst

Gioya Steinke (with her legal guardian) feeds the pigeons in Trafalgar Square.

people's minds were focused on resisting Hitler, a surreptitious democratic revolution was taking place, paving the way for the Beveridge Report and the creation of the welfare state.

In May 1941, however, Britain's main concern was the defeat of Nazi Germany. Six weeks after the end of the Blitz, Hitler launched *Operation Barbarossa* – the invasion of the Soviet Union. He believed that he could achieve a quick victory over Stalin before returning his attention to Britain. A bloody struggle ensued with the Soviet Union but, in fact, Hitler had already lost the battle for Britain. For the first time, a nation had successfully resisted him. There had been no invasion, no surrender, no negotiations. Before the United States had entered the war, the interests of the free world had been protected. In the face of extreme odds, thanks to the men and women of Fighter Command, thanks to Winston Churchill, thanks to the strength and spirit and courage of her people, Britain had survived.

Index of Contributors

Number in brackets denotes IWM Sound Archive catalogue number.
Page numbers in *italics* refer to photographs.

PM denotes Private Material supplied by the author

General Index

Page numbers in *italics* refer to photographs.